PAGODA TOEFL

90+ Reading Actual Test

파고다교육그룹 언어교육연구소 | 저

PAGODA Books

PAGODA
TOEFL

90+ Reading
Actual Test

초판   1쇄 발행 2014년 12월 15일
개정판 1쇄 발행 2021년   2월 26일
개정판 2쇄 발행 2022년   9월 16일

지 은 이 | 파고다교육그룹 언어교육연구소
펴 낸 이 | 박경실
펴 낸 곳 | Wit&Wisdom 도서출판 위트앤위즈덤
임프린트 | **PAGODA Books**
출판등록 | 2005년 5월 27일 제 300-2005-90호
주   소 | 06614 서울특별시 서초구 강남대로 419, 19층(서초동, 파고다타워)
전   화 | (02) 6940-4070
팩   스 | (02) 536-0660
홈페이지 | www.pagodabook.com

ISBN 978-89-6281-866-6 (14740)

도서출판 위트앤위즈덤   www.pagodabook.com
파고다 어학원   www.pagoda21.com
파고다 인강   www.pagodastar.com
테스트 클리닉   www.testclinic.com

PAGODA Books는 도서출판 Wit&Wisdom의 성인 어학 전문 임프린트입니다.
낙장 및 파본은 구매처에서 교환해 드립니다.

2019년 8월
New iBT TOEFL®의 시작!

2019년 5월 22일, TOEFL 주관사인 미국 ETS(Educational Testing Service)는 iBT TOEFL® 시험 시간이 기존보다 30분 단축되며, 이에 따라 Writing을 제외한 3가지 시험 영역이 다음과 같이 변경된다고 발표했다. 새로 바뀐 iBT TOEFL® 시험은 2019년 8월 3일 정기시험부터 시행되고 있다.

- 총 시험 시간 기존 약 3시간 30분 ┈➔ 약 3시간으로 단축
- 시험 점수는 각 영역당 30점씩 총 120점 만점으로 기존과 변함 없음

영역	2019년 8월 1일 이전	2019년 8월 1일 이후
Reading	지문 3~4개 각 지문 당 12~14문제 시험 시간 60~80분	지문 3~4개 각 지문 당 10문제 시험 시간 54~72분
Listening	대화 2~3개, 각 5문제 강의 4~6개, 각 6문제 시험 시간 60~90분	대화 2~3개, 각 5문제 강의 3~4개, 각 6문제 시험 시간 41~ 57분
Speaking	6개 과제 독립형 과제 2개 통합형 과제 4개 시험 시간 20분	4개 과제 독립형 과제 1개 통합형 과제 3개 시험 시간 17분
Writing	*변함 없음 2개 과제 시험 시간 50분	

목차

이 책의 구성과 특징

▶▶ New TOEFL 변경사항 및 최신 출제 유형 완벽 반영!

2019년 8월부터 변경된 새로운 토플 시험을 반영, iBT TOEFL® 90점 이상을 목표로 하는 학습자를 위해 최근 iBT TOEFL®의 출제 경향을 완벽하게 반영한 문제와 주제를 골고루 다루고 있습니다.

▶▶ 예제를 통한 문제 유형별 공략법 정리!

본격적으로 실전에 들어가기에 앞서, iBT TOEFL® Reading의 9가지 문제 유형을 정리해 자주 나오는 질문을 파악하고 예제를 풀어보면서 iBT TOEFL® 전문 연구원이 제시하는 문제풀이 필수 전략을 학습할 수 있도록 하였습니다.

▶▶ 7회분의 Actual Test로 실전 완벽 대비!

실제 시험과 동일하게 구성된 7회분의 Actual Test를 수록해 실전에 철저하게 대비할 수 있도록 구성하였습니다.

▶▶ 온라인 모의고사 체험 인증번호 제공!

PC에서 실제 시험과 유사한 형태로 모의 테스트를 볼 수 있는 시험 구현 시스템을 제공합니다. 본 교재에 수록되어 있는 Actual Test 2회분(Test 01, 02)과 동일한 내용을 실제 iBT TOEFL® 시험을 보듯 온라인 상에서 풀어보실 수 있습니다.

▶ 온라인 모의고사 체험 인증번호는 앞표지 안쪽에서 확인하세요.

▶▶ 그룹 스터디와 독학에 유용한 단어 시험지 생성기 제공!

자동 단어 시험지 생성기를 통해 교재를 학습하면서 외운 단어 실력을 테스트해 볼 수 있습니다.

▶ 사용 방법: 파고다북스 홈페이지(www.pagodabook.com)에 로그인한 후 상단 메뉴의 [모의테스트] 클릭 >모의테스트 메뉴에서 [단어 시험] 클릭 > TOEFL - PAGODA TOEFL 90+ Reading Actual Test를 고른 후 원하는 문제 수를 입력하고 문제 유형 선택 > '단어 시험지 생성'을 누르고 별도의 브라우저 창으로 뜬 단어 시험지를 PDF로 내려 받거나 인쇄

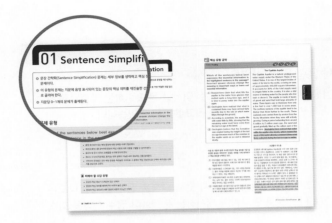

PART 01. Question Types

iBT TOEFL® 전문 연구원이 제안하는 9가지 문제 유형별 고득점 전략을 학습할 수 있습니다.

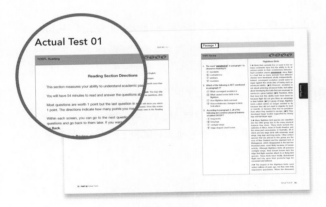

PART 02. Actual Tests

실제 시험과 동일하게 구성된 7회분의 Actual Test 를 통해 실전에 대비합니다. 본 교재의 Actual Test 2회분(Test 01, 02)은 온라인 모의고사로도 함께 제공되어 iBT TOEFL®과 유사한 환경에서 실제처럼 연습해 볼 수 있습니다.

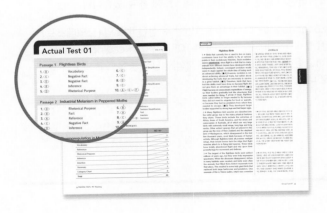

정답 및 해석

지문 및 문제에 대한 정답과 해석, 지문에서 등장한 주요 어휘 정리를 수록했습니다.

4주 완성 학습 플랜

DAY 1	DAY 2	DAY 3	DAY 4	DAY 5
PART 01				
01 Sentence Simplification • 문제 유형 및 전략 • Sample Questions	02 Fact / Negative Fact • 문제 유형 및 전략 • Sample Questions	03 Vocabulary • 문제 유형 및 전략 • Sample Questions	04 Reference • 문제 유형 및 전략 • Sample Questions	05 Rhetorical Purpose • 문제 유형 및 전략 • Sample Questions

DAY 6	DAY 7	DAY 8	DAY 9	DAY 10
PART 01				**PART 02**
06 Inference • 문제 유형 및 전략 • Sample Questions	07 Insertion • 문제 유형 및 전략 • Sample Questions	08 Summary • 문제 유형 및 전략 • Sample Questions	09 Category Chart • 문제 유형 및 전략 • Sample Questions	Actual Test 01 • 문제 풀이

DAY 11	DAY 12	DAY 13	DAY 14	DAY 15
PART 02				
Actual Test 02 • 문제 풀이	Actual Test 01~02 Review • 지문 다시 읽기 • 단락 요약하기 연습	Actual Test 03 • 문제 풀이	Actual Test 04 • 문제 풀이	Actual Test 03~04 Review • 지문 다시 읽기 • 단락 요약하기 연습

DAY 16	DAY 17	DAY 18	DAY 19	DAY 20
PART 02				
Actual Test 05 • 문제 풀이	Actual Test 06 • 문제 풀이	Actual Test 05~06 Review • 지문 다시 읽기 • 단락 요약하기 연습	Actual Test 07 • 문제 풀이	Actual Test 07 & Voca Review • 지문 다시 읽기 • 단락 요약하기 연습 • 학습한 단어 총정리

iBT TOEFL® 개요

1. iBT TOEFL® 이란?

TOEFL은 영어 사용 국가로 유학을 가고자 하는 외국인들의 영어 능력을 평가하기 위해 개발된 시험이다. TOEFL 시험 출제 기관인 ETS는 이러한 TOEFL 본연의 목적에 맞게 문제의 변별력을 더욱 높이고자 PBT(Paper-Based Test), CBT(Computer-Based Test)에 이어 차세대 시험인 인터넷 기반의 iBT(Internet-Based Test)를 2005년 9월부터 시행하고 있다. ETS에서 연간 30~40회 정도로 지정한 날짜에 등록함으로써 치르게 되는 이 시험은 Reading, Listening, Speaking, Writing 총 4개 영역으로 구성되며 총 시험 시간은 약 3시간이다. 각 영역별 점수는 30점으로 총점 120점을 만점으로 하며 성적은 시험 시행 약 10일 후에 온라인에서 확인할 수 있다.

2. iBT TOEFL®의 특징

1) 영어 사용 국가로 유학 시 필요한 언어 능력을 평가한다.

각 시험 영역은 실제 학업이나 캠퍼스 생활에 반드시 필요한 언어 능력을 측정한다. 평가되는 언어 능력에는 자신의 의견 및 선호도 전달하기, 강의 요약하기, 에세이 작성하기, 학술적인 주제의 글을 읽고 내용 이해하기 등이 포함되며, 각 영역에 걸쳐 고르게 평가된다.

2) Reading, Listening, Speaking, Writing 전 영역의 통합적인 영어 능력(Integrated Skill)을 평가한다.

시험이 4개 영역으로 분류되어 있기는 하지만 Speaking과 Writing 영역에서는 [Listening + Speaking], [Reading + Listening + Speaking], [Reading + Listening + Writing]과 같은 형태로 학습자가 둘 또는 세 개의 언어 영역을 통합해서 사용할 수 있는지를 평가한다.

3) Reading 지문 및 Listening 스크립트가 길다.

Reading 지문은 700단어 내외로 A4용지 약 1.5장 분량이며, Listening은 3~4분 가량의 대화와 6~8분 가량의 강의로 구성된다.

4) 전 영역에서 노트 필기(Note-taking)를 할 수 있다.

긴 지문을 읽거나 강의를 들으면서 핵심 사항을 간략하게 적어두었다가 문제를 풀 때 참고할 수 있다. 노트 필기한 종이는 시험 후 수거 및 폐기된다.

5) 선형적(Linear) 방식으로 평가된다.

응시자가 시험을 보는 과정에서 실력에 따라 문제의 난이도가 조정되어 출제되는 CAT(Computer Adaptive Test)방식이 아니라, 정해진 문제가 모든 응시자에게 동일하게 제시되는 선형적인 방식으로 평가된다.

6) 시험 응시일이 제한된다.

시험은 주로 토요일과 일요일에만 시행되며, 시험에 재응시할 경우, 시험 응시일 3일 후부터 재응시 가능하다.

7) Performance Feedback이 주어진다.

온라인 및 우편으로 발송된 성적표에는 수치화된 점수뿐 아니라 각 영역별로 수험자의 과제 수행 정도를 나타내는 표도 제공된다.

3. iBT TOEFL®의 구성

시험 영역	Reading, Listening, Speaking, Writing
시험 시간	약 3시간
시험 횟수	연 30~40회(날짜는 ETS에서 지정)
총 점	0~120점
영역별 점수	각 영역별 30점
성적 확인	응시일로부터 10일 후 온라인에서 성적 확인 가능

시험 영역	문제 구성	시간
Reading	● 독해 지문 3~4개, 총 30~40 문제가 출제된다. ● 각 지문 길이 700단어 내외, 지문당 10개 문제 ● 지문 3개가 출제될 경우 54분, 4개가 출제될 경우 72분이 주어진다.	54분~72분
Listening	● 대화(Conversation) 2~3개(각 5문제씩)와 강의(Lecture) 3~4개(각 6문제씩)가 출제된다. ● 듣기 5개가 출제될 경우 41분, 7개가 출제될 경우 57분이 주어진다.	41분~57분
Break		10분
Speaking	● 독립형 과제(Independent Task) 1개, 통합형 과제(Integrated Task) 3개 총 4개 문제가 출제된다.	17분
Writing	● 통합형 과제(Integrated Task) 1개(20분), 독립형 과제(Independent Task) 1개(30분) 총 2개 문제가 출제된다.	50분

4. iBT TOEFL®의 점수

1) 영역별 점수

Reading	0~30	Listening	0~30
Speaking	0~30	Writing	0~30

2) iBT, CBT, PBT 간 점수 비교

iBT	CBT	PBT	iBT	CBT	PBT
120	300	677	81~82	217	553
120	297	673	79~80	213	550
119	293	670	77~78	210	547
118	290	667	76	207	540~543
117	287	660~663	74~75	203	537
116	283	657	72~73	200	533
114~115	280	650~653	71	197	527~530
113	277	647	69~70	193	523
111~112	273	640~643	68	190	520
110	270	637	66~67	187	517
109	267	630~033	65	183	513
106~108	263	623~627	64	180	507~510
105	260	617~620	62~63	177	503
103~104	257	613	61	173	500
101~102	253	607~610	59~60	170	497
100	250	600~603	58	167	493
98~99	247	597	57	163	487~490
96~97	243	590~593	56	160	483
94~95	240	587	54~55	157	480
92~93	237	580~583	53	153	477
90~91	233	577	52	150	470~473
88~89	230	570~573	51	147	467
86~87	227	567	49~50	143	463
84~85	223	563	-	-	-
83	220	557~560	0	0	310

5. 시험 등록 및 응시 절차

1) 시험 등록

온라인과 전화로 시험 응시일과 각 지역의 시험장을 확인하여 신청할 수 있으며, 일반 접수는 시험 희망 응시일 7일 전까지 가능하다.

❶ 온라인 등록

ETS 토플 등록 사이트(https://www.ets.org/mytoefl)에 들어가 화면 지시에 따라 등록한다. 비용은 신용카드로 지불하게 되므로 American Express, Master Card, VISA 등 국제적으로 통용되는 신용카드를 미리 준비해둔다. 시험을 등록하기 위해서는 회원 가입이 선행되어야 한다.

❷ 전화 등록

한국 프로메트릭 콜센터(00-7981-4203-0248)에 09:00~17:00 사이에 전화를 걸어 등록한다.

2) 추가 등록

시험 희망 응시일 4일(공휴일을 제외한 업무일 기준) 전까지 US $40의 추가 비용으로 등록 가능하다.

3) 등록 비용

2021년 현재 US $210(가격 변동이 있을 수 있음)

4) 시험 취소와 변경

ETS 토플 등록 사이트나 한국 프로메트릭(00-7981-4203-0248)으로 전화해서 시험을 취소하거나 응시 날짜를 변경할 수 있다. 등록 취소와 날짜 변경은 시험 날짜 4일 전까지 해야 한다. 날짜를 변경하려면 등록 번호와 등록 시 사용했던 성명이 필요하며 비용은 US $60이다.

5) 시험 당일 소지품

❶ 사진이 포함된 신분증(주민등록증, 운전면허증, 여권 중 하나)

❷ 시험 등록 번호(Registration Number)

6) 시험 절차

❶ 사무실에서 신분증과 등록 번호를 통해 등록을 확인한다.

❷ 기밀 서약서(Confidentiality Statement)를 작성한 후 서명한다.

❸ 소지품 검사, 사진 촬영, 음성 녹음 및 최종 신분 확인을 하고 연필과 연습장(Scratch Paper)을 제공받는다.

❹ 감독관의 지시에 따라 시험실에 입실하여 지정된 개인 부스로 이동하여 시험을 시작한다.

❺ Reading과 Listening 영역이 끝난 후 10분간의 휴식이 주어진다.

❻ 시험 진행에 문제가 있을 경우 손을 들어 감독관의 지시에 따르도록 한다.

❼ Writing 영역 답안 작성까지 모두 마치면 화면 종료 메시지를 확인한 후에 신분증을 챙겨 퇴실한다.

7) 성적 확인

응시일로부터 약 10일 후부터 온라인으로 점수 확인이 가능하며 약 13일 후 우편 통지서도 발송된다.

6. 실제 시험 화면 구성

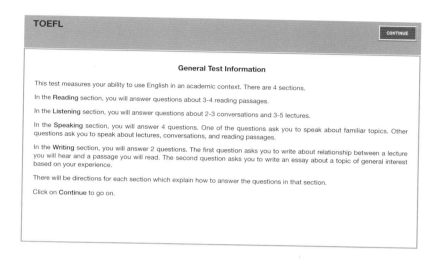

전체 Direction

시험 전체에 대한 구성 설명

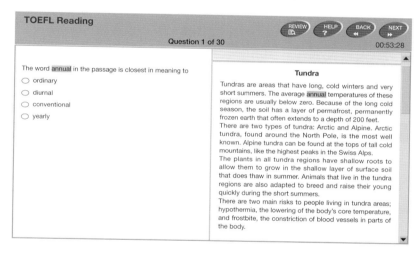

Reading 영역 화면

지문은 오른쪽에, 문제는 왼쪽에 제시

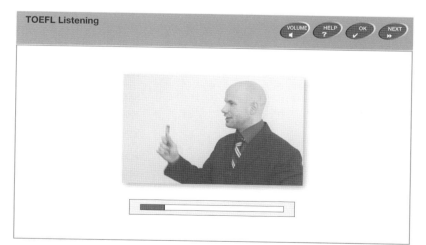

Listening 영역 화면

수험자가 대화나 강의를 듣는 동안 사진이 제시됨

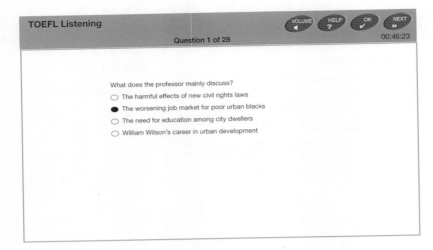

Listening 영역 화면

듣기가 끝난 후 문제 화면이
등장

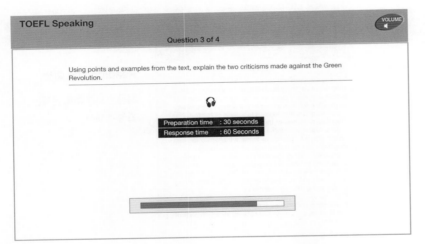

Speaking 영역 화면

문제가 주어진 후, 답변을 준
비하는 시간과 말하는 시간을
알려줌

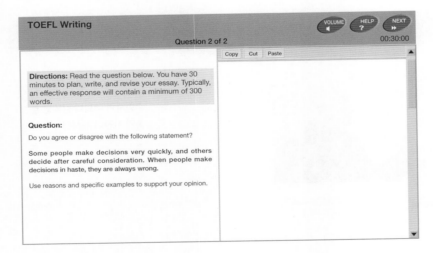

Writing 영역 화면

왼쪽에 문제가 주어지고 오른
쪽에 답을 직접 타이핑할 수
있는 공간이 주어짐

복사(Copy), 자르기(Cut), 붙
여넣기(Paste) 버튼이 위쪽
에 위치함

iBT TOEFL® Reading 개요

1. Reading 영역의 특징

1. 지문의 특징

Reading 영역에서는 영어권 대학의 학습 환경에서 접할 수 있는 전공별 강좌의 입문 내지 개론 수준의 지문이 다뤄지며 다양한 분야의 주제가 등장한다.

① 자연 과학: 화학, 수학, 물리학, 생물학, 의학, 공학, 천문학, 지질학 등

② 인문: 역사, 문화, 정부 정책, 문학, 그림, 조각, 건축, 연극, 춤, 특정 인물의 일대기 또는 업적 등

③ 사회 과학: 사회학, 심리학, 인류학, 경제학 등

Reading 영역에서 출제되는 글의 종류는 크게 설명(Exposition), 논증(Argumentation), 역사적인 인물 혹은 역사적인 사건의 서술(Historical / Biographical Event Narratives)로 나눌 수 있으며, 수필이나 문학 작품은 포함되지 않는다. 각 지문은 논지가 매우 분명하며 객관적인 논조로 전개되는 잘 짜인 글이다. 각 지문에는 제목이 주어지며 때로는 지문과 관련된 그림이나 사진, 도표, 그래프, 지도 등이 포함되기도 한다. 또한 용어 설명(Glossary) 기능이 있어 지문에서 밑줄 표시가 된 어휘에 마우스를 갖다 대면 그 영어 뜻이 화면 하단에 제공된다. 이러한 어휘는 일반적으로 난이도가 매우 높거나 특수한 용어다.

2. 문제의 특징

각 지문당 10개의 문제가 주어지며 크게 3가지 유형으로 나뉜다.

① 사지선다형

② 지문에 문장 삽입하기

③ 지문 전반에 걸쳐 언급된 주요 사항을 분류하여 요약표(Summary)나 범주표(Category Chart)에 넣기

※ 하나의 지문에는 Summary와 Category Chart 중 한 가지 유형의 문제만 출제되며, 이 두 문제 유형에는 부분 점수 (총점 2~3점)가 있다.

2. Reading 영역의 구성

Reading 영역에서는 총 10개의 문제 유형을 통해 지문에 대한 이해도를 다각도로 평가한다. 지문 길이가 700단어 내외로 상당히 긴 편이기 때문에 자칫 어렵다고 생각할 수 있지만, 문제 풀이에 필요한 정보는 모두 지문에서 찾을 수 있다. 따라서 다양한 주제의 지문을 접하면서 실제 시험 문제 유형에 익숙해지고 나면 TOEFL의 그 어느 영역보다도 고득점에 유리한 영역이다.

TOEFL 시험의 첫 번째 영역인 Reading은 3개 또는 4개의 지문으로 구성된다. 지문이 3개 출제될 경우 약 54분, 지문이 4개 출제될 경우 72분이 주어진다.

Part 구성	지문 수	문제 수	시험 시간
Part 1	3~4개	30~40 문제	54~72분

3. Reading 영역의 문제 유형

Reading 영역을 통해 평가하고자 하는 기본 능력은 다음과 같다.

- Basic Comprehension: 지문에 대한 기초적인 이해도
- Reading to Learn: 문장/문단 전후 관계 파악 및 전체 지문과의 연관성에 대한 이해도
- Inferencing: 지문 전체의 흐름에 대한 이해에 기반한 저자 의도 파악 능력

\<Reading 영역의 10가지 문제 유형\>

문제 유형	문제 설명	문제 개수
Basic Comprehension		
어휘 (Vocabulary)	문맥 안에서 특정 어휘가 어떤 뜻으로 사용되었는지 선택지 가운데 가장 비슷한 유의어를 고르는 문제	1~2
지시어 (Reference)	문맥에서 대명사나 관계대명사 등이 지칭하는 명사를 고르는 문제	0~1
문장 요약 (Sentence Simplification)	지문에서 음영 표시된 문장을 가장 잘 간결하게 바꾸어 쓴 것을 선택지 중에서 고르는 문제	0~1
사실 정보 찾기 (Factual Information)	지문을 바탕으로 문제를 통해 특정 정보의 사실 여부를 파악하거나 육하원칙에 따라 묻는 정보를 찾는 문제	2~3
틀린 정보 찾기 (Negative Fact)	지문에서 언급되지 않았거나 지문의 정보에 비춰볼 때 잘못된 것을 가려내는 문제	1

핵심 유형 공략

Which of the sentences below best expresses the essential information in the highlighted sentence in the passage? *Incorrect* answer choices change the meaning in important ways or leave out essential information.

Ⓐ Researchers claim that what fills the aquifer is the water from glaciers that melted quite a long time ago, and it is time to pump water into the aquifer again.

Ⓑ Geologists have realized that what is contained there may have arrived fairly recently due to the rate at which water filters through the ground.

Ⓒ According to scientists, the aquifer fills with water little by little, showing that the remaining water must have come from the last ice age at the latest.

Ⓓ Geologists believe that the formation was created during the height of the last ice age because much of the moisture in the aquifer exists as ice and is released slowly.

The Ogallala Aquifer

The Ogallala Aquifer is a natural underground water supply under the Western Plains of the United States. It is one of the largest bodies of water of its kind in the world, covering an area of approximately 450,000 square kilometers. It accounts for 30% of the total supply used to irrigate fields in the country. It is also a vital source of drinking water for the people who live near or above it. The aquifer is made of layers of gravel and sand that hold large amounts of water. These layers vary in thickness from only a few feet to over 1,000 feet in some areas. The northern sections of the aquifer tend to be thicker than those further to the south. These materials were carried there by erosion from the Rocky Mountains when they were still actively growing. During a period extending from around 6 million to 2 million years ago, the sand and gravel gradually filled up the valleys east of the mountains. Geologists have noticed that water refills the aquifer very slowly, which means that most of the water already contained there most likely collected during the last ice age or earlier.

다음 중 지문의 음영 표시된 문장의 핵심 정보를 가장 잘 표현한 문장은 무엇인가? 오답은 의미를 크게 왜곡하거나 핵심 정보를 누락하고 있다.

Ⓐ 연구자들은 대수층을 채우고 있는 것은 꽤 오래 전에 녹은 빙하의 물이며, 이제 다시 대수층으로 물을 퍼올릴 때라고 주장한다.

Ⓑ 지질학자들은 그곳에 들어 있는 것이 지면을 통과하는 물의 여과율 때문에 상당히 최근에 거기에 다다랐을 수 있다는 것을 깨달았다.

Ⓒ 과학자들에 따르면 대수층은 조금씩 물로 채워지며, 이는 남아 있는 물이 늦어도 마지막 빙하기로부터 왔을 것이라는 점을 보여준다.

Ⓓ 지질학자들은 대수층의 많은 습기가 얼음으로 존재하고 천천히 방출되기 때문에 마지막 빙하기가 한창일 때 대수층이 형성되었다고 믿는다.

오갈랄라 대수층

오갈랄라 대수층(Ogallala Aquifer)은 미국 서부 평원 산하의 천연 지하수 공급원이다. 그것은 세계에서 그런 종류의 가장 큰 수역 중 하나이며, 약 45만 평방 킬로미터의 면적에 달한다. 그것은 그 나라의 밭에 물을 대는 데 사용되는 전체 공급량의 30%를 차지한다. 그것은 또한 그 근처나 위에 사는 사람들에게 식수의 중요한 원천이다. 대수층은 많은 양의 물을 담을 수 있는 자갈과 모래 층들로 이루어져 있다. 이 층들의 두께는 불과 몇 피트부터 일부 지역에서는 1,000 피트 이상까지 다양하다. 대수층의 북쪽 지역은 남쪽으로 멀리 떨어진 지역보다 더 두꺼운 경향이 있다. 이 물질들은 로키 산맥이 아직 활발하게 형성되고 있을 때 침식에 의해 그곳에 운반되었다. 약 600만 년에서 200만 년 전에 걸친 기간 동안, 모래와 자갈은 산의 동쪽 골짜기를 점차 메웠다. 지질학자들은 물이 대수층을 매우 천천히 다시 채운다는 것을 알아냈는데, 이는 이미 그곳에 들어 있는 대부분의 물이 마지막 빙하기 혹은 그 이전에 모였을 가능성이 높다는 것을 의미한다.

해당 문장에서 핵심 정보 파악하기

해당 문장을 읽으며 중요 핵심 정보와 주변 세부 정보를 구분하여 표시해 둔다.

> Geologists have noticed that ① water refills the aquifer very slowly, which means that ② most of the water already contained there most likely collected during the last ice age or earlier.
>
> 핵심 정보 ① 물이 대수층을 천천히 다시 채우고 있음
> 핵심 정보 ② 대수층의 물은 대부분 마지막 빙하기로부터 온 것임

STEP 2 **정보가 모두 언급되어 있는 선택지 고르기**

문장의 핵심 정보를 담고 있는 선택지가 한 개 이상이므로 꼼꼼히 읽고 비교하여 고른다.

> Geologists have noticed that ① water refills the aquifer very slowly, which means that ② most of the water already contained there most likely collected during the last ice age or earlier.
>
> ⋯→ ⓒ According to scientists, ① the aquifer fills with water little by little, showing that ② the remaining water must have come from the last ice age at the latest.

STEP 3 **선택지들의 오답 여부를 재확인하여 정답 확정하기**

오답에는 해당 문장의 핵심 정보가 왜곡되었거나 누락되어 있으므로 이를 다시 확인한다.

> Ⓐ Researchers claim that what fills the aquifer is the water from glaciers that melted quite a long time ago, and it is time to pump water into the aquifer again (✘).
> ⋯→ 문장의 일부 핵심 정보가 왜곡되어 있음
>
> Ⓑ Geologists have realized that what is contained there may have arrived fairly recently (✘) due to the rate at which water filters through the ground.
> ⋯→ 문장의 일부 핵심 정보가 왜곡되어 있음
>
> Ⓓ Geologists believe that the formation was created during the height of the last ice age because much of the moisture in the aquifer exists as ice and is released slowly (✘).
> ⋯→ 문장의 일부 핵심 정보가 왜곡되어 있음
>
> 정답: ⓒ According to scientists, the aquifer fills with water little by little, showing that the remaining water must have come from the last ice age at the latest.

Sample Question 1

Which of the sentences below best expresses the essential information in the highlighted sentence in the passage? *Incorrect* answer choices change the meaning in important ways or leave out essential information.

(A) Merchants saw that they could utilize these skilled workers to produce cloth by giving them supplies and paying them with the money they made in the market.

(B) Farmers produced finished cloth for a share of the profits that merchants made by selling their products.

(C) Merchants began to purchase the cloth that farmers produced and sell it in markets to make a profit.

(D) The merchants collected raw materials from the farmers and gave them finished cloth from the market in return.

Population Growth in 18th Century Europe

The final factor that supported the surge in population was the growth of rural industry throughout Europe. In the cities, most industries like cloth production were managed by organizations called guilds that strictly regulated every stage of manufacturing. In the countryside, however, the people that farmed the land had long made their own clothing from local supplies of raw materials. As agriculture advanced, these rural poor also had increasing amounts of free time. Some merchants recognized the opportunity that such a large pool of skilled labor provided, and they began the putting-out system wherein they provided the farmers with raw materials for cloth and the tools needed to work with them, and the people produced finished material for a share of the profits. This provided the rural poor with a much needed source of income, particularly in the lean winter months when they could use the money to buy food and medicine. The influx of money also meant that young people could afford to marry and move out of their parents' homes. Since they had their children when they were younger, the children were more likely to survive.

18세기 유럽의 인구 증가

인구 급증을 뒷받침한 마지막 요소는 유럽 전역에 걸친 농촌산업 성장이었다. 도시에서는 직물 생산과 같은 대부분의 산업이 모든 제작 과정을 엄격하게 규제하는 길드라 불리는 조직에 의해 관리되었다. 그러나 지방에서는 농사를 짓던 사람들이 현지에서 공급되는 원자재로 오랫동안 직접 옷을 만들었다. 농업이 발전하자 지방의 빈곤계층은 갈수록 증가하는 여유 시간이 생겼다. 몇몇 상인들은 이렇게 대규모 숙련노동자 인력이 제공하는 기회를 알아보았고, 농부들에게 직물을 만들기 위해 필요한 원자재와 도구를 제공하고 사람들은 이익의 일부를 받는 대가로 완성물을 제공하는 선대제도를 시작했다. 이것은 지방의 빈곤계층에게 특히 수입이 적은 겨울철에 식량과 약을 구입하는 데 매우 필요한 수입원을 제공했다. 이런 돈의 유입은 젊은이들이 결혼하고 부모의 집에서 나올 수 있는 여유가 생긴다는 것을 뜻했다. 더 젊었을 때 아이를 낳았기 때문에 아이들은 생존할 가능성이 더 높았다.

다음 중 지문의 음영 표시된 문장의 핵심 정보를 가장 잘 표현한 문장은 무엇인가? 오답은 의미를 크게 왜곡하거나 핵심 정보를 누락하고 있다.

(A) 상인들은 이런 숙련 노동자들에게 재료를 주고 시장에서 자신들이 번 돈을 그들에게 지불함으로써 그들을 이용해 직물을 생산할 수 있다는 것을 알았다.

(B) 농부들은 자신들의 생산품을 상인들이 판매하여 생기는 이익의 일부를 받는 대가로 완성된 직물을 생산했다.

(C) 상인들은 농부들이 생산한 직물을 구입하고 돈을 벌기 위해 시장에서 그것을 팔기 시작했다.

(D) 상인들은 농부들에게서 원자재를 모으고 그 대가로 시장의 완성된 직물을 그들에게 주었다.

Sample Question 2

Which of the sentences below best expresses the essential information in the highlighted sentence in the passage? *Incorrect* answer choices change the meaning in important ways or leave out essential information.

Ⓐ Only what was left over from producing weaponry was devoted to manufacturing tools and utensils that were traded throughout the land.

Ⓑ Out of the ten thousand laborers who worked in government-owned plants, the majority produced weapons, while the rest produced nonmilitary equipment.

Ⓒ Most of the metal was produced in government-owned facilities which employed thousands of workers to transform it into weapons and armor.

Ⓓ The same government-owned plant which produced metal also hired laborers to manufacture tools and utensils that were traded throughout China.

Economic Changes in Postclassical China

The improvement of transportation infrastructure in Postclassical China also encouraged domestic trade along the canal and the Yangtze River. The increased demand for products stimulated industrial production, which led to improved production techniques and finer quality products. The government soon consolidated industrial production under its direct control, and it established massive factories that employed thousands of workers. One was a textile factory that had more than 10,000 workers engaged in silk manufacturing. Due to improved methods for iron and steel production, China's output skyrocketed. The majority of the metal was produced in government-owned arsenals that employed over 100,000 workers, who used the metal to manufacture weapons and armor, and the remainder was used for tools and utensils that were sold throughout China. Innovations in ceramics allowed craftsmen to create porcelain that was lighter, thinner, and more beautiful, and large factories were also built for its production. Other innovations of the time had enduring effects on the world, including movable-type printing, gunpowder, and a magnetic compass for sailing.

다음 중 지문의 음영 표시된 문장의 핵심 정보를 가장 잘 표현한 문장은 무엇인가? 오답은 의미를 크게 왜곡하거나 핵심 정보를 누락하고 있다.

Ⓐ 무기를 생산하는 것에서 남은 것만이 전국적으로 거래된 도구와 기구를 제작하는 데 사용됐다.

Ⓑ 정부 소유 공장에서 일한 노동자 1만 명 중에서 대다수는 무기를 생산했고 나머지는 비군사적인 용품을 생산했다.

Ⓒ 대부분의 금속은 수천 명의 노동자를 고용하여 그것을 무기와 갑옷으로 생산하는 정부 소유 시설에서 생산됐다.

Ⓓ 금속을 생산한 동일한 정부 소유 공장은 중국 전역에서 거래된 도구와 기구를 제작하기 위해 노동자들을 고용했다.

고전 시대 이후 중국의 경제 변화

고전 시대 이후 중국의 운송 기반 시설 개선은 운하와 양자강을 따라 국내 무역을 촉진했다. 상품에 대한 수요 증가는 산업 생산을 활성화시켰고 이것은 개선된 생산 기술과 양질의 상품으로 이어졌다. 정부는 곧이어 산업 생산을 통합해 직할 통제 아래 두었고 수천 명의 직원을 고용하는 거대한 공장들을 세웠다. 그중 하나는 비단 제조에 1만 명 이상의 직원을 투입한 직물 공장이었다. 철과 강철 생산 방법의 개선으로 인해 중국의 생산량은 급등했다. 금속의 대부분은 10만 명이 넘는 직원을 고용한 정부 소유의 무기고에서 생산됐고 그들은 금속을 사용해서 무기와 갑옷을 제작했다. 그리고 나머지는 중국 전역에 판매된 도구와 기구에 사용됐다. 도예에 있어서의 혁신은 공예가들이 더 가볍고 더 얇고 더 아름다운 자기를 만들 수 있게 해주었고 그 생산을 위해 큰 공장들이 지어졌다. 가동 활자판, 화약, 그리고 항해에 사용되는 자기 나침반을 포함한 당대의 다른 혁신들은 세계에 지속적인 영향을 끼쳤다.

PAGODA TOEFL 90+

READING

Actual Test

02 Fact / Negative Fact

- 사실/틀린 정보 찾기(Fact/Negative Fact) 문제는 지문에 제시된 세부 정보에 관해 묻는 문제로, Fact 문제는 선택지 중에서 지문의 내용과 일치하는 것을, Negative Fact 문제는 지문의 내용과 일치하지 않거나 지문에 언급되지 않은 것을 고르는 문제이다.

- 출제 빈도가 가장 높은 유형으로 지문당 1~4개의 문제가 출제되며, 질문이 출제된 단락의 번호가 문제와 함께 제시된다.

- 정답은 일반적으로 지문의 내용 중 핵심 정보는 넣되 주변 정보는 빼는 방식으로 패러프레이즈된다.

📖 문제 유형

Fact

- According to paragraph X, which of the following is true of Y?
  X단락에 따르면, 다음 중 Y에 대해 사실인 것은 무엇인가?

- In paragraph X, the author states that
  X단락에서 글쓴이가 제시하는 것은?

- According to paragraph X, why/what/how Y?
  X단락에 따르면, 왜/무엇이/어떻게 Y인가?

Negative Fact

- All of the following are mentioned in paragraph X EXCEPT
  다음 중 X단락에서 언급되지 않은 것은?

- According to the passage, which of the following is NOT true of X?
  지문에 따르면, 다음 중 X에 대해 사실이 아닌 것은 무엇인가?

💡 문제 풀이 전략

- 지문을 빠르게 훑어 읽으면서 문제의 키워드를 신속하게 찾을 수 있어야 한다. 이때, 고유명사, 숫자, 이름, 지명 등을 이용하면 좀 더 효율적이다.

- 지문에서 핵심어 포함 문장과 그 앞뒤 문장들을 꼼꼼히 살펴보면서 선택지와 비교한다.

- Fact와 Negative Fact 문제의 선택지에는 지문의 내용이 모두 패러프레이즈되어 있으므로 유의한다. 패러프레이징에 익숙해지려면 동의어 및 같은 의미를 나타내는 서로 다른 표현들을 잘 알고 있어야 한다.

🚨 피해야 할 오답 유형

- Fact: 지문에서 전혀 언급되지 않은 내용의 선택지, 지문에서 언급된 내용과 다른 선택지
- Negative Fact: 지문에서 언급된 내용이 패러프레이즈되어 있는 선택지

📖 핵심 유형 공략

TOEFL **Reading**

REVIEW · HELP ? · BACK ◀◀ · NEXT ▶▶

All of the following are mentioned in the passage about the flying method of the fish EXCEPT

(A) they use their tail to gain the driving force for jumping.

(B) they can fly up to 50 meters high and stay in the air for 400 meters.

(C) they use their fins like a bird's wings to ride on the wind.

(D) they can fly far longer with their tail moving in the water.

Flying Fish

Flying fish can be found in every ocean, but they typically prefer tropical areas. To begin a flight, the fish will rapidly swing its tail to gain speed. This pushes the fish up out of the water where it will extend its long wing-like fins. It will adjust the fins to lift its body above the water and then glide on the wind. Their flights are usually about 50 meters long. However, by putting only their tail in the water and moving it to maintain speed, they can travel up to 400 meters. They can move at speeds around 70 kilometers per hour while swimming. They can glide up to 6 meters above the water, which often lands them on the decks of boats. This flight is a tactic they evolved to avoid their many predators which include dolphins, marlin, tuna, and squid.

다음 중 이 물고기의 비행 방법에 대해 지문에서 언급되지 않은 것은?

(A) 점프하는 추진력을 얻기 위해 꼬리를 사용한다.

(B) 최대 50미터 높이까지 날 수 있고 400미터까지 공중에 머물 수 있다.

(C) 바람을 타기 위해 지느러미를 새의 날개처럼 사용한다.

(D) 꼬리를 물속에서 움직이면서 훨씬 더 오래 날 수 있다.

날치

날치는 모든 바다에서 발견될 수 있지만, 전형적으로 열대 지역을 선호한다. 비행을 시작하기 위해 이 물고기는 속도를 내려고 빠르게 꼬리를 흔든다. 이것은 이 물고기를 물 밖으로 밀어내고 물고기는 긴 날개 같은 지느러미를 뻗는다. 그것은 지느러미를 조절하여 몸을 물 위로 들어올린 다음 바람을 타고 활공한다. 그들의 비행은 보통 약 50미터에 달한다. 하지만 꼬리만 물에 넣고 속도를 유지하기 위해 움직이면 최대 400미터까지 이동할 수 있다. 그들은 수영하는 동안 시속 70킬로미터의 속도로 움직일 수 있다. 그들은 물 위로 6미터까지 활공할 수 있는데, 이로 인해 종종 보트 갑판에 내려앉는다. 이 비행은 돌고래, 청새치, 참치, 오징어를 포함한 많은 포식자들을 피하기 위해 진화한 전술이다.

질문의 요지와 핵심어 파악하기

질문을 읽고 난 후, Fact/Negative Fact 중 무엇을 묻는 문제인지와 질문의 핵심어를 파악한다.

지문에서 핵심어 주변 정보 확인하기

지문을 빠르게 훑어 읽으며 질문의 핵심어나 관련 내용을 찾아 앞뒤 문장의 세부 정보를 확인한다.

지문 내의 세부 정보와 선택지 대조해 보기

Negative Fact의 답은 지문에 아예 등장하지 않은 내용이거나, 지문에 언급된 사실을 약간만 왜곡해서 패러프레이즈한 내용일 수 있다.

Their flights are usually about 50 meters long. However, by putting only their tail in the water and moving it to maintain speed, they can travel up to 400 meters.

⋯▸ 날치는 보통 50미터 거리를 날지만, 꼬리만 물속에 넣은 상태로 움직이면 최대 400미터까지 이동할 수 있다고 했으므로 선택지 Ⓑ의 '400미터까지 공중에 머물 수 있다'와 일부 일치하지 않음

정답: Ⓑ they can fly up to 50 meters high and stay in the air for 400 meters.

Sample Question 1

According to the passage, which of the following is NOT true of the golden ratio of the Great Pyramids?

Ⓐ The Great Pyramid is one example which shows a close relationship between math and art.

Ⓑ Some scholars who study pyramids believe the presence of the golden ratio had a direct effect on the pyramids.

Ⓒ The difference between the golden ratio and the calculated proportions of Khufu's pyramid is more than 1%.

Ⓓ The existence of the golden ratio in the pyramid design still remains controversial among many renowned researchers.

Pyramids and the Golden Ratio

Mathematical influence on art is evident when you look at the Great Pyramids. This complex of pyramids was commissioned by Egyptian Pharaoh Khufu and completed in 2,560 BCE. Since the 19th century, pyramidologists have noted that the golden ratio is present in the design of these ancient monuments. Specifically, they point out that the length of the base edges of the Khufu Pyramid range from 755 to 756 feet, the height of the structure is 481.4 feet, and the slant height of the perpendicular bisector of the face of the pyramid is 612 feet. The ratio of the slant height to half its base length is 1.619, which is less than 1% shy of the golden ratio. This also indicates that half of the cross-section of Khufu's pyramid is actually a Kepler triangle. Of course, these findings resulted in debate between the world's most prominent pyramidologists. One faction claims that the evidence shows that the golden ratio was purposely made a part of the pyramid design while the other faction states that the golden ratio's presence is merely a coincidence.

PART 01
Question Types

지문에 따르면, 다음 중 대 피라미드의 황금 비율에 대해 사실이 아닌 것은 무엇인가?

Ⓐ 대 피라미드는 수학과 예술의 밀접한 관계를 보여주는 한 가지 예이다.

Ⓑ 피라미드를 연구하는 일부 학자들은 황금 비율의 존재가 피라미드에 직접적인 영향을 주었다고 믿는다.

Ⓒ 황금 비율과 계산된 쿠푸 피라미드 비율과의 오차는 1퍼센트 이상이다.

Ⓓ 피라미드 설계에 있는 황금 비율의 존재는 명성 있는 많은 연구자들 사이에서 아직도 논란이 되고 있다.

피라미드와 황금 비율

대 피라미드를 보면 수학이 예술에 미친 영향을 분명히 알 수 있다. 이 피라미드 단지는 이집트 파라오 쿠푸가 의뢰하였으며 기원전 2,560년에 완공되었다. 19세기 이래로 피라미드 연구학자들은 이런 기념비적인 고대 건축물들의 설계에 황금 비율이 존재한다고 언급했다. 구체적으로 학자들은 쿠푸 피라미드 하단 모서리 길이는 755~756피트(약 230미터), 높이는 481.4피트(약 147미터), 정면의 수직 이등분선인 경사면 높이는 612피트(약 187미터)라고 언급한다. 하단 길이의 절반에 대한 경사면 높이의 비율은 1.619이며, 이것은 황금 비율에서 1퍼센트가 부족한 것이다. 이는 또한 쿠푸 피라미드 횡단면의 절반이 실제로 케플러의 삼각형이라는 것을 나타낸다. 물론 이런 연구 결과는 세계에서 가장 저명한 피라미드 연구학자들 사이의 논쟁을 야기했다. 한 당파는 이것이 황금 비율이 피라미드 설계에 의도적으로 적용되었다는 증거라고 주장하는 반면 다른 당파는 황금 비율의 존재는 그저 우연의 일치일 뿐이라고 말한다.

Sample Question 2

Citizen's Arrest

In the event of a crime, the person or persons committing an illegal act may be arrested by someone who is not a sworn law enforcement officer. This is known as a citizen's arrest. This right is afforded to common citizens in many countries. The practice of allowing citizens to make arrests dates back to medieval English common law. In medieval England, the sheriff encouraged ordinary citizens to help catch criminals. However, making a citizen's arrest can actually lead to trouble for the person carrying it out. The citizen making an arrest could be exposing him or herself to the possibility of a lawsuit or serious criminal charges if an innocent person is arrested or if the suspect's civil rights are violated in some way. Some of the possible charges against the citizen making an arrest could include kidnapping, impersonating a police officer, and wrongful arrest. This may be the reason why stories of citizen's arrests actually taking place are uncommon.

According to the passage, those who make a citizen's arrest could be in trouble when

(A) they arbitrarily apprehend criminals without the permission of authorities.

(B) they are not officially designated citizens who have the right to exert governmental power.

(C) they abduct a suspect, represent themselves as a police officer, or arrest an innocent person.

(D) they don't take appropriate actions to place serious criminals under arrest.

시민 체포

범죄가 발생하면 불법 행위를 저지른 사람 또는 사람들은 정식 임명된 사법 기관 공무원이 아닌 사람에 의해 체포될 수 있다. 이것은 시민 체포라고 알려져 있다. 이런 권리는 많은 나라에서 일반 시민들에게 주어진다. 시민들이 체포를 할 수 있도록 허용하는 이 관행은 중세 영국의 관습법으로 거슬러 올라간다. 중세 영국에서는 주 장관이 일반 시민들에게 법을 어기는 자들을 잡도록 장려했다. 그러나 시민에 의한 범인 체포는 실제로 체포를 수행하는 사람을 곤경에 처하게 할 수 있다. 죄 없는 사람이 체포되거나 용의자의 인권이 어떤 식으로든 침해되었을 경우, 체포를 수행하는 시민은 소송이나 심각한 형사 기소를 당할 가능성에 스스로를 노출할 수 있다. 체포를 수행하는 시민을 상대로 있을 수 있는 기소들 중에는 납치, 경찰 사칭, 부당 체포가 있다. 이것이 시민 체포가 실제로 일어났다는 이야기가 흔치 않은 이유일 것이다.

지문에 따르면, 시민 체포를 하는 사람이 곤경에 처하게 되는 때는?

(A) 당국의 허가 없이 독단적으로 범죄자를 체포하는 때이다.

(B) 공권력을 행사할 권리를 가지고 있는 공식 지정 시민이 아닐 때이다.

(C) 용의자를 납치하거나 경찰을 사칭하거나 무고한 사람을 체포하는 때이다.

(D) 중범죄자를 체포하기 위한 적절한 조치를 취하지 않은 때이다.

PAGODA TOEFL 90+

READING

Actual Test

03 Vocabulary

- 어휘(Vocabulary) 문제는 주어진 어휘의 동의어(Synonym)를 묻는 문제이다.
- 지문당 1~2개의 문제가 출제되며, 해당 단어나 구는 지문에 음영으로 표시된다.

📖 문제 유형

- **The word "X" in paragraph Y is closest in meaning to**
  Y단락의 단어 "X"와 의미상 가장 가까운 것은?

- **The phrase "X" in paragraph Y is closest in meaning to**
  Y단락의 구 "X"와 의미상 가장 가까운 것은?

💡 문제 풀이 전략

- 빈출 어휘의 다양한 동의어와 관련 표현을 익혀두는 것이 좋다.
- 질문과 선택지에 등장하는 어휘의 다양한 의미를 고려해야 한다.
- TOEFL에서는 성, 수, 격의 일치 여부로 답을 고를 수 없음을 알아둔다.
- 해당 어휘의 앞뒤 문장에 동의어나 반의어의 단서가 있는지 찾아본다.
- 해당 어휘를 포함한 문장의 문맥을 살펴 가능한 답의 범위를 좁힌다.
- 가능한 선택지를 문장에 넣어 보고 문맥이 자연스럽게 연결되는지 확인한다.

🚨 피해야 할 오답 유형

- 지문의 내용과 관련이 있는 어휘
- 문장 속에서 무난하게 해석되는 어휘

📖 핵심 유형 공략

TOEFL Reading

REVIEW HELP ? BACK ◄◄ NEXT ►►

The word "incorporates" in paragraph 1 is closest in meaning to	(...) This technology incorporates the cable and pulley system of an elevator and the metal tracks and wheels of a railway train. (...)
Ⓐ persuades Ⓑ combines Ⓒ restrains Ⓓ determines	

1단락의 단어 "incorporates(결합하다)"와 의미상 가장 가까운 것은?

Ⓐ 설득하다　　　Ⓑ 결합하다
Ⓒ 억제하다　　　Ⓓ 결정하다

(…) 이 기술은 엘리베이터의 케이블과 도르래 시스템에 철도 열차의 철로와 바퀴를 결합한 것이다. (…)

STEP 1 어휘력 활용하기

평소 어휘력이 풍부하다면 문제의 어휘를 보고 선택지에서 바로 동의어를 고를 수 있다.

> **incorporate:** 포함하다. 결합하다 (≒ integrate, include, contain, take in)

STEP 2 문맥에서 단서 찾기

해당 어휘를 모른다면 앞뒤 문맥을 살펴보고 단서를 찾아 선택지에서 오답을 소거한다.

> This technology incorporates ① the cable and pulley system of an elevator and ② the metal tracks and wheels of a railway train.
> Ⓐ persuades　　Ⓑ combines　　Ⓒ restrains　　Ⓓ determines
> ⋯ 이 기술이 ①과 ②를 incorporates한다고 했으므로, Ⓐ persuades(설득하다), Ⓒ restrains(억제하다)는 문맥에 어울리지 않으므로 소거한다.

STEP 3 문장에 대입해 보기

오답 소거 후에 남은 선택지들을 문장에 대입해 보고 가장 적절한 것을 정답으로 고른다.

> This technology combines / determines the cable and pulley system of an elevator and the metal tracks and wheels of a railway train.
> ⋯ 이 기술은 엘리베이터의 케이블과 도르래 시스템에 철도 열차의 철로와 바퀴를 결합한 것이다 / 결정한 것이다.
> 정답: Ⓑ combines

Sample Question 1

The word "accountable" in the passage is closest in meaning to

(A) defendable

(B) acceptable

(C) responsible

(D) manageable

Spamming

Perhaps the largest annoyance to be found when connected to modern communication systems is "spam." Those who send spam are called "spammers," while the act of sending spam is known as "spamming." Spamming is basically defined as an abuse of electronic messaging systems in which unsolicited bulk messages are sent indiscriminately to a large number of recipients. The most widely recognized form of spam is e-mail spam, but the term is also applied to similar abuses of other forms of communication. Advertisers find spamming to be an effective strategy due to both the low cost and lack of regulation. The lack of regulation has made it difficult to hold spammers accountable for their mass mailings. Since it is cheaper and easier to reach more people, the number of spam messages has skyrocketed. However, the costs of spam on the public, such as lost productivity in the workplace and cases of fraud, have made spam the target of new legislation in many countries.

지문의 단어 "accountable(책임을 지는)"과 의미상 가장 가까운 것은?

(A) 방어할 수 있는

(B) 받아들일 수 있는

(C) 책임이 있는

(D) 관리할 수 있는

스패밍(스팸 메일 보내기)

아마도 현대 통신 시스템과 관련하여 가장 성가신 것으로 생각되는 것은 '스팸(메일)'일 것이다. 스팸 메일을 보내는 사람들은 '스패머'라고 불리며 스팸 메일을 보내는 행동은 '스패밍'이라고 알려져 있다. 스패밍은 기본적으로 원하지 않는 대규모의 메시지를 무차별적으로 많은 수신자들에게 보내서 전자 메시지 시스템을 남용하는 것으로 정의된다. 가장 널리 알려진 형태의 스팸은 이메일 스팸이지만, 스팸이라는 용어는 다른 종류의 통신 수단을 비슷하게 남용한 경우에도 또한 적용된다. 광고주들은 스팸 메일을 보내는 것이 비용이 저렴하고 규제가 적기 때문에 효과적인 전략이라고 생각한다. 규제의 부족으로 인해 스팸 메일을 보내는 사람들에게 대량 메일에 대한 책임을 지게 하기가 어려워졌다. 더 많은 사람들에게 연락하는 것이 더 저렴하고 더 쉽기 때문에 스팸 메시지의 수는 급증했다. 그러나 직장에서의 생산성 저하와 사기 사건과 같이 스팸이 대중에게 치르게 하는 비용으로 인해 많은 국가에서 스팸 메일을 새로운 법안의 대상으로 삼고 있다.

Sample Question 2

The phrase "once and for all" in the passage is closest in meaning to

Ⓐ immediately

Ⓑ conclusively

Ⓒ permanently

Ⓓ indefinitely

The Bombing of Hiroshima

In 1945, the United States made the decision to drop an atomic bomb and hopefully end World War II once and for all with a devastating strike upon their enemy, Japan. On August 6th of that year, a U.S. B-29 bomber flew through clear skies until it was approximately 10,000 meters above the Japanese city of Hiroshima. Once in position, the crew opened the craft's bomb bay doors and released a single bomb. At 8:15 A.M., only forty-three seconds after the bomb's release, two large pieces of uranium collided within the casing of the descending weapon. The explosion that resulted scorched the earth beneath in a matter of seconds, and an estimated 12 square kilometers of Hiroshima was effectively obliterated. The entire world was amazed, yet horrified, that a single bomb was capable of such destruction. The United States Military was deliberate in choosing Hiroshima for a target. The city had factories supplying Japan's military machine as well as serving as an inland port for their military missions into Korea, China, and Southeast Asia. In addition, as headquarters for Japan's Second Army, the city housed approximately 43,000 military personnel, 20,000 forced laborers and roughly 280,000 civilians.

히로시마의 폭격

지문의 구 "once and for all(완전히)"과 의미상 가장 가까운 것은?

Ⓐ 즉시

Ⓑ 확실히

Ⓒ 영원히

Ⓓ 무기한으로

1945년 미국은 적국 일본에 원자 폭탄을 투하하기로 결정했으며 파괴적인 공격으로 제2차 세계 대전을 완전히 끝내길 바랐다. 그해 8월 6일에 미국의 B-29 폭격기는 맑은 하늘을 날아 일본 히로시마의 약 1만 미터 상공에 이르렀다. 위치를 잡자마자 전투기 조종사는 전투기의 포문을 열고 폭탄 한 발을 투하했다. 폭탄 투하 후 단 43초 만인 오전 8시 15분에 낙하하는 무기의 외피 내부에서 두 개의 큰 우라늄 덩어리가 충돌했다. 그 결과로 인한 폭발이 몇 초 사이에 아래에 있는 땅을 불태웠고, 히로시마의 약 12제곱 킬로미터가 사실상 흔적도 없이 사라졌다. 전 세계는 폭탄 하나가 그런 파괴력을 가지고 있다는 것에 놀랐고 공포에 휩싸였다. 미군은 의도적으로 히로시마를 목표로 선택했다. 히로시마는 한국, 중국과 동남아로 군사 행동을 하기 위한 내륙 기지 역할을 해오고 있었을 뿐만 아니라 일본군에 장비를 공급하는 공장을 가지고 있었다. 또한 히로시마는 일본의 제2부대 본부로서 약 4만 3천 명의 군인들과 2만 명의 강제 노역자들, 그리고 약 28만 명의 민간인들이 거주하고 있었다.

PART 01
Question Types

04 Reference

- 지시어(Reference) 문제는 주어진 지시어가 지문 내에서 가리키는 대상이 무엇인지를 찾는 문제로, 해당 지시어나 구는 지문에 음영으로 표시된다.
- 지문당 1개의 문제가 출제되거나, 아예 출제되지 않을 때도 있다.

📖 문제 유형

- The word "*X*" in paragraph *Y* refers to   Y단락의 단어 "X"가 가리키는 것은
- The phrase "*X*" in paragraph *Y* refers to   Y단락의 구 "X"가 가리키는 것은

💡 문제 풀이 전략

- 지시 대상은 주로 지시어보다 먼저 언급되지만, 간혹 지시어가 먼저 나오는 경우도 있으므로 주의한다.
- 다양한 지시어의 성격과 쓰임을 미리 알아두면 지시 대상을 신속하게 찾을 수 있다. 지시 대상은 단어, 구, 절, 혹은 문장 전체가 될 수도 있다.
- 선택지에는 모두 성, 수, 격이 일치하는 단어가 등장하기 때문에 성, 수, 격의 일치 여부로는 정답의 범위를 좁힐 수 없다는 점을 염두에 둔다.
- 문맥을 보고 정답을 바로 고를 수 없는 경우에는 선택지를 하나씩 대입해 보며 오답을 소거한다.

지시어의 종류	지시어의 쓰임
인칭대명사	it, its [단수] ǀ they, their, them [복수]
지시대명사/형용사	this, that [+단수명사] ǀ these, those [+복수명사] the former 전자, the latter 후자
지시부사	there [장소], then [시간]
부정대명사/형용사	all 모두, none 아무도, several 몇몇, some 일부, others 다른 사람들/것들, both 둘 다, one 하나(의), another 또 다른 하나(의), neither (둘 중) 어느 것도 아닌, either (둘 중) 어느 하나(의)
관계대명사	who, which, that

🚨 피해야 할 오답 유형

- 지시어와 너무 멀리 떨어져 있는 대상
- 가까이에 있는 단어이지만 문맥에 맞지 않는 대상
- 지시어 이전에 전혀 언급되지 않은 대상

📖 핵심 유형 공략

TOEFL Reading   REVIEW HELP BACK NEXT

The word "them" in the passage refers to

(A) styles

(B) artists

(C) colors

(D) strokes

Pointillism

In the 1880s, Georges Seurat and Paul Signac developed a new style of painting. With most painting styles, artists blend colors and then brush them onto the canvas using strokes to create shape and texture. However, in their new technique, small distinct dots of pure color are placed in patterns. The viewers must use their eyes and minds to blend the colors into a more complete image.

지문의 단어 "them(그것들)"이 가리키는 것은?

(A) 화풍들

(B) 화가들

(C) 색깔들

(D) 붓질들

점선주의

1880년대에 조르주 쇠라와 폴 시냐크는 새로운 화풍을 개발했다. 대부분의 화풍에서는 형태와 질감을 나타내기 위해 화가가 색을 혼합한 후에 그것들을 붓질하여 화폭에 칠한다. 하지만 그들의 새로운 기법의 경우 순색의 작고 뚜렷한 점들을 일정한 무늬로 배치한다. 그림을 보는 사람들은 그들의 눈과 마음을 이용해 색을 섞어서 보다 완전한 그림으로 만들어야 한다.

STEP 1 지시어 포함 문장과 앞뒤 문장 살펴보기

지시어가 포함된 문장과 그 주변의 문장을 살펴보며 선택지에 제시된 대상들을 확인한다.

In the 1880s, Georges Seurat and Paul Signac developed a new style of painting. With most painting Ⓐ styles, Ⓑ artists blend Ⓒ colors and then brush them onto the canvas using Ⓓ strokes to create shape and texture. However, in their new technique, small distinct dots of pure color are placed in patterns.

STEP 2 선택지에서 문맥에 맞지 않는 대상 소거하기

정답을 바로 고를 수 없다면 앞뒤 문맥을 살펴보고 단서를 찾아 선택지에서 오답을 소거한다. '그것들을 화폭에 칠한다'는 것으로 보아 Ⓑ artists(화가), Ⓓ strokes(붓질)는 문맥에 어울리지 않으므로 소거한다.

STEP 3 정답 후보인 선택지를 해당 문장에 대입해 보기

확실한 오답을 소거한 후에 남은 선택지들을 해당 문장에 대입해 보고 최종 정답을 고른다.

With most painting Ⓐ styles, Ⓑ artists blend Ⓒ colors and then brush styles / colors onto the canvas using Ⓓ strokes to create shape and texture.
대부분의 화풍에서는 형태와 질감을 나타내기 위해 화가가 색을 혼합한 후에 화풍 / 색을 붓질하여 화폭에 칠한다.

정답: Ⓒ colors

Sample Question 1

Max Weber's Sociological Influence

German sociologist and political economist Maximilian Karl Emil "Max" Weber had a major influence on social theory and social research. Weber's major works, released just before the turn of the 20th century, dealt with the rationalization and disenchantment that he associated with the rise of the capitalist system and the age of modernity that accompanied **it**. Weber, along with others like Georg Simmel, was a central figure in the establishment of methodological anti-positivism. Anti-positivism presented sociology as a discipline in which one must study social action through resolutely subjective means. Of his works, Weber is most famous for his thesis on economic sociology: *The Protestant Ethic and the Spirit of Capitalism*. In this thesis, he argued that the Protestantism particular to the people of the Western Hemisphere (Europe) was a key player in the rise of capitalism, bureaucracy, and the rational-legal nation-state. He argued against the ideas of Karl Marx and Friedrich Engels, which he felt were overly materialistic interpretations of the development of capitalism. Instead, he emphasized the cultural influences firmly embedded in religion.

The word "**it**" in the passage refers to

(A) theory

(B) century

(C) rise

(D) age

PART 01 Question Types

막스 베버의 사회학적 영향

독일 사회학자이자 정치 경제학자인 막시밀리안 칼 에밀 '막스' 베버는 사회 이론과 사회 연구에 중요한 영향을 미쳤다. 20세기로 접어들기 바로 전에 발표된 베버의 대표작들은 합리화와 각성을 다루었는데 그는 그것을 자본주의 체제의 대두와 그것을 동반한 현대 시대와 연관지었다. 베버는 게오르그 짐멜과 같은 다른 이들과 함께 방법론적 반실증주의를 확립한 중심 인물이었다. 반실증주의는 사회학을 확실히 주관인 수단을 통해 사회적 행위를 연구해야 하는 지식 분야로 소개했다. 그의 작품들 중에서 베버는 〈프로테스탄트 윤리와 자본주의 정신〉이라는 경제 사회학 논문으로 가장 유명하다. 이 논문에서 그는 서반구(유럽) 사람들에게 각별한 프로테스탄트주의가 자본주의, 관료 제도, 그리고 합리적이며 합법적인 민족 국가의 발흥에 중요한 역할을 했다고 주장했다. 그는 칼 마르크스와 프리드리히 엥겔스의 사상에 반대론을 펼쳤는데, 그는 이 사상들이 자본주의 발달에 대한 지나친 유물론적인 해석이라고 생각했다. 대신에 그는 종교에 단단히 뿌리 박힌 문화적 영향을 강조했다.

지문의 단어 "it(그것)"이 가리키는 것은?

(A) 이론

(B) 세기

(C) 대두

(D) 시대

Sample Question 2

Earth's Atmosphere

Most people know that Earth is the third planet from the Sun, a medium-sized star. The Earth is approximately 4.5 billion years old, and it has been constantly changing during that time. However, few people realize that the Earth is now on its third atmosphere. The first atmosphere was helium and hydrogen, but it dissipated early on because the planet was so hot. As the planet cooled, volcanic eruptions produced a second atmosphere of steam and carbon dioxide. The water vapor from the steam condensed and formed the oceans that cover most of the planet. Around three billion years ago, bacteria evolved to consume carbon dioxide and excrete oxygen, while other bacteria released nitrogen. The concentration of these gases slowly increased, and organisms that could not adapt to them died out. The Earth's atmosphere is as violent as the land beneath it. At any moment, there are around 1,500 electrical storms in progress, and eleven lightning bolts strike the land each second. A tornado tears across the surface every six hours, and a giant cyclonic storm moves over the oceans at least once a week.

The word "them" in the passage refers to

Ⓐ oceans

Ⓑ bacteria

Ⓒ gases

Ⓓ organisms

지구의 대기

대부분의 사람들은 지구가 태양으로부터 세 번째에 있는 행성이고 중간 크기의 별이라는 것을 알고 있다. 지구는 대략 45억 살이며 그 세월 동안 끊임없이 변해왔다. 하지만 지구가 현재 세 번째 대기 상에 있다는 것을 아는 사람은 거의 없다. 첫 번째 대기는 헬륨과 수소 였지만, 지구가 너무 뜨거웠기 때문에 일찍 소멸되었다. 지구가 식자 화산 폭발이 증기와 이산화탄소로 이루어진 두 번째 대기를 만들어 냈다. 그 증기에서 나온 수증기가 응결하여 지구 대부분을 덮고 있는 대양을 형성했다. 약 30억 년 전, 박테리아들이 진화하여 이산화탄소 를 마시고 산소를 배출하게 되었으며 한편 다른 박테리아들은 질소 를 배출했다. 이러한 기체들의 농도는 서서히 증가했고, 그것들에 적 응할 수 없었던 생물들은 멸종되었다. 지구의 대기는 그 아래에 있는 대지만큼이나 격렬하다. 매 순간 약 1,500여 건의 뇌우가 일어나고 있으며, 초당 11번의 번개가 땅에 떨어진다. 6시간마다 토네이도가 표 면을 가르고, 적어도 일주일에 한 번씩은 거대한 저기압성 폭풍이 대 양 위를 이동한다.

지문의 단어 "them(그것들)"이 가리키는 것은?

Ⓐ 대양들

Ⓑ 박테리아들

Ⓒ 기체들

Ⓓ 생물들

PAGODA TOEFL 90+

READING

Actual Test

05 Rhetorical Purpose

⊙ 의도 파악(Rhetorical Purpose) 문제는 글쓴이가 지문에서 특정 어구나 설명 방식을 사용한 의도 및 역할을 묻는 문제이다.

⊙ 질문에 그대로 언급된 특정 어구는 지문에 음영 표시되어 있으며, 전체적인 설명 방식을 묻는 질문에는 지문의 단락 번호가 표시된다.

⊙ 지문당 1개의 문제가 출제되거나, 아예 출제되지 않을 때도 있다.

📖 문제 유형

- **Why does the author mention "X" in paragraph Y?**
  Y단락에서 글쓴이가 "X"를 언급하는 이유는 무엇인가?

- **What is the purpose of paragraph X?**
  X단락의 목적은 무엇인가?

- **The author mentions "X" in order to**
  글쓴이가 "X"를 언급하는 이유는?

- **In paragraph X, the author mentions "Y" to**
  X단락에서 글쓴이가 "Y"를 언급하는 이유는?

💡 문제 풀이 전략

- 문제에서 묻고 있는 특정 어구, 즉 키워드를 지문에서 신속하게 찾아 그 주변에서 관련 단서를 파악하는 것이 중요하다.

- 지문의 전체 구조나 개별 문장의 의미보다는 키워드와 해당 단락 사이의 논리 전개 방식에 초점을 맞춰야 한다.

- 글쓴이의 의도와 키워드의 역할에 관한 다양한 표현들을 알아두면 지문과 보기를 비교할 때 도움이 된다.

설명 / 예시	to illustrate ∣ to explain ∣ to describe ∣ to clarify ∣ to list ∣ to exemplify ∣ to give an example of
비교 / 대조	to compare ∣ to contrast
강조 / 부연	to emphasize ∣ to highlight ∣ to further develop the idea
주장 / 제안	to suggest ∣ to support ∣ to argue ∣ to present ∣ to propose
증명 / 입증	to demonstrate ∣ to show ∣ to prove ∣ to give a reason for
반박 / 반론	to contradict ∣ to repute

🚨 피해야 할 오답 유형

- 글쓴이의 의도 및 설명 방식 면에서는 맞는 것처럼 보이지만, 지문의 세부 정보와 다른 내용이 담긴 선택지

📖 핵심 유형 공략

TOEFL **Reading**

REVIEW HELP? BACK NEXT

The author mentions "**the opposite is becoming true for coins**" in the passage in order to

(A) demonstrate that coins have fewer problems than paper money.

(B) clarify a principle to determine the face value of metal coins.

(C) contradict the idea that coins are preferred over bills.

(D) suggest that the value of coins has declined due to the market.

Monetary Value

When bank notes were first introduced, they were greeted with disdain by many people. They trusted coins made of gold and silver and believed that paper money was worthless. Even today, people still say that money isn't worth the paper it's printed on. However, the opposite is becoming true for coins. Due to rising prices for silver, copper, zinc and other metals commonly used to make coins, they are becoming more expensive than their stated value. Many countries have sought cheaper alternatives like aluminum while other countries have chosen to phase out some coins altogether. For example, the Canadian government will soon stop making pennies. The coin is worth one cent, but they cost 1.6 cents to manufacture. The discontinuation of the penny is expected to save the Canadian government 11 million Canadian dollars a year. To compensate for this, retailers will increase or decrease prices to the nearest five cents.

통화 가치

지문에서 글쓴이가 "주화의 경우 그 반대 현상이 나타나고 있다"고 언급하는 이유는?

(A) 주화가 지폐보다 문제가 더 적다는 것을 증명하기 위해

(B) 금속 주화의 액면가를 결정하는 원칙을 명확히 하기 위해

(C) 주화가 지폐보다 선호된다는 생각에 반박하기 위해

(D) 시장으로 인해 주화의 가치가 하락했음을 시사하기 위해

지폐가 처음 도입되었을 때, 많은 사람들이 그것들을 멸시했다. 그들은 금과 은으로 만들어진 주화를 신뢰했고 지폐는 가치가 없다고 믿었다. 심지어 오늘날에도 사람들은 여전히 돈이 인쇄된 종이만큼의 가치가 없다고 말한다. 그러나 주화의 경우 그 반대 현상이 나타나고 있다. 일반적으로 주화를 만들 때 사용되는 은, 구리, 아연과 다른 금속의 가격 상승으로 인해 그것들은 명시된 가치보다 더욱 비싸지고 있다. 많은 나라들이 알루미늄과 같은 더 저렴한 대안을 모색하는 한편 다른 나라들은 일부 주화를 단계적으로 폐지하기로 결정했다. 예를 들어, 캐나다 정부는 곧 페니 발행을 중단할 것이다. 이 동전은 1센트의 가치가 있지만 제조하는 데 1.6센트가 든다. 페니의 단종으로 캐나다 정부는 연간 1,100만 캐나다 달러를 절약할 수 있을 것으로 예상된다. 이를 보완하기 위해 소매업체들은 가격을 가장 근접한 5센트로 올리거나 내릴 것이다.

지문에서 질문 대상인 특정 어구 찾기

질문에서 묻고 있는 대상을 지문에서 신속하게 찾아 해당 어구 앞뒤의 문장들을 살펴본다.

> 질문 The author mentions "the opposite is becoming true for coins" in the passage
>
> 지문 They trusted coins made of gold and silver and believed that paper money was worthless (...) However, the opposite is becoming true for coins. Due to rising prices for silver, copper, zinc and other metals commonly used to make coins, they are becoming more expensive than their stated value. (...)

지문에서 글쓴이의 의도 및 설명 방식 파악하기

질문 대상 주변에 있는 정보들을 참고해 글쓴이가 해당 어구를 사용한 의도를 파악해 본다.

> 지문 They trusted coins made of gold and silver and believed that paper money was worthless (...) However, the opposite is becoming true for coins. Due to rising prices for silver, copper, zinc and other metals commonly used to make coins, they are becoming more expensive than their stated value. (...)
>
> 설명 방식(의도) 반박/반론
> 세부 정보 과거에는 지폐보다 주화가 선호되었지만, 오늘날에는 이와 반대가 되었다.

지문의 설명 방식과 세부 정보를 선택지와 대조하기

지문에서 파악한 설명 방식 및 전달하고자 하는 내용을 선택지에 있는 정보와 비교, 대조한다.

> 설명 방식(의도) 반박/반론
> 세부 정보 화폐 선호도 – 과거: 주화>지폐 ⇒ 현재: 주화<지폐
>
> (A) **demonstrate** [증명] that coins have fewer problems than paper money. (주화의 문제가 더 적음)
> (B) **clarify** [설명] a principle to determine the face value of metal coins. (주화 액면가 결정 원칙)
> (C) **contradict the idea** [반박] that coins are preferred over bills. (선호도: 주화>지폐)
> (D) **suggest** [주장] that the value of coins has declined due to the market. (주화의 가치↓)
>
> 그런 다음, 이 두 가지 조건을 모두 만족하는 보기를 고른다.
> ① 지문에서 키워드가 하는 역할을 정확히 제시한 보기
> ② 지문에서 파악한 키워드 관련 세부 정보를 담고 있는 보기
>
> 정답: (C) contradict the idea that coins are preferred over bills.

Sample Question 1

The author mentions "acupuncture and moxibustion" in order to

Ⓐ highlight major tasks of UNESCO including festivals and rituals.

Ⓑ introduce assets awaiting designation on UNESCO's list.

Ⓒ show the increasing diversification of UNESCO's field of interest.

Ⓓ classify the broadened activities of UNESCO.

UNESCO – Preservation of Art Forms and Traditions

The United Nations Educational, Scientific and Cultural Organization (UNESCO) is better known for its work protecting world monuments and natural wonders, but in 2003, the organization started a list to promote the preservation of art forms and other traditions in the face of globalization. The aim of the list is to recognize particular elements of living cultural heritage, such as language and rituals, in order to protect and ensure the continuation of cultural diversity and to foster a sense of community. For a tradition to be recognized on the list, it must be deemed functional in the spread of knowledge of intangible heritage, and protective measures need to be taken in order to promote the continuation of this process. Most recently in 2010, the art of French gastronomy, traditional Mexican cuisine, the Mediterranean diet, and art forms like the Peking opera, Flamenco, and Gagok, among others, have been added to the list. The acupuncture and moxibustion of traditional Chinese medicine were also nominated to join the list.

유네스코 – 예술 형식과 전통의 보존

국제연합교육과학문화기구(유네스코)는 세계적인 기념물들과 자연의 경관들을 보호하는 업무로 더 잘 알려져 있지만, 2003년에 이 기구는 세계화에 직면하여 예술 형식과 그외 다른 전통의 보존을 장려하기 위해 목록을 만들기 시작했다. 이 목록의 목적은 언어와 의례와 같이 살아 있는 문화유산을 구성하는 구체적인 요소들을 공인하는 것인데, 이는 문화적 다양성이 지속되도록 보호하고 지키며 공동체 의식을 강화하기 위한 것이다. 어떠한 전통이 이 목록에 오르기 위해서는 무형 유산에 대한 지식 확산에 도움이 된다고 여겨져야 하고, 이 과정의 지속을 촉진하기 위해 보호 조치가 취해져야 한다. 가장 최근인 2010년에는 프랑스식 미식법, 멕시코의 전통 요리법, 지중해식 식습관, 그리고 경극, 플라멩코와 가곡과 같은 예술 형식들이 목록에 추가되었다. 전통 한의학의 침술과 뜸질도 이 목록에 오르도록 추천되었다.

글쓴이가 "침술과 뜸질"을 언급한 이유는?

Ⓐ 축제와 의례들을 포함해 유네스코의 주요 임무를 강조하기 위해

Ⓑ 유네스코 목록에 지정되기를 기다리는 유산들을 소개하기 위해

Ⓒ 유네스코의 관심 분야가 점점 다양해짐을 보여주기 위해

Ⓓ 유네스코의 확장된 활동을 분류하기 위해

Sample Question 2

Why does the author use "Loose lips sink ships" as an example of a slogan?

Ⓐ To reveal characteristics of censorship mostly related to physical expressions

Ⓑ To accentuate the significance of censorship during the wars of the past

Ⓒ To assert that censorship can't be justified even in case of emergency

Ⓓ To introduce popular proverbs which disagree with censorship

Censorship

Censorship usually strikes a sour note for most people in democratic societies, but it sometimes has its place. For instance, censorship is carried out during wartime with the purpose of preventing the release of information that might prove useful to the enemy. This typically involves keeping information concerning times and locations secret. At other times, the information may only be delayed in its release until it is of no use to the enemy. The reason why censorship is not considered as immoral during wartime as it is during peacetime is because the underlying circumstances have changed. The issue shifts from personal liberty to personal safety. During World Wars I and II, the personal letters of British soldiers were censored. At that time, censorship was an incredibly time-consuming process, for the process consisted of commanding officers going through their own men's letters with a black marker and crossing out anything their men wrote that could possibly compromise the security of any ongoing operations. Many slogans were created to remind the population about censorship. "Loose lips sink ships" was one of the most famous of these slogans.

검열

글쓴이가 "가벼운 입은 배를 가라앉힌다"를 표어의 예로 든 이유는 무엇인가?

Ⓐ 주로 신체 표현과 관련된 검열의 특징들을 나타내기 위해

Ⓑ 과거 전시에서의 검열의 중요성을 강조하기 위해

Ⓒ 비상시에도 검열이 정당화될 수 없음을 주장하기 위해

Ⓓ 검열에 반대하는 유명한 속담을 소개하기 위해

검열은 보통 민주주의 사회에서 대부분의 사람들에게 불쾌한 인상을 주지만, 가끔 검열이 자리할 곳이 있다. 예를 들면, 검열은 전시에 적에게 유용할 수도 있는 정보의 유출을 방지하려는 목적으로 실시된다. 이는 일반적으로 시간과 장소에 관한 정보를 기밀로 유지하는 것과 관련이 있었다. 다른 때는 적에게 그 정보가 쓸모 없어질 때까지 정보의 유출이 그저 지연될지도 모른다. 검열이 전시에는 평화로운 시기에 여겨지는 것만큼 비도덕적이라고 여겨지지 않는 이유는 근본적인 상황이 변했기 때문이다. 이 쟁점은 개인의 자유에서 개인의 안전으로 옮겨진다. 제1, 2차 세계 대전 동안 영국 군인들의 사적인 편지는 검열을 받았다. 그 당시 검열은 엄청나게 시간이 걸리는 과정이었다. 왜냐하면 이 과정에서 부대 지휘관들이 검은색 펜을 들고 부하들의 편지를 검토하다 그들이 쓴 것 중 현재 진행되고 있는 작전의 보안을 위태롭게 할 수 있는 모든 내용에 선을 그어 지웠기 때문이다. 사람들에게 검열에 대해 상기시키기 위해 많은 표어들이 만들어졌다. "가벼운 입은 배를 가라앉힌다"는 그 표어들 중에서 가장 유명했던 것 중 하나이다.

PAGODA TOEFL 90+

READING

Actual Test

06 Inference

- 추론(Inference) 문제는 지문의 내용을 근거로 하여 명시되어 있지 않은 함축적 내용을 추론해 내는 문제로, 논리적인 인과 관계에 근거하여 합리적인 결론을 도출해 내야 한다.
- 질문에 infer 혹은 imply라는 동사가 직접 언급되므로 문제 유형을 파악할 수 있다.
- 지문당 1~2개의 문제가 출제되거나, 아예 출제되지 않을 때도 있다.

📖 문제 유형

- According to paragraph X, what can be inferred about Y?
  X단락에 따르면, Y에 대해 추론할 수 있는 것은 무엇인가?
- It can be inferred from paragraph X that X단락에서 추론할 수 있는 것은?
- Which of the following can be inferred about X? 다음 중 X에 대해 추론할 수 있는 것은 무엇인가?
- Based on the information in paragraph X, what can be inferred about Y?
  X단락의 정보에 근거하여, Y에 대해 추론할 수 있는 것은 무엇인가?
- The author of the passage implies that 지문의 글쓴이가 암시하는 것은?
- What is X believed to indicate? X는 무엇을 가리킨다고 여겨지는가?

💡 문제 풀이 전략

- 주관적인 생각이나 상식에 의한 판단을 피하고, 항상 지문에 주어진 객관적 정보에만 근거하여 정답을 고르도록 한다.
- 지문 내용에 근거하여 추론하되 단순히 지문에 나와 있는 단어나 내용이 담긴 선택지를 정답으로 고르지 않도록 주의한다.
- 추론의 단서가 단락 전체에 광범위하게 분포되어 있는 경우에는 선택지를 먼저 읽고 해당 내용을 지문에서 확인하여 오답을 소거해 나가면서 정답의 범위를 좁히도록 한다.
- 추론 근거는 해당 문장이나 단락 내에 있기도 하지만 지문 전체에 분포되어 있기도 한다.

🚨 피해야 할 오답 유형

- 지문의 내용과 관련이 없는 선택지
- 지문에 추론 근거가 없는 배경 지식에 관한 선택지
- 논리적 비약이 심하거나 지나친 일반화의 오류를 범한 선택지

핵심 유형 공략

It can be inferred from the passage that

Ⓐ compasses easily malfunction at sea.

Ⓑ Polaris will not always be the North Star.

Ⓒ Earth's rotation has influenced Polaris.

Ⓓ other stars actually move in a circle.

Polaris

Polaris, also known as Alpha Ursae Minoris or the North Star, is a bright star, though not the brightest, located 434 light-years away from Earth. From Earth, however, it is positioned almost straight above Earth's North Pole. For this reason, while other stars appear to move in a circle in the sky due to Earth's rotation, Polaris seems to stay in the same place from anywhere it can be seen on Earth. This unique characteristic allowed sailors of the past to figure out which way was north, approximately where they were on the ocean, and in which direction they were moving. In fact, when lost, scientists have argued that it is safer to rely on Polaris than a compass. Nevertheless, when Egyptians built the pyramids 5,000 years ago, Thuban, in the constellation Draco the Dragon, was the North Star. In fact, the earliest document that refers to Polaris as the North Star was written after the birth of Christ. This is because the place in the sky the North Pole points at changes slowly over time due to small differences in Earth's rotation and Polaris's position.

지문에서 추론할 수 있는 것은?

Ⓐ 나침반은 바다에서 쉽게 오작동한다.

Ⓑ 폴라리스가 언제나 북극성이지는 않을 것이다.

Ⓒ 지구의 자전이 폴라리스에 영향을 끼쳤다.

Ⓓ 다른 별들은 실제로 원을 그리며 움직인다.

폴라리스

알파 우르새 미노리스 또는 북극성으로도 알려진 폴라리스는 지구에서 434광년 떨어진 곳에 위치해 있으며, 비록 가장 밝지는 않지만 밝은 별이다. 하지만 지구에서 봤을 때 그것은 지구 북극의 거의 바로 위에 위치해 있다. 이런 이유로, 지구의 자전 때문에 다른 별들이 하늘에서 원을 그리며 움직이는 것처럼 보이는 반면 폴라리스는 지구상에서 볼 수 있는 어느 곳에서도 같은 장소에 머물러 있는 것처럼 보인다. 이 독특한 특성은 옛날 선원들이 어느 쪽이 북쪽인지, 그들이 대략 바다 위 어디에 있는지, 그리고 어느 방향으로 움직이고 있는지 알아낼 수 있게 해주었다. 실제로 과학자들은 길을 잃었을 때 나침반보다 폴라리스에 의지하는 것이 더 안전하다고 주장해 왔다. 그럼에도 불구하고, 이집트인들이 5천 년 전에 피라미드를 지었을 때에는 용자리인 드라코 별자리에서 투반이 북극성이었다. 사실 폴라리스를 북극성이라고 지칭하는 가장 초기의 문서는 그리스도의 탄생 후에 쓰여졌다. 하늘에서 북극이 가리키는 지점이 지구의 자전과 폴라리스 위치의 작은 차이 때문에 시간이 지남에 따라 천천히 바뀌기 때문이다.

지문에서 질문 대상(핵심어) 찾기

질문의 핵심어 혹은 질문의 선택지에 등장하는 대상들을 지문 안에서 찾는다.

(...) For this reason, while Ⓓ other stars appear to move in a circle in the sky due to Earth's rotation, Polaris seems to stay in the same place from anywhere it can be seen on Earth. (...) In fact, when lost, scientists have argued that it is safer to rely on Polaris than a Ⓐ compass. Nevertheless, when Egyptians built the pyramids 5,000 years ago, Thuban, in the constellation Draco the Dragon, was Ⓑ the North Star. (...) This is because the place in the sky the North Pole points at changes slowly over time due to small differences in Ⓒ Earth's rotation and Polaris's position.

STEP 2 질문 대상의 주변에서 추론의 근거 파악하기

질문 대상이 언급된 문장과 그 주변에서 추론의 근거가 될 만한 내용을 파악한다.

(...) For this reason, while Ⓓ other stars appear to move in a circle in the sky due to Earth's rotation, Polaris seems to stay in the same place from anywhere it can be seen on Earth. (...) In fact, when lost, scientists have argued that it is safer to rely on Polaris than a Ⓐ compass. Nevertheless, when Egyptians built the pyramids 5,000 years ago, Thuban, in the constellation Draco the Dragon, was Ⓑ the North Star. (...) This is because the place in the sky the North Pole points at changes slowly over time due to small differences in Ⓒ Earth's rotation and Polaris's position.

Ⓐ 과학자들은 길을 잃었을 때 나침반(compass)보다 폴라리스에 의지하는 것이 더 안전하다고 주장해 왔다.
Ⓑ 5천 년 전에는 용자리인 드라코 별자리에서 투반이 북극성(the North Star)이었다.
Ⓒ 지구의 자전과 폴라리스의 위치(Earth's rotation & Polaris's position)에 작은 차이가 생기기 때문에 시간이 지나면서 북극이 가리키는 지점이 천천히 바뀐다.
Ⓓ 다른 별들(other stars)은 하늘에서 원을 그리며 움직이는 것처럼 보인다.

STEP 3 지문 내용을 근거로 추론할 수 있는 선택지 고르기

지문에서 찾은 추론의 근거 문장에서 함축된 의미를 파악하고, 이를 선택지와 비교해 본다.

Ⓐ compasses easily malfunction at sea. ⋯ 길을 잃었을 때 나침반보다 폴라리스에 의지하는 것이 더 안전하다는 주장이 있으나, 바다에서 나침반 고장이 잦다는 의미는 아님 (X)
Ⓑ Polaris will not always be the North Star.
　　⋯ 5천 년 전에는 다른 별이 북극성이었으므로 미래에 폴라리스가 북극성이 아니게 될 가능성 있음 (O)
Ⓒ Earth's rotation has influenced Polaris.
　　⋯ 지구의 자전 때문에 북극의 지점이 변하는 것이지 폴라리스에 영향을 주는 것은 아님 (X)
Ⓓ other stars actually move in a circle.
　　⋯ '다른 별들이 원을 그리며 움직이는 것처럼 보인다'고 했으므로 실제로 움직이는 것은 아님 (X)

정답: Ⓑ Polaris will not always be the North Star.

Sample Question 1

It can be inferred from the passage that Isaac Newton

(A) studied astronomy while he was at university.

(B) proposed that some objects repel each other.

(C) believed that celestial objects behave differently.

(D) encountered strong opposition to his theory.

Newton's Law of Gravitation

Physicists enjoy examining phenomena in order to show that a relationship can be found if they are only examined closely enough. This search for unification between phenomena has been going on for centuries. In 1665, Isaac Newton, a young man, who was only 23 at the time, made a fundamental contribution to physics when he showed that the force that holds the Moon in its orbit is the very same force that makes an apple fall. This is taken so much for granted now that it is difficult for us to imagine the past view that the motions of earthbound bodies and heavenly bodies were different kinds of motion and were governed by different sets of laws. Newton concluded that not only does the Earth attract an apple and the Moon, but that each object in the universe attracts every other object. This thought takes a little time to get used to because the familiar attraction of the Earth for earthbound bodies is so great that it overshadows the attractions that these same earthbound bodies have for each other.

뉴턴의 만유인력 법칙

지문에서 아이작 뉴턴에 대해 추론할 수 있는 것은?

(A) 대학에서 천문학을 공부했다

(B) 몇몇 물체가 서로를 밀어낸다고 제안했다

(C) 천체(天體)가 다르게 움직인다고 믿었다

(D) 그의 이론에 대한 강한 반박에 부딪혔다

물리학자들은 현상들을 충분히 면밀하게 조사하면 관련성이 발견될 수 있다는 것을 보여주기 위해 그것들에 대한 연구를 즐긴다. 현상 간의 통합을 위한 이런 연구는 수 세기 동안 지속되어 왔다. 1665년 당시 겨우 스물세 살이었던 젊은 청년 아이작 뉴턴은 달이 궤도를 돌게 하는 힘과 사과를 떨어지게 만드는 힘이 동일하다는 사실을 보여주며 물리학에 핵심적인 공헌을 했다. 이는 현재 매우 당연하게 받아들여져서, 우리는 땅에 있는 물체와 하늘에 있는 물체의 움직임이 다른 종류의 움직임이며 다른 법칙에 의해 지배된다는 과거의 시각을 상상하기 어렵다. 뉴턴은 지구가 사과와 달을 끌어당길 뿐만 아니라, 우주에 있는 물체 하나하나가 외부에 있는 모든 물체를 끌어당긴다는 결론을 내렸다. 이 개념에 익숙해지는 데에는 약간의 시간이 걸리는데, 그 이유는 지구가 땅 위에 있는 물체들을 끌어당기는 우리에게 익숙한 인력이 너무 커서 지상의 이 물체들끼리 서로를 끌어당기는 인력을 무색하게 만들기 때문이다.

Sample Question 2

It can be inferred from the passage that Somali pirates

(A) put their countrymen in danger as well as ships and crews of other countries.

(B) run training camps and purchase political influence with ransom money.

(C) gather thousands of applicants mostly consisting of former fishermen for their training.

(D) are forced to dispose of their arms by the government as their numbers are increasing.

Somali Pirates

Though we live in a progressive age, Somalia's 1,880-mile coastline is currently crawling with pirates. This is a serious problem for the Somali people given that the country is dependent on food aid from other nations, which arrives mostly by ship. The pirates are organized and work in teams. The pirates even have a spokesman. The pirates attack everything from yachts to oil tankers and usually demand millions of dollars in ransom for the ships and their crews. 2010 was one of the worst years on record, with more than 50 ships attacked, 25 hijacked, and at least 14 being held by pirates. Somali waters are now considered the most dangerous in the world. The Somali pirates are typically former fishermen who have turned to the more lucrative work of patrolling the seas with binoculars, rifles, and rocket-propelled grenades. They travel in light speedboats deployed from a mother ship and have attacked tankers as far as 300 miles from the coast. Somali officials say the number of pirates is increasing. With more than 1,000 gunmen at their disposal, they have evolved into a sophisticated, organized crime ring headquartered along the rocky shores of northern Somalia.

지문에서 소말리아 해적에 대해 추론할 수 있는 것은?

(A) 다른 국가의 배와 선원들뿐만 아니라 자기 나라 사람들까지 위험에 처하게 한다.

(B) 몸값으로 받은 돈으로 훈련 캠프를 운영하고 정치적 영향력을 얻는다.

(C) 훈련을 위해 주로 전직 어부로 구성된 수천 명의 지원자들을 모집한다.

(D) 숫자가 늘어남에 따라 정부로부터 무기를 처분하라는 압력을 받는다.

소말리아 해적

우리는 진보의 시대에 살고 있지만, 1,880마일에 이르는 소말리아의 해안선은 지금도 해적들로 들끓고 있다. 소말리아가 다른 나라로부터의 식량 원조에 의존하고 있으며 그 대부분이 배편으로 온다는 점에서 이는 소말리아 사람들에게 심각한 문제이다. 해적들은 조직화되어 있으며 팀으로 일한다. 해적들에게는 심지어 대변인도 있다. 해적들은 요트부터 유조선에 이르기까지 모든 것을 공격하며 배나 선원의 몸값으로 보통 수백만 달러를 요구한다. 2010년은 기록상 최악의 해 중 하나였는데, 그 해에는 50척 이상의 배가 공격을 당했고, 25척이 납치되었으며, 최소 14척이 해적들에게 억류되었다. 소말리아의 바다는 현재 세계에서 가장 위험한 곳으로 간주되고 있다. 소말리아 해적들은 쌍안경, 소총, 로켓 추진 유탄을 들고 바다를 순찰하는 좀 더 돈벌이가 되는 일로 전향한 전직 어부들인 경우가 일반적이다. 그들은 모선에 배치된 경쾌속정을 타고 이동하며 연안에서 300마일이나 떨어진 곳에 있는 유조선들을 공격한 적도 있다. 소말리아 정부 관계자들은 해적들의 수가 증가하고 있다고 말한다. 언제든 현장에 투입할 수 있는 1천여 명의 무장 병력을 거느리고 있는 그들은 소말리아 북부의 암석 해안에 본거지를 둔 정교하고 조직화된 범죄단으로 진화했다.

PAGODA TOEFL 90+

READING

Actual Test

07 Insertion

- 문장 삽입(Insertion) 문제는 글 전체의 논리적 흐름에 맞도록 주어진 문장을 적절한 위치에 삽입하는 문제로, 지문에 주어진 문장이 삽입될 수 있는 후보 네 곳이 박스[■]로 표시되어 있다.
- 지문당 1개의 문제가 출제되며, 항상 끝에서 두 번째 문제(9번)로 출제된다.

📖 문제 유형

Look at the four squares [■] that indicate where the following sentence could be added to the passage. 지문에 다음 문장이 들어갈 수 있는 위치를 나타내는 네 개의 사각형[■]을 확인하시오.

-------------------------------- [삽입 문장] ---------------------------------

Where would the sentence best fit? 이 문장이 들어가기에 가장 적합한 곳은?

💡 문제 풀이 전략

- 지문 전체를 빠르게 훑어 읽으면서 신속하게 삽입 문장과 주위 문장 간의 연결 관계를 파악하도록 한다.
- 삽입 문장이나 지문에서 단서를 파악하기 어려운 경우, 총 4개의 [■]에 문장을 차례대로 넣어서 살펴본다.
- 삽입 문장은 앞뒤 문장과의 관계가 유기적이어야 하며, 단락 전체 혹은 지문 전체의 논리적인 흐름에서도 벗어나지 않아야 한다.
- 삽입 문장에서 지시어, 연결어, the+명사, 반복어구, 유사어구 등의 단서를 찾는다.

지시어	it, they, this, these, that, those, one, some, both, the former, the latter
연결어	[예시] for example, for instance [부연] in addition, furthermore, in other words, also, besides, similarly [대조] but, however, in contrast, on the contrary, meanwhile, on the other hand [인과] therefore, so, as a result, because of, thus, due to, consequently, in conclusion
반복어구	삽입 문장의 중심 소재, 앞뒤 문장의 대응 표현

🚨 피해야 할 오답 유형

- 삽입 문장에 나온 단어들이 언급된 문장 주변의 위치
- 앞뒤 문장과는 연결되지만 전체 단락의 흐름을 저해하는 위치
- 문장을 삽입했을 때 크게 어색하지는 않지만 연결성이 부족한 위치

PAGODA TOEFL 90+

READING

Actual Test

08 Summary

- 요약(Summary) 문제는 주어진 도입 문장(Introductory sentence)을 읽고 6개의 선택지 중에서 지문의 핵심 내용을 담고 있는 3개의 선택지를 골라 요약문을 완성하는 문제이다.
- Drag-n-Drop 유형으로, 선택지를 골라 순서에 상관없이 요약표의 [•] 옆에 끌어다 놓으면 된다.
- 지문의 마지막 문제(10번)로 나오며 Category Chart 유형과 번갈아 가며 0~1개의 문제가 출제된다. 다만 Category Chart 문제보다 Summary 문제의 출제 비율이 훨씬 더 높다.
- 정답 3개를 모두 맞혔을 경우 2점이며, 이를 기준으로 오답 1개당 1점씩 감점된다.

📖 문제 유형

Directions: An introductory sentence for a brief summary of the passage is provided below. Complete the summary by selecting the THREE answer choices that express the most important ideas in the passage. Some sentences do not belong in the summary because they express ideas that are not presented in the passage or are minor ideas in the passage. ***This question is worth 2 points.***

지시문: 지문을 간략하게 요약한 글의 첫 문장이 아래 제시되어 있다. 지문의 가장 중요한 내용을 표현하는 세 개의 선택지를 골라 요약문을 완성하시오. 일부 문장들은 지문에 제시되지 않았거나 지문의 지엽적인 내용을 나타내기 때문에 요약문에 포함되지 않는다. *이 문제의 배점은 2점이다.*

-------------------------------- [도입 문장] --------------------------------

-
-
-

Answer Choices

(A) ---------------------------------   (D) ---------------------------------
(B) ---------------------------------   (E) ---------------------------------
(C) ---------------------------------   (F) ---------------------------------

Drag your answer choices to the spaces where they belong.
To remove an answer choice, click on it. To review the passage, click on **View Text**.

선택한 답안을 맞는 곳에 끌어다 넣으시오.

선택한 답안을 삭제하려면, 답안에 대고 클릭하시오. 지문을 다시 보려면 **지문 보기**를 클릭하시오

💡 문제 풀이 전략

- 지문 내용을 요약, 재구성하는 유형이므로 지문을 읽으며 노트 정리하는 습관을 들인다.
- 글의 중심 내용(major idea)과 부가 정보(minor idea)를 구분하는 연습을 해 두는 것이 좋다.
- 주어진 도입문과 노트 정리를 활용하면 지문을 다시 읽지 않아도 오답을 소거할 수 있어 시간을 단축할 수 있다.

🚨 피해야 할 오답 유형

- 지문에 언급되지 않았거나 지문과 다른 내용이 담긴 선택지
- 지문에 언급된 내용 중 부가적인 정보(minor idea)가 담긴 선택지

📖 핵심 유형 공략

STEP 1 단락별로 핵심 내용 정리하기

주어진 도입 문장을 읽고 6개의 선택지 중에서 중심 내용과 부가 정보를 구분한다. 시간 단축을 위해 처음 지문을 읽을 때 단락별 핵심 내용을 노트에 정리해 둔다.

노트 정리 예시
진공 활동
단락 1. 동물들의 행동은 학습이 아닌 유전적 영향의 결과
단락 2. 진공 활동은 경험이나 정상적 자극 없이 하는 유전적 행동
단락 3. 사육 동물들은 불가능한 상황에서도 야생 동물들의 습성을 모방

STEP 2 예상 오답 소거하기

노트 정리한 내용을 참고하여 지문에 언급되지 않은 선택지를 예상 오답으로 소거한다. 지문에 언급된 내용일지라도 부가 정보를 담고 있는 선택지는 예상 오답으로 소거한다. 노트에 정리해 놓은 단락별 요지와 가장 가까운 내용의 선택지 3개를 골라 표를 완성한다.

STEP 3 남은 선택지가 도입문을 뒷받침하는지 확인하기

위의 두 단계를 통해 정답을 확정하기 어려운 경우에는 지문을 다시 빠르게 훑어 읽으면서 관련 내용을 확인한다. 예상 오답을 소거하고 남은 선택지들이 도입 문장을 뒷받침하는 문장인지 확인하여 정답을 확정한다.

Sample Question 1

Divinization and the Roman Catholic Church

In the Catholic Church, divinization is the belief that people can be made divine or holy through the performance of particular religious rituals called sacraments. The practice of rituals is present in many religions, but perhaps it is most strongly associated with Catholics. This vital tenet of the Catholic religion is most strongly manifested through the taking of Holy Communion (Eucharist). The majority of Christian faiths also practice this ritual, but since they almost exclusively stemmed from the Catholic Church, any distinctions in how they partake of the Eucharist are minor. The essential nature of this ceremony is the belief that by reenacting the events of Christ's Last Supper with his disciples members of the church are also able to affirm themselves as loyal followers. At his final meal, Christ blessed the bread and the wine, calling them his body and blood, and the disciples ate and drank them, thereby taking some of his holiness into themselves. This gift, as the most authoritative of Catholic theologians Saint Thomas Aquinas wrote, "surpasses every capability of created nature, since it is nothing short of a partaking of the Divine Nature, which exceeds every other nature."

Directions: An introductory sentence for a brief summary of the passage is provided below. Complete the summary by selecting the THREE answer choices that express the most important ideas in the passage. Some sentences do not belong in the summary because they express ideas that are not presented in the passage or are minor ideas in the passage. *This question is worth 2 points.*

Divinization can be realized through the ceremony of Holy Communion in the Catholic Church.

-
-
-

Answer Choices

Ⓐ It was Saint Thomas Aquinas that emphasized the importance of divinization and Holy Communion.

Ⓑ Believers reproduce the sacred event of partaking of Christ's body and blood when performing Communion.

Ⓒ Followers believe they can testify their loyalty to Christ by imitating the Last Supper.

Ⓓ Christ's disciples ate and drank the sacred bread and wine to spread the holiness of Christ.

Ⓔ The core of Catholicism is well represented in the process of taking Communion.

Ⓕ The procedures of Holy Communion are quite different in other Christian religions.

Drag your answer choices to the spaces where they belong.
To remove an answer choice, click on it. To review the passage, click on **View Text**.

신성화와 로마 가톨릭 교회

가톨릭 교회에서 신성화는 성례라 불리는 특별한 종교 의식을 수행함으로써 사람이 신성해지거나 성스러워질 수 있다는 믿음이다. 의식의 실행은 많은 종교에서 찾아볼 수 있지만, 아마도 가톨릭교도와 가장 강하게 연관되어 있을 것이다. 가톨릭교의 필수 교리는 성찬식(성체 성사)에 참여함으로써 가장 강하게 드러난다. 대다수의 기독교 신앙에서도 이 의식을 행하지만, 그 신앙들이 거의 가톨릭 교회에서만 파생된 것이기 때문에 성체를 모시는 방법에 대한 차이는 작다. 이 의식의 중요한 본질은 그리스도가 최후의 만찬에서 그의 제자들과 함께 했던 일들을 재연함으로써 교회의 신자들도 스스로를 충실한 신앙인들이라고 주장할 수 있다는 믿음이다. 마지막 만찬에서 그리스도는 빵과 포도주를 그의 몸과 피라고 부르며 축성했고, 제자들은 그것들을 먹고 마심으로써 그리스도의 신성함을 받아들였다. 가톨릭 신학자들 중에서 최고 권위자인 성 토마스 아퀴나스는 이 선물이 "창조된 본성의 어떤 능력보다도 뛰어난데, 이는 다른 모든 본성을 능가하는 신성을 나누는 것이나 다름없기 때문이다"라고 기록했다.

지시문: 지문을 간략하게 요약한 글의 첫 문장이 아래에 제시되어 있다. 지문의 가장 중요한 내용을 표현하는 세 개의 선택지를 골라 요약문을 완성하시오. 일부 문장들은 지문에 제시되지 않았거나 지문의 지엽적인 내용을 나타내기 때문에 요약문에 포함되지 않는다. *이 문제의 배점은 2점이다.*

신성화는 가톨릭 교회의 성찬식 의식을 통해 이루어질 수 있다.

- Ⓑ 신도들은 성찬식을 거행할 때 그리스도의 몸과 피를 먹고마시는 신성한 사건을 재현한다.
- Ⓒ 신도들은 최후의 만찬을 모방함으로써, 그리스도에 대한 자신들의 충성을 증명할 수 있다고 믿는다.
- Ⓔ 가톨릭교의 핵심은 성찬식에 참여하는 과정을 통해 잘 나타난다.

Ⓐ 신성화와 성찬식의 중요성을 강조한 것은 성 토마스 아퀴나스였다.

Ⓓ 그리스도의 제자들은 그리스도의 거룩함을 전파하기 위해 성스러운 빵과 포도주를 먹고 마셨다.

Ⓕ 성찬식 절차가 다른 기독교에서는 상당히 다르다.

Sample Question 2

The Politician Illusion

In a sense, politics has always been something of a dishonest game. Voters in democratic societies insist upon their belief in a higher order. They cling to this politico-religion that promises a better life and passionately defend the illusion that the men and women that choose to lead them are of a finer nature than themselves. Traditionally, the successful politician maintains this illusion. To succeed today, a politician must exploit this illusion to the fullest extent, especially if he wishes to be president. In 1967, an advisor to President Richard Nixon wrote in a memorandum, "Potential presidents are measured against an ideal that's a combination of leading man, God, father, hero, pope, king, with maybe a touch of the avenging Furies thrown in." This same advisor, perhaps aware that Nixon qualified only as "father," discussed improvements that would have to be made, not upon Nixon himself, but upon the image of him which was perceived by the voters.

Directions: An introductory sentence for a brief summary of the passage is provided below. Complete the summary by selecting the THREE answer choices that express the most important ideas in the passage. Some sentences do not belong in the summary because they express ideas that are not presented in the passage or are minor ideas in the passage. ***This question is worth 2 points.***

Politics in democratic societies rely on the illusory hopes of the public.

-
-
-

Answer Choices

(A) Nowadays, political candidates need to maximize this illusion to win an election, especially for a presidential election.

(B) The admirable reflections on politicians are composed of figures such as leader, God, father, hero, pope, and king.

(C) This fantasy is usually due to the belief that politicians are men of more commendable qualities.

(D) According to a political consultant, successful politicians should possess all kinds of ideal images created by the public.

(E) Richard Nixon could not meet the needs of the general public at the moment of his presidential election.

(F) It is deceitful and vulgar for statesmen to make use of their fake fantasies in order to gain popularity.

Drag your answer choices to the spaces where they belong.
To remove an answer choice, click on it. To review the passage, click on **View Text**.

정치가의 환상

어떤 면에서 정치는 항상 일종의 부정적인 게임 같은 것이다. 민주주의 사회의 유권자들은 더 고차원적으로 자신들의 소신을 주장한다. 유권자들은 더 나은 삶을 약속하는 정치 종교에 의존하고 그들이 지도자로 선택한 남녀가 그들 자신보다 더 훌륭한 본성을 지니고 있을 것이라는 환상을 열렬히 옹호한다. 전통적으로, 성공한 정치가는 이런 환상을 유지한다. 오늘날 정치가가 성공하기 위해서는, 특히 대통령이 되고자 한다면 이러한 환상을 충분히 이용해야 한다. 1967년에 리처드 닉슨 대통령의 한 고문은 비망록에 다음과 같이 적었다. "대통령 후보자들은 지도자, 하나님, 아버지, 영웅, 교황과 왕을 합쳐 놓은 것에다가 복수의 세 여신까지 살짝 가미한 이상형과 비교하여 평가된다." 아마도 닉슨이 '아버지'로서의 자질밖에 없다는 것을 간파했던 그 고문은 닉슨 본인이 아니라 유권자들에게 인지되는 그의 이미지에 대해 이루어져야 할 개선점을 논한 것이었다.

지시문: 지문을 간략하게 요약한 글의 첫 문장이 아래 제시되어 있다. 지문의 가장 중요한 내용을 표현하는 세 개의 선택지를 골라 요약문을 완성하시오. 일부 문장들은 지문에 제시되지 않았거나 지문의 지엽적인 내용을 나타내기 때문에 요약문에 포함되지 않는다. *이 문제의 배점은 2점이다.*

민주주의 사회에서 정치는 대중들의 환상에 기반한 희망에 의존한다.

- Ⓐ 오늘날 정치 후보자들은 선거, 특히 대통령 선거에서 이기기 위해 이러한 환상을 극대화할 필요가 있다.
- Ⓒ 이러한 환상은 보통 정치가들이 더 훌륭한 성품을 지닌 사람들이라는 믿음에서 비롯된다.
- Ⓓ 한 정치 고문에 따르면, 성공한 정치가들은 대중들이 만들어낸 이상적인 모든 이미지를 지니고 있어야 한다.

Ⓑ 정치가들에게 투영되는 존경할 만한 모습은 지도자, 하나님, 아버지, 영웅, 교황, 왕 등의 인물로 이루어져 있다.

Ⓔ 리처드 닉슨은 대통령 선거 시기에 일반 대중의 요구를 충족시킬 수 없었다.

Ⓕ 정치가들이 인기를 얻기 위해 가짜 환상을 이용하는 것은 기만적이고 천박하다.

09 Category Chart

- 분류(Category Chart) 문제는 주어진 7개/9개의 선택지 중에서 5개/7개를 골라 지문에서 비교, 대조되고 있는 각각의 범주(category)에 분류해 넣는 문제이다.

- Drag-n-Drop 유형으로, 선택지를 골라 순서에 상관없이 표의 [•] 옆에 끌어다 놓으면 된다.

- 지문의 마지막 문제(10번)로 나오며 Summary 유형과 번갈아 가며 0~1개의 문제가 출제된다. 다만 Summary 유형에 비해 출제 빈도가 현저히 낮다.

- 선택지가 7개일 경우에는 정답 5개 기준으로 3점 만점, 선택지가 9개일 경우에는 정답 7개 기준으로 4점 만점이며, 오답 1개당 1점씩 감점된다.

📖 문제 유형

Directions: Complete the table by matching the sentences below. Select the appropriate sentences from the answer choices and match them to the category to which they relate. TWO of the answer choices will NOT be used. *This question is worth 3 points.*

지시문: 아래 문장들을 알맞게 넣어 표를 완성하시오. 선택지에서 적절한 문장을 골라 관계 있는 범주에 연결하시오. 선택지 중 두 개는 정답이 될 수 없다. *이 문제의 배점은 3점이다.*

Answer Choices	Category 1
Ⓐ ----------------------------------- Ⓑ ----------------------------------- Ⓒ -----------------------------------	• • •
Ⓓ -----------------------------------	**Category 2**
Ⓔ ----------------------------------- Ⓕ ----------------------------------- Ⓖ -----------------------------------	• •

Drag your answer choices to the spaces where they belong.
To remove an answer choice, click on it. To review the passage, click on **View Text**.

💡 문제 풀이 전략

- 노트 정리가 반드시 필요한 유형이므로, 지문의 제목이나 문제 유형을 미리 확인 후 지문 내용을 범주별로 정리해 두도록 한다.
- 노트 정리를 하기 전에 표에 어떤 범주가 제시되어 있는지 먼저 확인하는 것이 좋다.
- 비교, 대조 지문의 전개 방식(AB-AB방식/AA-BB방식)을 파악해 두면 노트 정리에 도움이 된다.
- 각 항목에 해당되는 정보를 고를 때, 이 선택지들이 지문 내용을 재진술하고 있음에 유의한다.

🚨 피해야 할 오답 유형

- 지문에 언급되지 않았거나 지문과 다른 내용이 담긴 선택지
- 단순히 지문에 쓰인 단어나 표현으로 이루어져 있는 선택지
- 지문과 화제는 같지만 두 범주의 정보가 혼재되어 있는 선택지
- 비교, 대조되는 두 개의 범주 중에 어디에도 해당되지 않는 선택지

Question Types

📖 핵심 유형 공략

STEP 1 지문을 읽으며 항목별로 노트 정리하기

노트 정리 예시	**Synthetic Diamonds**	**Simulated Diamonds**
	1. identical physical properties to natural gems but are made in a lab 2. jewelers have difficulty determining them 3. more perfect than natural stones (fewer flaws) 4. using the HPHT technique	1. look like other genuine stones 2. use the mineral (cubic zirconium) 3. simple examination → it is false

STEP 2 노트의 항목과 선택지를 비교하여 범주표 완성하기

노트에 정리하지 못한 내용은 View Text 버튼을 눌러 지문에서 다시 확인한다.

STEP 3 남은 선택지 2개의 오답 여부를 재확인하여 정답 확정하기

지문에 언급되지 않았거나 지문의 내용과 다른 선택지는 오답 처리하여 정답을 확정한다.

Sample Question

Bees in Agriculture

The bees utilized in agriculture have traditionally been honeybees because they pollinate farmers' crops and produce a substantial amount of honey. Honeybees live in large colonies that contain thousands of individuals, which means that they can cover large areas. They also communicate by dancing to tell their hive mates where a food source can be found. However, honeybees are not necessarily the best choice for pollinating certain crops. Honeybees are very sensitive to weather conditions, and they are only active during the daytime. Honeybees cannot tolerate temperatures below 10 degrees Celsius, and even light drizzle will make honeybees stay in their hives. Bumblebees, on the other hand, are able to handle a wider range of weather and light conditions. They can easily absorb heat even from weak sunlight, and their thicker body hair conserves warmth much better. They can also generate their own heat internally by vibrating their flight muscles. This technique is very similar to the shivering that mammals employ. They can also fly in much stronger wind conditions, and they are not deterred by light rain. Bumblebee tongues are longer than those of honeybees, so they can reach nectar in flowers that honeybees cannot. Bumblebees also visit flowers that do not offer nectar in order to collect pollen.

Directions: Complete the table by matching the sentences below. Select the appropriate sentences from the answer choices and match them to the category to which they relate. TWO of the answer choices will NOT be used. *This question is worth 3 points.*

Answer Choices	Honeybees
(A) Able to fly when there is precipitation	•
(B) Share locations of food sources with other bees	•
(C) Use shivering to maintain body temperature	•
(D) More active during daytime than in twilight	**Bumblebees**
(E) Transport pollen to other insects	
(F) Visit flowers that do not offer nectar	•
(G) Live in large colonies	•

Drag your answer choices to the spaces where they belong.
To remove an answer choice, click on it. To review the passage, click on **View Text**.

1. The word "paradoxical" in paragraph 1 is closest in meaning to

   (A) inevitable
   (B) contradictory
   (C) arbitrary
   (D) mundane

2. Which of the following is NOT mentioned in paragraph 1?

   (A) What convergent evolution is
   (B) What caused some birds to be flightless
   (C) How flightless birds survived
   (D) How evolutionary changes in birds took place

3. According to paragraph 2, all of the following are common physical features of ratites EXCEPT

   (A) long necks
   (B) long legs
   (C) vestigial wings
   (D) ridge-shaped chest bones

Flightless Birds

1 ➡ Birds that currently live or used to live on many continents have lost the ability to fly at various points in their evolutionary histories. Such evolution seems paradoxical, since flight is a trait that so many animals from different classes have developed wholly independently. Indeed, convergent evolution would seem to argue against the whole idea of losing such an advanced ability. [■A] However, evolution is not about achieving advanced traits, but rather about developing the traits that are necessary to survive in a given habitat. [■B] Therefore, birds that have lost this ability must have done so because flight did not give them an advantage in their habitat. [■C] A group of large, flightless birds called ratites no longer needed to fly because they did not need to migrate for food or warmth, or because they had no predators from which they needed to escape. [■D] They developed larger bodies supported by strong legs and laid larger eggs.

2 ➡ Many flightless bird species are classified into the ratite group due to the many physical features they share. These birds include the ostriches of Africa, rheas of South America, and the emus and cassowaries of Australia, all of which are very large birds with extremely small wings, long legs and long necks. Other extinct species that are placed in this group are the moa of New Zealand and the elephant bird of Madagascar, which disappeared in the last few thousand years, most likely because of human activity. Although flightless birds all possess vestigial wings, their breast bones lack the ridge that flight muscles attach to in flying bird species. These birds have totally abandoned flight and rely upon their powerful legs for movement and defense.

3 ➡ The largest of the flightless birds went extinct millions of years ago, but they were truly impressive specimens. When the dinosaurs

4. Which of the following can be inferred about terror birds from paragraph 3?

  (A) *Titanis walleri* was the largest land predator in the Western Hemisphere when it lived.

  (B) They were ultimately unable to compete with mammalian predators.

  (C) They lived alongside the dinosaurs and competed with them for food.

  (D) They were not as fast and agile as birds that hunt while flying.

5. Why does the author mention "Diatryma" in paragraph 3?

  (A) To cast doubt on its being classified as a "terror bird"

  (B) To explain why "terror birds" had large digestive organs

  (C) To draw a line between a giant bird and a large herbivore

  (D) To introduce a bird that was mistakenly categorized

6. In paragraph 4, which of the following is NOT mentioned about Gondwana?

  (A) It was an ancient supercontinent that broke up about 180 million years ago.

  (B) It incorporated the current continents of Africa, Australia, and South America.

  (C) It started to split when magma from below the Earth's crust began pushing upward.

  (D) Its breakup is believed to have isolated the animals living on it.

disappeared, niches in many habitats were vacated, and birds were often the animals that filled them before mammals took their place. This resulted in some truly giant birds that replaced both large herbivores and predators. One example of this is *Titanis walleri*, which was a member of the Phorusrhacidae family of the Americas also known as "terror birds." This hunter stood at 2.5 meters tall and would have weighed around 150 kilograms. It had powerful legs it used to hunt its prey, both for chasing the animals and knocking them to the ground. It also had a massive, hooked beak that was well-suited to tearing flesh. Another ancient bird called the Diatryma was included in the same group, but scientists now believe it was a large herbivore. Although it was of similar size and had a powerful beak, recent data shows that its diet consisted primarily of tough plant matter. For this reason, it would have needed a large caecum, an organ used to digest such a diet, which would have made flight difficult.

4 ➡ The wide distribution of ratite species has long puzzled scientists. For many decades, the most popular theory was that they descended from a common flightless ancestor. The continents that they live on, Africa, Australia and South America, were once connected into one landmass called Gondwana that split apart about 180 million years ago. This would have isolated the animals and allowed them to evolve independently. However, geologic evidence shows that the supercontinent of Gondwana broke apart far too long ago for that to be the case. A recent genetic survey of ratite species supports the more likely theory that the flightless giants evolved from a common ancestor that could fly. Members of this species spread across the world to the already divided continents, and then lost their ability to fly.

5 ➡ However, members of the ratite family are not exclusively large. The kiwi of New Zealand and the tinamou of South America are ratites with stout, robust bodies despite their diminutive

7. According to paragraph 5, what advantage do huge eggs bring to the kiwi?

   (A) Their large size prevents predators from eating them easily.

   (B) They give kiwi chicks a competitive edge over flying birds.

   (C) The chicks do not need to be fed after they hatch.

   (D) A female can only lay one egg at a time, which requires less energy.

8. Which of the sentences below best expresses the essential information in the highlighted sentence in the passage? *Incorrect* answer choices change the meaning in important ways or leave out essential information.

   (A) The ostrich has the largest egg compared to the body of the adult bird, while the kiwi has the smallest compared to its body.

   (B) Although it is a much smaller bird, the kiwi actually lays larger eggs than the ostrich does.

   (C) Since it is the largest bird in the world, it is not surprising that the ostrich lays the largest egg, but the kiwi actually lays a very large egg as well.

   (D) The ostrich actually has the smallest egg compared to the adult's body although it is the largest bird, whereas the kiwi has the largest egg compared to its body.

size. Still, they have another important trait that they share with other ratites: very large eggs. It makes sense for the ostrich to lay the biggest egg as the largest bird in the world, but the kiwi actually lays the largest egg relative to its own body size, and the ostrich egg is the smallest in comparison to the size of the adult bird. It remains unclear why kiwis lay such large eggs, but there are two possibilities. Either kiwis have always been small and their eggs have grown, or kiwis used to be much larger, and their eggs have not shrunk very much. Either way, a large egg provides definite survival advantages for kiwi chicks. They hatch with an extra supply of yolk that they can live off of for over two weeks, which means they are born pretty much ready to run. This makes it possible for them to better evade flying predators, so it might be worth carrying such outsized eggs.

PART 02
Actual Tests

9. Look at the four squares [■] that indicate where the following sentence could be added to the passage.

   Flight became an unnecessary expenditure of energy, so their bodies gradually lost the structures that were needed for flying.

   Where would the sentence best fit?

   Click on a square [■] to add the sentence to the passage.

10. **Directions:** An introductory sentence for a brief summary of the passage is provided below. Complete the summary by selecting the THREE answer choices that express the most important ideas in the passage. Some sentences do not belong in the summary because they express ideas that are not presented in the passage or are minor ideas in the passage. *This question is worth 2 points.*

    Many species of birds like the ratites have lost the ability to fly as they adapted to the habitats in which they live.

    -
    -
    -

Answer Choices

Ⓐ Many of the early flightless birds evolved to fill niches that had been left vacant by the dinosaurs when they went extinct.

Ⓑ *Titanis walleri* was the largest of the "terror birds" at 2.5 meters tall.

Ⓒ Scientists originally thought that ratites were flightless when the continents separated, but they have since learned that their ancestors must have flown across the oceans.

Ⓓ Ratite species live in Australia, Africa, and South America today.

Ⓔ Some scientists believe that the ancestors of modern kiwis must have been much larger than their descendants.

Ⓕ The smallest ratite species is the kiwi, which lays disproportionally large eggs.

Drag your answer choices to the spaces where they belong.
To remove an answer choice, click on it. To review the passage, click on **View Text**.

1. Why does the author mention "natural selection" in paragraph 1?

   Ⓐ To demonstrate that Darwin had a thorough insight concerning evolution

   Ⓑ To question the veracity of Darwin's theory of evolution

   Ⓒ To introduce various hypotheses about the evolution of species

   Ⓓ To explain the concept of evolution and give examples of it

2. According to paragraph 2, which of the following is the factor that accelerated the pace of evolution?

   Ⓐ Introduction of a new predator

   Ⓑ A sudden change in the environment

   Ⓒ Genetic diseases and mutations

   Ⓓ Competition for resources

3. The word "it" in paragraph 2 refers to

   Ⓐ morph

   Ⓑ bark

   Ⓒ content

   Ⓓ color

4. All of the following are mentioned in paragraph 3 EXCEPT

   Ⓐ the influence of air pollution on human lives.

   Ⓑ how the pollution changed the natural environment.

   Ⓒ the number of peppered moths that died from air pollution.

   Ⓓ the radical change in population of the melanic morph.

Industrial Melanism in Peppered Moths

1 ➡ According to the theory of evolution, organisms evolve through a process called natural selection. When they are subjected to changes in their environment, some organisms possess genetic traits that allow them to survive. These survivors mate and pass on their genes to future generations. Over time, the genetic trait becomes the norm for their population, and the species can be said to have evolved. Charles Darwin famously illustrated this theory through his studies of the finches living on the Galapagos Islands. However, this process was also happening in his home country, England, at the same time and at a much faster pace. The organism involved in this rapid adaptation was the peppered moth.

2 ➡ While evolution usually occurs over thousands of years, sometimes the environmental pressure is so extreme that the rate speeds up. For the peppered moths, their motivation to adapt was increased predation. Peppered moths in England typically come in two different morphs or types that are determined by their genes. The more commonly seen morph was grey, often with speckled patterns that helped it blend in with light colored tree bark and lichens. The less commonly observed morph had a much higher melanin content, which makes its body and wings dark grey to black in color. However, the melanic trait is actually the dominant allele. The lighter morphs were more common because they could blend in more easily, making it more difficult for birds to see and then eat them. But, something shifted the situation in favor of the melanic morph.

3 ➡ During the Industrial Revolution in England, air pollution in the form of soot from burned coal increased dramatically. This pollution eventually became so severe that thousands of people in London died from breathing it. This

5. Based on paragraph 3, what can be inferred about the peppered moths in the middle of the 19th century?

    Ⓐ Light colored moths were less resistant to air pollution than darker ones.

    Ⓑ The Industrial Revolution threatened their survival and reproduction.

    Ⓒ There was a rapid increase in the moth population due to industrialization.

    Ⓓ Their color had changed so that they could blend in with the surroundings.

6. Which of the sentences below best expresses the essential information in the highlighted sentence in the passage? *Incorrect* answer choices change the meaning in important ways or leave out essential information.

    Ⓐ Lighter moths in rural areas were stronger than the melanistic moths in urban areas.

    Ⓑ In contrast to urban areas where the melanistic moths were prevalent, lighter moths were still dominant in rural areas.

    Ⓒ It was the melanistic moths that occupied urban areas, and they eventually spread to rural areas.

    Ⓓ Lighter moths in rural areas had smaller populations than the melanistic ones in urban areas due to some regional differences.

7. According to paragraph 5, why were only a few of the lighter moths recovered in Kettlewell's experiment?

    Ⓐ Their color made it easy for their predators to find and eat them.

    Ⓑ Great Tits had difficulty in discovering them on matching surfaces.

    Ⓒ Kettlewell marked the underside of their wings.

    Ⓓ All of the darker moths were eaten by birds.

pollution also affected the peppered moths. Throughout England, but particularly in cities, the rocks and trees that the moths rested on became covered in a layer of soot, killing much of the lichen and making everything darker. Prior to industrialization, the melanic morph only accounted for about .01% of the moth population, by the middle of the 19th century it had increased noticeably, and by 1895 it had reached a staggering 98% in some areas, which puzzled many naturalists.

4 ➡ In urban areas, the melanistic moths became overwhelmingly dominant, but in rural areas, the lighter moths continued to have the advantage. In an attempt to explain such a dramatic shift, J. W. Tutt offered a hypothesis in 1896 that birds were eating one morph in the city and the other morph in the country. Over the years, many experiments have been conducted to test this hypothesis, and the data gathered has consistently supported it. The most famous of these experiments were conducted by Bernard Kettlewell and his associates between 1952 and 1972.

5 ➡ In his first experiment, Kettlewell captured both light and dark moths and released them into an aviary to observe the results. The birds that ate the most moths were Great Tits, and they usually took the moths that were resting on a contrastingly colored surface. When the moths sat on matching surfaces, he had trouble seeing them, and the birds clearly did as well. In his following experiments, Kettlewell raised his own population of both morphs and marked the concealed underside of their wings with paint. If he had placed the markings on the top of the wing, they would all have become easier prey. Then, he released them into a heavily polluted forest near Birmingham and recaptured as many survivors as he could. Very few of the moths that he recovered were the lighter morph, which he interpreted to mean that the melanism was necessary to survival in such a habitat.

8. The word "vital" in paragraph 6 is closest in meaning to

  (A) notable

  (B) tangible

  (C) essential

  (D) trivial

6 ➡ He later repeated this experiment, but he chose an unpolluted forest near Dorset. Again, he observed that the moths' coloring was vital to their survival. [■A] Kettlewell concluded that factories like those in Birmingham were responsible for causing industrial melanism, which is when animals evolve darker coloration to survive in a habitat darkened by pollution. [■B] In the decades since his experiments, study has continued and provided further support for the theory that melanism in moths is a response to natural selection based on camouflage and predation. [■C] In particular, researchers have found that since stricter pollution laws were imposed, the population of lighter morphs near urban areas has rebounded. [■D]

PART 02
Actual Tests

9. Look at the four squares [■] that indicate where the following sentence could be added to the passage.

The dark moths did better in polluted woods, and the lighter ones did better in cleaner woods.

Where would the sentence best fit?

Click on a square [■] to add the sentence to the passage.

10. **Directions:** An introductory sentence for a brief summary of the passage is provided below. Complete the summary by selecting the THREE answer choices that express the most important ideas in the passage. Some sentences do not belong in the summary because they express ideas that are not presented in the passage or are minor ideas in the passage. *This question is worth 2 points.*

The melanism of peppered moths in the 19th century in England was the result of adaptation to environmental changes, which exemplified Darwin's theory of evolution by natural selection.

-
-
-

Answer Choices

Ⓐ Darwin claimed that evolution occurs over a long period of time.

Ⓑ Rapid industrialization increased the pollutants in the air, which covered trees and rocks and brought about changes in the moths' color.

Ⓒ The patterns which peppered moths have on their bodies help them blend in with light colored objects such as tree bark and lichens.

Ⓓ Kettlewell carried out a test by releasing both light moths and melanistic ones into a specific area, recapturing them, and counting the survivors.

Ⓔ Kettlewell concluded that the increased risk of predation caused the melanism of the peppered moths.

Ⓕ Kettlewell's experiment demonstrated that melanism strengthened moths' biological resistance to the polluted air.

Drag your answer choices to the spaces where they belong.
To remove an answer choice, click on it. To review the passage, click on **View Text**.

PART 02
Actual Tests

1. The word "sustained" in paragraph 2 is closest in meaning to

   (A) continued

   (B) intensive

   (C) compulsory

   (D) vigorous

2. According to paragraph 2, the rapidly swimming fish in the tuna family keep their body temperature higher than the water around them so they can

   (A) supply energy to their red aerobic muscles.

   (B) generate heat at the core of their body.

   (C) increase their metabolism for prolonged activity.

   (D) swim deep into the ocean chasing prey.

3. According to paragraph 3, why are some marine organisms not classified as truly ectothermic?

   (A) They are found in intertidal areas.

   (B) They have the ability to reflect or absorb solar energy.

   (C) Their blood circulation system is different from that of ectothermic species.

   (D) They maintain temperatures lower than their environment.

Thermoregulation in Marine Organisms

1 ➡ Living organisms have a variety of ways in which they regulate their body temperature, but they are generally divided into two larger categories. [■A] Endothermic organisms are those whose metabolisms allow them to maintain a relatively stable temperature that is generally hotter than their ambient conditions. [■B] The key reason behind the difference in core body temperature between these organisms is the fact that water is much more conductive than air, and they lose more of their heat into their environment. [■C] The majority of marine creatures regulate their body temperature by matching that of their surroundings, which puts them in the second broad category of ectothermic organisms. [■D]

2 ➡ Most species of fish and invertebrates that dwell in the open ocean below tidal areas are ectothermic, but not all marine organisms fit neatly into either of the categories. Some organisms possess abilities that allow them to exist somewhere between the two by maintaining a temperature that is higher than the water around them, but well below what truly endothermic creatures are capable of. One such exception is the rapidly swimming fish in the tuna family. They are able to keep their body temperature significantly higher than the water around them through their unique musculature. Unlike most fish whose swimming muscles are distributed evenly under their skin, their red aerobic muscle is located along their spine. This not only makes them powerful swimmers, but it also generates heat at the core of their body. In combination with a retention system, this allows them to generate the heat required to increase their metabolic rate and engage in sustained activity.

3 ➡ Other marine creatures cannot truly be classified as ectothermic because they actually try to maintain temperatures that are lower than

4. All of the following are mentioned in paragraph 4 as ways endothermic animals lose heat EXCEPT

(A) skin coming into contact with water.

(B) absorbing solar energy close to the equator.

(C) warm blood flowing to the extremities.

(D) breathing in cold air.

5. What is the function of paragraph 5 as it relates to paragraph 4?

(A) To explain ways marine animals deal with the problems mentioned in paragraph 4

(B) To discuss how the problems described in paragraph 4 affect some animals more than others

(C) To provide examples of animals to which the problems mentioned in paragraph 4 do not apply

(D) To suggest possible causes of the problems mentioned in paragraph 4

6. What is implied by comparing land mammals to marine mammals of similar size in paragraph 5?

(A) Relatively smaller-sized land mammals lose less heat than the relatively bigger-sized marine mammals.

(B) Land mammals are more efficient at preventing heat loss than marine mammals.

(C) Land animals are exposed to significantly colder temperatures.

(D) There are other factors responsible for metabolic rate than body size.

their surroundings. These animals are found in intertidal areas where they are exposed to greater amounts of sunlight, which heats the small tidal pools they are trapped in at different times of the day. They circulate and expel bodily fluids to cool themselves by evaporation. They are so effective at this that they will have lower temperatures than inanimate objects near them even if they are of the same size and shape. They also use color to their advantage as lighter colors absorb less heat than darker colors do, so the predominant colors of organisms will vary in order to reflect or collect solar energy depending upon their distance from the equator.

4 ➡ Since ocean temperatures are typically below 30 degrees centigrade, and may plunge below zero depending upon depth, completely endothermic organisms like whales and dolphins suffer from a constant loss of body heat. This mainly occurs due to their skin's contact with the water, which can rapidly lower their temperature. This is exacerbated when their blood flows outward from their core to their extremities, is cooled, and returns to the core. When they surface to breathe, they expel heat along with their breath and often breathe in cold air, which only lowers their temperature even further. Since a considerable lowering of internal temperature can be fatal for endotherms, those that live in the marine environment have developed various tactics to prevent this outcome.

5 ➡ Sea birds like penguins have developed a dual coat of feathers that prevents heat loss. They have a thick layer of downy feathers covered with a layer of rigid interconnecting feathers that hold air stationary between them, acting as an insulating layer. Cetaceans and pinnipeds, however, rely upon a thick layer of fat underneath their skin called blubber. Unlike whales and seals, sea otters lack blubber, but they have an incredibly thick coat of fur that keeps their skin from coming into direct contact with the water. In addition, these marine mammals have accelerated metabolisms in

7. Which of the sentences below best expresses the essential information in the highlighted sentence in the passage? *Incorrect* answer choices change the meaning in important ways or leave out essential information.

(A) The shape of their limbs allows the animals to maintain their body temperature more easily by utilizing a unique heat exchange that avoids releasing heat.

(B) The limbs have a greater surface area to inner volume ratio than the rest of the body, which makes it difficult for them to receive warm arterial blood.

(C) Their heat exchange system allows them to minimize heat loss through limbs which lose heat more quickly than other parts of the body due to their shape.

(D) Because their limbs have a greater surface area to inner volume ratio than other parts of the body, these animals have developed a system that prevents blood flow to the limbs.

8. According to paragraph 6, how do some marine mammals minimize heat loss through their limbs?

(A) By placing veins closer to the core of the body

(B) By having the blood flowing back to the core colder than the blood flowing out

(C) By having veins carrying cold blood around the arteries carrying warm blood

(D) By cooling down warm blood in the veins before it reaches the core

comparison with similarly sized land mammals to produce much more internal heat.

6 ➡ For whales and dolphins, these measures are still insufficient due to the large fins and tail flukes that they need for swimming. These limbs have a far greater surface area to inner volume ratio than the rest of the body, which means that they rapidly shed heat, but they still must receive arterial blood, so they have developed a heat exchange system to minimize the effect. The veins that carry cold blood back in from the limbs wind around the arteries which carry out warm blood from the core. This warms the venous blood so it doesn't cool the core, and cools the arterial blood so that it doesn't release much warmth into the water through the limbs. This system is not unique to mammals, as some fish species, like the aforementioned tuna and some sharks, possess overall similar systems to reduce heat loss through their fins and gills.

9. Look at the four squares [■] that indicate where the following sentence could be added to the passage.

    The average body temperature of most land mammals tends to be around 40 degrees Celsius, but that of marine mammals is usually a few degrees lower.

    Where would the sentence best fit?

    Click on a square [■] to add the sentence to the passage.

10. **Directions:** An introductory sentence for a brief summary of the passage is provided below. Complete the summary by selecting the THREE answer choices that express the most important ideas in the passage. Some sentences do not belong in the summary because they express ideas that are not presented in the passage or are minor ideas in the passage. *This question is worth 2 points.*

    Organisms that maintain body temperatures higher than the ambient temperature are called endothermic, and organisms that match their body temperature to their surroundings are called ectothermic.

    -
    -
    -

    Answer Choices

    Ⓐ Many do not fall into either category, as some keep their temperature between the two categories, while others keep their temperature even lower than their environment.

    Ⓑ The rapidly swimming fish in the tuna family have their swimming muscles concentrated just below their skin.

    Ⓒ Many endothermic organisms possess features such as fur coats and blubber to keep their body temperature high enough.

    Ⓓ For body parts with a greater surface area to inner volume ratio, they have developed a blood circulation system which prevents heat loss.

    Ⓔ Sea otters do not have blubber, but they have a thick coat of fur preventing their skin from coming into direct contact with water.

    Ⓕ The fact that intertidal organisms have lower temperatures than inanimate objects proves that land mammals have a lower metabolic rate than marine mammals.

    Drag your answer choices to the spaces where they belong.

    To remove an answer choice, click on it. To review the passage, click on **View Text**.

Actual Test 02

정답 및 해석 ㅣ P. 19

Reading Section Directions

This section measures your ability to understand academic passages in English.

You will have 54 minutes to read and answer the questions about 3 passages.

Most questions are worth 1 point but the last question in each set is worth more than 1 point. The directions indicate how many points you may receive.

Within each screen, you can go to the next question by clicking **Next**. You may skip questions and go back to them later. If you want to return to previous questions, click on **Back**.

You can click on **Review** at any time and the review screen will show you which questions you have answered and which you have not answered. From this review screen, you may go directly to any questions you have already seen in the Reading section.

You may now begin the Reading section.

Click on **Continue** to go on.

The Fall of the Mayan Civilization

1. **Based on paragraph 1, what can be inferred about the Mayan civilization?**

   Ⓐ Nobody truly knows how the Mayan civilization collapsed.

   Ⓑ The golden age of the Mayan civilization began with the ending of the Classical Period.

   Ⓒ Most of the Mayan population lived in cities.

   Ⓓ The Mayan civilization eventually recovered from the Spanish conquest.

2. **According to paragraph 2, which of the following is NOT true of the Classical Period?**

   Ⓐ It was a period of constant warfare with their neighbors.

   Ⓑ It was a period during which the number of aristocrats grew.

   Ⓒ It was a period of flourishing trade.

   Ⓓ It was a period during which many buildings were constructed.

1 ➡ The Mayan civilization that once covered much of modern day Guatemala and Southern Mexico was inarguably one of the greatest civilizations ever to exist in Pre-Columbian America. Their settlements date back to around 2,000 BCE, and some existed until the Spanish conquest of the region. They are known for their monumental step-pyramids, stonemasonry, understanding of astronomy and mathematics, and a fully developed hieroglyphic writing system. Their civilization reached its peak during what is called its Classical Period, extending from 250 CE to around 900 CE, when their cities reached their highest state of development. However, their flourishing society suffered a catastrophic collapse at this time from which they never fully recovered. Many theories have been suggested to explain such a sudden decline, including natural disasters, war, and plague. While these may have contributed to the overall decline, the root cause appears to have been an interconnected series of events involving agriculture, conflict, and climate change.

2 ➡ In the Classical Period, the Maya experienced rapid expansion and their population reached into the millions. Most of their large religious and political complexes were built during this time, and their civilization developed into a large politically and economically interconnected society comprised of many small kingdoms and empires. By the 8th century, populations surrounding the central lowlands had reached new peaks of size and density. This was also the area that held the most political influence. Their growing aristocracy, who enjoyed luxuries and the best food, are believed to have expanded rapidly. The outlying kingdoms served as the primary centers for trade, and they brought in goods from throughout Mesoamerica. While relationships with their neighbors were not always peaceful,

3. Which of the sentences below best expresses the essential information in the highlighted sentence in the passage? *Incorrect* answer choices change the meaning in important ways or leave out essential information.

Ⓐ The increased rainfall quickly diminished the minerals and nutrients in the soil, so it was hard for them to shorten their fallow cycles.

Ⓑ The farmers resisted the temptation to shorten fallow cycles because the increased rainfall fostered growth on the farms where minerals and nutrients were replenished.

Ⓒ The farmers probably wanted to shorten rest periods because the increased rainfall replenished their farms and made it easier to grow crops.

Ⓓ The farmers began to use shorter rest periods for their farms because the soil was washed away by water coming from the surrounding countryside.

4. According to paragraph 3, what is one possible cause for the increase in population?

Ⓐ Significantly higher rainfall

Ⓑ Shorter fallow cycle

Ⓒ Reduced expanses of rainforest

Ⓓ Increased food production

5. What is the main purpose of paragraph 4?

Ⓐ To demonstrate the negative effects of reckless expansion

Ⓑ To discuss the effects of rainfall on competition between large urban centers

Ⓒ To explain what began the downfall of the Mayan civilization

Ⓓ To highlight the social divide between peasants and aristocrats

and warfare did indeed occur, they were generally friendly. The greatest danger to the Maya, although they were probably oblivious to the fact, came from within.

3 ➡ Early in the Classical Period, from about 440 to 660 CE, the area the Maya lived in experienced significantly higher rainfall than it had in the past. This extended wetter period allowed them to expand their agriculture and produce unprecedented amounts of food. The food surplus allowed the population to grow, and fueled the civilization's rapid expansion. The Maya used permanent farms and raised terraces for cultivation, and their usual method of crop rotation involved fallow cycles, leaving the land uncultivated in order to allow it to recover. However, the increased rainfall would have meant that the minerals and nutrients in the soil of their farms would be replenished more quickly by the mountain runoff, and the temptation to shorten fallow cycles must have been nearly irresistible in a climate that fostered such growth. In addition, the Maya began cutting down expanses of rainforest to clear land for farming and to provide lumber and firewood, reducing the amount of groundcover. Since they raised little livestock, they were also rapidly depleting the area of the animals they relied on for meat. The Maya were overtaxing the carrying capacity of their environment, but they would not realize this until it was too late.

4 ➡ As their civilization continued to expand throughout the 8th and 9th centuries, the advantageous rainfall began to lessen. As this trend continued, pressures began to grow within Mayan society. The large urban centers with their aristocratic populations were a huge drain on agriculture, so as the output decreased, they had to compensate by importing food. This transferred the burden out onto the surrounding communities, which increased competition and conflict between cities and regions. As the societal and economic divide between the peasants and the aristocrats widened further,

6. According to paragraph 4, what was the likely result of importing food?

   Ⓐ It increased the number of aristocrats.

   Ⓑ The farmers began to revolt against the traders.

   Ⓒ It caused conflicts amongst those in large urban centers.

   Ⓓ The social divide between the upper class and lower class widened.

7. The word "exacerbated" in paragraph 5 is closest in meaning to

   Ⓐ evoked

   Ⓑ placated

   Ⓒ aggravated

   Ⓓ controlled

8. According to paragraph 5, why was the drought especially devastating for the Mayan civilization?

   Ⓐ It was a symptom of a global shift in climate.

   Ⓑ Deforestation worsened the drought.

   Ⓒ The Maya fought for water.

   Ⓓ It was a result of unchecked expansion.

the lower classes began to revolt against the established order, and food shortages only worsened the situation. Their whole society was teetering on the brink of an abyss.

5 ➡ Then around 1,000 CE, the already faltering civilization was struck by a true disaster: a prolonged drought struck the southern regions. [■A] The drought was a symptom of a global shift in climate that seriously affected other areas in the world, but for the Mayan civilization it was devastating. [■B] Their practice of clearing forest exacerbated the problem in two ways. The land that had been cleared was poor for farming, and the lack of trees disrupted the normal evaporation cycle. [■C] Internal warfare escalated as supplies dwindled, and eventually their whole system collapsed. [■D] The Mayan civilization was ultimately a victim of its own unchecked expansion. The drought did not completely destroy their culture as some of the city states in the north survived and continued to expand, but they too fell after the arrival of the Spanish.

9. Look at the four squares [■] that indicate where the following sentence could be added to the passage.

    Therefore, when the drought reduced rainfall by 25 to 40%, their agricultural system became completely unsustainable.

    Where would the sentence best fit?

    Click on a square [■] to add the sentence to the passage.

10. **Directions:** An introductory sentence for a brief summary of the passage is provided below. Complete the summary by selecting the THREE answer choices that express the most important ideas in the passage. Some sentences do not belong in the summary because they express ideas that are not presented in the passage or are minor ideas in the passage. *This question is worth 2 points.*

    While there are many theories that attempt to explain the fall of the Mayan civilization, there seems to have been several interlinked factors that led to the sudden decline of one of the greatest civilizations ever to exist in Pre-Columbian America.

    -
    -
    -

    Answer Choices

    (A) The Maya reached the peak of their civilization by the 9th century CE.
    (B) The widening gap and deepening conflict between the aristocrats worsened the economic situation.
    (C) With less rainfall, the farms were not able to produce enough food, resulting in food shortages that applied critical pressure to Mayan society.
    (D) The drought was the final straw for the weakened Mayan society, completely collapsing their already dysfunctional agricultural system.
    (E) The prolonged drought forced the Maya to import food from surrounding communities.
    (F) Relying heavily on increased rainfall, the Maya overtaxed the natural resources of the land.

    Drag your answer choices to the spaces where they belong.
    To remove an answer choice, click on it. To review the passage, click on **View Text**.

Continental Drift

1 ➡ During the Age of Exploration, European travelers sailed the world's oceans searching for new land and resources to exploit. During these great voyages of discovery, their crews usually included cartographers and scientists who documented the regions where they traveled. Over the centuries, the cartographers' maps gradually became more complete and accurate, allowing other Europeans to learn about the shape of the world, and some startling ideas began to develop. Initially, the famous intellectual Francis Bacon noted the similarity in shape between the eastern coast of South America and the western coast of Africa, which he thought meant that they had been formed by similar processes. As the scientists collected specimens of organisms they encountered, they marveled at the diversity of life, but when they compared the specimens from different landmasses, they were surprised to see how similar some of them were. In fact, many were identical, despite being collected from different continents. These observations formed the foundation for the theory of continental drift.

2 ➡ One such explorer was Joseph D. Hooker, a botanist who traveled to Antarctica as a ship's surgeon on Ross's expedition. He traveled extensively throughout the Southern Hemisphere and compiled many books about the flora of New Zealand, Australia, and Tasmania. Later, Charles Darwin invited him to classify the plants that he had collected in South America, some of which were very similar to ones he had found on earlier voyages. This led him to surmise that the major landmasses of the Southern Hemisphere had at one point been connected, although exactly how he could not be certain. He proposed that they had originally formed one supercontinent that had been loosely connected by land bridges that had since disappeared due to either geologic forces or climatic events. Although they agreed upon many things,

1. Why does the author mention "Francis Bacon" in paragraph 1?

   Ⓐ To suggest that Bacon was a gifted cartographer

   Ⓑ To show where the idea of one great landmass may have come from

   Ⓒ To point out that Bacon was not qualified to speak on such matters

   Ⓓ To question whether maps were good enough to make such an observation

2. Which of the sentences below best expresses the essential information in the highlighted sentence in the passage? *Incorrect* answer choices change the meaning in important ways or leave out essential information.

   Ⓐ As the scientists collected specimens they encountered on different landmasses, they were surprised by their diversity.

   Ⓑ When scientists compared specimens of organisms they collected, they were amazed at both the diversity and similarity of specimens from different landmasses.

   Ⓒ When the scientists compared specimens of organisms they collected from different landmasses, they were surprised to see they were similar to those from the ocean.

   Ⓓ While the scientists collected specimens of organisms, they were no longer surprised to see the similarities between specimens from different landmasses.

3. According to paragraph 2, Hooker's ideas were novel because

   Ⓐ he proposed the possibility that the Earth's crust could move.

   Ⓑ he had definitive proof that the southern continents had been connected into one.

   Ⓒ the standard by which he classified the plants from South America was strict.

   Ⓓ he argued that land bridges had enabled similar plants to spread to different areas.

4. According to paragraph 3, why did Suess name the hypothetical supercontinent after Gondwana?

   Ⓐ Gondwana is an area where the Earth had clearly cooled and contracted.

   Ⓑ Gondwana represented a legendary supercontinent in central India.

   Ⓒ He believed that the region was located in the center of the supercontinent.

   Ⓓ Geologic features and fossils in Gondwana gave him clues for the supercontinent.

5. According to paragraph 4, why was Wegener's theory disregarded by other scientists?

   Ⓐ It could not provide a clear explanation of what caused continental drift.

   Ⓑ It was against the dominant scientific paradigm of the time.

   Ⓒ It was thought to be theoretically impossible despite all the evidence he had collected.

   Ⓓ It was supported by pieces of evidence that were inconsistent with one another.

Darwin discounted this theory and said that the similarity was due to dispersal: the plants had migrated along ocean currents. Still, the idea of one southern continent had been proposed.

3 ➡ This concept was further solidified by Austrian geologist Eduard Suess. Through his studies, he became convinced that India, South America, Australia, Africa and Antarctica had all once been connected. He was led to this conclusion by examples of glossopteris fossils that had been found in all of those locations. He developed the theory that the oceans had changed levels and locations over time and that this could be mapped across all of the continents. He also imagined a fragmented supercontinent connected by gateways that had disappeared beneath the waves. He named this supercontinent Gondwanaland after the Gondwana region in central India, which had similar geologic formations and fossils compared to the other areas. However, his theories were based upon the concept that the Earth is cooling and contracting, creating mountain ranges and relocating oceans; a theory that was later disproven.

4 ➡ In the early 20th century, Alfred Wegener also noted how the continents appeared to fit together like a giant puzzle. He believed that the continents had all once been a single landmass that had broken apart and drifted apart from, and in some cases back into, each other. He analyzed continental shelves on both sides of the Atlantic, looking for geologic structures, rock types, and fossils, and found that they were quite similar. He published a paper detailing his theory of continental drift, but his evidence was observational and failed to answer an important question. What was the mechanism causing the drift? Without a clear cause, much of the scientific community ignored his theory. They believed that the seafloor crust was too solid for the continents to move through it. One scientist who pursued the theory was Alexander du Toit, a South African geologist. He traveled extensively

6. The word "spreading" in paragraph 5 is closest in meaning to

   Ⓐ expansion

   Ⓑ circulation

   Ⓒ separation

   Ⓓ acceleration

7. All of the following are mentioned in paragraph 5 EXCEPT

   Ⓐ the way sonar helped the process of mapping.

   Ⓑ the role of satellite mapping in researching the Earth's surface.

   Ⓒ the mineral composition of the crust.

   Ⓓ the mechanism behind plate tectonics.

8. Which of the following can be inferred from paragraph 5?

   Ⓐ Only a few scientists in the past had the foresight to predict the future.

   Ⓑ It sometimes requires time for an innovative idea to be widely accepted.

   Ⓒ Some evidence has recently been discovered to refute the concept of tectonic plates.

   Ⓓ With advances in technology, it became possible to support the continental drift theory.

throughout Africa and South America, locating and documenting many geologic features that showed the two continents had not only formed similarly, but had once been a single landmass. This was seen as a very significant find and bolstered the theory of continental drift.

5 ➡ [■A] The mechanism behind continental drift was discovered in the latter half of the 20th century. The development of sonar allowed for much more accurate mapping of the seafloor. [■B] Instead, it is a zone of seafloor spreading, where new crust wells up from within the Earth. [■C] In addition, many trenches were revealed to be areas where crust is plunging back down into the Earth. [■D] Satellite mapping has allowed scientists to confirm that the Earth's surface is not a single solid crust, but rather a complex arrangement of crust plates that float on the mantle below and are constantly moving. This process is called plate tectonics, and it proves that the continents were once all one, and that they did indeed separate and migrate as so many scientists had theorized in the past.

9. Look at the four squares [■] that indicate where the following sentence could be added to the passage.

This revealed that the Mid Atlantic Ridge was not simply a mountain range extending the length of the ocean.

Where would the sentence best fit?

Click on a square [■] to add the sentence to the passage.

10. **Directions:** An introductory sentence for a brief summary of the passage is provided below. Complete the summary by selecting the THREE answer choices that express the most important ideas in the passage. Some sentences do not belong in the summary because they express ideas that are not presented in the passage or are minor ideas in the passage. *This question is worth 2 points.*

Although it is widely accepted as fact today, the theory of continental drift faced strong opposition throughout its development.

-
-
-

Answer Choices

(A) It was early European travelers who figured out the connection between the fossils they had found and the supercontinent Gondwana.

(B) When the supercontinent hypothesis was first proposed, it was dismissed by most contemporary scientists due to lack of detailed evidence.

(C) Charles Darwin was one of the scientists who presumed that different continents had once formed one large landmass.

(D) The research and discoveries of Wegener and du Toit contributed to verifying the theory of continental drift.

(E) The development of science and technology helped reveal the mechanism behind continental drift.

(F) Currents and winds dispersed the seeds and spores of plants, causing similar plant specimens to be found all over the world.

Drag your answer choices to the spaces where they belong.
To remove an answer choice, click on it. To review the passage, click on **View Text**.

Altruism in Meerkats

1 ➡ Meerkats are small members of the mongoose family that live in the Kalahari and Namib Deserts of southern Africa. Scientists have studied them for centuries due to their complex societal structure and their altruism, which they practice to a level not often seen in nature. Meerkats breed cooperatively, which means that a group will consist of a dominant breeding pair and up to 40 male and female assistants who do not breed. These assistants spend most of their time taking care of the young by feeding them, training them, and protecting them from danger. As a social predator, it is not unusual that meerkats should do these things as a group, but the extent they carry this behavior to is remarkable.

2 ➡ Meerkats are primarily insectivores, but they will also eat small reptiles, mammals, fungi, and occasionally birds. The majority of the group will usually go out to gather food together, leaving a few to guard the young. Once the pack locates prey, it is difficult for that animal to escape as meerkats are extremely fast and excellent diggers. [■A] Surprisingly, one of their preferred prey animals is scorpions. [■B] While many members of the mongoose family are immune to various snake and insect venoms, it is unclear how much immunity meerkats possess, but this does not deter them. [■C] When a meerkat pounces on a scorpion, the arachnid often has no time to prepare a strike, and the meerkat circumvents any attack by swiftly biting off the scorpion's stinger. [■D] The meerkat can then devour the disarmed creature at its leisure, or use it as a teaching tool for the young.

3 ➡ Young meerkats feed on milk like any other mammal as infants, but that milk is not always produced by their mother. If the mother is away hunting, other females will actually lactate to feed the infant young. Once they are weaned, however, they must be taught to forage with the

1. According to paragraph 1, what sets apart the meerkats from other animals?
   - (A) They are one of the few mammal species that breed cooperatively.
   - (B) They are a popular subject of study for scientists.
   - (C) They are the smallest member of the mongoose family.
   - (D) They are altruistic to an extent rarely observed.

2. Which of the sentences below best expresses the essential information in the highlighted sentence in the passage? *Incorrect* answer choices change the meaning in important ways or leave out essential information.
   - (A) Because many members of the mongoose family hold immunity to various venoms, meerkats do not fear venomous animals.
   - (B) Unlike with other members of the mongoose family, we don't know how much immunity meerkats possess, but this isn't an obstacle for the meerkats.
   - (C) Compared to many members of the mongoose family which have immunity to various venoms, meerkats are not aware if they possess immunity.
   - (D) While it is unclear how much immunity meerkats possess, other members of the mongoose family are weak against most venoms, and this discourages them.

3. The word "circumvents" in paragraph 2 is closest in meaning to

 (A) overcomes
 (B) eradicates
 (C) preserves
 (D) avoids

4. What is the purpose of paragraph 3 as it relates to paragraph 2?

 (A) To describe the training young meerkats go through to participate in hunting mentioned in paragraph 2
 (B) To provide an example of how young meerkats develop the immunity to venoms mentioned in paragraph 2
 (C) To explain why meerkats prefer to hunt dangerous prey as mentioned in paragraph 2
 (D) To differentiate the feeding practices of young meerkats from those of adults as discussed in paragraph 2

5. According to paragraph 4, what is the reasoning against regarding sentry behavior as altruistic?

 (A) Sentries are the first to enter their burrows.
 (B) Sentries do not participate in high-risk duties such as hunting dangerous prey.
 (C) Sentries give false warnings to steal food.
 (D) Sentries are safe from predator attacks.

6. Based on paragraph 4, what can be inferred about meerkats?

 (A) Meerkats are quite vulnerable to predator attacks.
 (B) Meerkats have poor vision.
 (C) Meerkats takes turns acting as sentries.
 (D) Meerkats dig many burrows in their territory.

adults. To teach them how to hunt dangerous prey like scorpions or centipedes, the adults will start with dead and disarmed prey. Once the young learn how to eat solid food, they will give them prey that has been disarmed but remains very much alive. After they get used to killing their own food, the adults will then show them how to remove the stinger. At that point, it becomes the young animals' turn, and they either succeed or receive a painful and potentially fatal wound. Apart from this kind of training, the adults normally go to great lengths to protect all of the members of their clan.

4 ➡ While most of the clan goes foraging or tends to the young, a few animals will find a place to act as a sentry, either by standing on their hind legs on high ground or by climbing up into a nearby bush, but this also makes them visible to predators. If a sentry spots danger, it will bark, and the entire clan will flee to the nearest burrows. Some researchers have claimed that since the sentries often are the first animals to run, it shows that this behavior may not be entirely altruistic. However, the first animal to reemerge is usually the same sentry animal, and it will continue to give warning barks until it has confirmed that the surface is safe. This behavior is truly selfless, because the animal is not only exposing itself to potential danger, but also announcing its presence to any nearby predators with its barking.

5 ➡ When the clan is unable to avoid a threat in this way, they exhibit further altruistic behavior. If they are threatened in a group, the adults will bunch together and attack the creature en masse in an action called mobbing. This behavior is meant to scare away the predator by making the group appear to be a single larger animal. This is not always effective against snakes, and sometimes individuals get bitten. When there is danger, the babysitter will quickly usher the young underground, but this is not always possible. When there is no safe place to hide, she will gather the young into a group and

7. The word "usher" in paragraph 5 is closest in meaning to

   Ⓐ move
   Ⓑ lead
   Ⓒ carry
   Ⓓ push

8. Which of the following is NOT mentioned in the passage about meerkats?

   Ⓐ Defensive mechanisms
   Ⓑ Foraging behavior
   Ⓒ Domestication by humans
   Ⓓ Breeding habits

then lie on top of them. Ideally, this will keep them from attracting attention, but it may result in the female sacrificing herself for the lives of the young.

9. Look at the four squares [■] that indicate where the following sentence could be added to the passage.

   Then, it uses sand to wash away any venom that may remain on the scorpion's exoskeleton.

   Where would the sentence best fit?

   Click on a square [■] to add the sentence to the passage.

10. **Directions:** An introductory sentence for a brief summary of the passage is provided below. Complete the summary by selecting the THREE answer choices that express the most important ideas in the passage. Some sentences do not belong in the summary because they express ideas that are not presented in the passage or are minor ideas in the passage. *This question is worth 2 points.*

   Meerkats, one of the mostly widely studied mammals living in southern Africa, are well known for their exceptionally altruistic behavior.

   -
   -
   -

   Answer Choices

   Ⓐ Male and female assistants in a group do not breed until the dominant pair permits them to.

   Ⓑ When sentries spot a predator, they issue a series of distinct barks until the danger has passed.

   Ⓒ When meerkats are attacked by predators, they display altruistic behavior by mobbing the predator and placing the safety of their young first.

   Ⓓ Every adult member of the group plays a role in feeding, training, and protecting the young, even though they are not their own offspring.

   Ⓔ The training for foraging and hunting for food is done in a multi-step process.

   Ⓕ Meerkats bite off the scorpion's stinger first to ensure that the arachnid does not strike them with its venom.

   Drag your answer choices to the spaces where they belong.
   To remove an answer choice, click on it. To review the passage, click on **View Text**.

Actual Test 03

정답 및 해석 ∣ P. 36

Reading Section Directions

This section measures your ability to understand academic passages in English.

You will have 54 minutes to read and answer the questions about 3 passages.

Most questions are worth 1 point but the last question in each set is worth more than 1 point. The directions indicate how many points you may receive.

Within each screen, you can go to the next question by clicking **Next**. You may skip questions and go back to them later. If you want to return to previous questions, click on **Back**.

You can click on **Review** at any time and the review screen will show you which questions you have answered and which you have not answered. From this review screen, you may go directly to any questions you have already seen in the Reading section.

You may now begin the Reading section.

Click on **Continue** to go on.

Deep Sea Biology

1 ➡ After centuries of exploration, scientists have revealed that life exists nearly everywhere on the surface of the Earth. This includes the deepest trenches in the ocean. However, proof of such life remained elusive for a long time because we lacked the technology to reach such depths. Therefore, many hypotheses that supposed that life could not survive there arose. These ideas were logical and convinced many experts that the reason that specimens could not be collected was because they did not exist. However, as evidence of organisms from the depths mounted, many of these ideas were proven wrong. One of the most famous mistaken theories about deep sea biology was created by Edward Forbes.

2 ➡ Edward Forbes was a naturalist and marine biologist from the Isle of Man who had a short but prolific career. He is best known for his time spent upon the HMS Beacon in the Aegean Sea on its survey voyage and the theory on oceanic life that he developed there. Using a dredging rig, he conducted a study of ocean life at varying depths, and came to the conclusion that life did not exist below 300 fathoms (1 fathom is about 2 meters). This belief became known as the azoic hypothesis and was widely accepted by the scientific community until it was disproven by later expeditions of discovery.

3 ➡ Forbes was invited to take part in the expedition by the commander of the ship, Captain Thomas Graves, in 1841. The majority of the trip was spent in the Greek Islands and Asia Minor, where Forbes devoted his time on land to botany. At sea, however, he was constantly dredging, completing at least 150 dredges at depths from 1 fathom to 130 fathoms. His goal was to catalogue how depth, pressure and the geology of the seafloor affected the sizes and types of organisms present. Unsurprisingly, his dredges proved that organisms became smaller

---

1. The word "elusive" in paragraph 1 is closest in meaning to

   (A) undefined
   (B) apparent
   (C) complicated
   (D) recognizable

2. Which of the sentences below best expresses the essential information in the highlighted sentence in the passage? *Incorrect* answer choices change the meaning in important ways or leave out essential information.

   (A) After conducting expeditions of discovery, the scientific community was found to be wrong about the azoic hypothesis.
   (B) The discoveries and expeditions made by the scientific community helped to disprove the azoic hypothesis.
   (C) The azoic hypothesis had been considered as true until it was proven to be erroneous by later discoveries.
   (D) It was the scientific community that revealed the error of the azoic hypothesis, which had been widely accepted before.

3. According to paragraph 2, which of the following can be inferred about Edward Forbes?

   (A) As an experienced biologist, he took part in the survey voyage of the HMS Beacon.
   (B) During the survey in the Aegean Sea, he developed a theory about marine life.
   (C) He became a well-respected member of the scientific community.
   (D) He correctly concluded that there was no life in the deep sea.

4. According to paragraph 3, why did Forbes participate in the expedition?

ⓐ To collect a variety of botanical samples in the Greek Islands and Asia Minor

ⓑ To find evidence to support his hypothesis that organisms could not inhabit the deep sea

ⓒ To develop an effective dredging device with which to study the seabed ecosystem

ⓓ To research the effects of depth, pressure and the geology under the sea on organisms

5. According to paragraph 4, why did Forbes conclude that life did not exist in the deepest ocean?

ⓐ He thought the environment was too tough for organisms to survive.

ⓑ He was unable to discover anything when he reached a certain depth.

ⓒ He faced unexpected obstacles while dredging.

ⓓ He successfully classified the zones according to species diversity.

6. Why does the author mention "the device he used to collect samples and the location" in paragraph 5?

ⓐ To describe how poor the technology was in Forbes's time

ⓑ To point out what caused Forbes to draw an erroneous conclusion

ⓒ To explain how Forbes collected samples from the ocean

ⓓ To emphasize the difficulty Forbes experienced during his exploration

and fewer in number the deeper he searched.

4 ➡ Based upon the specimens and data he recovered, Forbes divided the depths of the ocean into eight fairly distinct zones based upon the fauna present. However, due to the fact that he could only dredge up to a certain depth, he was forced to extrapolate what conditions were like deeper down. This led him to believe that the deepest ocean abysses were utterly devoid of life. He could not conceive how organisms could withstand the brutal pressure, cold and absolute darkness that would be present, and his dredges seemed to support his logic. So, he called this the azoic zone, which literally means "without life." His hypothesis was greeted with general support, and became a dominant theory until it was proven utterly wrong many years later.

5 ➡ The reasons for his mistaken hypothesis come down to particular details of his investigation: the device he used to collect samples and the location. The dredge Forbes used was actually quite poorly designed for its intended use. The opening on the front of the dredge was actually fairly small, meaning that more animals were deflected by it than were captured. To make matters worse, the net on the back of it that was intended to hold the specimens until they were brought to the surface had holes that were large enough for many smaller organisms to freely pass through. In addition, the Aegean Sea had considerably lower levels of fauna than other seas of comparable size and depth. Combined, these factors actually limited the amount of data he could collect.

6 ➡ Another popular but erroneous hypothesis was created by the French naturalist François Peron. Prior to Forbes's survey of the Aegean, Peron explored the depths of the Baltic Sea, paying particular attention to the temperatures he recorded. He correctly noted that the temperature of the water falls as you descend. Pressure also increases with depth, so he

7. All of the following are mentioned in paragraph 5 as reasons for Forbes's mistaken hypothesis EXCEPT

  Ⓐ the dredge was originally designed for use on the surface of the sea rather than in the deep sea.

  Ⓑ the device Forbes used had a small hole which made it difficult to capture animals.

  Ⓒ the net of the dredge did not function efficiently and failed to hold tiny organisms.

  Ⓓ the Aegean Sea had lower levels of life compared to other seas.

8. According to paragraph 6, all of the following are true about Peron's hypothesis EXCEPT

  Ⓐ Peron's hypothesis was similar to that of Forbes in that it was lifeless in the deep sea.

  Ⓑ Peron found that the temperature becomes lower with depth by recording temperatures in the Baltic Sea.

  Ⓒ Peron thought ice was present at the bottom of the ocean due to the low seawater temperature.

  Ⓓ Peron's hypothesis was correct in that the high pressure at the ocean floor makes it impossible for organisms to inhabit it.

believed that the water at the ocean floor was so cold and dense that there must be ice at the bottom of the ocean. These ideas led him to also conclude that the deep sea was lifeless. Like Forbes, Peron's theory also received wide support, even though it later turned out to be false.

7 ➡ As technology advanced, subsequent exploration of the ocean's depths revealed just how flawed these ideas were. [■A] Improved dredging equipment allowed much more effective collection of specimens, and organisms were found at depths well below 300 fathoms. [■B] Forbes's theory that life could not exist below that mark was shattered by Charles Wyville Thomson in 1868 when he collected specimens from over 2,400 fathoms (4,389 meters). [■C] The Challenger expedition measured the Mariana Trench in 1875 and found that it was over 4,475 fathoms (8,184 meters) deep. [■D] Today, the trench is known to reach a maximum depth of 5,960 fathoms (10,900 meters), and life has been found even there.

PART 02
Actual Tests

9. Look at the four squares [■] that indicate where the following sentence could be added to the passage.

   Scientists also discovered that the oceans were far deeper than they had ever imagined.

   Where would the sentence best fit?

   Click on a square [■] to add the sentence to the passage.

10. **Directions:** An introductory sentence for a brief summary of the passage is provided below. Complete the summary by selecting the THREE answer choices that express the most important ideas in the passage. Some sentences do not belong in the summary because they express ideas that are not presented in the passage or are minor ideas in the passage. *This question is worth 2 points.*

    Many hypotheses that have been presented to suggest that no life exists in the deepest ocean have since been disproven.

    -
    -
    -

    Answer Choices

    (A) Forbes divided the depths of the sea into eight regions based on the data he had collected and concluded it is lifeless in the abysmal depths of the ocean.
    (B) Forbes found that the size and number of organisms decrease as you descend deeper into the sea.
    (C) Forbes's theory had been generally supported in the contemporary scientific field before it was revealed to be wrong.
    (D) The defective device Forbes used for his research and environmental conditions in the Aegean Sea led Forbes to the incorrect conclusion.
    (E) Peron was the first to discover the link between the pressure and the temperature under the sea.
    (F) Peron also developed a hypothesis that no living things existed in the depths of the ocean because of the low temperature and high pressure there.

    Drag your answer choices to the spaces where they belong.
    To remove an answer choice, click on it. To review the passage, click on **View Text**.

Water in the Desert

1 ➡ Despite their reputation as the most extreme environments on Earth, the world's great deserts have not always been so hostile. In fact, there is ample evidence suggesting that many of the driest places once flourished with life. The Sahara Desert, the Earth's largest desert, contains caves adorned with paintings of animals that only live in the grasslands of the savannah today. In addition, many species have specially adapted to the harsh conditions, and others like crocodiles linger on in the remnants of rivers and lakes that form oases. All of this evidence points to an environment that was very different from what prevails today, an environment that was blessed with far more water than what it currently possesses.

2 ➡ During a 1981 mission of the space shuttle Columbia, scientists used a radar array on board to scan the eastern Sahara, and they revealed a very different terrain beneath the dunes. They found that bedrock underlies the sand, and that ancient rivers had carved valleys through it. These features appear to have been created during the Tertiary period around 35 million years ago. As they dried up about 2.5 million years ago, they began to fill with sand. Archaeological data shows that these sand sheets have advanced and retreated many times in a cycle that takes about 10,000 years, and that the region has had its current appearance for about 5,000 years. Further geological research was carried out by an Egyptian petroleum company using microwaves to penetrate the shifting sands in search of water. They subsequently drilled wells that revealed that freshwater aquifers are still present.

3 ➡ These massive climatic shifts are thought to be the result of plate tectonics. The surface of the planet is composed of plates of crust that move slowly but relentlessly, and over time they have moved entire continents great distances,

1. Which of the sentences below best expresses the essential information in the highlighted sentence in the passage? *Incorrect* answer choices change the meaning in important ways or leave out essential information.

   (A) The environment, which was under water in the past, has gone through drastic changes.

   (B) Various scientific findings show that unlike its current state, the environment used to be one of the driest places.

   (C) Evidence shows that the environment will be blessed with far more water than what it currently contains and will become very different.

   (D) Evidence shows that the environment possessed more water in the past than it does today.

2. What can be inferred about the Sahara Desert in paragraph 1?

   (A) It thrived with animal life in the past.

   (B) It has only recently become the Earth's largest desert.

   (C) It was the home to many artists who drew cave paintings.

   (D) It is home to many different species of crocodiles.

3. Based on paragraph 2, what can be inferred from the data collected on the Sahara Desert?

   (A) It is one of the oldest deserts in the world.

   (B) It was formed during the Tertiary period.

   (C) It has bodies of seawater trapped in its bedrock.

   (D) It might have a different ecosystem 5,000 years from now.

4. The word "relentlessly" in paragraph 3 is closest in meaning to

Ⓐ conventionally
Ⓑ interminably
Ⓒ gradually
Ⓓ eventually

5. According to paragraph 3, what do Antarctica and the Sahara have in common?

Ⓐ Both were habitats for dinosaurs.
Ⓑ Both have shifted to different continents.
Ⓒ Both have extreme climates.
Ⓓ Both used to be deserts.

6. What is the main purpose of paragraph 3?

Ⓐ To compare and contrast Antarctica and the Sahara
Ⓑ To provide an explanation for the climate changes
Ⓒ To suggest how dinosaurs became extinct
Ⓓ To introduce a new theory regarding plate tectonics

7. All of the following are mentioned in paragraphs 4 and 5 as effects of water on the desert EXCEPT

Ⓐ shattering boulders
Ⓑ forming shallow lakes
Ⓒ creating sand
Ⓓ forming aquifers

resulting in massively different climates. In many cases, this movement has led to decreased precipitation, drying up rivers and lakes and transforming lush forests into barren wilderness. One extreme example of this is Antarctica, where dinosaurs once wandered through primeval forests but now ice sheets 2 kilometers thick dominate the landscape. Antarctica seems about as different from the Sahara as can be imagined, but it is also a desert as it only receives an average of 20 centimeters of precipitation per year. Both areas are subject to frequent wind storms, but Antarctica's polar location makes it extremely cold while the Sahara is in the tropics. Although water is scarcer in the Sahara, it is in a form more conducive to life.

4 ➡ Just as water manages to sustain life in the desert, it is also the major force behind continued changes there. In the rare event of actual rain, there is nothing to resist its power, and it rapidly carves new channels and forms great, shallow lakes. However, it usually affects the environment in a much more subtle way caused by the dramatic temperature changes between night and day. [■A] During the night and early morning, fog from the ocean and dew deposit their moisture on stones in the desert. [■B] This water is absorbed directly into the rocks, but the heat of day evaporates it once again. [■C] The results are not readily observable, but given enough time, it has a dramatic effect, causing the outer layers of the rocks to flake off. [■D] Sometimes, however, the process occurs more rapidly.

5 ➡ After a fierce downpour saturates stones already damaged by the daily water cycle, the rapid drying caused by the sun can sometimes shatter the stone. The energy released in such explosions can even split apart boulders. This explains how some rocks appear to move themselves without the help of wind or flowing water. Taken together, this evidence suggests that although deserts are defined by their lack of precipitation, water is the chief influence on

8. According to paragraph 5, what is a key characteristic of a desert?

Ⓐ Stones damaged by the daily water cycle

Ⓑ Powerful solar energy

Ⓒ Oceans of sand

Ⓓ Lack of precipitation

their existence. It forms the terrain that underlies them, creates the oceans of sand that cover many, and continues to reshape them through both gradual and more rapid processes.

9. Look at the four squares [■] that indicate where the following sentence could be added to the passage.

As this cycle repeats daily, the stones expand and contract, damaging them on a microscopic level.

Where would the sentence best fit?

Click on a square [■] to add the sentence to the passage.

10. **Directions:** An introductory sentence for a brief summary of the passage is provided below. Complete the summary by selecting the THREE answer choices that express the most important ideas in the passage. Some sentences do not belong in the summary because they express ideas that are not presented in the passage or are minor ideas in the passage. **This question is worth 2 points.**

Areas that are deserts today were once lush land inhabited by animals and even people.

-
-
-

Answer Choices

Ⓐ An Egyptian petroleum company penetrated sand sheets to determine the presence of freshwater aquifers beneath the sand dunes.

Ⓑ Over the years, advanced technology has allowed evidence of the ancient landscape beneath the desert dunes to be unearthed.

Ⓒ Scientists have discovered that the region which is currently the Sahara Desert undergoes cyclic climatic changes every 10,000 years.

Ⓓ Changes in the Earth's plates have caused drastic climatic changes around the world, as is evident in Antarctica and the Sahara Desert.

Ⓔ Water, which is crucial for sustaining life in the desert, still plays a significant role in creating and reshaping the terrain there.

Ⓕ The phenomenon in which rocks in the desert appear to move on their own is explained by the shattering of boulders damaged by the daily water cycle.

Drag your answer choices to the spaces where they belong.
To remove an answer choice, click on it. To review the passage, click on **View Text**.

New York City Urban Planning

1 ➡ Originally settled by the Dutch under the name of New Amsterdam, New York is one of the oldest planned cities in the United States. Like many early colonial cities, it began its existence as a fortification and was constructed along military guidelines. They eventually surrendered it to England, which in turn lost it when the United States achieved its independence. As the city expanded, a great deal of effort went into keeping the city organized. In fact, in 1811, the city council adopted a plan that divided up the mostly undeveloped northern portion of Manhattan Island and employed a strict grid pattern, regardless of terrain. However, due to the city's rampant growth, these measures often proved insufficient, and there were many serious problems involving health, sanitation and safety.

2 ➡ New York City has always been an important port city, but few anticipated the number of immigrants it would receive, and many buildings had to be rapidly constructed to accommodate the new arrivals. By 1800, the city's population had reached 30,000 people, most of whom lived in an area that only comprises a fraction of the modern city. Some historians estimate that New York's population increased at a rate of around 100 percent every ten years, which meant that even more people were forced to live in hastily constructed tenements. Such massive immigration and overcrowding inevitably created conditions that were perfect for infectious diseases to ravage the city. Epidemics of cholera, malaria, and typhoid swept through the population in the early 19th century, killing thousands in some of the worst outbreaks the country has ever seen. The demolition of many apartment buildings and the development of the northern part of the island served to alleviate the overcrowding, but these diseases would return again. One famous case was an outbreak of typhoid in the early 1900s. A woman whom the press labeled

1. The word "They" in paragraph 1 refers to
   - (A) the Dutch
   - (B) colonial cities
   - (C) guidelines
   - (D) the United States

2. The word "inevitably" in paragraph 2 is closest in meaning to
   - (A) relentlessly
   - (B) unavoidably
   - (C) perversely
   - (D) allegedly

3. Based on paragraph 2, what can be inferred about epidemics in New York City in the early 19th century?
   - (A) They caused many people to resettle on the northern part of the island.
   - (B) Immigration declined due to the unsanitary conditions.
   - (C) The authorities were unable to locate the sources of outbreaks.
   - (D) Population growth slowed because of massive outbreaks of disease.

4. According to paragraph 3, what was the main role of horses in New York?

   Ⓐ Pulling cabs and wagons

   Ⓑ Disposing of waste in residential areas

   Ⓒ Fertilizing farmland

   Ⓓ Clearing snow in the winter

5. Which of the sentences below best expresses the essential information in the highlighted sentence in the passage? *Incorrect* answer choices change the meaning in important ways or leave out essential information.

   Ⓐ The population was unable to filter the water from the polluted wells, leading to severe cholera outbreaks.

   Ⓑ The wells were used as sewers, polluting the aquifer and causing severe outbreaks of cholera amidst the growing population.

   Ⓒ The aquifer which the wells reached into, already insufficient with population growth, became polluted and led to increased disease.

   Ⓓ As the population grew, the wells could no longer reach the aquifer, which led to epidemics.

6. According to paragraph 4, what did the Old Croton Aqueduct achieve?

   Ⓐ It linked the Croton River to the Great Lakes.

   Ⓑ It provided an ample supply of clean water to the city.

   Ⓒ It paved the way for additional population growth.

   Ⓓ It improved the quality of life in the city.

Typhoid Mary was a carrier of the disease who caused the deaths of over fifty people while working as a maid.

3 ➡ Along with overcrowding, New York also suffered from an inadequate sanitation system. All of the cabs and wagons that transported people and goods through the city streets were pulled by horses, and an estimated 200,000 of them were living there by the beginning of the 20th century. By necessity, most of these animals lived on the island of Manhattan, often in residential areas. [■A] These animals generated large amounts of waste that piled up throughout the city due to a lack of infrastructure. [■B] This waste made the streets reek in the summer, and it mixed with heavy snow in the winter, sometimes accumulating in frozen piles up to two meters high. [■C] Not only that, but the horses also were often overworked and otherwise mistreated to the extent that many of them died in the streets, where their bodies would remain since no one had the responsibility of cleaning them up. [■D] This situation was not remedied until 1909, when the Queensboro Bridge was opened to traffic. This allowed the waste to be transported over to rural Queens where it was used to fertilize farmland.

4 ➡ Waste from animals and humans led to an even more serious health problem: contaminated drinking water. Manhattan Island had never had a reliable water supply, with its brackish rivers forcing people to rely upon well water. Already insufficient, as the population grew, the aquifer those wells reached into became seriously polluted, which led to severe outbreaks of cholera. To cope with this problem, they had to look far outside of the city to find a viable source of water. The city undertook a large and complex project to bring fresh water from the Croton River to the island. Built between 1837 and 1842, the Old Croton Aqueduct brought water 66 kilometers to reservoirs in the city. Life in the city rapidly improved, but its growth did not slow down, and many additional aqueducts

7. Why does the author mention "Great Fire of New York" in paragraph 5?

- (A) To prove that fire has a more disastrous effect on society than poor sanitation
- (B) To highlight the unexpected consequences of constructing the Erie Canal
- (C) To point out an aspect of urban planning the city planners neglected
- (D) To introduce the history of fire safety regulations in New York City

8. Which of the following is NOT mentioned in the passage as a source of misfortune in New York City?

- (A) Massive immigration
- (B) Poor sanitation system
- (C) Lack of drinking water
- (D) Wooden buildings

have been built since.

5 ➡ As serious as the health and sanitation issues were, a serious safety issue went largely ignored until disaster struck. After years of construction, the Erie Canal opened, successfully linking the Hudson River to the Great Lakes in 1825. This shipping lane dramatically increased trade in New York, and warehouses sprang up throughout the financial district to accommodate the merchants' goods. Unfortunately, like most of the city's other buildings, these warehouses were made of wood, and a calamitous fire started in a warehouse on the bitterly cold and windy evening of December 16, 1835. Before its flames were finally put out, the Great Fire of New York razed southeastern Manhattan, destroying most of the buildings in Wall Street and the New York Stock Exchange. The builders had ignored the dangers of constructing so many wooden buildings in such close proximity, and the fire took full advantage of their oversight. Following the conflagration, city planners regulated the minimum distance between buildings and created newer, stricter fire prevention policies.

9. Look at the four squares [■] that indicate where the following sentence could be added to the passage.

   Most often, waste was left in the middle of the street, as horse owners were far less likely to clean up after their horses if they were not on their own property.

   Where would the sentence best fit?

   Click on a square [■] to add the sentence to the passage.

10. **Directions:** An introductory sentence for a brief summary of the passage is provided below. Complete the summary by selecting the THREE answer choices that express the most important ideas in the passage. Some sentences do not belong in the summary because they express ideas that are not presented in the passage or are minor ideas in the passage.
    This question is worth 2 points.

    New York, one of the oldest planned cities in the United States, underwent significant trial and error in tackling problems such as public health, sanitation, and fire safety during its development.

    - •
    - •
    - •

    Answer Choices

    Ⓐ The huge number of immigrants settling down in New York rapidly increased the city's population, resulting in overcrowding and epidemic outbreaks.

    Ⓑ The lack of a proper sanitation system or a reliable water supply resulted in outbreaks of cholera, prompting the city to transport clean water to the island.

    Ⓒ The horse owners did not clean up after their horses, and often left the remains of dead horses on the streets, providing a trigger for epidemic outbreaks.

    Ⓓ Frequent outbreaks of infectious diseases led the city to demolish apartment buildings, and it was effective at curbing the death tolls.

    Ⓔ After the fire in 1835, a greater awareness of fire safety led to stricter regulations about constructing buildings.

    Ⓕ The building of the Queensboro Bridge allowed the waste accumulated in Manhattan to be transported to Queens, where it was used as fertilizer.

    Drag your answer choices to the spaces where they belong.
    To remove an answer choice, click on it. To review the passage, click on **View Text**.

Actual Test 04

정답 및 해석 | P. 53

Reading Section Directions

This section measures your ability to understand academic passages in English.

You will have 54 minutes to read and answer the questions about 3 passages.

Most questions are worth 1 point but the last question in each set is worth more than 1 point. The directions indicate how many points you may receive.

Within each screen, you can go to the next question by clicking **Next**. You may skip questions and go back to them later. If you want to return to previous questions, click on **Back**.

You can click on **Review** at any time and the review screen will show you which questions you have answered and which you have not answered. From this review screen, you may go directly to any questions you have already seen in the Reading section.

You may now begin the Reading section.

Click on **Continue** to go on.

Biodiversity in the Hawaiian Islands

1 ➡ The flora and fauna of the Hawaiian Islands display a level of biodiversity that is particularly remarkable due to their isolation. Located in the middle of the Pacific Ocean, the Hawaiian archipelago is about 4,000 kilometers from the nearest continent, and the islands were never attached to any large landmass. They are the tops of mountains created by a volcanic hot spot under the seafloor. None of the organisms found there could have taken an overland route from Asia, Australia, or the Americas, yet these areas share many of the same species. Some of the current species were introduced by humans, either when Polynesian people settled there around 500 CE or after Europeans reached the islands in the 1600s, but many of the organisms are different enough from other organisms that they must have arrived there much earlier and evolved in isolation. Therefore, the plants and animals that had lived there before humans arrived must have used other means of transportation to reach the islands.

2 ➡ The organisms that predate human colonization of Hawaii arrived by what are referred to as the "3 Ws." The first is "wind," which transported small, light seeds through the air. The second is "wings," which refers both to flying insects and birds and the seeds and other organisms that they carried with them. These animals did not deliberately transport seeds, but they did carry them lodged in their feathers and resting in their stomachs after eating fruit. After they reached the islands, the seeds were dislodged or released in their excrement. Many seeds actually require passing through an animal's digestive tract to germinate, so this method of transportation is widespread. The third "W" is "waves," which refers to all organisms that were brought over on ocean waves and currents. In some cases these were individual seeds like coconuts, but the category

1. Which of the following questions is answered by paragraph 1?

   (A) Who named the islands?

   (B) When were the Hawaiian Islands created?

   (C) How many native species live in the Hawaiian Islands?

   (D) What caused the unique biodiversity of the Hawaiian Islands?

2. Which of the sentences below best expresses the essential information in the highlighted sentence in the passage? *Incorrect* answer choices change the meaning in important ways or leave out essential information.

   (A) Both the Polynesians and European explorers introduced new species to the Hawaiian Islands.

   (B) Many of the species that live in Hawaii were introduced by people, but others are so unique that they must have evolved there on their own.

   (C) Most of the animals that live in Hawaii were brought there by people around 500 CE.

   (D) Even though many species did not arrive there until the 1600s, they have rapidly adapted to their environment and become distinct from their original species.

3. According to paragraph 2, which of the following is NOT a way seeds made their way to the Hawaiian archipelago?

   (A) Transported through the air by wind

   (B) Embedded in birds' feathers

   (C) Drifting with volcanic ash

   (D) Resting in animals' digestive organs

4. What is the purpose of paragraph 3 as it relates to paragraph 2?

   Ⓐ To continue the explanation of the transportation of the organisms described in paragraph 2

   Ⓑ To suggest another way of transportation in addition to the ways mentioned in paragraph 2

   Ⓒ To explain the environmental conditions that the organisms described in paragraph 2 would have faced on the islands

   Ⓓ To explain how the organisms described in paragraph 2 adapted to the unique environment of the islands

5. According to paragraph 3, which of the following is true about the climate of Hawaii?

   Ⓐ Volcanism raises temperatures at higher altitudes.

   Ⓑ There is little annual variation in temperatures at sea level.

   Ⓒ The islands are hardly vulnerable to changes in the weather.

   Ⓓ It has two main seasons: a warm winter and a hot summer.

6. Which of the following is NOT mentioned in paragraph 4 as effects of trade winds on the Hawaiian Islands?

   Ⓐ Trade winds soak the eastern faces of the islands with rain.

   Ⓑ The windward side of an island is more fertile than the leeward.

   Ⓒ Trade winds make the air drier by carrying off evaporated ocean water.

   Ⓓ Frost and snow that fall on the mountain slopes prevent many plants from growing there.

also includes rafts of tree branches and other drifting vegetation that carry their seeds and animal passengers. Such drifting rafts are how most land-based animals reach islands without human help.

3 ➡ The climate of Hawaii is typical for the tropics, but it varies with altitude and weather. The Hawaiian Islands sit atop volcanoes that range in age from 28 million years old for the northwestern-most Kure Atoll to a mere 400,000 years old for the main island. Despite the young geologic age of some, the islands have been heavily weathered, and they provide a wide variety of habitats. The smaller lower western islands are mostly rock with little protection from the wind. The larger eastern islands have peaks that reach up to 2.5 kilometers above sea level, which creates a variety of climatic zones. Since the islands are in the tropics, the temperature at sea level varies little throughout the year. At higher elevations, the climate becomes more temperate, and eventually transforms into alpine tundra at the summits of the tallest peaks. Some of the volcanoes are still active, which obviously puts pressure on any species that try to live in the immediate vicinity.

4 ➡ Being in the tropics also means that the islands are constantly buffeted by the trade winds that blow from the Eastern Pacific. Due to these winds, the eastern faces of the tall islands capture most of the rain that falls on the islands. This means that the windward side of an island supports much more plant life than the side that is out of the wind. Therefore, the windward sides are covered by lush rainforests filled with a myriad of species, while the leeward sides are open grassland with scattered shrubs. On the high mountain slopes, only hardy bushes and flowering plants can survive the colder weather that brings frequent frost and occasional snow.

5 ➡ The environmental extremes that characterize the Hawaiian Islands have forced any species that managed to survive there to adapt rapidly. [■A] The endemic species

7. **According to paragraph 5, what is true about endemism in the Hawaiian Islands?**

   Ⓐ Native reptiles and amphibians have gone completely extinct.

   Ⓑ Most of the remaining mammals are considered endangered.

   Ⓒ Termites and ants are representative native species of Hawaii.

   Ⓓ Many native species are unable to survive the competition with introduced species.

8. **Which of the following can be inferred about the species in Hawaii from paragraph 5?**

   Ⓐ There are over 800 different fly species in Hawaii, the majority of which are native.

   Ⓑ The endemic species of Hawaii have developed sophisticated defense mechanisms.

   Ⓒ Most of the animals that reached the islands without human help are able to fly.

   Ⓓ Many of the animals that people have introduced are predators that have decimated native species.

include a staggering array of plant, bird, and insect species, but there are no native reptiles or amphibians and only a few mammals. [■B] However, even among the categories with abundant species there is often a surprising lack of different types. [■C] For example, there are about 800 species of flies, but only about 15 percent of the world's insect families are represented, and termites, ants, and mosquitoes were wholly introduced by people. [■D] When new species successfully migrated to the islands, they adapted to fill many niches, which resulted in this kind of selective diversity. Since there are no large native predator species, most of the organisms also lack the defensive mechanisms that their distant cousins use like camouflage, armor, and venom. As a result, many of the native flora and fauna species have gone extinct since humans began introducing new organisms.

9. Look at the four squares [■] that indicate where the following sentence could be added to the passage.

   About 90 percent of the organisms in Hawaii are native to the islands, and they exist nowhere else.

   Where would the sentence best fit?

   Click on a square [■] to add the sentence to the passage.

10. **Directions:** An introductory sentence for a brief summary of the passage is provided below. Complete the summary by selecting the THREE answer choices that express the most important ideas in the passage. Some sentences do not belong in the summary because they express ideas that are not presented in the passage or are minor ideas in the passage. **This question is worth 2 points.**

    The location of the Hawaiian Islands has caused them to have unusual biodiversity.

    -
    -
    -

    Answer Choices

    (A) The species that reached the Hawaiian Islands before people were carried by wind, flew or were carried by flying organisms, or floated on waves.

    (B) The Hawaiian Islands are geologically young, but some are very tall, so they have a variety of climate zones.

    (C) The islands are all old volcanoes, and it is difficult for new species to adapt to such a harsh environment.

    (D) The islands are near the equator, so they are influenced by the trade winds.

    (E) Many of the species in Hawaii evolved in isolation, so they are vulnerable to invasive species.

    (F) The windward sides of the larger islands have dense rain forests while the leeward sides are covered with grassland.

    Drag your answer choices to the spaces where they belong.
    To remove an answer choice, click on it. To review the passage, click on **View Text**.

Passage 2

The Purpose of Extrafloral Nectar

1 ➡ Many flowering plants produce nectar as a way to attract insects that are beneficial to their life cycle. Most of them produce nectar from the sepal, a structure at the base of the inside of the flower. Any organism that wishes to feed on the nectar has to brush past the flower's reproductive structures, which deposit pollen on the organism that it then transports to another flower. However, many plant species produce nectar on other parts of the plant in what are referred to as extrafloral nectaries, which clearly must serve another purpose. Most of the empirical evidence that has been gathered shows that extrafloral nectaries are a defensive mechanism that attracts insects to protect the plant. As a reward, the insects may freely feed upon the nectar provided.

2 ➡ Nectar is a complex brew of many chemicals which are designed to attract and provide sustenance to other organisms. About 95% of all nectars is natural sugars, but many types contain amino acids. In fact, all of the twenty amino acids that naturally occur in proteins have been found in various nectars. Many of the other compounds present in nectar are designed to attract specific organisms by their scent. These are often volatiles that carry long distances on breezes. However, other chemicals present in some nectars actually discourage the organism from taking a second sip. For example, tobacco plants include some nicotine in their nectar, which is very bitter and less aromatic, meaning that the organism will eagerly feed once, but most likely move on soon afterward. This allows the plant to conserve its nectar, which most plants reabsorb after fertilization to use in seed production.

3 ➡ Unlike flowers, extrafloral nectaries produce nectar continuously, regardless of whether the plant has reproduced. This is due to the fact that they attract insects for an entirely

---

1. According to paragraph 1, what is the primary function of extrafloral nectar?

   (A) It induces pollination.

   (B) It provides nutrients to insects.

   (C) It poisons organisms that feed on plants.

   (D) It serves as a defense mechanism.

2. Which of the sentences below best expresses the essential information in the highlighted sentence in the passage? *Incorrect* answer choices change the meaning in important ways or leave out essential information.

   (A) Insects will move on to other tobacco plants after feeding on the nectar of one tobacco plant because it includes a certain amount of nicotine in its nectar.

   (B) Because insects feeding on the nectar of tobacco plants find it bitter, they move on after only feeding once.

   (C) Some insects are attracted to the nicotine present in tobacco plants because it is bitter and less aromatic, so they do not move on to other plants after feeding.

   (D) Because the nicotine in the nectar of tobacco plants is poisonous, insects will only feed eagerly on the nectar once before moving on.

3. Based on paragraph 2, it can be inferred that

(A) the chemical composition of nectar varies little from plant to plant.

(B) most plants do not want organisms to feed on their nectar indefinitely.

(C) nectars contain all the building blocks of proteins.

(D) flowers stop producing nectar after they have been fertilized.

4. All of the following are mentioned in paragraph 3 EXCEPT

(A) ants can defend against animals much larger than them.

(B) aphids, which reproduce asexually, are a significant pest.

(C) the purpose of extrafloral nectaries is different from those in flowers.

(D) parasitic wasps provide protection against caterpillar eggs.

5. The word "secrete" in paragraph 4 is closest in meaning to

(A) emit

(B) secure

(C) conclude

(D) absorb

6. What is the function of paragraph 6 as it relates to paragraph 5?

(A) To show similarities between the work of Wheeler and Bentley

(B) To provide support for Delpino's work

(C) To illustrate what Bentley's experiment was about

(D) To cast doubt on the validity of Bentley's experiment

different reason. Scientists have observed ladybird beetles, wasps, and particularly ants feeding on extrafloral nectar, and they all provide protection to the plant as well. Ladybird beetles are voracious predators that are very fond of eating aphids, which are a significant pest because they can reproduce asexually. Parasitic wasps will stun, remove, and lay eggs inside of caterpillars that consume leaves. Ants provide the most protection as they will attack and consume any insects that attack the plant and are also capable of discouraging larger herbivores from feeding on the plants.

4 ➡ Although such relationships may seem obvious today, they were not always so well understood. Initially, many scientists thought that extrafloral nectaries were purely excretory organs, including Charles Darwin. In fact, his disagreement with Federico Delpino about this led the latter to engage in some of the first serious study of the phenomenon. Many experts at the time argued that the structures were actually hydathodes. Hydathodes are a type of specialized plant tissue that is very similar to stomata. However, they are actually used to secrete excess water instead of regulating gas exchange. Delpino published a paper based on his observations in 1886 that contended that plants deliberately attract ants with this nectar to gain their protection.

5 ➡ [■A] Delpino's work later received support from the research of entomologist William Morton Wheeler and botanist Barbara Bentley. [■B] Based upon his own observations, Wheeler proposed in 1910 that not only did the ants feed on the nectar, but that the plants were actually dependent upon the ants for their survival. [■C] He observed that plants that produced extrafloral nectar were almost entirely unable to reproduce without ants present and often died. [■D]

6 ➡ In Bentley's experiment, she deliberately set out to determine whether plants genuinely benefited from ants and vice versa. She

7. According to paragraph 6, Bentley conducted the experiment by

Ⓐ introducing different types of insects to each environment.

Ⓑ delaying the stages of development of plants in one environment.

Ⓒ controlling the number of plants in each environment.

Ⓓ comparing plants in an ant-free environment to those in one with ants.

8. Based on paragraph 7, it can be inferred that

Ⓐ extrafloral nectaries are a product of evolution.

Ⓑ a positive symbiotic relationship between insects and plants is rare.

Ⓒ over time, the ants developed enzymes that could easily digest the amino acids present in nectar.

Ⓓ more careful observation is needed to fully understand the relationship between extrafloral nectarine plants and their predators.

compared plants living in a carefully controlled environment free of ants to others in an environment that contained them. She found that after the plants had reproduced, there was a marked difference in the number of viable seeds that they produced. The plants that were exposed to ants produced an average of 215 seeds, whereas the plants in the controlled environment produced a mere 45. The ants protected the flowers throughout their stages of development, thereby providing the plants with a better opportunity to reproduce.

7 ➡ As the research by Wheeler and Bentley shows, these organisms depend upon each other for their survival. The ants provide the plants with much needed protection, while the plants provide the ants with an easily digestible energy source and protection against their predators. Most insects have parasitic relationships with plants, wherein the plants suffer for the insect's benefit. However, the relationships between extrafloral nectarine plants and their protectors appear to be wholly beneficial to both species. This means that they have evolved to share a mutualistic form of symbiosis. When this occurred or how long it took to happen remains unclear, but their interaction is clearly observable.

9. Look at the four squares [■] that indicate where the following sentence could be added to the passage.

Barbara Bentley conducted an experiment in 1977 that added further support to the theory.

Where would the sentence best fit?

Click on a square [■] to add the sentence to the passage.

10. **Directions:** An introductory sentence for a brief summary of the passage is provided below. Complete the summary by selecting the THREE answer choices that express the most important ideas in the passage. Some sentences do not belong in the summary because they express ideas that are not presented in the passage or are minor ideas in the passage. **This question is worth 2 points.**

While nectar produced inside flowers attracts insects to help pollinate them, nectar produced on other parts of the plant attracts insects to protect the plant.

-
-
-

Answer Choices

Ⓐ Nectar, which is primarily composed of natural sugars, includes other chemical compounds that give off scents to attract insects.

Ⓑ Both hydathodes and stomata are types of specialized plant tissues, but hydathodes secrete excess water while stomata regulate gas exchange.

Ⓒ While many scientists mistakenly assumed that extrafloral nectaries were excretory organs, Delpino was right in his argument that extrafloral nectar attracts insects to gain their protection.

Ⓓ Bentley's experiment, which showed that plants produced more seeds when ants were present, revealed the symbiotic relationship between insects and plants with extrafloral nectaries.

Ⓔ In fact, plants exposed to ants produced an average of 215 seeds while those in an ant-free environment produced an average of 45 seeds.

Ⓕ Insects such as parasitic wasps and ants feed on extrafloral nectar, consume pests which attack the plant, and deter larger herbivores from feeding on the plant.

Drag your answer choices to the spaces where they belong.
To remove an answer choice, click on it. To review the passage, click on **View Text**.

1. According to paragraph 1, the boundaries of some species' ranges are fluid due to
   - Ⓐ population density
   - Ⓑ seasonal migration
   - Ⓒ average life span
   - Ⓓ abiotic factors

2. What is the function of paragraph 2 as it relates to paragraph 1?
   - Ⓐ To outline the similarities and differences between biotic and abiotic factors
   - Ⓑ To provide an explanation about factors influencing population distribution
   - Ⓒ To give an example of how climatic factors affect the environment
   - Ⓓ To suggest that abiotic factors are no different from biotic factors

3. What can be inferred about species distribution in paragraph 3?
   - Ⓐ Animals form clumped groups with their kin.
   - Ⓑ Animals in deserts typically display clumped distribution.
   - Ⓒ Clumped distribution is found primarily amongst predators.
   - Ⓓ Water is the main resource around which animals form clumps.

Population Distribution

1 ➡ All species of organisms that live on Earth inhabit an area that is referred to as that species' range. The boundaries of such an area are usually fluid as individuals may occasionally stray outside their normal range, and many species migrate seasonally. [■A] Within a species' range, the distribution of individuals usually takes on one of three forms of population distribution: clumped, regular, or random. [■B] These different types of distribution can greatly affect the population density of a species as they determine the number of animals that are going to be found in a given region within the species' range. [■C] The ways in which the population is distributed are determined by various factors that are categorized as abiotic or biotic. [■D]

2 ➡ Abiotic factors include any non-living physical or chemical factors in the environment. These factors are broken down into three subcategories: climatic factors, edaphic factors, and social factors. Climatic factors are those that determine the atmospheric environment, and they include the availability of sunlight, humidity, temperature, and salinity. Edaphic factors are those that determine the quality of the soil in a region, consisting of the local geology, the coarseness of the soil, acidity, and air penetration. Social factors that are categorized as abiotic include water availability and land use. Biotic factors are behaviors of organisms which directly or indirectly affect other organisms. These include competition for resources like mates, food, and water, predation, and disease. Taken together, these many factors determine which pattern of species distribution a population of a species will adopt.

3 ➡ The most common form of species distribution found in nature is clumped distribution, wherein space between individuals is minimized to form close groups that are separated from other groups of the same

4. Which of the following tactics are mentioned in paragraph 4? Click on two answers.

- (A) Hunting in groups
- (B) Attacking a predator as a group
- (C) Forming selfish herds
- (D) Scattering when being hunted

5. The word "apparent" in paragraph 5 is closest in meaning to

- (A) peculiar
- (B) obsolete
- (C) pertinent
- (D) evident

6. According to paragraph 5, what factor causes plants to grow in a uniform pattern?

- (A) Competition
- (B) Distribution of sunlight
- (C) Size of roots
- (D) Length of branches

species. Clumped distribution is typically found in environments where resources are unevenly distributed. In very arid regions, where water is continuously in short supply, most species will clump together around permanent water sources called oases. In other areas where resource availability varies seasonally, animals will clump together around resources when they are scarce and disperse when they are plentiful. Clumped distribution is also useful in defending against predation or increasing the likelihood of capturing prey.

4 ➡ Prey animals often form into herds for protection through safety in numbers, and this can occur deliberately or accidentally. Many species of animals will organize into groups with the young in the center and large adults around the perimeter to deter predators. Others form what are called selfish herds, where safety is achieved by moving towards the middle of the group, increasing that organism's chances for survival with no thought for its fellow creatures. Predatory animals also form into groups such as wolf packs and prides of lions to maximize their hunting potential against prey herds. The greater the number of hunters working in coordination, the more likely they are to catch enough of their prey to survive.

5 ➡ Conversely, the availability of resources can also have an opposite effect, maximizing the distance between individual members of a population, which results in regular or even distribution. Some species not only compete with their own population and others for resources, but they can effectively deny others from using their resources. This is particularly apparent in the trees which form the canopy of a forest. Their outstretched branches collect the maximum amount of sunlight possible, with only a small amount filtering through to the forest floor. This results in the widely spaced arrangement of trees that often appears to be deliberate or planned. In reality, it is the result of successful tree saplings utilizing resources

7. Which of the sentences below best expresses the essential information in the highlighted sentence in the passage? *Incorrect* answer choices change the meaning in important ways or leave out essential information.

   Ⓐ When organisms live in an environment where competition between members of the population is virtually nonexistent, they are able to share access to resources.

   Ⓑ Living in an environment in which they have no access to resources, animals have no need to group together or disperse.

   Ⓒ In an environment with access to sufficient resources, the pressure to gather together or disperse is absent because of the lack of competition.

   Ⓓ When competition for resources between members of a population is nonexistent, there is no advantage for animals to either group together or separate.

8. According to paragraph 6, why is random distribution not common in nature?

   Ⓐ In most environments, resources are unevenly distributed.

   Ⓑ Not many organisms disperse their offspring randomly throughout the environment.

   Ⓒ Not all members of a population have equal access to resources.

   Ⓓ Animals like arachnids are not common in nature.

more effectively than other members of their population, and discouraging the others from growing any further.

6 ➡ However, there are also species whose population distribution seems to have no inherent logic behind it. These organisms live in an environment where they have equal access to sufficient resources, so competition between members of the population is virtually nonexistent, and they are neither encouraged to group together nor to separate. Random distribution of a population is comparatively rare because abiotic and biotic factors typically cause populations to group together or to spread out. Therefore, this pattern of distribution is typically seen in organisms whose offspring disperse randomly throughout the environment. Plants whose seeds are carried on the wind often follow this pattern, as do animals with little social interaction apart from mating such as shellfish or arachnids.

9. Look at the four squares [■] that indicate where the following sentence could be added to the passage.

   However, most organisms live within one or more fairly well-defined areas throughout their lifetimes.

   Where would the sentence best fit?

   Click on a square [■] to add the sentence to the passage.

10. **Directions:** Complete the table by matching the sentences below. Select the appropriate phrases from the answer choices and match them to the category to which they relate. TWO of the answer choices will NOT be used. *This question is worth 3 points.*

Answer Choices	Climatic Factors
Ⓐ availability of sunlight	•
Ⓑ disease	•
Ⓒ coarseness of the soil	•
Ⓓ temperature	**Edaphic Factors**
Ⓔ local geology	•
Ⓕ average life span	•
Ⓖ salinity	

Drag your answer choices to the spaces where they belong.
To remove an answer choice, click on it. To review the passage, click on **View Text**.

Actual Test 05

정답 및 해석 ㅣ P. 70

Reading Section Directions

This section measures your ability to understand academic passages in English.

You will have 54 minutes to read and answer the questions about 3 passages.

Most questions are worth 1 point but the last question in each set is worth more than 1 point. The directions indicate how many points you may receive.

Within each screen, you can go to the next question by clicking **Next**. You may skip questions and go back to them later. If you want to return to previous questions, click on **Back**.

You can click on **Review** at any time and the review screen will show you which questions you have answered and which you have not answered. From this review screen, you may go directly to any questions you have already seen in the Reading section.

You may now begin the Reading section.

Click on **Continue** to go on.

Fire Management

1 ➡ Many people consider wildfires to be only a force of rampant destruction that devastates forests and consumes everything in its path. However, this is only partially true, as they actually play an important role in the life cycle of forests. Under normal circumstances, a wildfire will burn the dead plant matter that accumulates on the forest floor, and leave the adult trees largely intact. In doing so, they provide a readily available source of nutrients and space for new plants to grow. While it is true that many fires destroy large sections of forests as well as the homes of animals and humans alike, this is not part of the natural cycle. In fact, the severity of many wildfires and the massive destruction they cause is usually a direct result of human activity, much of which was undertaken with the goal of protecting the forests.

2 ➡ Without human intervention, wildfires play a vital role in the survival of forests. Although the damage they cause may seem severe, and it may take the forest an extended period to recover, they actually ensure the forest's survival. Over time, the trees in the forest drop branches, leaves and needles, which accumulate on the forest floor. This material takes about half a century to break down enough for other plants to utilize it, but if it burns it can be used much faster. This vegetable matter also piles up faster than it can decompose, often creating a thick layer that prevents new saplings from taking root in the soil and replacing the older trees. Not only that, but if periodic minor fires are prevented, this ever-thickening layer will only serve to intensify the magnitude of the inevitable blaze that will occur. A prime example of this situation is the fires that ravaged Yellowstone National Park in 1988.

3 ➡ Since its establishment as the first national park in 1872, efforts have been made to maintain the park and its many geological and natural

1. The author begins the passage by
   - (A) comparing two types of forest fires.
   - (B) giving an example of threatening wildfires.
   - (C) refuting the common notion about wildfires.
   - (D) emphasizing the importance of fire prevention.

2. The word "extended" in paragraph 2 is closest in meaning to
   - (A) harsh
   - (B) uncertain
   - (C) long
   - (D) extreme

3. In paragraph 2, the author implies that
   - (A) wildfires hinder the decomposition process of dead leaves.
   - (B) wildfires help forests by burning the layer of dead branches and leaves.
   - (C) wildfires may develop into a conflagration unless preventative measures are taken.
   - (D) wildfires destroy old trees, allowing young ones to grow.

4. According to paragraphs 3 and 4, what is the underlying cause of the fire at Yellowstone National Park?

   Ⓐ The natural geological wonders of the park

   Ⓑ The opposition against wildlife protection

   Ⓒ The operation of the park as a tourist attraction

   Ⓓ The fire suppression policy of the park

5. According to paragraph 4, all of the following are true about the fire at Yellowstone National Park EXCEPT

   Ⓐ the weather conditions aggravated the situation.

   Ⓑ the fire started from a small fire at one spot.

   Ⓒ the efforts to extinguish the fire cost a great deal.

   Ⓓ natural phenomena helped to put out the fire.

6. According to paragraph 5, the purpose of using prescribed fire is

   Ⓐ to lower levels of wildfire damage.

   Ⓑ to learn how to control large-scale fires.

   Ⓒ to burn useless farms and grassland.

   Ⓓ to estimate the damage caused by wildfires more accurately.

wonders for future generations. Initially, this meant protecting its wildlife from poaching, the ground from miners, and its forests from logging. There was considerable opposition from nearby communities that wished to exploit the park's resources, but as its staff gradually increased, and its importance as a tourist attraction grew, this diminished. By 1940, the chief danger to the park was believed to be fire, so legislation was passed to make fire suppression a top priority. Therefore, the National Park Service extinguished any fires that started as quickly as possible. This policy allowed dead vegetation and thick undergrowth to accumulate for nearly 50 years, and set the stage for disaster.

4 ➡ In the summer of 1988, severe drought and strong, gusting winds made conditions in the park critical. Park officials admitted that they had knowledge of a number of small fires, but they had assumed that they would be put out naturally. As they looked on, those smaller fires merged into one of the largest conflagrations in the park's history. After raging for several months, the fire destroyed approximately 800,000 acres within the park boundaries, and more outside. Around 13,000 firefighters and military personnel were called upon to put out the blaze, and the effort cost the government 120 million dollars. Despite such efforts, they were unsuccessful, and the fire was ultimately defeated by precipitation that came in the fall and winter. This fire served as a wakeup call to fire control authorities, revealing how inadequate their current fire control policies were and how serious the need was for new techniques for protecting natural environments and managing forests.

5 ➡ Following the fires, a great deal of research was carried out to determine the exact role of fires in forest ecology and how they should be managed. Fires control growth in the understory of the forest, dispose of shed vegetation, and make way for new growth. In fact, some pinecones will not open to release their seeds

7. All of the following are mentioned in paragraph 5 EXCEPT

(A) the roles of fire in forest ecology.

(B) the changes in people's view of fire.

(C) the purpose of using controlled burning.

(D) research conducted to find out the cause of wildfires.

8. Which of the sentences below best expresses the essential information in the highlighted sentence in the passage? *Incorrect* answer choices change the meaning in important ways or leave out essential information.

(A) Since the late 1970s, officials have let around 300 natural fires burn out, which resulted in improvement in those areas.

(B) Since the late 1970s, around 300 natural fires have struck flourishing areas, but officials could hardly control them.

(C) Since the late 1970s, officials have set around 300 fires in order to make the areas flourish.

(D) Since the late 1970s, around 300 natural fires which officials failed to control burned some thriving areas.

unless exposed to fire. These conclusions led many people to provide more support for prescribed fire, which is also referred to as controlled burning. These fires are used in farming and grassland management to reduce the risk of wildfires. Some even condemned park officials for not having used controlled burns, saying that they could have prevented the firestorm in 1988. However, many scientists contend that in order for fires to be beneficial to forests, they would have to reach sizes that are uncontrollable.

6 ➡ [■A] The current policy is to let fires that begin naturally burn and monitor them closely. [■B] Fire management only intervenes when the parameters of weather, size, and potential danger to wildlife and nearby human communities are exceeded. [■C] To protect park structures and nearby communities, underbrush and other fuel sources are manually removed within 400 feet of any structure. [■D] They are also removed from risk areas as designated by the Hazard Fuels Reduction Plan. There have been around 300 natural fires since the late 1970s that officials have allowed to burn with little or no effort to control them, and the areas where they struck have since flourished.

9. Look at the four squares [■] that indicate where the following sentence could be added to the passage.

    Fires that are caused by humans are still quickly suppressed though.

    Where would the sentence best fit?

    Click on a square [■] to add the sentence to the passage.

10. **Directions:** An introductory sentence for a brief summary of the passage is provided below. Complete the summary by selecting the THREE answer choices that express the most important ideas in the passage. Some sentences do not belong in the summary because they express ideas that are not presented in the passage or are minor ideas in the passage. *This question is worth 2 points.*

    Wildfires can be beneficial to forests and the ecosystem when controlled properly.

    -
    -
    -

    ### Answer Choices

    Ⓐ Occasional wildfires remove dead branches and leaves, thus stimulating the decay process and allowing new plants to flourish.

    Ⓑ In order to prevent devastating fires, immediate and thorough fire suppression is required.

    Ⓒ Through a number of research projects, misuse of prescribed fire was found to be the cause of the fire at Yellowstone National Park.

    Ⓓ Causing extreme loss of life and property, the fire at Yellowstone National Park showed how important it was to prevent wildfires.

    Ⓔ The conflagration in Yellowstone National Park provided an opportunity to change the pre-existing fire control policy.

    Ⓕ The fire control policy of Yellowstone National Park provided an environment where a disastrous fire could break out.

    Drag your answer choices to the spaces where they belong.
    To remove an answer choice, click on it. To review the passage, click on **View Text**.

1. According to paragraph 1, what is NOT one of the factors that led to the development of the steam engine in Britain?

   (A) The dwindling supply of timber in Europe

   (B) The growing population

   (C) The flooding in coal mines

   (D) The expanding British empire

2. Why does the author mention the "aeolipile" in paragraph 2?

   (A) To point out that the conceptual device served no real purpose

   (B) To explain Beaumont's source of inspiration for his steam operated pump

   (C) To prove that Roman Egypt was very advanced in science

   (D) To illustrate how long the concept of steam power has existed

The Steam Engine in Britain

1 ➡ By the late 17th century, England was facing a crisis of a kind it had never faced before. Its rapidly growing population and expanding empire demanded huge amounts of timber to supply fuel to provide energy for homes and industry and wood for its mighty fleet of ships. Unfortunately, its own forests had already dwindled down far too low to meet the demand. [■A] To supplement their shipbuilding, timber was imported, but a new source of fuel had to be found. [■B] This need was met with coal, of which the British Isles had an ample supply. [■C] As the coal miners delved ever deeper, however, they encountered a new problem with water seeping into the shafts, making the work dangerous and often impossible. [■D] The creation of a viable steam engine ultimately not only resolved this dilemma, but also ushered in the modern industrial age.

2 ➡ The concept of a steam powered engine actually dates back to 1st century Roman Egypt. Writings describe a device called an aeolipile which created steam within a closed vessel and released it through opposite facing vents on a ball, making the ball rotate. While illustrating the principle of steam power, this primitive example served no real purpose. Over the intervening centuries, more sophisticated designs were developed, but few were ever built. In 1606, a Spanish engineer named Jeronimo de Ayanz y Beaumont made a steam operated pump that he used to drain flooded mines. Denis Papin later designed a piston that operated by boiling water and letting the steam condense, creating a vacuum. The action of this device was used to lift small weights, but his machine had to be completely reassembled for each use. He saw that the steam would need to be created in a separate boiler to create an automatic cycle of movement, but he took his research no further.

3. Based on paragraph 3, it can be inferred that

Ⓐ Savery's machine did not achieve commercial success.

Ⓑ Savery incorporated Papin's invention in his machine.

Ⓒ Savery eventually overcame the limitations of the chamber.

Ⓓ Savery's machine provided a final solution to the English miners.

4. Which of the sentences below best expresses the essential information in the highlighted sentence in the passage? *Incorrect* answer choices change the meaning in important ways or leave out essential information.

Ⓐ Condensation of steam inside the chamber caused water to be sucked up into the vacuum.

Ⓑ When the cold water poured over the chamber rapidly condensed, the vacuum created by this opened the valve and sucked water up into the chamber.

Ⓒ The vacuum created by the condensation of steam allowed cold water to be sucked up into the chamber through the valve.

Ⓓ When the cold water rapidly condensed the steam, the vacuum created inside the chamber caused water to be sucked up through the valve.

5. According to paragraph 4, what was the main difference between Newcomen's and Savery's designs?

Ⓐ Newcomen's engine relied on creating a vacuum in the chamber.

Ⓑ Savery's engine could pull water up much farther than Newcomen's.

Ⓒ Savery's engine drew up water directly into the vacuum chamber.

Ⓓ Newcomen's engine was connected to a beam on an axle.

3 ➡ In 1698, Thomas Savery improved upon Beaumont's design, and came to the English miners' rescue. His machine consisted of a vessel where the water was boiled, and the steam was sent into a second chamber. When cold water was poured over the outside of the chamber, the steam rapidly condensed, creating a vacuum that opened the valve and sucked water up into the chamber. The valve only opened in this direction, so when it shut, it kept the water from falling back down the pipe. The water could then be drained off through a different valve. There were a few flaws with his design. Firstly, the vacuum could only pull water up from a short distance, so a series of pumps had to be used to draw water up to the surface. In addition, the condensing chambers had weak walls and sometimes exploded.

4 ➡ In 1712, Thomas Newcomen took Savery's design and incorporated Papin's piston. With his machine, the steam was driven into the piston chamber, and then a small injection of cold water condensed the steam creating a vacuum. However, instead of drawing up water into the chamber like in Savery's design, the vaccum pulled down the piston, which was attached to a chain. This chain was connected to a beam on an axle, and a chain at the other end of the beam operated the pump. When a new charge of steam filled the piston, it would rise and a weight on the pump end of the beam reset the system. Newcomen's steam engine could pull water up much farther, so it enjoyed great success, and over 100 had been installed by 1735.

5 ➡ Although Savery and Newcomen inarguably employed steam technology in their machines, the creation of the modern steam engine is usually attributed to one individual: James Watt. Watt was trained as an instrument maker in London and employed near Glasgow University. While there, he was asked to repair one of Newcomen's engines. As he worked, he realized why it was so inefficient: fuel, steam, and

6. The word "inarguably" in paragraph 5 is closest in meaning to

    Ⓐ incongruently

    Ⓑ indisputably

    Ⓒ irrevocably

    Ⓓ unlikely

7. According to paragraph 6, what effect did Watt's innovations have in Britain? Click on two answers.

    Ⓐ They replaced water wheels in factories.

    Ⓑ They automated the manufacturing process in British factories.

    Ⓒ They reduced Britain's dependency on timber.

    Ⓓ They provided increased power output with the same amount of steam.

8. According to the passage, why is the creation of the modern steam engine attributed to James Watt?

    Ⓐ He added a separate condenser to Newcomen's engines.

    Ⓑ He allowed factories to be built away from rivers.

    Ⓒ He made significant improvements to prior inefficient designs.

    Ⓓ He trained as an instrument maker at Glasgow University.

time were being wasted by having the steam condense inside of the piston. He remedied this by creating a separate condenser, and he partnered with Matthew Boulton.

6 ➡ They subsequently created two more improvements that not only further increased the engine's power output, but also allowed the engines to be used to power factories in addition to pumps. The first was a double-acting engine, which used steam to push the piston both up and down. This used steam that formerly was wasted and provided more power. The second was a spinning device called a fly-ball governor. This device's rotation was used to open and close valves automatically, and it changed the engine's back-and-forth motion into a circular one. Before this invention, factories used water wheels to power their machines, but the rotating steam engine replaced them. This meant that factories could be built away from rivers, and Britain's manufacturing output skyrocketed. These innovations are why James Watt is typically given the most credit for modern steam engines.

9. Look at the four squares [■] that indicate where the following sentence could be added to the passage.

    Initially, they used manually powered pumps driven by animals, but this soon proved insufficient.

    Where would the sentence best fit?

    Click on a square [■] to add the sentence to the passage.

10. **Directions:** An introductory sentence for a brief summary of the passage is provided below. Complete the summary by selecting the THREE answer choices that express the most important ideas in the passage. Some sentences do not belong in the summary because they express ideas that are not presented in the passage or are minor ideas in the passage. **This question is worth 2 points.**

    Growing energy demands prompted England to turn from timber to coal and finally to the steam engine for a reliable source of energy, paving the way for the modern industrial age.

    -
    -
    -

    Answer Choices

    Ⓐ Because there was an abundant supply of coal in the British Isles, England was temporarily saved from a potentially disastrous energy crisis.

    Ⓑ Newcomen improved Savery's design by introducing pistons, and this modification increased the effectiveness of the steam engine.

    Ⓒ Together, the double-acting engine and the fly-ball governor changed the engine's motion into a circular pattern.

    Ⓓ Utilizing steam power was a concept various engineers experimented with, but without significant application in real life.

    Ⓔ Watt's improvements to Newcomen's design transformed it into an efficient rotating steam engine, which contributed to the industrial age.

    Ⓕ Because Watt made it possible for the steam engine to be applied in factories, he is called the creator of the steam.

    Drag your answer choices to the spaces where they belong.
    To remove an answer choice, click on it. To review the passage, click on **View Text**.

Agricultural Pest Control

1 ➡ Without the adoption and subsequent development of agriculture, human society would never have been able to develop to the extent that it has, nor could our population have grown so rapidly. In order to farm, humans deliberately disrupt natural ecosystems to create the best possible conditions for the crops they wish to grow. [■A] They remove large numbers of the native species, alter the distribution of water, and enrich the soil with fertilizers. In addition, most farms practice monoculture to a certain extent, which means that one section to all of their land is used to grow the same plants. [■B] Such massive disruption of nature often leads to the explosion of species that consume those plants. [■C] In order to control pest organisms, farmers typically use chemical or biological controls; however, a more moderate approach appears to be the most effective in the long run. [■D]

2 ➡ Chemical controls are the most widely used method for limiting pest populations today, but they have a surprisingly long past. Around 2,500 BCE, ancient Sumerians used elemental sulfur powder to discourage pests, and a text called the Rig Veda, which dates back to around 4,000 years ago, mentions the use of poisonous plants for similar purposes. By the Renaissance, toxic chemicals like mercury, lead, and arsenic were being widely used to kill pests. Although these chemicals are toxic to humans as well, they were also used in makeup and medicines. At the time, people believed that small doses of poison were good for one's health, and no doubt thought that using them on crops would have little effect on them.

3 ➡ Beginning in the 17th century, people began extracting chemicals from plants to use as pesticides: nicotine sulfide from tobacco, pyrethrum from chrysanthemum flowers, and rotenone from the roots of tropical plants. All

1. All of the following are mentioned in paragraph 2 about past pest control EXCEPT

Ⓐ Sumerians used powdered sulfur to deter pests.

Ⓑ farmers used toxins that made produce unsafe for consumption.

Ⓒ ancient farmers were aware of plants that are toxic to pests.

Ⓓ texts on agriculture have been written for over 4,000 years.

2. Which of the sentences below best expresses the essential information in the highlighted sentence in the passage? *Incorrect* answer choices change the meaning in important ways or leave out essential information.

Ⓐ At that time, people thought using a little poison on crops was helpful for their health.

Ⓑ At that time, people took small doses of poison for their health by using them on the crops that they grew.

Ⓒ At that time, the poisons which people used on their crops were not very dangerous, so they took them for their health.

Ⓓ At that time, people thought that using poisons would not affect crops seriously since they were thought to be beneficial when used in small quantities.

3. According to paragraph 3, all of the following are true about DDT EXCEPT

  Ⓐ DDT replaced natural chemicals from plants that had been used to kill pests.

  Ⓑ DDT was the first synthetic pesticide, and it came to be used widely in the 20th century.

  Ⓒ DDT was originally synthesized to help agriculture by eliminating insects.

  Ⓓ DDT was adapted to be available in various physical forms.

4. According to paragraph 4, how does intentional control of pest populations affect the food chain?

  Ⓐ Pesticides make it unnecessary for natural predators to depend upon pests for food.

  Ⓑ The use of pesticides may kill natural predators as well as pest species.

  Ⓒ Pesticides affect the whole ecosystem by causing mutations in natural predators.

  Ⓓ Pesticides often weaken the immunity of predators, allowing pests to thrive.

5. According to paragraph 5, the Chinese introduced ant hives to their orchards to

  Ⓐ identify the organisms affecting their trees.

  Ⓑ remove undesired plants from the rows of trees.

  Ⓒ keep their citrus trees safe from fruit-damaging insects.

  Ⓓ make their citrus trees more resistant to insects and disease.

of these pesticides existed in nature, even the toxic elemental chemicals. However, in the early 20th century, synthesized chemicals became dominant. The first of these was DDT, which was initially used to control human parasites like mosquitoes and lice. Scientists soon learned to deliver DDT in any physical form, which led to its widespread use in agriculture. Since then, chemical pesticides have become the dominant control for agricultural pests, and their use has revealed many side effects of pest control.

4 ➡ Any attempt at controlling the population of a pest species entails the risk of affecting other species. Initially, this is caused by disrupting the predator-prey system. Even though local predators are unable to control the pest species, they may still depend upon them for food. However, chemical controls introduce additional problems. Firstly, the pesticides often kill organisms other than the intended pests, including their natural predators. Secondly, continuously exposing pests to chemicals will inevitably cause them to develop a resistance. Through natural immunity or repeated low level exposure, some will always survive to reproduce, and their population will rebound. Nearly every pesticide known to man has been used on mosquitoes, and they have always quickly adapted. Thirdly, pesticides spread into the surrounding environment, particularly through the water system. This can have far-reaching effects on organisms with no connection to the farms whatsoever, like birds that eat fish.

5 ➡ Thus, many farmers have decided to return to nature by introducing predatory species. Again, this is hardly a new idea as the Chinese are credited with deliberately introducing ant hives to their fruit orchards. After noticing that a particular species of ants attacked insects on their citrus trees, they began collecting and transplanting the ants' nests into their trees. Today, many farmers introduce spiders, wasps and other predatory animals to their fields. However, they must take great care with the

6. Why does the author mention the cane toad in paragraph 5?

   (A) To give an example of a species with great adaptability

   (B) To explain how to domesticate introduced species effectively

   (C) To claim that any attempt to control a pest population is fruitless

   (D) To show the danger of introducing foreign species indiscriminately

7. The word "tactics" in paragraph 6 is closest in meaning to

   (A) alliances

   (B) strategies

   (C) standards

   (D) advantages

8. What can be inferred about IPM from paragraph 6?

   (A) It was designed to guarantee both ecological safety and productivity improvement.

   (B) It aims to eradicate any kind of pest by introducing predator species.

   (C) It puts the highest priority on environmental value and the protection of species.

   (D) It was intended to expand agricultural fields and maximize crop yields.

organisms which they select. The introduction of any non-indigenous species can have serious unforeseen side effects. These organisms often have no natural predators in their new environment, so their population can grow unchecked. In addition, there is no guarantee that they will eat the correct organisms, or even remain in the desired area. This has occurred widely with the cane toad, which often fled farmers' fields due to insufficient ground cover. Since the toads are poisonous, they have had a disastrous impact on local predatory animals with no immunity to their toxin.

6 ➡ In order to avoid such problems and still maintain maximum possible crop yield, many experts recommend an approach called Integrated Pest Management (IPM). IPM involves many tactics, but it begins with determining the threat level to the crops. Merely sighting a possible pest is not sufficient cause to begin using pesticides. The situation should be carefully monitored until an identified pest becomes an economic threat to the farm. At that point, preventative measures like removing the affected plants, rotating crops, or selecting more resistant varieties of a plant are recommended. If these are ineffective, then introducing reliable predator species may be an option, but spraying of broad-spectrum pesticides should only be used as a last resort.

9. Look at the four squares [■] that indicate where the following sentence could be added to the passage.

   These species that endanger crops are labeled as pests.

   Where would the sentence best fit?

   Click on a square [■] to add the sentence to the passage.

10. **Directions:** An introductory sentence for a brief summary of the passage is provided below. Complete the summary by selecting the THREE answer choices that express the most important ideas in the passage. Some sentences do not belong in the summary because they express ideas that are not presented in the passage or are minor ideas in the passage. *This question is worth 2 points.*

    There have been various efforts to raise agricultural productivity by controlling pest organisms throughout human history.

    -
    -
    -

                                 Answer Choices

    Ⓐ Thanks to the development of agriculture, mankind could flourish and build civilizations.
    Ⓑ In the past, a variety of chemicals from nature were generally used as pesticides.
    Ⓒ To avoid the adverse effects of chemical pesticides on the ecosystem, some farmers began to make use of the predator-prey system.
    Ⓓ Before the advent of DDT, people had mainly depended upon specific predator species to discourage pests.
    Ⓔ These days, the introduction of non-indigenous species is recommended for pest eradication since it has few side effects.
    Ⓕ IPM is an approach which requires care for the balance between economic values and the ecosystem.

         Drag your answer choices to the spaces where they belong.
    To remove an answer choice, click on it. To review the passage, click on **View Text**.

Actual Test 06

정답 및 해석 ㅣ P. 87

TOEFL Reading

Reading Section Directions

This section measures your ability to understand academic passages in English.

You will have 54 minutes to read and answer the questions about 3 passages.

Most questions are worth 1 point but the last question in each set is worth more than 1 point. The directions indicate how many points you may receive.

Within each screen, you can go to the next question by clicking **Next**. You may skip questions and go back to them later. If you want to return to previous questions, click on **Back**.

You can click on **Review** at any time and the review screen will show you which questions you have answered and which you have not answered. From this review screen, you may go directly to any questions you have already seen in the Reading section.

You may now begin the Reading section.

Click on **Continue** to go on.

The Development of Islamic Bookmaking

1 ➡ Bookmaking flourished in the Middle East between the 9th and 15th centuries. Islamic books from this period were finely hand-crafted with luxurious materials and had detailed and artistically wrought covers and interior illustrations. This flowering of literary artistry was the result of two major events in the Muslim world. The first was the development of an official language with a codified alphabet and an accepted writing style. The second was the importation of paper-making technology, which allowed books to be produced on a vaster scale. These books were one of the main venues for artistic expression in the Arab world, and they employed not only calligraphers and painters, but also leather and paper makers and professional binders. This bookmaking industry was financially supported by princes and caliphs and lasted until printing presses were imported.

2 ➡ Islamic bookmaking extends back to the beginning of the religion it supports. According to the teachings of Islam, the Quran was imparted to the Prophet Muhammad by the archangel Gabriel between 610 and 632 CE, and he in turn translated the word of Allah into his own native Arabic. At first, his followers memorized his words and verbally relayed them to others, but this method of spreading the word was inconvenient, and worse yet, unreliable. In order to faithfully repeat his words, his assistants began writing down the Quran on any available material. These were eventually collected together, but a problem emerged: there was no unified Arabic alphabet. This was resolved during the rule of caliph Abd al-Malik, who made Arabic the official language of his empire and codified it into a single alphabet. This was eventually developed into calligraphy by Ibn Muqla in the 9th century, which was perfected by the 11th century calligrapher Ibn al-Bawwab.

1. Based on paragraph 1, it can be inferred that
   - (A) bookmaking flourished because of the varieties of writing styles.
   - (B) printing presses were probably imported around the 15th century.
   - (C) there were no other channels for artistic expression in the Arab world.
   - (D) the upper class did not support bookmaking.

2. The author mentions "Ibn Muqla" in paragraph 2 to indicate who
   - (A) developed the Arabic handwriting system
   - (B) collected the Quran into a single volume
   - (C) made Arabic the official language of Islam
   - (D) codified the Arabic alphabet

3. According to paragraph 2, what was one problem of spreading the Quran?
   - (A) Verbally spreading the word was slow.
   - (B) Most of the recorded Quran were illegible.
   - (C) Calligraphy was not perfected until the 11th century.
   - (D) There was no unified Arabic alphabet.

4. The word "**extracted**" in paragraph 3 is closest in meaning to

   Ⓐ converged

   Ⓑ purified

   Ⓒ accumulated

   Ⓓ removed

5. According to paragraph 4, what was the result of a flourishing bookmaking industry?

   Ⓐ Books became trade goods in other parts of the world.

   Ⓑ There was a growth in the number of literature writers.

   Ⓒ Secular texts became more popular than the Quran.

   Ⓓ Lower quality materials were used to keep up with demand.

6. The word "**ostentatious**" in paragraph 4 is closest in meaning to

   Ⓐ extravagant

   Ⓑ expensive

   Ⓒ decorated

   Ⓓ obnoxious

3 ➡ [■A] What contributed most to the expansion of books throughout the Muslim world was an innovation from China that was introduced in the 9th century: paper. [■B] Muslim forces that captured Chinese prisoners in Samarkand who knew how to make paper allowed this to happen. [■C] Their method of paper production involved three main steps. [■D] First, pulp was extracted from various plant types by boiling them down in water. Next, a fine mesh screen was used to catch these fibers and form a thin layer of pulp. Finally, these screens were carefully dried to make flexible sheets of paper. Despite the labor intensive process, this method actually produced writing material much more quickly and inexpensively than the prior method of curing goat hides. Qurans were soon being produced with pages made of this paper, and later other secular and scientific ideas were also spread through such books.

4 ➡ The first books produced in this way were religious texts, but later history, scientific treatises, poetry, and romantic literature were also written down and transformed into books. Many of these secular texts were just as richly decorated as the Quran, and many people were employed in their manufacture. They often featured leather covers that were embossed with gold in geometric and floral patterns. For the Qurans, this usually involved a fairly consistent pattern with a circle or oval at the center of the design that symbolized the sun. Of course, the degree of decoration varied, with books that were made for important patrons or public use being the richest, whereas those for personal use were often less ostentatious. These books became valuable trade goods, and often could be found far from where they were produced.

5 ➡ As paper spread through the Arab world, it revolutionized more than just bookmaking. Parchments were limited in size by the animals killed to make the original leather, but paper was limited only by the size of the screen it was dried upon. This meant that huge, incredibly detailed

maps could be produced, and blueprints could be made large enough to clearly show building elements. In addition, the limitations of paper also made it popular for some purposes. Because the paper was so thin and absorbent, ink marks on it were nearly impossible to change, unlike parchment which allowed for corrections, or even worse, fraudulent alterations. For this reason, it quickly became the chief material used for official documents in Baghdad. Paper and its various uses rapidly spread throughout the Muslim world, stretching across northern Africa, and even into Spain, where it was first introduced to Europeans.

7. Which of the sentences below best expresses the essential information in the highlighted sentence in the passage? *Incorrect* answer choices change the meaning in important ways or leave out essential information.

    (A) While parchment allowed for the correction of ink marks, fraudulent alterations on paper were impossible to change because it was so thin and absorbent.

    (B) Paper's resistance to ink allowed for criminal alterations, while corrections on parchment were nearly impossible.

    (C) While alterations could be made on parchment, the thin nature of paper made it impossible for corrections to be made.

    (D) Because it was thin and absorbent, parchment allowed for corrections, sometimes even fraudulent alterations.

8. Based on paragraph 5, what can be inferred about paper?

    (A) Paper was introduced to Europe before the 9th century.

    (B) Using paper increased the sizes of books and documents.

    (C) The concept of drawing up blueprints was nonexistent until the widespread production of paper.

    (D) The Chinese were unwilling to reveal the secrets of manufacturing paper to the Europeans.

9. Look at the four squares [■] that indicate where the following sentence could be added to the passage.

   Paper was originally developed much earlier, but before this time the technology had not spread westward.

   Where would the sentence best fit?

   Click on a square [■] to add the sentence to the passage.

10. **Directions:** An introductory sentence for a brief summary of the passage is provided below. Complete the summary by selecting the THREE answer choices that express the most important ideas in the passage. Some sentences do not belong in the summary because they express ideas that are not presented in the passage or are minor ideas in the passage. *This question is worth 2 points.*

    Development of a unified alphabet and the introduction of paper-making technology allowed the bookmaking industry to flourish in the Middle East.

    -
    -
    -

    ### Answer Choices

    (A) Arabic calligraphy wasn't perfected until the 11th century, crippling the caliph's effort at spreading the language.

    (B) Widespread production of paper in the Middle East allowed non-religious literature to be made into books, and the use of paper quickly spread to other continents.

    (C) With a unified alphabet, the teachings of Muhammad could be written down, which was more convenient and reliable than the previous oral means.

    (D) Paper had many advantages over animal hides, and it quickly became the preferred writing material for books, blueprints, and official documents.

    (E) The books were richly decorated with gold, with some books being more ostentatious than others.

    (F) While paper was invented much earlier, it wasn't until the 9th century that the technology spread westward.

    Drag your answer choices to the spaces where they belong.
    To remove an answer choice, click on it. To review the passage, click on **View Text**.

PART 02
Actual Tests

The First Life on Earth

1. According to paragraph 1, all of the following are true about the LHB EXCEPT

   Ⓐ it lasted for about 300 million years.

   Ⓑ a great number of asteroid collisions occurred then.

   Ⓒ it provided the appropriate environment for the birth of life on Earth.

   Ⓓ life does not appear to have existed on Earth before it.

2. According to paragraphs 2 and 3, what did scientists incorrectly presume about the formation of life?

   Ⓐ They presumed that the first life forms did not need oxygen to metabolize.

   Ⓑ They presumed that the first life forms created oxygen by photosynthesis.

   Ⓒ They presumed that the early atmosphere contained little oxygen.

   Ⓓ They presumed that the early atmosphere was filled with water vapor.

3. According to paragraph 3, why did the earliest life forms start deep in the ocean?

   Ⓐ They needed oxygen to breathe and metabolize.

   Ⓑ The seawater contained abundant hydrogen and oxygen then.

   Ⓒ The ocean functioned as chemical soup which had the necessary materials.

   Ⓓ The necessary chemicals for life were vulnerable to oxygen in the atmosphere.

1 ➡ Although there is still disagreement in scientific circles regarding what is the earliest evidence of life on Earth, the majority of experts agree that it could not have existed before the end of the Late Heavy Bombardment (LHB). The LHB was a period extending from approximately 4.1 to 3.8 billion years ago during which an unusually large number of asteroids collided with the inner planets of the solar system. Before this stellar assault, the inner planets had accreted most of their current mass and become fairly stable and solid. The severity of the LHB returned the Earth to a semi-molten state, and no evidence of life has been found that predates it. However, once the planet stabilized, life began gradually to take shape.

2 ➡ The popular theory of the origins of life held that it began in pools of water containing amino acids and other building blocks that were suddenly activated by an electric shock delivered by lightning. Indeed, subsequent laboratory experiments confirmed that such was possible. However, the planet's original atmosphere contained only trace amounts of oxygen, the element which so many organisms rely upon. Therefore, they concluded that these first life forms must have created the oxygen that permeates our atmosphere. They theorized that these organisms must have developed photosynthesis, the process by which plants use sunlight and carbon dioxide to sustain themselves and release oxygen as a byproduct.

3 ➡ However, there was a flaw in this theory. While the early atmosphere lacked oxygen, it was rich in water vapor, which readily reacts to ultraviolet radiation from the sun, splitting its molecules into hydrogen and oxygen. This means that the chemical soup from which life supposedly came would have been exposed to oxygen, which would have destroyed the amino acids. This means that the earliest life forms

4. The word "crevices" in paragraph 4 is closest in meaning to

   Ⓐ pebbles

   Ⓑ cliffs

   Ⓒ gaps

   Ⓓ flanks

5. Why does the author mention "Crustaceans" in paragraph 4?

   Ⓐ To explain how life evolved around deep sea vents

   Ⓑ To indicate how organisms feed on volcanic chemicals

   Ⓒ To show the complexity of life in the deep ocean

   Ⓓ To illustrate the food chain that exists near volcanic fissures

6. Which of the sentences below best expresses the essential information in the highlighted sentence in the passage? *Incorrect* answer choices change the meaning in important ways or leave out essential information.

   Ⓐ They share many similarities with bacteria and eukaryotes, which are definitely unique and classified as prokaryotes and further divided into four different phyla.

   Ⓑ They are very similar to bacteria and eukaryotes, but these two domains are separately classified as prokaryotes, which are further divided into four different phyla.

   Ⓒ While they are similar to bacteria and eukaryotes in many ways, they are distinctly categorized as prokaryotes and further divided into four different phyla.

   Ⓓ They are very similar to bacteria and eukaryotes, which are the two domains with which they are classified as prokaryotes and further categorized into four different phyla.

could not have formed in areas exposed to the atmosphere. So, life could only have started where the oxygenated atmosphere could not reach: deep in the ocean.

4 ➡ The cold, dark, high-pressure environment of the seafloor seems like the most inhospitable environment imaginable, but even today life thrives there. The majority of the seabed is barren, but around volcanic vents, a whole ecosystem exists that depends upon them for warmth and the chemicals that pour out of them. Crustaceans feed upon worms, which in turn rely upon bacteria for their food. These bacteria are able to metabolize the chemicals that pour from crevices in the seabed, and they are very similar to their ancient cousins. Like their ancestors, they absorb the chemicals before they react to their new environment, and absorb the energy released when those inevitable reactions occur. The fossil record confirms that such bacteria existed up to 3.5 billion years ago, and they are called archaebacteria.

5 ➡ Despite their distant origins, archaebacteria still exist today, and they are typically found in harsh environments like the ocean floor, hot springs, and even highly acidic mine drainage. They share many similarities with bacteria and eukaryotes, the other two domains, but they are undeniably unique and have their own domain in the classification of organisms called prokaryotes, which is divided into four different phyla. They have no nucleus or any other form of organelles with membranes within their cells, but they do contain genes, which have allowed scientists to trace their lineage. Researchers have compared their genome to that of many extant bacteria, and the results have revealed that they share common ancestry.

6 ➡ [■A] Unfortunately, archaebacteria lack defined cell walls or shapes, so fossilized samples are impossible to find. [■B] Instead, scientists have found characteristic chemical fossils in the form of lipids that do not exist in other organisms. [■C] Along with bacteria and

7. According to paragraph 5, all of the
   following are true about archaebacteria
   EXCEPT

   (A) they are similar to other bacteria and
   eukaryotes in many ways.

   (B) they are classified as prokaryotes and
   still exist today in severe environments.

   (C) they are the oldest single-celled
   organisms to possess a nucleus.

   (D) they have genes though they lack any
   organelles with membranes.

8. According to paragraph 6, why
   is it difficult to discover fossils of
   archaebacteria?

   (A) They do not have cell walls, which
   makes it impossible to be fossilized.

   (B) A long period of time has destroyed
   the remaining fossils.

   (C) They consist only of lipids which other
   organisms lack.

   (D) They are minuscule and invisible to the
   naked eye.

other single-celled organisms, archaebacteria
were the only life on Earth for around 2 billion
years. [■D] Over time, these organisms evolved
and became more complex, leading to the
existence of all other life on the planet, including
humans.

9. Look at the four squares [■] that indicate where the following sentence could be added to the passage.

These samples vary in age from 2.7 to 3.8 billion years old, which makes them absolutely among the oldest organisms on the planet.

Where would the sentence best fit?

Click on a square [■] to add the sentence to the passage.

10. **Directions:** An introductory sentence for a brief summary of the passage is provided below. Complete the summary by selecting the THREE answer choices that express the most important ideas in the passage. Some sentences do not belong in the summary because they express ideas that are not presented in the passage or are minor ideas in the passage. *This question is worth 2 points.*

The earliest life forms, which are called archaebacteria, arose in the deep sea.

-
-
-

Answer Choices

Ⓐ Scientists assumed that the first organisms came from small bodies of water that had materials necessary for starting life.

Ⓑ The first organisms are believed to have emerged in the deep sea since the early Earth's atmospheric conditions were improper for the birth of new life forms.

Ⓒ The first life forms might have been able to feed from volcanic vents by absorbing the energy emitted in the process of chemical reactions.

Ⓓ Much about archaebacteria remains unknown since fossilized samples of them are unobtainable.

Ⓔ The only way to trace the origin of archaebacteria is to compare their genetic information with that of other bacteria.

Ⓕ Archaebacteria are believed to be the first life forms on Earth because they share similarities with the genomes of extant bacteria.

Drag your answer choices to the spaces where they belong.
To remove an answer choice, click on it. To review the passage, click on **View Text**.

Soil Formation

1 ➡ The definition of soil varies between different scientific disciplines, with the most basic being any loose material on the surface of the Earth. However, this ignores the complex nature of soil and the processes that are involved in its creation. Soil formation is determined by five main factors: the parent materials from which it forms, the weathering it is exposed to, the geography of the area, the flora and fauna that are present, and time. Changing the type or amount of any of these factors will dramatically affect the type and quality of soil that forms in a given region. However, the most significant factor as far as the soil's fertility is concerned is the life forms that are present.

2 ➡ The nature of soil depends first and foremost on the parent material from which it forms. All soils begin as bedrock, which is broken down into progressively smaller particles. The rocks that make up the Earth's crust are divided into three overall categories: igneous, sedimentary, and metamorphic. Igneous rocks like granite or basalt form directly from the cooling of magma, sedimentary rocks like sandstone and limestone aggregate from tiny particles of weathered material and minerals from organisms, and metamorphic rock is created by subjecting the other two kinds to extreme heat and pressure underground. Soils may be created on site from the weathering of parent material or from weathered rock that is transported from other areas.

3 ➡ Weathering of stone is caused by one of two processes: physical disintegration and chemical decomposition. In physical disintegration, the parent material is broken down without changing its molecular or crystalline structure; it simply becomes smaller pieces. This is caused by temperature changes that make the rocks expand and contract, cycles where water permeates the rock then evaporates

1. The word "this" in paragraph 1 refers to
   - (A) definition
   - (B) material
   - (C) surface
   - (D) nature

2. The word "subjecting" in paragraph 2 is closest in meaning to
   - (A) exposing
   - (B) absorbing
   - (C) handling
   - (D) subduing

3. In paragraph 2, what does the author indicate about the rocks that make up the Earth's crust?
   - (A) Sedimentary rocks are the final phase of formation.
   - (B) All of the rocks are formed inside of the Earth.
   - (C) There are only two types of sedimentary rocks.
   - (D) Igneous rocks are formed directly from magma.

4. Which of the sentences below best expresses the essential information in the highlighted sentence in the passage? *Incorrect* answer choices change the meaning in important ways or leave out essential information.

   (A) Temperature changes, water, and rock particles carried across the surface break down the stone.

   (B) Expansion and contraction of rocks allows particles of rock to be carried across the rock surface.

   (C) The cycles of temperature change freezes the rock, making it stronger.

   (D) Temperature changes cause water that had permeated the rock to expand and contract.

5. Based on paragraph 4, what can be inferred about soil formation?

   (A) Sediments deposited in valleys and plains below mountains are composed of rich organic deposits.

   (B) The geography of a region does not play a minor role in determining where soil sediments are deposited.

   (C) Mountains are shaped by the amount of precipitation in that region.

   (D) Sediments of rock particles on their own cannot be considered fertile soil.

6. What is the main purpose of paragraph 5?

   (A) To provide examples of how minerals and gases in soil are utilized by bacteria

   (B) To demonstrate the advantages of having decomposers speeding up the process of breaking down dead material into humus

   (C) To explain how microscopic organisms help transform soil into an environment where plants can flourish

   (D) To emphasize the sheer number of bacteria living in soil

or freezes and thaws, and particles of rock that wind or water carry across the surface, abrading the stone. Chemical decomposition happens when reactions occur in the rock, breaking chemical bonds and causing the stone to fragment. Apart from wind weathering, these processes are directly dependent upon the amount of water an area has.

4 ➡ The amount of precipitation an area receives is important to soil composition, but the amount of water the soil can retain is even more important. This is determined by the geography of the region. Mountains and high plateaus do not tend to allow water to penetrate deeply, and their steepness means that it also will not collect on their surface. Instead it will pour down their sides, carrying away sediments and leaving little soil in place. This material collects further down slope, in valleys and plains where it forms layers of sediment that can make thick soil. However, while rich in minerals and nutrients released by chemical decomposition, soil at this point is still inorganic rock particles. In order to form fertile soil, organisms need to be present.

5 ➡ The first organisms that infiltrate soil are microscopic organisms, and there are usually millions of them living in just a cubic centimeter. These organisms include both flora and fauna, but the flora dominates. These organisms utilize the minerals and gases in the soil to create the nutrients that plants need in order to thrive. [■A] These include bacteria that fix nitrogen, combining it into compounds that the plants can use. [■B] They also help the soil particles to clump together, allowing more water and air to penetrate. [■C] These decomposers speed up a process that would otherwise take many years to accomplish, and they exist in huge numbers. [■D] In fact, 1 acre of soil, depending on depth, may contain 40 metric tons of bacteria.

6 ➡ While bacteria are of vital importance, other organisms also play important roles in fertile soil creation. The next most important organisms are earthworms, which tunnel through the soil

7. Why does the author mention "earthworms" in paragraph 6?

   Ⓐ To prove that bacteria are not the most important organisms in soil development

   Ⓑ To provide an example of an organism that helps process soil

   Ⓒ To contrast earthworms with burrowing animals like moles

   Ⓓ To discuss the various habitats of earthworms

8. In paragraph 7, what does the author mention about the development of fertile soil? Click on two answers.

   Ⓐ Areas with high levels of erosion are not exposed to much precipitation.

   Ⓑ Well-developed fertile soil usually has distinct layers.

   Ⓒ Many years must pass for precipitation to create solid bedrock.

   Ⓓ Well-developed soil forms where sediments are deposited.

by the thousands. Not only do their tunnels help water and air to spread through the soil, but they process the soil they move through their digestive tract. This chemically affects the soil, releasing even more nutrients, and the material they excrete as casts acts as natural fertilizer. Other burrowing animals like moles also mechanically mix the soil below the surface, while land mammals break down and mix the material above. Tree roots help water reach down into the soil, and shrubs and grasses hold the soil in place.

7 ➡ Of course, all of these factors require time to exert their influence on soil formation. In order to go from solid bedrock to fertile soil, many years must pass. The more time that the soil surface has seen exposure to precipitation and plant growth, the more developed the soil will be. Well-developed soil usually forms on stable, fairly flat areas and will often have distinct layers. Areas that are exposed to high levels of erosion usually form only thin soils, but the areas where those removed sediments are deposited may become very rich soil in the future.

9. Look at the four squares [■] that indicate where the following sentence could be added to the passage.

Other bacteria are responsible for breaking down the dead material that plants shed, converting it into a rich mixture known as humus.

Where would the sentence best fit?

Click on a square [■] to add the sentence to the passage.

10. **Directions:** An introductory sentence for a brief summary of the passage is provided below. Complete the summary by selecting the THREE answer choices that express the most important ideas in the passage. Some sentences do not belong in the summary because they express ideas that are not presented in the passage or are minor ideas in the passage. **This question is worth 2 points.**

The development of soil unfolds over many years, with several key factors playing their roles in transforming solid bedrock into rich soil.

-
-
-

Answer Choices

Ⓐ Wind and water abrade rocks into small particles, which are swept down by rainwater and deposited in plains.

Ⓑ The amount of water retained in a region is fundamental in supporting the activity of microscopic organisms.

Ⓒ Microscopic organisms and other organisms work the inorganic sediment into an environment rich with nutrients that support a variety of plant life.

Ⓓ The material that earthworms excrete becomes natural fertilizer in important soil formation.

Ⓔ The more time a given region is allowed for plant growth and development, the richer the soil will be.

Ⓕ Harsh weather conditions have serious repercussions on the processes of soil formation.

Drag your answer choices to the spaces where they belong.
To remove an answer choice, click on it. To review the passage, click on **View Text**.

Actual Test 07

정답 및 해석 | P. 104

Reading Section Directions

This section measures your ability to understand academic passages in English.

You will have 54 minutes to read and answer the questions about 3 passages.

Most questions are worth 1 point but the last question in each set is worth more than 1 point. The directions indicate how many points you may receive.

Within each screen, you can go to the next question by clicking **Next**. You may skip questions and go back to them later. If you want to return to previous questions, click on **Back**.

You can click on **Review** at any time and the review screen will show you which questions you have answered and which you have not answered. From this review screen, you may go directly to any questions you have already seen in the Reading section.

You may now begin the Reading section.

Click on **Continue** to go on.

Uneven Distribution of Gliding Animals

1 ➡ Many species of animals around the world have developed gliding as a way to cover long distances, and this mode of transportation is typically used to avoid predation. It also provides a means to conserve the valuable energy that they would expend descending from one tree, crossing the forest floor, and climbing another when searching for scattered food sources. These organisms have provided intensely interesting subjects of study for scientists since gliding often requires extreme body modification. Biologists have also observed that the rainforests of Southeast Asia seem to have an unusually large concentration of such creatures in a surprising variety of animal classes. A number of theories have been suggested to explain why such proliferation exists in this particular region, and many of them focus on the particular flora of their environment.

2 ➡ The first theory focuses upon the extreme height of the dipterocarp trees and how this is conducive to gliding, so it is called the tall tree theory. [■A] As animals glide, they are engaged in a kind of controlled fall, so they lose altitude fairly rapidly as they move forward. [■B] However, observed animal behavior does not generally support this theory. [■C] Many gliders do not take off from the canopy of the trees they are in; rather, many initiate their trips from closer to the middle of the trunk. [■D] Not only that, but the gliders are not confined to these extremely tall forests and may be found in the relatively shorter canopy of the northern rainforests, on plantations, and even in urban areas. So, tall trees are not necessarily a requirement of gliding animals.

3 ➡ Another theory called the broken forest hypothesis speculates that Asian forests lack vegetation connecting them to one another because the dipterocarp trees are so much taller than the other trees in the canopy, which

1. The word "scattered" in paragraph 1 is closest in meaning to
   (A) evenly distributed
   (B) seasonally available
   (C) widely separated
   (D) hardly visible

2. According to paragraph 1, why have many species living in forests developed gliding?
   (A) It is an energy-efficient way of climbing down the tree.
   (B) It makes them less vulnerable to predation.
   (C) It allows for extreme body modification.
   (D) It means they can travel long distances that were not possible before.

3. According to paragraph 2, what evidence highlights the problems with the tall tree theory? Click on two answers.
   (A) Gliding animals lose altitude swiftly as they descend.
   (B) Gliding animals begin their descent from the middle of the trunk.
   (C) More gliding species live in forests that have a relatively short canopy.
   (D) The gliding animals are found in other environments.

PART 02
Actual Tests

4. Based on paragraph 3, what can be inferred about forests which have dense liana growth?

Ⓐ Lack of sunlight on the forest floor limits the number of predators in the forest.

Ⓑ The tree canopies of these forests are more uneven in height.

Ⓒ Animals utilize the vines to travel between trees.

Ⓓ Climatic conditions concentrate them in Central and South America.

5. According to paragraph 3, what is one problem with the broken forest hypothesis?

Ⓐ The height difference between the tall dipterocarp trees and the other shorter trees makes gliding between trees more difficult, not easier.

Ⓑ According to botanists, Southeast Asian rainforests have the most dense liana growth in the world.

Ⓒ There are other animal species in Southeast Asian rainforests that have not developed gliding abilities.

Ⓓ Contrary to popular belief, woody vines do not grow profusely in the Amazon rainforest.

6. Why is the theory explained in paragraph 4 called the food desert theory?

Ⓐ The majority of the gliding species living in Southeast Asian rainforests are also found living in deserts in other countries.

Ⓑ The poisonous dipterocarp leaves have caused other leaves in the forest to become inedible also.

Ⓒ Species like the colugo have adapted themselves to the dry, hot, desert-like surroundings.

Ⓓ Herbivores are unable to eat the majority of the leaves in the region because they are poisonous.

made gliding the most viable option. In the Central and South American rainforests, woody vines called lianas grow in profusion, creating a dense network of vines throughout the forest that animals exploit. However, botanists working in various parts of the world have concluded that vine proliferation is more dependent upon other conditions like climate, soil, elevation, and slope than the height of the trees. Indeed, many sections of Southeast Asian rainforests have dense liana growth, just as many parts of the Amazon possess very little. The many mammalian species that dwell in the canopy but do not glide or spend much time on the ground also detract from this theory.

4 ➡ A third explanation, called the food desert theory, purports that it is other aspects of dipterocarps that are providing such tremendous impetus for gliding adaptation. The majority of the gliding species are herbivores that subsist on leaves and fruit or carnivores that eat insects and some smaller vertebrates like frogs. Unfortunately for the mammals that prefer to feed upon leaves, the trees in the dipterocarp family often have poisonous leaves. In a habitat where 95 percent of the tall trees and over 50 percent of the total canopy foliage are dipterocarp trees, so much of their surroundings are inedible that they may as well be living in a desert. Gliding allows them to conserve energy while they seek out leaves that are palatable. There is a type of primate called the colugo that utilizes flaps of skin that extend from its front to rear paws to create a broad flat surface that includes its tail, granting it great control in the air. Unfortunately, this degree of control comes at a price as colugos are not very skilled climbers.

5 ➡ The herbivores that prefer to consume fruit encounter another problem entirely. The fruit that the trees produce contains much less toxin in comparison to the leaves, so it is actually edible. However, dipterocarps have very unusual reproductive cycles that recur every 2 to 7 years,

7. Which of the sentences below best expresses the essential information in the highlighted sentence in the passage? *Incorrect* answer choices change the meaning in important ways or leave out essential information.

    Ⓐ The lack of fruit means the reptiles that rely on them suffer, causing a serious effect on the carnivorous gliders.

    Ⓑ Scarcity of fruit means that the insects and small vertebrates that feed upon them as a vital part of their diet suffer, causing a serious effect on the food chain.

    Ⓒ The lack of fruit has a serious effect on the food chain because the carnivorous gliders compete with reptiles that eat insects and small vertebrates for food.

    Ⓓ When fruit is scarce, it affects the gliding carnivores which feed on herbivores that feed upon the fruit.

8. All of the following are mentioned in paragraphs 4 and 5 to be responsible for the lack of food in Southeast Asian forests EXCEPT

    Ⓐ a forest comprised mainly of poisonous dipterocarp leaves.

    Ⓑ the relatively small number of carnivorous gliders.

    Ⓒ the unusual reproductive cycles of dipterocarp trees.

    Ⓓ the extended periods when fruit is scarce.

and most of them bloom en masse. This makes fruit scarce most of the time, which also has a serious effect on the carnivorous gliders as these reptiles that eat insects and small vertebrates suffer since their prey feeds upon the fruit directly or indirectly as a vital part of their food chain. So, they must also travel extensively to locate their prey, and they are quite adept at gliding. Lizards in the genus Draco have greatly elongated ribs joined by skin which act as a very effective wing when extended. Some have even been observed to gain altitude while traveling from tree to tree.

PART 02
Actual Tests

9. Look at the four squares [■] that indicate where the following sentence could be added to the passage.

    Therefore, the taller the tree that they leap from, the longer the distance they could cover.

    Where would the sentence best fit?

    Click on a square [■] to add the sentence to the passage.

10. **Directions:** An introductory sentence for a brief summary of the passage is provided below. Complete the summary by selecting the THREE answer choices that express the most important ideas in the passage. Some sentences do not belong in the summary because they express ideas that are not presented in the passage or are minor ideas in the passage. *This question is worth 2 points.*

    Many theories have been put forth to explain why such proliferation of gliding animals exists in Southeast Asian rainforests.

    -
    -
    -

    Answer Choices

    Ⓐ Botanists have discovered that 95 percent of the tall trees in Southeast Asian forests have poisonous leaves.

    Ⓑ Most gliding animals in the forest have gone through extreme body modifications, sometimes sacrificing the ability to climb.

    Ⓒ The extreme height of dipterocarp trees has led to the development of many gliding species.

    Ⓓ The Amazon rainforest possesses very dense liana growth, and scientists say this explains the lack of gliding animals there.

    Ⓔ Dipterocarp trees create a desert-like environment that made it necessary for animals to develop gliding abilities to travel widely to find food.

    Ⓕ The canopy structure and the lack of woody vines in Southeast Asian forests are the main factors behind the concentration of gliding animals in the region.

    Drag your answer choices to the spaces where they belong.
    To remove an answer choice, click on it. To review the passage, click on **View Text**.

1. The word "dedicated" in paragraph 1 is closest in meaning to

   Ⓐ reserved

   Ⓑ staunch

   Ⓒ resolute

   Ⓓ purposeful

2. Based on paragraph 2, it can be inferred that

   Ⓐ the construction of the Transcontinental Railway lasted for more than 10 years.

   Ⓑ England had the most tracks in the world before the development of the Transcontinental Railway.

   Ⓒ the government dictated the route of the railroad that would connect the Atlantic and Pacific coasts.

   Ⓓ the construction of the Transcontinental Railway began from both California and Nebraska simultaneously.

Railroad Development in the United States

1 ➡ The completion of the Transcontinental Railway in 1869 was a watershed event in United States history. Prior to the construction of railways, the primary means of transportation other than horses was by water. Boats traversed rivers and canals hauling both cargo and passengers. However, this meant that only cities that were on major waterways could benefit, and goods had to be transported by wagon to reach towns that were not. The earliest railways were short, dedicated routes that were used to connect things like quarries to rivers, and they were pulled by horses. When the steam engine was applied to railways in England, Americans were quick to follow suit. The first steam railways were built to connect cities in New England, but they soon spread both south and westward.

2 ➡ By 1850, approximately 14,400 kilometers of tracks had been laid down, but it was during the following decade that construction really began in earnest. By 1860, there was about 48,000 kilometers of railroad tracks, which meant that the United States had the most tracks in the world. The idea for a railroad that would connect the Atlantic and Pacific coasts dates back to 1832, but it did not receive government approval until 1862. The railway was built in three sections: from Oakland, California to Sacramento, California, from Sacramento to Promontory Summit, Utah, and from Omaha, Nebraska to Promontory Summit. When the two lines met at Promontory Summit, Utah, they were connected with a ceremonial golden spike on May 10, 1869.

3 ➡ The benefits of railway construction were many, but the most significant was their effect on the economy. [■A] They allowed the rapid transportation of food and other products to areas that previously had little to no access to such items. [■B] Previously, dairy products

3. According to paragraph 4, what effect did railroad construction have on the West?

   Ⓐ Existing towns along the railroad became important hubs.

   Ⓑ Displaced Native Americans established new cities and towns.

   Ⓒ It forced mail to be transported along wagon trails during the period of railroad construction.

   Ⓓ Maps had to be redrawn to include locations where trains stopped to replenish their supplies.

4. Why does the author mention "Indian Wars" in paragraph 5?

   Ⓐ To discuss the negative effects of targeting railroad tracks for destruction

   Ⓑ To explain the role General Sherman played in the military after the American Civil War

   Ⓒ To provide further support for the argument that the railroads had significant military value

   Ⓓ To provide an earlier example of how railroads played a strategic role in warfare

5. Based on paragraph 5, it can be inferred that

   Ⓐ the South's railway network was more extensive than the North's.

   Ⓑ General Sherman fought in the South's army.

   Ⓒ the March to the Sea was a failed military operation.

   Ⓓ the South's lack of infrastructure contributed to its defeat.

had to be produced and consumed locally, but now they could be transported long distances, allowing people to also increase production. [■C] Most of the farmers in the western territories had practiced subsistence agriculture before, selling what little surplus they produced to local markets or using it for barter with neighbors. [■D] The railways allowed them to plant cash crops that they could send all over the country. Along with improvements in plow and harvester technology, this allowed the farms in the Midwest to expand rapidly, transforming the prairie into oceans of wheat and corn.

4 ➡ The railroads also facilitated settlement of the vast reaches of the West. Prior to the completion of the Transcontinental Railway, the only way to reach the West Coast was by wagon trail or by sailing around South America, both of which took many months. By rail, it could be achieved in a matter of days. The railroads also helped these people keep in touch with their families back east as mail came to be transported by train. Settlers flooded into the West, displacing Native Americans as they rapidly established cities and towns. Towns that already existed along the route also grew in response as they became important layovers where trains were supplied with fuel and water. As populations swelled, more states were admitted to the Union, and maps had to be redrawn to reflect the new boundaries.

5 ➡ The extensive rail system also proved to have significant military value. During the American Civil War, both sides transported troops to the front by train whenever possible, and many battles were fought in order to secure vital railway hubs. The North's ability to exploit its more extensive railway network was an important factor in its ultimate victory in 1865. Their importance is further clarified by General Sherman's infamous March to the Sea, wherein his troops specifically targeted railroad tracks for destruction to economically weaken the Confederacy. Later, they helped transport

6. The word "freight" in paragraph 6 is closest in meaning to

Ⓐ weapons

Ⓑ vehicles

Ⓒ cargo

Ⓓ mail

7. According to paragraph 7, what is true about the railroad companies?

Ⓐ The railroad companies were owned by the same group of people that owned the banks.

Ⓑ The Interstate Commerce Commission was successful in regulating the railroad companies.

Ⓒ The federal government bought railroad tracks that were left without management.

Ⓓ Railroad companies eventually allocated more locomotives to transporting freight than passengers.

8. Which of the sentences below best expresses the essential information in the highlighted sentence in the passage? *Incorrect* answer choices change the meaning in important ways or leave out essential information.

Ⓐ Distrust led owners of remaining railroad companies to gain control of tracks left without management.

Ⓑ Distrust of railroad companies arose when railroad company owners sold tracks that were left without management.

Ⓒ This resulted in distrust of railroad companies which grew stronger after other company owners teamed up to buy the abandoned tracks.

Ⓓ Distrust grew as other railroad company owners fought to gain control over railroad tracks that were left without management.

mounted cavalry throughout the West during the many conflicts of the Indian Wars.

6 ➡ By 1880, there were 17,800 locomotives transporting freight and 22,200 of them transporting passengers all over the country. The industrialists who owned these railways became incredibly wealthy as some of the larger companies spanned across many states. However, the federal government viewed such complete control as monopolistic, and it disapproved of some of the owners' excesses, particularly when they were lax about regulations. Congress responded to the situation by establishing the Interstate Commerce Commission, which controlled their business activities through heavy regulation. This was effective for a while, but then disaster struck.

7 ➡ In 1893, railroad overbuilding and unstable railroad financing resulted in the largest economic crisis ever at that time. By the middle of 1894, one quarter of the railroad companies had failed, and as they collapsed, they took a series of banks with them. This led to a distrust of the railroad companies that only intensified when the remaining owners joined forces to gain control of the railroad tracks left without management. Eventually, the invention of the automobile created competition that the railroads couldn't cope with, and passenger trains dwindled. In the United States today, most of the trains carry only freight.

9. Look at the four squares [■] that indicate where the following sentence could be added to the passage.

Seafood could also be transported further inland than ever before.

Where would the sentence best fit?

Click on a square [■] to add the sentence to the passage.

10. **Directions:** An introductory sentence for a brief summary of the passage is provided below. Complete the summary by selecting the THREE answer choices that express the most important ideas in the passage. Some sentences do not belong in the summary because they express ideas that are not presented in the passage or are minor ideas in the passage. *This question is worth 2 points.*

The Transcontinental Railway, which was completed in 1869, greatly impacted the United States, which already had the most tracks in the world by the mid-19th century.

-
-
-

Answer Choices

Ⓐ Despite the government's efforts to regulate the monopoly, railroad company owners retained their dominance until it was broken by the automobile.

Ⓑ Prior to railway construction, farmers could not attempt mass production because produce had to be consumed locally, with any surplus being sold to neighbors.

Ⓒ Not only did increased accessibility encourage settlers to rush into the West, but the railway system also proved to be of strategic military value.

Ⓓ The construction of the railway began in 1862, and it eventually spanned across the continent, connecting the cities in New England to Promontory Summit.

Ⓔ The railway system allowed farmers to increase crop production as products could be transported to other areas rapidly.

Ⓕ During the American Civil War, General Sherman focused on destroying railway tracks to prevent troops from being transported to the frontlines.

Drag your answer choices to the spaces where they belong.
To remove an answer choice, click on it. To review the passage, click on **View Text**.

Geographic Speciation

1 ➡ The evolutionary paths of all species are influenced by three factors: mutation, natural selection, and genetic drift. A mutation occurs when there is a random, sudden change in an individual's genetic code, making it distinct from other members of its species. This may occur at any time, but if it does not give the organism any advantage over other members of the species, the change is unlikely to be passed down for many generations. Genetic drift also involves chance, but it is a much more gradual process. Genes govern particular traits of an organism, but they can yield different results each time the organisms reproduce. These possible results are called alleles, but as a species evolves, the number of possible alleles becomes smaller, gradually homogenizing the species. Natural selection, often referred to as survival of the fittest, occurs when environmental factors force organisms to adapt in order to survive and reproduce, which inevitably changes the species as a whole. These factors often act in combination, and the end result of the changes they cause are new species. Therefore, this evolutionary process is called speciation.

2 ➡ Each species is the result of its own genetic history and how it was influenced by unpredictable interactions. Every genetic history is unique, but they can be grouped according to some recurring patterns. The origin of any new species can usually be traced back to a physical separation of the original population, which is called allopatric speciation. The separation is usually caused by an impassable physical object like a river, canyon, mountain range, or ocean. Once the population is divided into two or more groups, they begin to take separate evolutionary paths from each other as different traits become dominant, gradually altering them into populations that can no longer successfully mate when reintroduced, thereby creating new species.

1. According to paragraph 1, what is the difference between mutation and natural selection?

   (A) Natural selection is a much quicker process than mutation.

   (B) Mutation is a result of an organism's attempt to accommodate itself to sudden changes.

   (C) Natural selection is a result of environmental changes while mutation is one of genetic changes.

   (D) Natural selection occurs randomly, whereas mutation occurs only when there is a great change in the genes of organisms.

2. The word "recurring" in paragraph 2 is closest in meaning to

   (A) developing
   (B) limiting
   (C) laboring
   (D) reappearing

3. Which of the sentences below best expresses the essential information in the highlighted sentence in the passage? *Incorrect* answer choices change the meaning in important ways or leave out essential information.

   (A) After the population divides into different groups, this prevents them from successfully mating with each other, and as a result, different traits become dominant.

   (B) As the population divides into several groups, this results in the creation of new species that take separate evolutionary paths by successfully mating with each other to become populations with different dominant traits.

C Once the population is reunited, each group exhibits different traits that have become dominant that make the species stronger after they mate successfully.

D The division of a population into different groups essentially creates new species that display different dominant traits and are unable to successfully mate with each other.

4. According to paragraph 2, all of the following are true about allopatric speciation EXCEPT

A it occurs due to a physical separation.

B it refers to changes caused by encounters between two different species.

C each group steadily develops traits which are different from the other.

D geographic factors such as rivers, mountain ranges, and oceans contribute to it.

5. The word "it" in paragraph 3 refers to

A speciation

B process

C Grand Canyon

D population

6. Why does the author mention "Isthmus of Panama" in paragraph 3?

A To give an example of geographic isolation that caused the speciation of an organism

B To show what affects the speciation of marine species as opposed to terrestrial species

C To demonstrate the consequences of long-term geological changes on rodent populations

D To point out how important volcanic eruptions are in the evolution of species

3 ➡ The likelihood of a physical barrier dividing a species is completely dependent upon that organism's regular means of travel. For example, small rivers in the Amazon have proven sufficient to create new species of leaf-cutter ants, but much larger barriers are usually required. This means that speciation due to geographic isolation is usually a very slow process. The Grand Canyon took millions of years to form, but it eventually divided a rodent population, resulting in different species living to the north and south of it. A similarly slow geological process occurred in Central America. Originally, North and South America were not connected, and a species of shrimp lived in the ocean between them. However, a chain of volcanoes grew, creating what is now the Isthmus of Panama, separating the population into two groups which evolved differently.

4 ➡ Within this larger concept there are two subgroups. In the first, one of the populations is much smaller than the other, which causes it to change much more rapidly. A smaller population equals a smaller gene pool, meaning that certain traits can become dominant much faster. As a result, the larger parent population remains largely unchanged, while the isolated smaller group may be radically different. This form of speciation is called peripatric. In the other, the population is not divided or isolated by a physical barrier, but by distance. The parent population is spread out over a vast area, and while they are capable of mating with members of any other group, members of a particular group only mate with each other. These small groups often exist in different environments than the rest of the population, causing them to express different genetic traits. This form of speciation is called parapatric.

5 ➡ One of the best areas to observe these forms of speciation is within archipelagos like the Galapagos Islands or the Hawaiian Islands. These island chains are located neither too far from the continents around the Pacific Ocean

7. According to paragraph 4, all of the following are true EXCEPT

   Ⓐ both peripatric and parapatric speciation occur in small groups which are separated from the rest of the parent population.

   Ⓑ a group with a smaller population is likely to develop specific traits faster due to its smaller gene pool.

   Ⓒ parapatric speciation occurs when members of a small group that lives away from the rest mate only with each other.

   Ⓓ parapatric speciation involves a physical barrier which divides the larger population of organisms into smaller groups.

8. According to paragraph 5, all of the following are true EXCEPT

   Ⓐ Darwin's theory of evolution is based upon the finches in the Galapagos Islands.

   Ⓑ some archipelagos in the Pacific Ocean are ideal places to observe the evolution of species.

   Ⓒ the Galapagos Islands were a proper place to observe speciation because of their climate.

   Ⓓ the physical traits of the finches changed in response to the environment of the islands.

nor too close to them. So, when animals do survive the journey to them, they usually remain. If they manage to reproduce, then they have the potential to become firmly established on the islands. [■A] This is because they left their natural predators behind on the mainland, and their population is often only limited by the available food supply. [■B] One example of this is the Galapagos finches, which contributed greatly to Darwin's theories regarding evolution. [■C] As they settled in their new home, they began to change physically to exploit the local food supply (allopatric speciation). [■D] Individual islands could not support a large population, so the necessary traits to eat the food available on each quickly became dominant. Large, blunt beaks developed to eat seeds and nuts, long, thin ones to feed on nectar, and medium ones to eat insects (peripatric speciation). And, although the finches were perfectly capable of traveling to other islands, the majority of them did not, which resulted in the 15 species that eventually developed (parapatric speciation).

PART 02
Actual Tests

9. Look at the four squares [■] that indicate where the following sentence could be added to the passage.

    These birds came to the islands from South America, effectively isolating themselves from their parent population.

    Where would the sentence best fit?

    Click on a square [■] to add the sentence to the passage.

10. **Directions:** An introductory sentence for a brief summary of the passage is provided below. Complete the summary by selecting the THREE answer choices that express the most important ideas in the passage. Some sentences do not belong in the summary because they express ideas that are not presented in the passage or are minor ideas in the passage. *This question is worth 2 points.*

    Speciation is the evolutionary process that occurs when a group of organisms is geographically isolated from the original population.

•
•
•

    Answer Choices

    (A) Mutation, genetic drift, and natural selection take place in combination, thus causing species to evolve.

    (B) The advent of new species is the result not of genetic alteration, but of a physical separation.

    (C) The definition of a species includes organisms which can mate and produce viable offspring.

    (D) It is not easy to observe how a new species emerges since there are various forms of speciation.

    (E) Physical barriers separate a species into two or more groups, and speciation gradually progresses afterward.

    (F) The Galapagos finches, which were provided with an ideal environment for evolution, are a great example of speciation.

    Drag your answer choices to the spaces where they belong.
    To remove an answer choice, click on it. To review the passage, click on **View Text**.

PAGODA TOEFL 90+

READING

Actual Test

PAGODA TOEFL 90+

READING

Actual Test

PAGODA TOEFL

90+ Reading Actual Test

정답 및 해석

PAGODA Books

PAGODA TOEFL

90+
Reading
Actual Test

파고다교육그룹 언어교육연구소 | 저

정답 및 해석

Actual Test 01

본서 | P. 72

Passage 1   Flightless Birds

1. Ⓑ	Vocabulary	6. Ⓒ	Negative Fact
2. Ⓒ	Negative Fact	7. Ⓒ	Fact
3. Ⓓ	Negative Fact	8. Ⓓ	Sentence Simplification
4. Ⓑ	Inference	9. Ⓒ	Insertion
5. Ⓓ	Rhetorical Purpose	10. Ⓐ, Ⓒ, Ⓕ	Summary

Passage 2   Industrial Melanism in Peppered Moths

1. Ⓓ	Rhetorical Purpose	6. Ⓑ	Sentence Simplification
2. Ⓑ	Fact	7. Ⓐ	Fact
3. Ⓐ	Reference	8. Ⓒ	Vocabulary
4. Ⓒ	Negative Fact	9. Ⓐ	Insertion
5. Ⓓ	Inference	10. Ⓑ, Ⓓ, Ⓔ	Summary

Passage 3   Thermoregulation in Marine Organisms

1. Ⓐ	Vocabulary	6. Ⓓ	Inference
2. Ⓒ	Fact	7. Ⓒ	Sentence Simplification
3. Ⓓ	Fact	8. Ⓒ	Fact
4. Ⓑ	Negative Fact	9. Ⓑ	Insertion
5. Ⓐ	Rhetorical Purpose	10. Ⓐ, Ⓒ, Ⓓ	Summary

● 내가 맞은 문제 유형의 개수를 적어 보고 어느 유형에 취약한지 확인해 봅시다.

문제 유형	맞은 개수
Sentence Simplification	3
Fact / Negative Fact	11
Vocabulary	3
Reference	1
Rhetorical Purpose	3
Inference	3
Insertion	3
Summary	3
Category Chart	0
Total	30

Flightless Birds

1 ➡ Birds that currently live or used to live on many continents have lost the ability to fly at various points in their evolutionary histories. Such evolution seems paradoxical, since flight is a trait that so many animals from different classes have developed wholly independently. Indeed, convergent evolution would seem to argue against the whole idea of losing such an advanced ability. [■A] However, evolution is not about achieving advanced traits, but rather about developing the traits that are necessary to survive in a given habitat. [■B] Therefore, birds that have lost this ability must have done so because flight did not give them an advantage in their habitat. [■C] Flight became an unnecessary expenditure of energy, so their bodies gradually lost the structures that were needed for flying. A group of large, flightless birds called ratites no longer needed to fly because they did not need to migrate for food or warmth, or because they had no predators from which they needed to escape. [■D] They developed larger bodies supported by strong legs and laid larger eggs.

2 ➡ Many flightless bird species are classified into the ratite group due to the many physical features they share. These birds include the ostriches of Africa, rheas of South America, and the emus and cassowaries of Australia, all of which are very large birds with extremely small wings, long legs and long necks. Other extinct species that are placed in this group are the moa of New Zealand and the elephant bird of Madagascar, which disappeared in the last few thousand years, most likely because of human activity. Although flightless birds all possess vestigial wings, their breast bones lack the ridge that flight muscles attach to in flying bird species. These birds have totally abandoned flight and rely upon their powerful legs for movement and defense.

3 ➡ The largest of the flightless birds went extinct millions of years ago, but they were truly impressive specimens. When the dinosaurs disappeared, niches in many habitats were vacated, and birds were often the animals that filled them before mammals took their place. This resulted in some truly giant birds that replaced both large herbivores and predators. One example of this is *Titanis walleri*, which was a member

날지 못하는 새

1 ➡ 현재 많은 대륙에 살고 있거나 과거에 살았던 새들이 그들의 진화 역사의 다양한 순간에서 나는 능력을 상실했다. 나는 것은 다른 종의 수많은 동물들이 완전히 독자적으로 발달시켜 온 특성이기에 이러한 진화는 모순적인 것으로 보인다. 사실상 수렴진화는 그토록 진보된 능력을 잃는다는 생각에 반박하는 것처럼 보일 수 있다. [■A] 하지만 진화란 진보된 특성을 얻는 것이 아니라, 주어진 환경에서 생존하기 위해 필요한 특성을 발달시키는 것이다. [■B] 따라서 이 능력을 잃은 새들은 자신들의 서식지에서 나는 것이 그들에게 별다른 이득을 주지 못했기 때문에 그 능력을 잃은 것임이 틀림없다. [■C] 나는 것은 에너지를 불필요하게 소모했기 때문에, 그들의 몸은 점차 나는 것에 필요한 구조를 잃게 되었다. 몸집이 크고 날지 못하는 주금류(走禽類)라고 불리는 새들은 더 이상 날 필요가 없었는데 왜냐하면 먹이를 찾거나 따뜻한 곳을 찾아 이동을 할 필요가 없었거나, 또는 피해야 할 포식자가 없었기 때문이었다. [■D] 이들은 튼튼한 다리로 버틸 수 있는 큰 몸을 발달시켰으며, 더 큰 알을 낳았다.

2 ➡ 날지 못하는 많은 종의 새들은 공통적으로 가지고 있는 많은 신체적 특징 때문에 주금류로 분리되고 있다. 주금류에는 아프리카의 타조, 남미의 레아, 그리고 호주의 에뮤와 화식조(火食鳥)가 포함되는데, 이들 모두는 아주 작은 날개와 긴 다리, 긴 목을 가진 거대한 새들이다. 이 그룹에 속한 다른 멸종된 새 중에는 뉴질랜드의 모아와 마다가스카르의 에피오르니스가 있는데, 이들은 지난 몇 천 년 사이에 사라졌고, 아마도 인간 활동 때문이었을 것이다. 비록 이 날지 못하는 새들 모두 날개의 흔적이 남아 있긴 하지만, 그들의 흉골에는 나는 종의 새에게 있는 비상근(飛翔筋)이 붙어 있는 길쭉하게 솟은 뼈가 없다. 이 새들은 완전히 나는 것을 포기했고 이동과 방어를 위해 자신들의 강한 다리에 의존한다.

3 ➡ 날지 못하는 새 중 가장 큰 새들은 수백만 년 전에 멸종됐지만, 그들은 실로 인상적인 종들이었다. 공룡이 사라졌을 때, 많은 서식지의 적소들이 비어 있어서 포유류가 자리를 차지하기 전에 새들이 종종 그곳을 차지했다. 그 결과 큰 초식동물과 포식자를 대체한 정말로 거대한 새들이 출현했다. 티타니스 왈레리(Titanis walleri)가 그 예 중 하나인데, 이것은 공포새라고 알려진 미대륙의 공포새과에 속하는 동물이었다. 이 새는 키가 2.5미터에 몸무게는 약 150

of the Phorusrhacidae family of the Americas also known as "terror birds." This hunter stood at 2.5 meters tall and would have weighed around 150 kilograms. It had powerful legs it used to hunt its prey, both for chasing the animals and knocking them to the ground. It also had a massive, hooked beak that was well-suited to tearing flesh. Another ancient bird called the Diatryma was included in the same group, but scientists now believe it was a large herbivore. Although it was of similar size and had a powerful beak, recent data shows that its diet consisted primarily of tough plant matter. For this reason, it would have needed a large caecum, an organ used to digest such a diet, which would have made flight difficult.

4 ➡ The wide distribution of ratite species has long puzzled scientists. For many decades, the most popular theory was that they descended from a common flightless ancestor. The continents that they live on, Africa, Australia and South America, were once connected into one landmass called Gondwana that split apart about 180 million years ago. This would have isolated the animals and allowed them to evolve independently. However, geologic evidence shows that the supercontinent of Gondwana broke apart far too long ago for that to be the case. A recent genetic survey of ratite species supports the more likely theory that the flightless giants evolved from a common ancestor that could fly. Members of this species spread across the world to the already divided continents, and then lost their ability to fly.

5 ➡ However, members of the ratite family are not exclusively large. The kiwi of New Zealand and the tinamou of South America are ratites with stout, robust bodies despite their diminutive size. Still, they have another important trait that they share with other ratites: very large eggs. It makes sense for the ostrich to lay the biggest egg as the largest bird in the world, but the kiwi actually lays the largest egg relative to its own body size, and the ostrich egg is the smallest in comparison to the size of the adult bird. It remains unclear why kiwis lay such large eggs, but there are two possibilities. Either kiwis have always been small and their eggs have grown, or kiwis used to be much larger, and their eggs have not shrunk very much. Either way, a large egg provides definite survival advantages for kiwi chicks. They hatch with an extra

킬로그램에 달했을 것이다. 이것은 먹이감을 사냥할 때 강한 다리로 동물들을 쫓고 바닥에 때려눕혔다. 또한 매우 크고 갈고리 모양으로 구부러진 부리는 살점을 찢는 데 아주 적합했다. 디아트리마(Diatryma)라고 불리는 또 다른 고대 새는 티타니스 왈레리와 같은 종에 속하긴 하지만, 현재 과학자들은 그것이 거대 초식동물이었다고 믿는다. 비록 크기가 비슷하고 강력한 부리를 가지고 있긴 했지만, 최근의 데이터에 의하면 그것이 먹던 음식물은 주로 질긴 식물들로 구성되어 있었다. 이러한 이유로 그것은 아마 그러한 음식물을 소화하기 위해 필요한 장기인 커다란 맹장을 필요로 했을 것이며, 이로 인해 나는 것이 힘들어졌을 것이다.

4 ➡ 주금류가 널리 분포되어 있는 점은 오랫동안 과학자들을 어리둥절하게 만들었다. 수십 년 동안, 가장 대중적인 이론은 그들이 공통의 날지 못하는 조상으로부터 내려왔다는 것이다. 그들이 살고 있는 아프리카, 호주, 남아메리카 대륙들은 한때는 곤드와나 불리는 하나의 대륙으로 연결되어 있었으며 약 1억 8천만년 전에 나뉘었다. 이로 인해 동물들이 고립되며 독자적으로 진화하게 되었을 것이다. 하지만 지질학적 증거에 따르면 곤드와나라는 초대륙은 그러기엔 너무 오래 전에 분리되었다. 최근 주금류 새들에 대한 유전자 조사는 거대한 날지 못하는 새들이 날 수 있는 공통의 조상으로부터 진화했다는 더욱 그럴싸한 이론을 뒷받침했다. 이 종에 속하는 새들은 전 세계에 걸쳐 이미 나뉘어진 대륙으로 퍼져나갔고, 그 과정에서 나는 능력을 상실했다.

5 ➡ 하지만 주금류에 속하는 새들이 단지 거대하기만 한 것은 아니다. 뉴질랜드의 키위와 남미의 티나무는 아주 작은 크기에도 불구하고 튼튼하고, 강건한 몸을 가진 주금류 새이다. 여전히 그들이 다른 주금류와 공유하는 또 다른 중요한 특성이 있다. 바로 매우 큰 알이다. 타조가 세상에서 가장 큰 새로서 가장 큰 알을 낳는 것은 이해가 가지만, 사실상 키위가 몸 크기에 비해 가장 큰 알을 낳으며, 타조의 알은 성체의 크기에 비해 가장 작다. 키위가 왜 이토록 큰 알을 낳는지 그 이유는 아직 명확하지 않지만, 두 가지 가능성이 있다. 키위는 항상 작았는데 알만 커졌거나, 키위가 예전에는 훨씬 더 컸는데, 알은 크기가 그리 많이 줄어들지 않은 경우이다. 어느 쪽이든 간에, 큰 알은 새끼 키위들에게 분명히 생존상의 이점을 제공한다. 그들은 생후 2주 이상 먹고 살 수 있는 여분의 노른자를 가지고 부화하는데, 이것은 그들이 태어나면서부터 뛸 준비가 상당히 되어 있다는 의미이다. 이것은 그들로 하여금 날아다니는 포식자

supply of yolk that they can live off of for over two weeks, which means they are born pretty much ready to run. This makes it possible for them to better evade flying predators, so it might be worth carrying such outsized eggs.

를 더 잘 피할 수 있게 해주므로, 그토록 거대한 알을 지니고 다닐 만한 가치가 있을지도 모른다.

1. Vocabulary

The word "paradoxical" in paragraph 1 is closest in meaning to

- (A) inevitable
- **(B) contradictory**
- (C) arbitrary
- (D) mundane

2. Negative Fact

Which of the following is NOT mentioned in paragraph 1?

- (A) What convergent evolution is
- (B) What caused some birds to be flightless
- **(C) How flightless birds survived**
- (D) How evolutionary changes in birds took place

3. Negative Fact

According to paragraph 2, all of the following are common physical features of ratites EXCEPT

- (A) long necks
- (B) long legs
- (C) vestigial wings
- **(D) ridge-shaped chest bones**

4. Inference

Which of the following can be inferred about terror birds from paragraph 3?

- (A) *Titanis walleri* was the largest land predator in the Western Hemisphere when it lived.
- **(B) They were ultimately unable to compete with mammalian predators.**
- (C) They lived alongside the dinosaurs and competed with them for food.
- (D) They were not as fast and agile as birds that hunt while flying.

1.

1단락의 단어 "paradoxical(모순적인)"과 의미상 가장 가까운 것은?

- (A) 불가피한
- (B) 모순적인
- (C) 임의적인
- (D) 일상적인

2.

다음 중 1단락에서 언급되지 않은 것은 무엇인가?

- (A) 수렴진화가 무엇인지
- (B) 일부 새들이 날지 못하게 된 것이 무엇 때문인지
- (C) 날지 못하는 새들이 어떻게 생존했는지
- (D) 조류에게 진화의 변화가 어떻게 발생했는지

3.

2단락에 따르면, 다음 중 주금류의 공통된 신체적 특징이 아닌 것은?

- (A) 긴 목
- (B) 긴 다리
- (C) 흔적만 남아 있는 날개
- (D) 길쭉하게 솟은 가슴뼈

4.

다음 중 3단락에서 공포새에 대해 추론할 수 있는 것은 무엇인가?

- (A) 생존했을 당시 티타니스 왈레리가 서반구에서 가장 큰 육식동물이었다.
- (B) 그들은 결국 포유류 포식자와 경쟁할 수 없었다.
- (C) 그들은 공룡과 함께 살았고 먹이를 두고 그들과 경쟁했다.
- (D) 그들은 날면서 사냥하는 새들만큼 빠르고 민첩하지 못했다.

5. Rhetorical Purpose

Why does the author mention "Diatryma" in paragraph 3?

- (A) To cast doubt on its being classified as a "terror bird"
- (B) To explain why "terror birds" had large digestive organs
- (C) To draw a line between a giant bird and a large herbivore
- (D) **To introduce a bird that was mistakenly categorized**

6. Negative Fact

In paragraph 4, which of the following is NOT mentioned about Gondwana?

- (A) It was an ancient supercontinent that broke up about 180 million years ago.
- (B) It incorporated the current continents of Africa, Australia, and South America.
- (C) **It started to split when magma from below the Earth's crust began pushing upward.**
- (D) Its breakup is believed to have isolated the animals living on it.

7. Fact

According to paragraph 5, what advantage do huge eggs bring to the kiwi?

- (A) Their large size prevents predators from eating them easily.
- (B) They give kiwi chicks a competitive edge over flying birds.
- (C) **The chicks do not need to be fed after they hatch.**
- (D) A female can only lay one egg at a time, which requires less energy.

8. Sentence Simplification

Which of the sentences below best expresses the essential information in the highlighted sentence in the passage? *Incorrect* answer choices change the meaning in important ways or leave out essential information.

- (A) The ostrich has the largest egg compared to the body of the adult bird, while the kiwi has the smallest compared to its body.
- (B) Although it is a much smaller bird, the kiwi actually lays larger eggs than the ostrich does.
- (C) Since it is the largest bird in the world, it is not surprising that the ostrich lays the largest egg, but the kiwi actually lays a very large egg as well.
- (D) **The ostrich actually has the smallest egg compared to the adult's body although it is the largest bird, whereas the kiwi has the largest egg compared to its body.**

5.

3단락에서 글쓴이가 "디아트리마"를 언급하는 이유는 무엇인가?

- (A) 그것이 공포새로 분류되는 것에 대한 의구심을 제기하기 위해
- (B) 공포새들이 큰 소화기관을 가졌던 이유를 설명하기 위해
- (C) 거대 새와 거대 초식동물을 비교하기 위해
- (D) 잘못 분류된 새를 소개하기 위해

6.

4단락에서 다음 중 곤드와나에 대해 언급되지 않은 것은 무엇인가?

- (A) 약 1억 8천만년 전에 분열된 고대의 초대륙이었다.
- (B) 현재의 아프리카, 호주, 남아메리카 대륙을 포함함.
- (C) 지구의 지각 아래에서 올라온 마그마가 위로 밀기 시작했을 때 분열되기 시작했다.
- (D) 그것의 분열로 인해 그곳에 살던 동물들이 고립되었다고 여겨진다.

7.

5단락에 따르면, 거대한 알이 키위새에게 가져다 주는 이점은 무엇인가?

- (A) 크기가 커서 포식자들이 쉽게 먹을 수 없게 한다.
- (B) 새끼 키위새가 나는 새들과의 경쟁에서 우위에 서게 한다.
- (C) 새끼 새들이 부화한 이후에 먹이를 받아먹을 필요가 없다.
- (D) 암컷이 한 번에 하나의 알만 낳을 수 있으므로 에너지를 덜 필요로 한다.

8.

다음 중 지문의 음영 표시된 문장의 핵심 정보를 가장 잘 표현한 문장은 무엇인가? 오답은 의미를 크게 왜곡하거나 핵심 정보를 누락하고 있다.

- (A) 타조는 성체의 몸에 비해 가장 큰 알을 낳는 반면, 키위는 몸에 비해 가장 작은 알을 낳는다.
- (B) 비록 키위가 타조보다 훨씬 더 작은 새지만, 사실상 타조보다 더 큰 알을 낳는다.
- (C) 세계에서 가장 큰 새이기 때문에, 타조가 가장 큰 알을 낳는 것이 놀랍지 않지만, 키위도 역시 아주 큰 알을 낳는다.
- (D) 타조는 가장 큰 새임에도 불구하고 사실상 성체의 크기에 비해 가장 작은 알을 낳는 반면, 키위는 몸에 비해 가장 큰 알을 낳는다.

9. Insertion

Look at the four squares [■] that indicate where the following sentence could be added to the passage.

Flight became an unnecessary expenditure of energy, so their bodies gradually lost the structures that were needed for flying.

Where would the sentence best fit? [■ C]

10. Summary

Directions: An introductory sentence for a brief summary of the passage is provided below. Complete the summary by selecting the THREE answer choices that express the most important ideas in the passage. Some sentences do not belong in the summary because they express ideas that are not presented in the passage or are minor ideas in the passage. *This question is worth 2 points.*

Many species of birds like the ratites have lost the ability to fly as they adapted to the habitats in which they live.

> Ⓐ **Many of the early flightless birds evolved to fill niches that had been left vacant by the dinosaurs when they went extinct.**
> Ⓒ **Scientists originally thought that ratites were flightless when the continents separated, but they have since learned that their ancestors must have flown across the oceans.**
> Ⓕ **The smallest ratite species is the kiwi, which lays disproportionally large eggs.**

Ⓑ *Titanis walleri* was the largest of the "terror birds" at 2.5 meters tall.

Ⓓ Ratite species live in Australia, Africa, and South America today.

Ⓔ Some scientists believe that the ancestors of modern kiwis must have been much larger than their descendants.

9.

지문에 다음 문장이 들어갈 수 있는 위치를 나타내는 네 개의 사각형[■]을 확인하시오.

나는 것은 에너지를 불필요하게 소모하기 때문에, 그들의 몸은 점차 나는 것에 필요한 구조를 잃게 되었다.

이 문장이 들어가기에 가장 적합한 곳은? [■ C]

10.

지시문: 지문을 간략하게 요약한 글의 첫 문장이 아래 제시되어 있다. 지문의 가장 중요한 내용을 표현하는 세 개의 선택지를 골라 요약문을 완성하시오. 일부 문장들은 지문에 제시되지 않았거나 지문의 지엽적인 내용을 나타내기 때문에 요약문에 포함되지 않는다. *이 문제의 배점은 2점이다.*

주금류와 같은 많은 종의 새들이 자신들이 사는 서식지에 적응하면서 나는 능력을 잃게 되었다.

> Ⓐ 초기의 날지 못하는 많은 새들이 공룡이 멸종되면서 남기고 간 적소를 채우는 것으로 진화했다.
> Ⓒ 원래 과학자들은 대륙이 분리될 당시 주금류는 날지 못했다고 생각했으나, 그 이후에 그들의 조상이 바다를 건너 날아온 것이 틀림없다는 것을 알게 되었다.
> Ⓕ 가장 작은 주금류 새는 키위이며, 이들은 불균형하게 커다란 알을 낳는다.

Ⓑ 티타니스 왈레리는 키가 2.5미터로 공포새 중 가장 컸다.

Ⓓ 주금류는 오늘날 호주, 아프리카, 남아메리카에서 서식한다.

Ⓔ 일부 과학자들은 현대 키위새의 조상들이 그들의 자손들보다 틀림없이 훨씬 더 컸을 것이라고 믿는다.

🔖 어휘

1 **advanced** adj 진보한, 선진의, (발달 단계상) 후기의 | **predator** n 포식자, 포식 동물
2 **be classified into** ~로 분류되다 | **extinct** adj 멸종된, 더 이상 존재하지 않는 | **possess** v 소유하다, 보유하다 | **vestigial** adj 남아 있는 | **abandon** v 버리다, 유기하다, 포기하다
3 **specimen** n 견본, 표본 | **knock** v 때리다, 타격하다 | **massive** adj 거대한, 엄청난 | **beak** n 부리 | **tear** v 찢다, 뜯다 | **herbivore** n 초식 동물
4 **distribution** n 분포, 분배 | **landmass** n 광대한 토지, 대륙 | **geologic** adj 지질학상의, 지질의
5 **stout** adj 튼튼한, 통통한 | **robust** adj 강건한, 원기 왕성한, 팔팔한 | **diminutive** adj 아주 작은 | **in comparison to** ~와 비교할 때 | **outsized** adj 대형의

Industrial Melanism in Peppered Moths

1 ➡ According to the theory of evolution, organisms evolve through a process called natural selection. When they are subjected to changes in their environment, some organisms possess genetic traits that allow them to survive. These survivors mate and pass on their genes to future generations. Over time, the genetic trait becomes the norm for their population, and the species can be said to have evolved. Charles Darwin famously illustrated this theory through his studies of the finches living on the Galapagos Islands. However, this process was also happening in his home country, England, at the same time and at a much faster pace. The organism involved in this rapid adaptation was the peppered moth.

2 ➡ While evolution usually occurs over thousands of years, sometimes the environmental pressure is so extreme that the rate speeds up. For the peppered moths, their motivation to adapt was increased predation. Peppered moths in England typically come in two different morphs or types that are determined by their genes. The more commonly seen morph was grey, often with speckled patterns that helped it blend in with light colored tree bark and lichens. The less commonly observed morph had a much higher melanin content, which makes its body and wings dark grey to black in color. However, the melanic trait is actually the dominant allele. The lighter morphs were more common because they could blend in more easily, making it more difficult for birds to see and then eat them. But, something shifted the situation in favor of the melanic morph.

3 ➡ During the Industrial Revolution in England, air pollution in the form of soot from burned coal increased dramatically. This pollution eventually became so severe that thousands of people in London died from breathing it. This pollution also affected the peppered moths. Throughout England, but particularly in cities, the rocks and trees that the moths rested on became covered in a layer of soot, killing much of the lichen and making everything darker. Prior to industrialization, the melanic morph only accounted for about .01% of the moth population, by the middle of the 19th century it had

점박이 나방에게서 나타나는 공업 흑화

1 ➡ 진화 이론에 따르면, 생명체들은 자연 선택이라고 불리는 과정을 통해 진화한다. 환경의 변화에 놓이게 되면 몇몇 생명체들은 그들을 생존 가능하게 하는 유전적 특성들을 가진다. 이 살아남은 개체들은 서로 짝짓기를 하여 자신들의 유전자를 미래의 세대에게 전달한다. 시간이 흘러 이 유전적 특성이 그들의 개체군에 표준이 되면 이 종은 진화했다고 말할 수 있다. 찰스 다윈은 갈라파고스 제도에 살던 핀치에 대한 연구를 통해 이 이론을 설명한 것으로 유명하다. 그러나 이 과정은 그의 모국인 영국에서도 같은 시기에 훨씬 더 빠른 속도로 일어나고 있었다. 이 빠른 적응에 관련된 생명체는 점박이 나방이었다.

2 ➡ 진화는 보통 수천 년에 걸쳐 일어나지만 때때로 환경적인 압박이 너무나 극단적이어서 이 속도가 빨라진다. 점박이 나방의 경우, 그들이 적응해야만 했던 동기는 포식의 증가였다. 영국의 점박이 나방들은 보통 유전자에 따라 결정되는 두 종류의 형태 혹은 변종이 있다. 더 흔히 볼 수 있는 변종은 회색이었는데, 그것이 연한 색의 나무 껍질과 이끼에 섞여드는 데 도움이 되는 작은 반점 무늬를 종종 가지고 있었다. 덜 흔하게 관찰할 수 있는 변종은 훨씬 더 높은 멜라닌의 함량으로 인해 몸과 날개가 짙은 회색에서 검은 색이었다. 그러나 이 흑생증의 특성은 사실 우성대립인자였다. 더 연한 색의 변종들이 더 흔한 이유는 그들이 더 쉽게 주위 환경에 섞여들어 새들이 그들을 보고 잡아먹기가 더 어려웠기 때문이었다. 그러나 무언가가 이 상황을 흑색 변종에 우세하도록 바꾸었다.

3 ➡ 영국의 산업 혁명 동안, 석탄을 태움으로 인해 발생한 그을음의 형태로 공기 오염이 급격히 늘었다. 이 오염은 결국 너무 극심해져서 런던에서 수천 명의 사람들이 이것을 들이마심으로 인해 사망했다. 이 오염은 점박이 나방에게도 영향을 주었다. 영국 전역에서, 특히 도심에서 이 나방들이 앉는 바위와 나무가 그을음에 덮이게 되었고 많은 이끼가 죽었으며 모든 것이 더 진한 색이 되었다. 산업화 이전에 흑색 변종은 나방 개체수의 단 0.01퍼센트밖에 되지 않았지만 19세기 중반에 이르러 눈에 띄게 개체수가 증가했으며, 1895년에 어떤 지역들에서는 98퍼센트라는 어마어마한 수치를 기록하여 많은 동식물 연구가들을 어리둥절하게 했다.

increased noticeably, and by 1895 it had reached a staggering 98% in some areas, which puzzled many naturalists.

4 ➡ In urban areas, the melanistic moths became overwhelmingly dominant, but in rural areas, the lighter moths continued to have the advantage. In an attempt to explain such a dramatic shift, J. W. Tutt offered a hypothesis in 1896 that birds were eating one morph in the city and the other morph in the country. Over the years, many experiments have been conducted to test this hypothesis, and the data gathered has consistently supported it. The most famous of these experiments were conducted by Bernard Kettlewell and his associates between 1952 and 1972.

5 ➡ In his first experiment, Kettlewell captured both light and dark moths and released them into an aviary to observe the results. The birds that ate the most moths were Great Tits, and they usually took the moths that were resting on a contrastingly colored surface. When the moths sat on matching surfaces, he had trouble seeing them, and the birds clearly did as well. In his following experiments, Kettlewell raised his own population of both morphs and marked the concealed underside of their wings with paint. If he had placed the markings on the top of the wing, they would all have become easier prey. Then, he released them into a heavily polluted forest near Birmingham and recaptured as many survivors as he could. Very few of the moths that he recovered were the lighter morph, which he interpreted to mean that the melanism was necessary to survival in such a habitat.

6 ➡ He later repeated this experiment, but he chose an unpolluted forest near Dorset. Again, he observed that the moths' coloring was vital to their survival. [■A] The dark moths did better in polluted woods, and the lighter ones did better in cleaner woods. Kettlewell concluded that factories like those in Birmingham were responsible for causing industrial melanism, which is when animals evolve darker coloration to survive in a habitat darkened by pollution. [■B] In the decades since his experiments, study has continued and provided further support for the theory that melanism in moths is a response to natural selection based on camouflage and predation. [■C] In particular, researchers have found that since stricter pollution laws were imposed, the population of lighter morphs near urban areas has rebounded. [■D]

4 ➡ 도심 지역에서는 흑색증 나방들이 압도적으로 우세하게 되었지만, 시골 지역에서는 더 옅은 색의 나방들이 계속해서 우위를 점했다. 이러한 극적인 변화를 설명하기 위해 J. W. 터트는 1896년에 한 가지 가설을 제시했는데, 새들이 도시에서 한 가지 변종 나방을 먹고, 시골에서 다른 변종을 잡아먹고 있다는 것이었다. 몇 년에 걸쳐 많은 실험들이 이 가설을 시험하기 위해 행해졌고, 수집된 자료는 끊임없이 이 가설을 뒷받침했다. 이 실험들 중 가장 잘 알려진 것은 버나드 케틀웰과 그의 동료들이 1952년부터 1972년까지 실시했던 실험들이었다.

5 ➡ 케틀웰은 그의 첫 번째 실험에서 연한 색과 진한 색 두 나방들을 잡아 새장에 풀어주고 결과를 관찰했다. 대부분의 나방을 잡아먹은 새들은 박새들이었고, 이 새들은 주로 자신의 색과 대비되는 색의 표면에 앉아 있던 나방들을 잡아먹었다. 나방들이 자신의 색과 비슷한 표면에 앉아 있었을 때 케틀웰은 나방들을 잘 보지 못했고, 새들 역시 확실히 그러했다. 그 이후의 실험들에서 케틀웰은 그가 보유한 두 변종의 개체수를 늘렸고 눈에 띄지 않는 날개 안쪽에 페인트로 표시를 했다. 만약 표시를 날개 바로 위에 하면 더 쉬운 표적이 되었을 것이다. 그런 뒤 그는 나방들을 버밍엄 근처의 심각하게 오염된 숲에 풀어주었고, 나중에 할 수 있는 한 많이 그 나방들을 다시 잡았다. 그가 다시 잡은 나방들 중 아주 소수만이 색이 더 연한 나방들이었는데, 이 결과를 그는 그러한 서식지에서의 생존을 위해 흑화가 필요하다는 의미라고 해석했다.

6 ➡ 그는 나중에 이 실험을 반복했지만, 도싯 근처의 오염되지 않은 숲을 선택했다. 그는 다시 한 번 나방들의 색이 그들의 생존에 필수적인 것이라는 것을 관찰했다. [■A] 색이 진한 나방들은 오염된 숲에서 더 잘 살아남았고, 더 연한 색 나방들은 더 깨끗한 숲에서 더 잘 살아남았다. 케틀웰은 버밍엄에 있는 것과 같은 공장들이 공업 흑화를 야기하는 원인이라고 결론내렸는데, 공업 흑화는 오염으로 인해 검게 변한 서식지에서 살아남기 위해 동물들이 더 진한 색을 진화시킬 때 일어난다. [■B] 그의 실험 뒤에도 수십 년 동안 연구는 계속되었고, 나방의 흑화는 위장과 포식에 근거한 자연 선택에 대한 반응이라는 이론을 더욱 뒷받침했다. [■C] 특히, 연구원들은 더욱 엄격한 공해방지법이 시행된 이후 도심 지역의 더 연한 색 변종 개체수가 다시 증가했다는 사실을 발견했다. [■D]

1. Rhetorical Purpose
Why does the author mention "natural selection" in paragraph 1?
- (A) To demonstrate that Darwin had a thorough insight concerning evolution
- (B) To question the veracity of Darwin's theory of evolution
- (C) To introduce various hypotheses about the evolution of species
- **(D) To explain the concept of evolution and give examples of it**

2. Fact
According to paragraph 2, which of the following is the factor that accelerated the pace of evolution?
- (A) Introduction of a new predator
- **(B) A sudden change in the environment**
- (C) Genetic diseases and mutations
- (D) Competition for resources

3. Reference
The word "it" in paragraph 2 refers to
- (A) **morph**
- (B) bark
- (C) content
- (D) color

4. Negative Fact
All of the following are mentioned in paragraph 3 EXCEPT
- (A) the influence of air pollution on human lives.
- (B) how the pollution changed the natural environment.
- **(C) the number of peppered moths that died from air pollution.**
- (D) the radical change in population of the melanic morph.

5. Inference
Based on paragraph 3, what can be inferred about the peppered moths in the middle of the 19th century?
- (A) Light colored moths were less resistant to air pollution than darker ones.
- (B) The Industrial Revolution threatened their survival and reproduction.
- (C) There was a rapid increase in the moth population due to industrialization.
- **(D) Their color had changed so that they could blend in with the surroundings.**

1.
1단락에서 글쓴이가 "자연 선택"을 언급하는 이유는 무엇인가?
- (A) 다윈이 진화와 관련해 깊은 통찰력을 가지고 있었다는 것을 보여주기 위해
- (B) 다윈의 진화 이론의 정확성에 의문을 던지기 위해
- (C) 종의 진화에 대한 다양한 가설들을 제시하기 위해
- (D) 진화의 개념을 설명하고 그 예시들을 보여주기 위해

2.
2단락에 따르면, 다음 중 진화의 속도를 더 빠르게 만든 요인은 무엇인가?
- (A) 새로운 포식자의 도입
- (B) 환경의 갑작스러운 변화
- (C) 유전 질병과 돌연변이
- (D) 자원을 얻기 위한 경쟁

3.
2단락의 단어 "it(그것)"이 가리키는 것은?
- (A) 변종
- (B) 나무 껍질
- (C) 함량
- (D) 색

4.
다음 중 3단락에서 언급되지 않은 것은?
- (A) 사람들의 삶에 공기 오염이 미치는 영향
- (B) 오염이 자연 환경을 어떻게 바꾸었는지
- (C) 공기 오염으로 죽은 점박이 나방의 수
- (D) 흑색 변종 개체수의 급격한 변화

5.
3단락에 근거하여 19세기 중반의 점박이 나방에 대해 추론할 수 있는 것은 무엇인가?
- (A) 연한 색 나방들은 더 진한 색 나방들보다 공기 오염에 대한 저항력이 덜했다.
- (B) 산업 혁명은 나방들의 생존과 번식을 위협했다.
- (C) 산업화로 인해 나방 개체수에 급격한 증가가 있었다.
- (D) 주변 환경에 섞여들 수 있도록 그들의 색이 바뀌었다.

6. Sentence Simplification

Which of the sentences below best expresses the essential information in the highlighted sentence in the passage? *Incorrect* answer choices change the meaning in important ways or leave out essential information.

(A) Lighter moths in rural areas were stronger than the melanistic moths in urban areas.

(B) **In contrast to urban areas where the melanistic moths were prevalent, lighter moths were still dominant in rural areas.**

(C) It was the melanistic moths that occupied urban areas, and they eventually spread to rural areas.

(D) Lighter moths in rural areas had smaller populations than the melanistic ones in urban areas due to some regional differences.

7. Fact

According to paragraph 5, why were only a few of the lighter moths recovered in Kettlewell's experiment?

(A) **Their color made it easy for their predators to find and eat them.**

(B) Great Tits had difficulty in discovering them on matching surfaces.

(C) Kettlewell marked the underside of their wings.

(D) All of the darker moths were eaten by birds.

8. Vocabulary

The word "vital" in paragraph 6 is closest in meaning to

(A) notable

(B) tangible

(C) **essential**

(D) trivial

9. Insertion

Look at the four squares [■] that indicate where the following sentence could be added to the passage.

The dark moths did better in polluted woods, and the lighter ones did better in cleaner woods.

Where would the sentence best fit? [■A]

6.

다음 중 지문의 음영 표시된 문장의 핵심 정보를 가장 잘 표현한 문장은 무엇인가? 오답은 의미를 크게 왜곡하거나 핵심 정보를 누락하고 있다.

(A) 시골 지역의 더 연한 색 나방들은 도심 지역의 흑색증 나방들보다 더 강했다.

(B) 흑색증 나방들이 우세했던 도심 지역과 달리 더 연한 색 나방들은 여전히 시골 지역에서 우세했다.

(C) 도심 지역을 점령한 것은 흑색증 나방들이었고, 그들은 결국 시골 지역으로 퍼지게 되었다.

(D) 시골 지역의 더 연한 색 나방들은 몇몇 지역적 차이로 인해 도심 지역의 흑색증 나방들보다 개체수가 더 적었다.

7.

5단락에 따르면, 케틀웰의 실험에서 더 연한 색 나방들이 소수만 발견된 이유는 무엇인가?

(A) 그들의 색이 포식자가 그들을 찾아내어 잡아먹기 쉽도록 만들었다.

(B) 색이 비슷한 표면에서는 박새들이 그들을 찾는 데 어려움을 겪었다.

(C) 케틀웰이 그들의 날개 안쪽에 표시를 해 두었다.

(D) 색이 더 진한 나방들은 새들이 모두 잡아먹었다.

8.

6단락의 단어 "vital(필수적인)"과 의미상 가장 가까운 것은?

(A) 눈에 띄는

(B) 실재하는

(C) 필수적인

(D) 하찮은

9.

지문에 다음 문장이 들어갈 수 있는 위치를 나타내는 네 개의 사각형[■]을 확인하시오.

색이 진한 나방들은 오염된 숲에서 더 잘 살아남았고, 더 연한 색 나방들은 더 깨끗한 숲에서 더 잘 살아남았다.

이 문장이 들어가기에 가장 적합한 곳은? [■A]

10. Summary

Directions: An introductory sentence for a brief summary of the passage is provided below. Complete the summary by selecting the THREE answer choices that express the most important ideas in the passage. Some sentences do not belong in the summary because they express ideas that are not presented in the passage or are minor ideas in the passage. *This question is worth 2 points.*

The melanism of peppered moths in the 19th century in England was the result of adaptation to environmental changes, which exemplified Darwin's theory of evolution by natural selection.

- Ⓑ Rapid industrialization increased the pollutants in the air, which covered trees and rocks and brought about changes in the moths' color.
- Ⓓ Kettlewell carried out a test by releasing both light moths and melanistic ones into a specific area, recapturing them, and counting the survivors.
- Ⓔ Kettlewell concluded that the increased risk of predation caused the melanism of the peppered moths.

- Ⓐ Darwin claimed that evolution occurs over a long period of time.
- Ⓒ The patterns which peppered moths have on their bodies help them blend in with light colored objects such as tree bark and lichens.
- Ⓕ Kettlewell's experiment demonstrated that melanism strengthened moths' biological resistance to the polluted air.

10.

지시문: 지문을 간략하게 요약한 글의 첫 문장이 아래 제시되어 있다. 지문의 가장 중요한 내용을 표현하는 세 개의 선택지를 골라 요약문을 완성하시오. 일부 문장들은 지문에 제시되지 않았거나 지문의 지엽적인 내용을 나타내기 때문에 요약문에 포함되지 않는다. *이 문제의 배점은 2점이다.*

19세기 영국에 있었던 점박이 나방의 흑화는 환경적 변화에 적응한 결과였으며, 이는 다윈의 자연 선택으로 인한 진화 이론의 예시가 되었다.

- Ⓑ 급격한 산업화는 공기 오염을 급증시켰고, 이는 나무와 바위를 덮어 나방 색의 변화를 초래했다.
- Ⓓ 케틀웰은 연한 색 나방과 흑색증 나방 두 종을 특정 지역에 풀어 주고 다시 잡아서 살아남은 나방의 수를 세는 실험을 했다.
- Ⓔ 케틀웰은 포식의 위험이 증가함으로 인해 점박이 나방의 흑화가 일어났다고 결론을 내렸다.

- Ⓐ 다윈은 진화가 오랜 시간에 걸쳐 일어난다고 주장했다.
- Ⓒ 점박이 나방들이 몸에 지닌 반점들은 나무 껍질과 이끼와 같은 연한 색의 사물에 그들이 잘 섞여드는 데 도움이 된다.
- Ⓕ 케틀웰의 실험은 흑화가 오염된 공기에 대한 나방의 생물학적 저항을 강하게 한다는 것을 보여주었다.

어휘

1 **natural selection** 자연 선택 | **be subjected to** ~을 받다[당하다] | **genetic** adj 유전적인 | **trait** n 특성 | **norm** n 표준 | **home country** 모국 | **adaptation** n 적응

2 **environmental** adj 환경의 | **pressure** n 압박, 압력 | **predation** n 포식 | **morph** n 어떤 종(種)의 한 변종 | **speckled** adj 작은 반점들이 있는 | **blend in** 조화를 이루다, (주위 환경에) 섞여들다 | **content** n 함량, 내용물 | **dominant** adj 우세한, 지배적인 | **shift** v 옮기다, 이동하다 | **in favor of** ~의 이익이 되도록

3 **soot** n 그을음 | **severe** adj 극심한 | **industrialization** n 산업[공업]화 | **account for** (부분, 비율을) 차지하다 | **noticeably** adv 두드러지게, 현저히 | **staggering** adj 믿기 어려운, 경이적인, 충격적인 | **puzzle** v 어리둥절하게 만들다 | **naturalist** n 동식물 연구가

4 **overwhelmingly** adv 압도적으로 | **consistently** adv 일관하여, 지속적으로

5 **contrastingly** adv 대조적으로 | **concealed** adj 감춰진 | **recover** v 되찾다, 회복하다 | **interpret** v 설명[해석]하다 | **habitat** n 서식지

6 **vital** adj 필수적인 | **camouflage** n 위장, 속임수 | **impose** v 도입[시행]하다 | **rebound** v 되돌아오다

Thermoregulation in Marine Organisms

1 ➡ Living organisms have a variety of ways in which they regulate their body temperature, but they are generally divided into two larger categories. [■A] Endothermic organisms are those whose metabolisms allow them to maintain a relatively stable temperature that is generally hotter than their ambient conditions. [■B] The average body temperature of most land mammals tends to be around 40 degrees Celsius, but that of marine mammals is usually a few degrees lower. The key reason behind the difference in core body temperature between these organisms is the fact that water is much more conductive than air, and they lose more of their heat into their environment. [■C] The majority of marine creatures regulate their body temperature by matching that of their surroundings, which puts them in the second broad category of ectothermic organisms. [■D]

2 ➡ Most species of fish and invertebrates that dwell in the open ocean below tidal areas are ectothermic, but not all marine organisms fit neatly into either of the categories. Some organisms possess abilities that allow them to exist somewhere between the two by maintaining a temperature that is higher than the water around them, but well below what truly endothermic creatures are capable of. One such exception is the rapidly swimming fish in the tuna family. They are able to keep their body temperature significantly higher than the water around them through their unique musculature. Unlike most fish whose swimming muscles are distributed evenly under their skin, their red aerobic muscle is located along their spine. This not only makes them powerful swimmers, but it also generates heat at the core of their body. In combination with a retention system, this allows them to generate the heat required to increase their metabolic rate and engage in sustained activity.

3 ➡ Other marine creatures cannot truly be classified as ectothermic because they actually try to maintain temperatures that are lower than their surroundings. These animals are found in intertidal areas where they are exposed to greater amounts of sunlight, which heats the small tidal pools they are trapped in at different times of the day. They circulate and expel

해양생물의 체온 조절

1 ➡ 생물체들은 체온을 조절하는 다양한 방법을 갖고 있지만, 이것은 대체적으로 두 개의 커다란 범주로 나누어진다. [■A] 내온성 생물의 신진대사는 그들로 하여금 주변 환경보다 대체적으로 더 높은 온도를 상대적으로 안정적으로 유지하게끔 한다. [■B] 대다수의 육지 포유류의 평균 체온은 섭씨 40도 정도에 머무는 반면, 해양 포유류의 경우에는 보통 이것보다 몇 도 더 낮다. 이 생물들 간에 심부 체온의 차이가 생기는 주된 이유는 물이 공기보다 훨씬 더 전도성이 뛰어나서 해양생물들이 주변 환경에 더 많은 열을 손실한다는 점이다. [■C] 해양생물들의 대다수는 체온을 주변 환경에 맞추는 방식으로 조절하기 때문에 외온성 생물이라는 두 번째 범주에 포함된다. [■D]

2 ➡ 감조 구역 아래 외해에 사는 대다수의 어종과 무척추동물 종은 외온성이지만, 모든 해양생물이 이 두 개의 범주 중 어느 한쪽으로 분명하게 구분되는 것은 아니다. 어떤 생물체는 주변의 수온보다 더 높지만 진정한 내온성 생물들에게 가능한 것보다는 훨씬 낮은 온도를 유지함으로써 이 두 개의 범주 중간쯤에 머무르는 능력을 가지고 있다. 이런 예외적인 동물 중 하나는 참치과의 빠르게 헤엄치는 물고기다. 이들은 독특한 근육계를 통해 주변의 물보다 훨씬 높은 체온을 유지할 수 있다. 유영 근육이 피부 아래 균일하게 분포되어 있는 대다수의 물고기와는 다르게, 그들의 유산소 적색근은 척추를 따라 위치해 있다. 이것은 그들을 뛰어난 유영 물고기로 만들 뿐만 아니라, 심부에 열을 발생시킨다. 보존 체계와 함께, 이는 신진대사율 증가와 계속되는 활동에 필요한 열을 발생시키도록 해 준다.

3 ➡ 다른 해양생물들은 주변 환경보다 더 낮은 체온을 유지하려고 노력하기 때문에 사실 진정한 외온성으로 분류될 수 없다. 이 동물들은 많은 양의 태양열에 노출되는 조간대 영역에서 발견되는데, 이는 하루의 다른 시간대에 그들이 갇혀 있는 작은 조수 웅덩이들을 뜨겁게 만든다. 그들은 증발을 통해 몸을 식히기 위해 체액을 순환시키고 배출한다. 그들은 이것을 매우 효과적으로 하기에 근처에 있는 동일

bodily fluids to cool themselves by evaporation. They are so effective at this that they will have lower temperatures than inanimate objects near them even if they are of the same size and shape. They also use color to their advantage as lighter colors absorb less heat than darker colors do, so the predominant colors of organisms will vary in order to reflect or collect solar energy depending upon their distance from the equator.

4 ➡ Since ocean temperatures are typically below 30 degrees centigrade, and may plunge below zero depending upon depth, completely endothermic organisms like whales and dolphins suffer from a constant loss of body heat. This mainly occurs due to their skin's contact with the water, which can rapidly lower their temperature. This is exacerbated when their blood flows outward from their core to their extremities, is cooled, and returns to the core. When they surface to breathe, they expel heat along with their breath and often breathe in cold air, which only lowers their temperature even further. Since a considerable lowering of internal temperature can be fatal for endotherms, those that live in the marine environment have developed various tactics to prevent this outcome.

5 ➡ Sea birds like penguins have developed a dual coat of feathers that prevents heat loss. They have a thick layer of downy feathers covered with a layer of rigid interconnecting feathers that hold air stationary between them, acting as an insulating layer. Cetaceans and pinnipeds, however, rely upon a thick layer of fat underneath their skin called blubber. Unlike whales and seals, sea otters lack blubber, but they have an incredibly thick coat of fur that keeps their skin from coming into direct contact with the water. In addition, these marine mammals have accelerated metabolisms in comparison with similarly sized land mammals to produce much more internal heat.

6 ➡ For whales and dolphins, these measures are still insufficient due to the large fins and tail flukes that they need for swimming. These limbs have a far greater surface area to inner volume ratio than the rest of the body, which means that they rapidly shed heat, but they still must receive arterial blood, so they have developed a heat exchange system to minimize the effect. The veins that carry cold blood

한 크기와 모양의 무생물보다 더 낮은 체온을 갖고 있다. 또한 그들은 더 밝은 색이 어두운 색보다 열을 덜 흡수하므로 색깔을 그들에게 유리한 쪽으로 사용하며, 적도로부터 떨어진 거리에 따라서 생물들의 주색은 태양열을 반사하거나 흡수하기 위해 달라진다.

4 ➡ 해수 온도는 보통 섭씨 30도 아래이며 깊이에 따라서 0도 아래로 내려갈 수도 있기 때문에, 고래 및 돌고래와 같은 완전히 내온성인 생물들은 꾸준한 체열 손실을 겪는다. 이는 주로 체온을 급격히 내려가게 하는 피부와 물의 접촉으로 일어난다. 이것은 피가 심부에서 사지 방향인 바깥으로 흐르고, 식어서 심부로 돌아올 때 더 심해진다. 수면 위로 올라와 호흡할 때, 그들은 호흡과 함께 열을 배출하고 흔히 차가운 공기를 들이마시는데, 이것은 체온을 훨씬 더 낮추기만 한다. 내부 체온의 상당한 감소는 온혈 동물에게 치명적일 수 있기 때문에 해양 환경에 살고 있는 동물들은 이런 결과를 막기 위해 다양한 전략을 발달시켜왔다.

5 ➡ 펭귄과 같은 해양 조류는 열 손실을 막는 두 겹의 깃털을 발달시켰다. 그들은 솜털로 덮인 두꺼운 깃털층을 가지고 있는데, 그것은 그 사이에 공기를 붙잡아주는 단단하고 서로 연결된 깃털층으로 덮여있고 전열층의 역할을 한다. 반면에, 고래류와 기각류 동물들은 피부 아래의 고래지방이라 불리는 두꺼운 지방층에 의존한다. 고래와 물개와는 다르게 해달은 고래지방을 갖고 있지 않지만, 피부가 물과 직접적으로 접촉하지 않게 막아주는 대단히 두꺼운 털 외피를 갖고 있다. 또한, 이 해양 포유류들은 훨씬 더 많은 내부의 열을 발생시키기 위해 비슷한 크기의 육지 포유류에 비해 높은 신진대사를 갖고 있다.

6 ➡ 유영에 필요한 커다란 지느러미와 꼬리를 가진 고래와 돌고래에게 이런 방식은 여전히 충분하지 않다. 이러한 사지는 몸의 다른 부위보다 내부 부피에 비해 표면적이 훨씬 크며, 이것은 열을 빠르게 잃어버린다는 것을 뜻하지만, 그래도 동맥혈을 공급받아야 하기 때문에 이 현상을 최소화하기 위해 열 교환 시스템을 발달시켰다. 사지에서 차가운 피를 안쪽으로 운반하는 정맥은 심부에서 따뜻한 피를 바깥으로 운반하는 동맥을 감싼다. 이것은 정

back in from the limbs wind around the arteries which carry out warm blood from the core. This warms the venous blood so it doesn't cool the core, and cools the arterial blood so that it doesn't release much warmth into the water through the limbs. This system is not unique to mammals, as some fish species, like the aforementioned tuna and some sharks, possess overall similar systems to reduce heat loss through their fins and gills.

맥혈을 따뜻하게 해서 심부를 식히지 않게끔 하고, 사지를 통해서 너무 많은 열을 물에 방출하지 않게 동맥혈을 식힌다. 이 시스템은 포유류 고유의 것이 아니며, 앞서 언급된 참치류와 일부 상어들과 같은 몇몇 어종들도 지느러미와 아가미를 통한 열 손실을 줄이기 위해 전반적으로 비슷한 시스템을 갖고 있다.

---

1. Vocabulary

The word "**sustained**" in paragraph 2 is closest in meaning to

(A) **continued**
(B) intensive
(C) compulsory
(D) vigorous

2. Fact

According to paragraph 2, the rapidly swimming fish in the tuna family keep their body temperature higher than the water around them so they can

(A) supply energy to their red aerobic muscles.
(B) generate heat at the core of their body.
(C) **increase their metabolism for prolonged activity.**
(D) swim deep into the ocean chasing prey.

3. Fact

According to paragraph 3, why are some marine organisms not classified as truly ectothermic?

(A) They are found in intertidal areas.
(B) They have the ability to reflect or absorb solar energy.
(C) Their blood circulation system is different from that of ectothermic species.
(D) **They maintain temperatures lower than their environment.**

4. Negative Fact

All of the following are mentioned in paragraph 4 as ways endothermic animals lose heat EXCEPT

(A) skin coming into contact with water.
(B) **absorbing solar energy close to the equator.**
(C) warm blood flowing to the extremities.
(D) breathing in cold air.

1.

2단락의 단어 "sustained(계속된)"와 의미상 가장 가까운 것은

(A) 계속된
(B) 집중적인
(C) 필수의
(D) 격렬한

2.

2단락에 따르면, 참치과의 빠르게 헤엄치는 물고기가 주변의 물보다 체온을 높게 유지하는 이유는?

(A) 유산소 적색근에 에너지를 공급하기 위하여
(B) 몸의 심부에 열을 발생시키기 위하여
(C) 지속적인 활동을 위해 신진대사를 증가시키기 위하여
(D) 먹이를 쫓아서 바다 깊은 곳으로 헤엄치기 위하여

3.

3단락에 따르면, 몇몇 해양생물이 진정한 외온성으로 분류되지 않는 이유는 무엇인가?

(A) 그들은 조간대 영역에서 발견된다.
(B) 그들은 태양 에너지를 반사하거나 흡수할 수 있는 능력을 갖고 있다.
(C) 그들의 혈액 순환 시스템은 외온성 종의 것과 다르다.
(D) 그들은 환경보다 더 낮은 체온을 유지한다.

4.

다음 중 4단락에서 내온성 동물들이 열을 상실하는 방식으로 언급되지 않은 것은?

(A) 피부가 물과 접촉하는 것
(B) 적도와 근접해서 태양 에너지를 흡수하는 것
(C) 따뜻한 혈액이 사지로 흘러가는 것
(D) 차가운 공기를 들이마시는 것

5. Rhetorical Purpose

What is the function of paragraph 5 as it relates to paragraph 4?

(A) **To explain ways marine animals deal with the problems mentioned in paragraph 4**

(B) To discuss how the problems described in paragraph 4 affect some animals more than others

(C) To provide examples of animals to which the problems mentioned in paragraph 4 do not apply

(D) To suggest possible causes of the problems mentioned in paragraph 4

6. Inference

What is implied by comparing land mammals to marine mammals of similar size in paragraph 5?

(A) Relatively smaller-sized land mammals lose less heat than the relatively bigger-sized marine mammals.

(B) Land mammals are more efficient at preventing heat loss than marine mammals.

(C) Land animals are exposed to significantly colder temperatures.

(D) **There are other factors responsible for metabolic rate than body size.**

7. Sentence Simplification

Which of the sentences below best expresses the essential information in the highlighted sentence in the passage? *Incorrect* answer choices change the meaning in important ways or leave out essential information.

(A) The shape of their limbs allows the animals to maintain their body temperature more easily by utilizing a unique heat exchange that avoids releasing heat.

(B) The limbs have a greater surface area to inner volume ratio than the rest of the body, which makes it difficult for them to receive warm arterial blood.

(C) **Their heat exchange system allows them to minimize heat loss through limbs which lose heat more quickly than other parts of the body due to their shape.**

(D) Because their limbs have a greater surface area to inner volume ratio than other parts of the body, these animals have developed a system that prevents blood flow to the limbs.

8. Fact

According to paragraph 6, how do some marine mammals minimize heat loss through their limbs?

(A) By placing veins closer to the core of the body

5.

4단락과의 관계에 비추어 5단락의 역할은 무엇인가?

(A) 4단락에서 언급된 문제들을 해양동물들이 처리하는 방법을 설명하기 위해

(B) 4단락에 묘사된 문제들이 어떻게 특정 동물들에게 더 큰 영향을 끼치는지 논의하기 위해

(C) 4단락에서 언급된 문제들이 적용되지 않는 동물들의 예시를 들기 위해

(D) 4단락에서 언급된 문제들의 가능한 원인들을 제시하기 위해

6.

5단락에서 육지 포유류를 그와 비슷한 크기의 해양 포유류와 비교함으로써 추론할 수 있는 것은 무엇인가?

(A) 상대적으로 크기가 더 작은 육지 포유류는 상대적으로 크기가 큰 해양 포유류보다 열을 덜 상실한다.

(B) 육지 포유류는 해양 포유류보다 열 손실을 막는 것에 더 효율적이다.

(C) 육지 포유류는 훨씬 더 낮은 온도에 노출된다.

(D) 몸의 크기 외에 신진대사율을 결정짓는 다른 요소들이 있다.

7.

다음 중 지문의 음영 표시된 문장의 핵심 정보를 가장 잘 표현한 문장은 무엇인가? 오답은 의미를 크게 왜곡하거나 핵심 정보를 누락하고 있다.

(A) 이 동물들의 사지 형태는 열 방출을 피하는 독특한 열 교환을 이용하여 이들이 체온을 더 쉽게 유지하도록 해준다.

(B) 이 사지는 몸의 다른 부위보다 내부 부피에 비해 표면적이 훨씬 크며, 이것은 그들로 하여금 따뜻한 동맥혈을 공급받는 것을 어렵게 만든다.

(C) 그들의 열 교환 시스템은 형태 때문에 몸의 다른 부위에 비해 열을 훨씬 빠르게 상실하는 사지를 통한 열 손실을 최소화한다.

(D) 사지가 몸의 다른 부위보다 내부 부피에 비해 표면적이 훨씬 크기 때문에, 이 동물들은 사지로 혈액이 흘러가는 것을 막는 시스템을 발달시켰다.

8.

6단락에 따르면, 몇몇 해양생물들은 사지를 통한 열 손실을 어떻게 최소화하는가?

(A) 정맥을 몸의 심부에 더 가깝게 위치시킴으로써

Ⓑ By having the blood flowing back to the core colder than the blood flowing out

Ⓒ **By having veins carrying cold blood around the arteries carrying warm blood**

Ⓓ By cooling down warm blood in the veins before it reaches the core

9. Insertion

Look at the four squares [■] that indicate where the following sentence could be added to the passage.

The average body temperature of most land mammals tends to be around 40 degrees Celsius, but that of marine mammals is usually a few degrees lower.

Where would the sentence best fit? [■ B]

10. Summary

Directions: An introductory sentence for a brief summary of the passage is provided below. Complete the summary by selecting the THREE answer choices that express the most important ideas in the passage. Some sentences do not belong in the summary because they express ideas that are not presented in the passage or are minor ideas in the passage. *This question is worth 2 points.*

Organisms that maintain body temperatures higher than the ambient temperature are called endothermic, and organisms that match their body temperature to their surroundings are called ectothermic.

Ⓐ **Many do not fall into either category, as some keep their temperature between the two categories, while others keep their temperature even lower than their environment.**

Ⓒ **Many endothermic organisms possess features such as fur coats and blubber to keep their body temperature high enough.**

Ⓓ **For body parts with a greater surface area to inner volume ratio, they have developed a blood circulation system which prevents heat loss.**

Ⓑ The rapidly swimming fish in the tuna family have their swimming muscles concentrated just below their skin.

Ⓔ Sea otters do not have blubber, but they have a thick coat of fur preventing their skin from coming into direct contact with water.

Ⓕ The fact that intertidal organisms have lower temperatures than inanimate objects proves that land mammals have a lower metabolic rate than marine mammals.

Ⓑ 심부로 흘러가는 혈액을 바깥으로 흘러가는 혈액보다 더 차갑게 유지함으로써

Ⓒ 차가운 혈액을 운반하는 정맥을 따뜻한 혈액을 운반하는 동맥 주변에 위치시킴으로써

Ⓓ 정맥의 따뜻한 혈액을 심부에 다다르기 전에 식힘으로써

9.

지문에 다음 문장이 들어갈 수 있는 위치를 나타내는 네 개의 사각형[■]을 확인하시오.

대다수 육지 포유류의 평균 체온은 섭씨 40도 정도에 머무는 반면, 해양 포유류의 경우에는 보통 이것보다 몇 도 더 낮다.

이 문장이 들어가기에 가장 적합한 곳은? [■ B]

10.

지시문: 지문을 간략하게 요약한 글의 첫 문장이 아래 제시되어 있다. 지문의 가장 중요한 내용을 표현하는 세 개의 선택지를 골라 요약문을 완성하시오. 일부 문장들은 지문에 제시되지 않았거나 지문의 지엽적인 내용을 나타내기 때문에 요약문에 포함되지 않는다. *이 문제의 배점은 2점이다.*

체온을 주변 온도보다 더 높게 유지하는 생물들은 내온성이라 부르고, 주변 환경에 체온을 맞추는 생물들은 외온성이라 부른다.

Ⓐ 많은 동물들이 둘 중 그 어느 범주에도 포함되지 않으며, 몇몇은 두 범주의 중간 정도로 체온을 유지하고, 다른 동물들은 체온을 환경보다 훨씬 더 낮게 유지한다.

Ⓒ 많은 내온성 생물들은 털 외피와 고래지방과 같은 특징들이 있어 체온을 충분히 높게 유지한다.

Ⓓ 내부 부피에 비해 표면적이 훨씬 큰 신체 부위가 있어 그들은 열 손실을 방지하는 혈액 순환 시스템을 발달시켰다.

Ⓑ 참치과의 빠르게 헤엄치는 물고기는 유영 근육들이 피부 바로 아래에 집중적으로 위치한다.

Ⓔ 해달은 고래지방을 갖고 있지 않지만, 피부가 물과 직접적으로 접촉하지 않게 막아주는 두꺼운 털 외피를 갖고 있다.

Ⓕ 조간대 생물들이 무생물보다 더 낮은 체온을 갖고 있다는 것은 육지 포유류들이 해양 포유류에 비해 더 낮은 신진대사율을 갖고 있다는 것을 입증한다.

1 **regulate** v 조절[조정]하다, 규제하다 I **metabolism** n 신진대사 I **maintain** v 유지하다 I **relatively** adv 비교적, 상대적으로 I **stable** adj 안정적인, 차분한 I **ambient** adj 주위[주변]의 I **core** n (사물의) 중심부

2 **neatly** adv 적절하게, 깔끔하게, 맵시 있게 I **capable** adj ~ 할 수 있는 I **exception** n (일반적인 상황의) 예외, (법칙을 따르지 않는) 이례[예외] I **distribute** v 분포시키다, 분배[배부]하다 I **evenly** adv 고르게, 반반하게 I **generate** v 발생시키다, 만들어 내다 I **engage** v 관여[참여]하다 I **sustained** adj 지속된, 한결같은

3 **expose** v 노출시키다, 드러내다, 폭로하다 I **circulate** v 순환시키다, 돌아다니다 I **expel** v 배출[방출]하다, 쫓아내다 I **evaporation** n 증발(작용), 발산 I **inanimate** adj 무생물의 I **to one's advantage** ~에게 유리하게 I **absorb** v 흡수하다, 빨아들이다 I **predominant** adj 우세한, 지배적인 I **equator** n 적도

4 **plunge** v 급락하다, 거꾸러지다 I **exacerbate** v 악화시키다 I **extremities** n (pl.) 심장에서 가장 먼 신체 부위, 손발 I **surface** v 수면으로 올라오다 I **considerable** adj 상당한 I **fatal** adj 치명적인 I **tactic** n 전략, 전술 I **outcome** n 결과

5 **stationary** adj 움직이지 않는, 정지된 I **insulating** adj 절연[단열/방음]을 위한 I **rely** v 의지하다, 신뢰하다 I **lack** v 없다, 부족하다 I **incredibly** adv 믿을 수 없을 정도로, 엄청나게 I **accelerated** adj 가속된, 속도가 붙은 I **internal** adj 내부의, 체내의

6 **measure** n 방법, 조치, 정책 I **insufficient** adj 불충분한 I **surface area** 표면적 I **volume** n 부피, 용량, 용적 I **minimize** v 최소화하다 I **aforementioned** adj 앞서 언급한 I **overall** adj 종합[전반]적인, 전체의

Actual Test 02

본서 | P. 85

Passage 1   The Fall of the Mayan Civilization

1. Ⓐ	Inference	6. Ⓓ	Fact
2. Ⓐ	Negative Fact	7. Ⓒ	Vocabulary
3. Ⓒ	Sentence Simplification	8. Ⓑ	Fact
4. Ⓓ	Fact	9. Ⓒ	Insertion
5. Ⓒ	Rhetorical Purpose	10. Ⓒ, Ⓓ, Ⓕ	Summary

Passage 2   Continental Drift

1. Ⓑ	Rhetorical Purpose	6. Ⓐ	Vocabulary
2. Ⓑ	Sentence Simplification	7. Ⓒ	Negative Fact
3. Ⓓ	Fact	8. Ⓓ	Inference
4. Ⓓ	Fact	9. Ⓑ	Insertion
5. Ⓐ	Fact	10. Ⓑ, Ⓓ, Ⓔ	Summary

Passage 3   Altruism in Meerkats

1. Ⓓ	Fact	6. Ⓓ	Inference
2. Ⓑ	Sentence Simplification	7. Ⓑ	Vocabulary
3. Ⓓ	Vocabulary	8. Ⓒ	Negative Fact
4. Ⓐ	Rhetorical Purpose	9. Ⓓ	Insertion
5. Ⓐ	Fact	10. Ⓑ, Ⓒ, Ⓓ	Summary

● 내가 맞은 문제 유형의 개수를 적어 보고 어느 유형에 취약한지 확인해 봅시다.

문제 유형	맞은 개수
Sentence Simplification	3
Fact / Negative Fact	11
Vocabulary	4
Reference	0
Rhetorical Purpose	3
Inference	3
Insertion	3
Summary	3
Category Chart	0
Total	30

The Fall of the Mayan Civilization

1 ➡ The Mayan civilization that once covered much of modern day Guatemala and Southern Mexico was inarguably one of the greatest civilizations ever to exist in Pre-Columbian America. Their settlements date back to around 2,000 BCE, and some existed until the Spanish conquest of the region. They are known for their monumental step-pyramids, stonemasonry, understanding of astronomy and mathematics, and a fully developed hieroglyphic writing system. Their civilization reached its peak during what is called its Classical Period, extending from 250 CE to around 900 CE, when their cities reached their highest state of development. However, their flourishing society suffered a catastrophic collapse at this time from which they never fully recovered. Many theories have been suggested to explain such a sudden decline, including natural disasters, war, and plague. While these may have contributed to the overall decline, the root cause appears to have been an interconnected series of events involving agriculture, conflict, and climate change.

2 ➡ In the Classical Period, the Maya experienced rapid expansion and their population reached into the millions. Most of their large religious and political complexes were built during this time, and their civilization developed into a large politically and economically interconnected society comprised of many small kingdoms and empires. By the 8th century, populations surrounding the central lowlands had reached new peaks of size and density. This was also the area that held the most political influence. Their growing aristocracy, who enjoyed luxuries and the best food, are believed to have expanded rapidly. The outlying kingdoms served as the primary centers for trade, and they brought in goods from throughout Mesoamerica. While relationships with their neighbors were not always peaceful, and warfare did indeed occur, they were generally friendly. The greatest danger to the Maya, although they were probably oblivious to the fact, came from within.

3 ➡ Early in the Classical Period, from about 440 to 660 CE, the area the Maya lived in experienced significantly higher rainfall than it had in the past. This

마야 문명의 몰락

1 ➡ 한때 현재의 과테말라와 멕시코 남부 대부분을 포함했던 마야 문명은 논쟁의 여지없이 콜럼버스가 미 대륙을 발견하기 전에 존재한 가장 위대한 문명 중 하나였다. 그들의 정착지는 기원전 2,000년경까지 거슬러 올라가며, 그 중 일부는 스페인이 그 지역을 점령하기 전까지 존재했다. 그들은 엄청난 계단 피라미드, 석공술, 천문학과 수학에 대한 이해, 그리고 완전히 발달한 상형 문자 체계로 알려져 있다. 그들의 문명은 기원후 250년에서 약 900년까지에 걸친 고전 시대라 불리는 시기에 정점에 달했는데, 그 당시 그들의 도시는 최고의 발전 상태에 이르렀다. 그러나 그들의 번영하는 사회는 이때 다시는 회복할 수 없는 대규모의 심각한 붕괴를 겪었다. 그러한 갑작스런 쇠퇴를 설명하기 위해 자연 재해, 전쟁, 전염병을 비롯해 많은 이론들이 제시되었다. 이 모두가 전체적인 쇠퇴의 원인이 되었을 수도 있지만, 근본 원인은 농업, 갈등, 기후 변화를 포함한 상호 연결된 일련의 사건들인 듯하다.

2 ➡ 고전 시대에 마야인들은 급격한 확장을 경험했고 인구는 수백만에 달했다. 대부분의 거대한 종교, 정치 복합 시설이 이 시기에 건설되었고, 그들의 문명은 많은 작은 왕국과 제국으로 이루어진 정치적, 경제적으로 상호 연결된 하나의 커다란 사회로 발달했다. 8세기에 중앙 저지대를 둘러싼 인구는 크기와 밀도에 있어서 새로운 정점에 달했다. 이곳은 대부분의 정치적 영향력을 가진 지역이기도 했다. 사치를 누리고 최고의 음식을 즐겼던, 증가 추세이던 귀족층이 급격히 늘어난 것으로 생각된다. 외곽의 왕국들은 교역의 중심지 역할을 했으며, 메소아메리카 전 지역으로부터 상품을 들여왔다. 이웃 국가들과의 관계가 언제나 평화롭지는 않았고 전쟁이 실제 발발했지만, 이들은 일반적으로 우호적이었다. 비록 그들은 사실을 의식하지 못했겠지만, 마야인들에게 가장 큰 위협은 내부에서 비롯되었다.

3 ➡ 고전 시대 초기(기원후 약 440년에서 660년)에 마야인들이 살고 있던 지역에는 과거보다 훨씬 많은 비가 내렸다. 이와 같이 길어진 우기는 마야인들이 농업을 확대하고,

extended wetter period allowed them to expand their agriculture and produce unprecedented amounts of food. The food surplus allowed the population to grow, and fueled the civilization's rapid expansion. The Maya used permanent farms and raised terraces for cultivation, and their usual method of crop rotation involved fallow cycles, leaving the land uncultivated in order to allow it to recover. However, the increased rainfall would have meant that the minerals and nutrients in the soil of their farms would be replenished more quickly by the mountain runoff, and the temptation to shorten fallow cycles must have been nearly irresistible in a climate that fostered such growth. In addition, the Maya began cutting down expanses of rainforest to clear land for farming and to provide lumber and firewood, reducing the amount of groundcover. Since they raised little livestock, they were also rapidly depleting the area of the animals they relied on for meat. The Maya were overtaxing the carrying capacity of their environment, but they would not realize this until it was too late.

4 ➡ As their civilization continued to expand throughout the 8th and 9th centuries, the advantageous rainfall began to lessen. As this trend continued, pressures began to grow within Mayan society. The large urban centers with their aristocratic populations were a huge drain on agriculture, so as the output decreased, they had to compensate by importing food. This transferred the burden out onto the surrounding communities, which increased competition and conflict between cities and regions. As the societal and economic divide between the peasants and the aristocrats widened further, the lower classes began to revolt against the established order, and food shortages only worsened the situation. Their whole society was teetering on the brink of an abyss.

5 ➡ Then around 1,000 CE, the already faltering civilization was struck by a true disaster: a prolonged drought struck the southern regions. [■A] The drought was a symptom of a global shift in climate that seriously affected other areas in the world, but for the Mayan civilization it was devastating. [■B] Their practice of clearing forest exacerbated the problem in two ways. The land that had been cleared was poor for farming, and the lack of trees disrupted the normal evaporation cycle. [■C] Therefore, when

전례 없는 양의 식량을 수확할 수 있게 해주었다. 식량 과 잉은 인구가 증가하도록 했으며, 문명의 급속한 발전을 가 속화했다. 마야인들은 경작을 위해 영구적 농장과 높이 올 린 계단식 밭을 이용했고, 그들의 윤작 방법은 휴경 주기를 포함했는데, 그것은 토양이 회복할 수 있도록 경작하지 않 고 묵혀 두는 것이었다. 그러나 늘어난 강수량은 농장 토양 의 광물과 영양분이 산으로부터의 유출로 인해 더 빠르게 보충된다는 것을 의미했을 것이며, 따라서 휴경 주기를 단 축하려는 유혹은 그처럼 성장이 빠른 기후에서는 참기 힘 들었을 것이다. 게다가 마야인들은 농작을 위한 땅을 확보 하고 목재와 땔감을 제공하기 위해 숲을 잘라내기 시작했 고 이것은 지표식물의 양을 감소시켰다. 그들은 가축을 거 의 기르지 않았기 때문에 고기를 얻기 위해 의존했던 동물 이 사는 지역을 빠르게 고갈시켰다. 마야인들은 그들 환경 의 수용력을 넘어 무리하게 사용했지만, 깨달았을 때는 너 무 늦었다.

4 ➡ 마야 문명이 8세기와 9세기에 걸쳐 확장을 지속하 고 있을 때, 이로운 강수량이 줄기 시작했다. 이러한 경향 이 지속되며 마야 사회 내부에서 압박이 커지기 시작했다. 귀족 인구로 이루어진 대형 도시 중심지들은 농업에 있어 서 거대한 고갈 원천이었고, 따라서 생산량이 줄기 시작하 자 식량을 수입함으로써 보충해야 했다. 이는 그 부담을 주 변의 지역 사회에 떠넘겼고, 도시와 지역 간의 경쟁과 갈등 을 증가시켰다. 농민과 귀족 사이의 사회적, 경제적 차이가 더 벌어짐에 따라 하층민들은 기존 질서에 반발하기 시작 하였고, 식량 부족은 상황을 악화시키기만 했다. 사회 전체 가 나락의 구렁텅이 가장자리에서 불안정하게 흔들리고 있 었다.

5 ➡ 그리고 기원후 1,000년경에 이미 흔들리던 문명 은 진정한 재난의 타격을 받았다. 지속된 가뭄이 남부 지 역을 강타했다. [■A] 가뭄은 전 세계의 다른 지역에 심 각하게 영향을 주었던 지구 전체적인 기후 변화의 한 징 후였지만, 마야 문명에 있어서는 대단히 파괴적이었다. [■B] 숲을 개간하는 그들의 행태는 문제를 두 가지 방 식으로 악화시켰다. 개간된 땅은 농업을 하기에는 어 려웠고, 나무 부족은 정상적인 증발 주기를 교란했다. [■C] 따라서 가뭄이 강수량을 25~40퍼센트 정도 감소시 켰을 때 마야인들의 농경 체계는 완전히 유지 불가능하게

the drought reduced rainfall by 25 to 40%, their agricultural system became completely unsustainable. Internal warfare escalated as supplies dwindled, and eventually their whole system collapsed. [■D] The Mayan civilization was ultimately a victim of its own unchecked expansion. The drought did not completely destroy their culture as some of the city states in the north survived and continued to expand, but they too fell after the arrival of the Spanish.

되었다. 내부 전쟁은 공급이 감소함에 따라 증가했고, 결국에는 시스템 전체가 무너졌다. [■D] 결국 마야 문명은 억제되지 않은 확장의 희생자였다. 북쪽의 도시국가 일부가 살아남아 확장을 계속하면서 가뭄은 이들의 문명을 완전히 파괴하지는 않았지만, 이 도시국가들 역시 스페인 사람들의 등장 이후 무너졌다.

---

1. Inference

Based on paragraph 1, what can be inferred about the Mayan civilization?

Ⓐ **Nobody truly knows how the Mayan civilization collapsed.**

Ⓑ The golden age of the Mayan civilization began with the ending of the Classical Period.

Ⓒ Most of the Mayan population lived in cities.

Ⓓ The Mayan civilization eventually recovered from the Spanish conquest.

1.

1단락에 근거하여, 마야 문명에 대해 추론할 수 있는 것은 무엇인가?

Ⓐ 누구도 마야 문명이 어떻게 붕괴되었는지 정확히 알지 못한다.

Ⓑ 마야 문명의 황금기는 고전 시대의 종말과 함께 시작되었다.

Ⓒ 마야 인구의 대부분은 도시에 살았다.

Ⓓ 마야 문명은 결국 스페인 침략으로부터 회복했다.

2. Negative Fact

According to paragraph 2, which of the following is NOT true of the Classical Period?

Ⓐ **It was a period of constant warfare with their neighbors.**

Ⓑ It was a period during which the number of aristocrats grew.

Ⓒ It was a period of flourishing trade.

Ⓓ It was a period during which many buildings were constructed.

2.

2단락에 따르면, 다음 중 고전 시대에 대해 사실이 아닌 것은 무엇인가?

Ⓐ 이웃 국가들과 끊임없는 전쟁이 있던 시기였다.

Ⓑ 귀족의 수가 늘어난 시기였다.

Ⓒ 교역이 번영한 시기였다.

Ⓓ 많은 건물들이 건설된 시기였다.

3. Sentence Simplification

Which of the sentences below best expresses the essential information in the highlighted sentence in the passage? *Incorrect* answer choices change the meaning in important ways or leave out essential information.

Ⓐ The increased rainfall quickly diminished the minerals and nutrients in the soil, so it was hard for them to shorten their fallow cycles.

Ⓑ The farmers resisted the temptation to shorten fallow cycles because the increased rainfall fostered growth on the farms where minerals and nutrients were replenished.

3.

다음 중 지문의 음영 표시된 문장의 핵심 정보를 가장 잘 표현한 문장은 무엇인가? 오답은 의미를 크게 왜곡하거나 핵심 정보를 누락하고 있다.

Ⓐ 강수량의 증가는 토양의 광물과 영양분을 빠르게 감소시켰고, 따라서 그들이 휴경 주기를 단축하는 것은 어려웠다.

Ⓑ 강수량의 증가가 광물과 영양분이 보충된 농장의 작물 성장을 도왔기 때문에 농부들은 휴경 주기를 단축하고자 하는 유혹을 이겨냈다.

© The farmers probably wanted to shorten rest periods because the increased rainfall replenished their farms and made it easier to grow crops.

Ⓓ The farmers began to use shorter rest periods for their farms because the soil was washed away by water coming from the surrounding countryside.

4. Fact
According to paragraph 3, what is one possible cause for the increase in population?

Ⓐ Significantly higher rainfall

Ⓑ Shorter fallow cycle

Ⓒ Reduced expanses of rainforest

Ⓓ **Increased food production**

5. Rhetorical Purpose
What is the main purpose of paragraph 4?

Ⓐ To demonstrate the negative effects of reckless expansion

Ⓑ To discuss the effects of rainfall on competition between large urban centers

Ⓒ **To explain what began the downfall of the Mayan civilization**

Ⓓ To highlight the social divide between peasants and aristocrats

6. Fact
According to paragraph 4, what was the likely result of importing food?

Ⓐ It increased the number of aristocrats.

Ⓑ The farmers began to revolt against the traders.

Ⓒ It caused conflicts amongst those in large urban centers.

Ⓓ **The social divide between the upper class and lower class widened.**

7. Vocabulary
The word "exacerbated" in paragraph 5 is closest in meaning to

Ⓐ evoked

Ⓑ placated

Ⓒ **aggravated**

Ⓓ controlled

© 강수량의 증가가 농장을 채워주고, 작물이 쉽게 자라게 해주었기 때문에 농부들은 아마 휴경 주기를 단축하고 싶어했을 것이다.

Ⓓ 토양이 주변의 시골 지역에서 오는 물에 씻겨나갔기 때문에 농부들은 농장에 더 짧은 휴경 주기를 두기 시작했다.

4.
3단락에 따르면, 인구 증가의 원인이 될 수 있는 것은 무엇인가?

Ⓐ 훨씬 많은 강수량

Ⓑ 더 짧은 휴경 주기

Ⓒ 감소한 우림 지역

Ⓓ 증가한 식량 생산량

5.
4단락의 주요 목적은 무엇인가?

Ⓐ 부주의한 확장의 부정적인 결과를 입증하기 위해

Ⓑ 대형 도심지 간의 경쟁에 미친 강수량의 영향을 논의하는 것

Ⓒ 마야 문명의 몰락이 무엇에 의해 시작되었는지 설명하는 것

Ⓓ 농민과 귀족 간의 사회적 차이를 강조하는 것

6.
4단락에 따르면, 식량을 수입한 결과는 무엇인가?

Ⓐ 귀족의 수를 증가시켰다.

Ⓑ 농부들이 상인들에게 반발하기 시작했다.

Ⓒ 대형 도심지에 사는 사람들 간의 갈등을 야기했다.

Ⓓ 상류층과 하층 계급 간의 사회적 차이가 커졌다.

7.
5단락의 단어 "exacerbated(악화시켰다)"와 의미상 가장 가까운 것은?

Ⓐ 불러일으켰다

Ⓑ 달랬다

Ⓒ 악화시켰다

Ⓓ 억제했다

8. Fact

According to paragraph 5, why was the drought especially devastating for the Mayan civilization?

Ⓐ It was a symptom of a global shift in climate.

Ⓑ **Deforestation worsened the drought.**

Ⓒ The Maya fought for water.

Ⓓ It was a result of unchecked expansion.

9. Insertion

Look at the four squares [■] that indicate where the following sentence could be added to the passage.

Therefore, when the drought reduced rainfall by 25 to 40%, their agricultural system became completely unsustainable.

Where would the sentence best fit? [■C]

10. Summary

Directions: An introductory sentence for a brief summary of the passage is provided below. Complete the summary by selecting the THREE answer choices that express the most important ideas in the passage. Some sentences do not belong in the summary because they express ideas that are not presented in the passage or are minor ideas in the passage. *This question is worth 2 points.*

While there are many theories that attempt to explain the fall of the Mayan civilization, there seems to have been several interlinked factors that led to the sudden decline of one of the greatest civilizations ever to exist in Pre-Columbian America.

Ⓒ With less rainfall, the farms were not able to produce enough food, resulting in food shortages that applied critical pressure to Mayan society.

Ⓓ The drought was the final straw for the weakened Mayan society, completely collapsing their already dysfunctional agricultural system.

Ⓕ Relying heavily on increased rainfall, the Maya overtaxed the natural resources of the land.

Ⓐ The Maya reached the peak of their civilization by the 9th century CE.

Ⓑ The widening gap and deepening conflict between the aristocrats worsened the economic situation.

Ⓔ The prolonged drought forced the Maya to import food from surrounding communities.

8.

5단락에 따르면, 왜 가뭄은 특히 마야 문명에 대단히 파괴적이었는가?

Ⓐ 그것은 전 지구적인 기후 변화의 한 징후였다.

Ⓑ 삼림 파괴가 가뭄을 악화시켰다.

Ⓒ 마야인들이 물을 위해 싸웠다.

Ⓓ 그것은 억제되지 않은 확장의 결과였다.

9.

지문에 다음 문장이 들어갈 수 있는 위치를 나타내는 네 개의 사각형[■]을 확인하시오.

따라서 가뭄이 강수량을 25~40퍼센트 정도 감소시켰을 때, 마야인들의 농경 체계는 완전히 유지 불가능하게 되었다.

이 문장이 들어가기에 가장 적합한 곳은? [■C]

10.

지시문: 지문을 간략하게 요약한 글의 첫 문장이 아래 제시되어 있다. 지문의 가장 중요한 내용을 표현하는 세 개의 선택지를 골라 요약문을 완성하시오. 일부 문장들은 지문에 제시되지 않았거나 지문의 지엽적인 내용을 나타내기 때문에 요약문에 포함되지 않는다. *이 문제의 배점은 2점이다.*

마야 문명의 몰락을 설명하고자 하는 많은 이론들이 있지만, 콜럼버스가 미 대륙을 발견하기 전에 존재한 가장 위대한 문명 중 하나였던 마야 문명의 갑작스런 쇠퇴에는 상호 연관된 여러 가지 요소들이 있는 것으로 보인다.

Ⓒ 강수량이 적어지자 농장들은 충분한 식량을 생산할 수 없었고, 그것은 마야 사회에 결정적인 압력을 가한 식량 부족의 결과로 이어졌다.

Ⓓ 가뭄은 약해진 마야 사회의 결정타였으며 이미 제대로 기능하지 못하는 농경 체계를 완전히 무너뜨렸다.

Ⓕ 마야인들은 증가한 강수량에 크게 의존하며 토양의 천연 자원을 무리하게 사용했다.

Ⓐ 마야인들은 기원후 9세기에 문명의 정점에 달했다.

Ⓑ 귀족 간의 넓어지는 격차와 깊어지는 갈등은 경제적 상황을 악화시켰다.

Ⓔ 길어진 가뭄은 마야인들이 주변 지역에서 식량을 수입하게 만들었다.

1 cover ⓥ ~에 이르다, 포함하다, 덮다 | inarguably adv 논쟁의 여지가 없이, 명백하게 | settlement ⓝ 정착지 | conquest ⓝ 정복 | monumental adj 기념비적인, 엄청난, 대단한 | understanding ⓝ 이해 | hieroglyphic adj 상형 문자의 | flourishing adj 번영하는, 성대한 | catastrophic adj 파멸의, 비극적인 | collapse ⓝ 붕괴 | decline ⓝ 쇠퇴, 감소, 하락, 축소 | natural disaster 자연 재해 | plague ⓝ 전염병 | contribute ⓥ ~의 원인이 되다, 기여하다 | interconnected adj 상호 연결된 | conflict ⓝ 갈등, 충돌

2 expansion ⓝ 확장, 발전 | comprise ⓥ ~으로 구성되다[이루어지다] | aristocracy ⓝ 귀족(계층) | outlying adj 외딴, 외진, 외곽의 | oblivious adj ~을 감지하지 못하는

3 extended adj (보통 때나 예상보다) 길어진[늘어난] | unprecedented adj 전례 없는 | surplus ⓝ 과잉, 잉여 | fuel ⓥ 부채질하다 | cultivation ⓝ 재배, 경작 | replenish ⓥ 보충하다, 다시 채우다 | irresistible adj 저항할 수 없는, 너무 유혹적인 | foster ⓥ 조성하다, 발전시키다 | deplete ⓥ 대폭 감소시키다, 고갈시키다 | capacity ⓝ 수용력

4 advantageous adj 이로운, 유리한 | drain ⓝ (많은 시간·돈 등을) 고갈시키는[잡아먹는] 것 | compensate ⓥ 보상하다, 보충하다 | order ⓝ 질서

5 prolonged adj 오래 계속되는, 장기적인 | devastating adj 대단히 파괴적인 | exacerbate ⓥ 악화시키다 | disrupt ⓥ 방해하다, 지장을 주다 | unsustainable adj 지속 불가능한 | escalate ⓥ 확대[증가/악화]되다 | dwindle ⓥ 점점 줄어들다 | unchecked adj 억제하지[손을 쓰지] 않고 놔 둔

Passage 2

Continental Drift

1 ➡ During the Age of Exploration, European travelers sailed the world's oceans searching for new land and resources to exploit. During these great voyages of discovery, their crews usually included cartographers and scientists who documented the regions where they traveled. Over the centuries, the cartographers' maps gradually became more complete and accurate, allowing other Europeans to learn about the shape of the world, and some startling ideas began to develop. Initially, the famous intellectual Francis Bacon noted the similarity in shape between the eastern coast of South America and the western coast of Africa, which he thought meant that they had been formed by similar processes. As the scientists collected specimens of organisms they encountered, they marveled at the diversity of life, but when they compared the specimens from different landmasses, they were surprised to see how similar some of them were. In fact, many were identical, despite being collected from different continents. These observations formed the foundation for the theory of continental drift.

2 ➡ One such explorer was Joseph D. Hooker, a botanist who traveled to Antarctica as a ship's surgeon on Ross's expedition. He traveled extensively throughout the Southern Hemisphere and compiled many books about the flora of New Zealand, Australia, and Tasmania. Later, Charles

대륙이동설

1 ➡ 대항해 시대에 유럽 탐험가들은 새로운 땅과 개발할 자원을 찾기 위해 전 세계의 바다를 항해했다. 이 위대한 발견의 항해 중에, 선원들에는 그들이 탐험한 지역을 기록하는 지도 제작자들과 과학자들이 포함되어 있었다. 수세기에 걸쳐 지도 제작자들의 지도는 점차 더욱 완전해지고 정확해졌는데, 이것은 다른 유럽인들로 하여금 세계의 형태에 대해 알게 만들었고 이로 인해 놀랄 만한 아이디어들이 발달하기 시작했다. 처음에 저명한 지식인인 프랜시스 베이컨은 남미의 동쪽 해안과 아프리카의 서쪽 해안 사이의 형태상의 유사점을 알아차렸고, 그는 그것들이 비슷한 과정을 통해 형성되었다는 것을 의미한다고 생각했다. 과학자들은 그들이 마주하게 된 생명체의 표본들을 수집하면서 생명의 다양함에 경이로움을 느꼈지만 그들은 각기 다른 땅덩어리에서 수집한 표본들을 비교하면서 표본 중 일부가 매우 유사한 것에 놀라워했다. 실제로, 다른 대륙에서 수집되었음에도 불구하고 많은 것들이 동일했다. 이러한 관찰 결과들은 대륙이동설의 기초를 형성했다.

2 ➡ 그러한 탐험가 중 한 명인 조셉 D. 후커는 로스 탐험대에서 배의 의사로서 남극대륙을 탐험한 식물학자였다. 그는 남반구 전체를 광범위하게 탐험했고 뉴질랜드, 호주, 그리고 태즈매니아의 식물에 대한 많은 책을 편집했다. 후에, 찰스 다윈은 자신이 남미에서 수집한 식물을 분류하기 위해 후커를 초대했는데, 그러한 식물 중 일부는 그가 초기

Darwin invited him to classify the plants that he had collected in South America, some of which were very similar to ones he had found on earlier voyages. This led him to surmise that the major landmasses of the Southern Hemisphere had at one point been connected, although exactly how he could not be certain. He proposed that they had originally formed one supercontinent that had been loosely connected by land bridges that had since disappeared due to either geologic forces or climatic events. Although they agreed upon many things, Darwin discounted this theory and said that the similarity was due to dispersal: the plants had migrated along ocean currents. Still, the idea of one southern continent had been proposed.

3 ➡ This concept was further solidified by Austrian geologist Eduard Suess. Through his studies, he became convinced that India, South America, Australia, Africa and Antarctica had all once been connected. He was led to this conclusion by examples of glossopteris fossils that had been found in all of those locations. He developed the theory that the oceans had changed levels and locations over time and that this could be mapped across all of the continents. He also imagined a fragmented supercontinent connected by gateways that had disappeared beneath the waves. He named this supercontinent Gondwanaland after the Gondwana region in central India, which had similar geologic formations and fossils compared to the other areas. However, his theories were based upon the concept that the Earth is cooling and contracting, creating mountain ranges and relocating oceans; a theory that was later disproven.

4 ➡ In the early 20th century, Alfred Wegener also noted how the continents appeared to fit together like a giant puzzle. He believed that the continents had all once been a single landmass that had broken apart and drifted apart from, and in some cases back into, each other. He analyzed continental shelves on both sides of the Atlantic, looking for geologic structures, rock types, and fossils, and found that they were quite similar. He published a paper detailing his theory of continental drift, but his evidence was observational and failed to answer an important question. What was the mechanism causing the drift? Without a clear cause, much of the scientific

탐험에서 발견한 것들과 매우 유사했다. 이것은 후커로 하여금 비록 어떻게인지는 정확히 몰라도, 남반구의 주요 땅덩어리들이 한때 연결되어 있었다고 추정하게 만들었다. 그는 그러한 땅덩어리들이 지질학적 힘이나 기후적 변화에 의해 지금은 사라진 지협들로 느슨하게 연결되어 있던 하나의 초대륙을 원래 형성하고 있었다고 주장했다. 비록 그들은 많은 것에 동의했지만, 다윈은 이 이론을 무시하였고 그러한 유사성은 확산에 기인한 것이라고 말했다. 확산은 식물들이 해류를 따라 이동했다는 것을 말한다. 그러나 여전히, 하나의 남쪽 대륙에 대한 가능성이 제안되었다.

3 ➡ 더 나아가 이 개념은 오스트리아의 지질학자 에두아르트 쥐스에 의해 강화되었다. 연구를 통해, 그는 인도, 남미, 호주, 아프리카와 남극대륙이 모두 한때 연결되어 있었음을 확신하게 되었다. 그는 위에 언급한 모든 장소에서 발견된 글로소프테리스 화석의 표본을 토대로 이러한 결론에 이르렀다. 그는 대양들이 시간을 따라 수위와 위치를 바꾸었으며 이것이 모든 대륙에서 발견될 수 있다는 이론으로 발전시켰다. 그는 또한 파도 밑으로 사라진 출입 통로로 연결된 조각난 초대륙을 상상했다. 그는 이 초대륙을 중앙 인도의 곤드와나 지역의 이름을 따서 곤드와나 대륙이라고 명명했는데, 그 지역은 다른 지역과 비교해 유사한 지질학적 형성 과정과 화석을 가지고 있었다. 그러나 그의 이론은 지구가 식어가고 수축하며, 산맥을 형성하고 대양을 재배치한다는 가설에 기초하고 있었는데, 이 가설은 후에 틀렸음이 입증되었다.

4 ➡ 20세기 초에 알프레트 베게너 역시 어떻게 대륙들이 마치 하나의 큰 퍼즐처럼 맞아떨어지는지에 대해 주목했다. 그는 대륙들이 한때 하나의 큰 땅덩어리였는데 쪼개지고 멀리 떨어졌다가, 어떤 경우에는 다시 붙었다고 믿었다. 그는 대서양의 양쪽 대륙붕을 분석하여 지질학적 구조, 암석 형태와 화석을 찾았고 그들이 매우 비슷하다는 것을 알아냈다. 그는 자신의 대륙이동설을 상세히 설명한 논문을 발표했지만, 그의 증거는 관측상의 것이었고 중요한 질문에 답하는 데 실패했다. 이동을 야기하는 메커니즘은 무엇인가? 확실한 원인이 없어서 대부분의 과학계는 그의 이론을 무시했다. 그들은 해저 지각이 너무 딱딱해서 대륙이 해저 지각 사이를 이동할 수 없다고 믿었다. 이 이론을 계속 추구한 과학자는 남아프리카의 지질학자 알렉산더 두 토이

community ignored his theory. They believed that the seafloor crust was too solid for the continents to move through it. One scientist who pursued the theory was Alexander du Toit, a South African geologist. He traveled extensively throughout Africa and South America, locating and documenting many geologic features that showed the two continents had not only formed similarly, but had once been a single landmass. This was seen as a very significant find and bolstered the theory of continental drift.

5 ➡ [■A] The mechanism behind continental drift was discovered in the latter half of the 20th century. The development of sonar allowed for much more accurate mapping of the seafloor. [■B] This revealed that the Mid Atlantic Ridge was not simply a mountain range extending the length of the ocean. Instead, it is a zone of seafloor spreading, where new crust wells up from within the Earth. [■C] In addition, many trenches were revealed to be areas where crust is plunging back down into the Earth. [■D] Satellite mapping has allowed scientists to confirm that the Earth's surface is not a single solid crust, but rather a complex arrangement of crust plates that float on the mantle below and are constantly moving. This process is called plate tectonics, and it proves that the continents were once all one, and that they did indeed separate and migrate as so many scientists had theorized in the past.

였다. 그는 아프리카와 남미를 광범위하게 여행하며, 두 대륙이 비슷하게 형성되었을 뿐만 아니라, 한때 하나의 땅덩어리였다는 지질학적 특징들을 찾아내고 기록했다. 이것은 매우 중요한 발견으로 여겨졌으며 대륙이동설을 강화했다.

5 ➡ [■A] 대륙이동의 메커니즘은 20세기 후반에 발견되었다. 수중음파탐지기의 발달은 보다 더 정확한 해저 지도화를 가능하게 만들었다. [■B] 이것은 대서양 중앙산령이 그저 대양 길이만큼 뻗어 있는 산맥이 아님을 밝혀냈다. 대신, 그것은 새로운 지각이 지구 내부에서 솟아오르는 해저 확장 구역이다. [■C] 게다가 많은 해구는 지각이 지구 내부로 다시 들어가는 지역인 것으로 밝혀졌다. [■D] 인공위성 지도 제작은 과학자들로 하여금 지구 표면이 하나의 단단한 껍질이 아니라 맨틀 위에 떠 있으며 끊임없이 움직이는 지각판들이 복잡하게 배치되어 있는 것이라고 확신하게 만들었다. 이러한 과정은 판구조론이라 불리며, 이것은 과거에 수많은 과학자들이 이론으로 제시했던 것처럼 대륙들이 한때 하나였으며, 분리되었고 이동했다는 것을 입증한다.

---

1. **Rhetorical Purpose**

Why does the author mention "Francis Bacon" in paragraph 1?

(A) To suggest that Bacon was a gifted cartographer

(B) **To show where the idea of one great landmass may have come from**

(C) To point out that Bacon was not qualified to speak on such matters

(D) To question whether maps were good enough to make such an observation

2. **Sentence Simplification**

Which of the sentences below best expresses the essential information in the highlighted sentence in the passage? *Incorrect* answer choices change the meaning in important ways or leave out essential information.

1.

1단락에서 글쓴이가 "프랜시스 베이컨"을 언급하는 이유는 무엇인가?

(A) 베이컨이 재능이 뛰어난 지도 제작자라는 것을 제안하기 위해

(B) 하나의 큰 대륙이라는 생각이 어디서 왔는지 보여주기 위해

(C) 베이컨이 그러한 문제에 대해 말할 자격이 없다는 것을 지적하기 위해

(D) 지도들이 그러한 관찰을 하기에 충분했는지 의문점을 제시하기 위해

2.

다음 중 지문의 음영 표시된 문장의 핵심 정보를 가장 잘 표현한 문장은 무엇인가? 오답은 의미를 크게 왜곡하거나 핵심 정보를 누락하고 있다.

Ⓐ As the scientists collected specimens they encountered on different landmasses, they were surprised by their diversity.

Ⓑ **When scientists compared specimens of organisms they collected, they were amazed at both the diversity and similarity of specimens from different landmasses.**

Ⓒ When the scientists compared specimens of organisms they collected from different landmasses, they were surprised to see they were similar to those from the ocean.

Ⓓ While the scientists collected specimens of organisms, they were no longer surprised to see the similarities between specimens from different landmasses.

3. Fact

According to paragraph 2, Hooker's ideas were novel because

Ⓐ he proposed the possibility that the Earth's crust could move.

Ⓑ he had definitive proof that the southern continents had been connected into one.

Ⓒ the standard by which he classified the plants from South America was strict.

Ⓓ **he argued that land bridges had enabled similar plants to spread to different areas.**

4. Fact

According to paragraph 3, why did Suess name the hypothetical supercontinent after Gondwana?

Ⓐ Gondwana is an area where the Earth had clearly cooled and contracted.

Ⓑ Gondwana represented a legendary supercontinent in central India.

Ⓒ He believed that the region was located in the center of the supercontinent.

Ⓓ **Geologic features and fossils in Gondwana gave him clues for the supercontinent.**

5. Fact

According to paragraph 4, why was Wegener's theory disregarded by other scientists?

Ⓐ **It could not provide a clear explanation of what caused continental drift.**

Ⓑ It was against the dominant scientific paradigm of the time.

Ⓐ 과학자들은 각기 다른 땅덩어리에서 마주한 표본들을 수집하면서 그것들의 다양성에 놀라워했다.

Ⓑ 과학자들은 수집한 생명체의 표본들을 비교했을 때, 각기 다른 땅덩어리에서 나온 표본들의 다양성과 유사성에 놀라워했다.

Ⓒ 과학자들은 각기 다른 땅덩어리에서 수집한 생명체의 표본들을 비교했을 때, 그것들이 대양의 것들과 유사하다는 점에 놀라워했다.

Ⓓ 과학자들은 생명체의 표본들을 수집했지만 각기 다른 땅덩어리에서 나온 표본들 간의 유사성에 더 이상 놀라지 않았다.

3.

2단락에 따르면, 후커의 아이디어가 참신했던 이유는?

Ⓐ 그는 지구의 지각이 움직일 가능성을 제안했다.

Ⓑ 그는 남반구의 대륙들이 하나로 연결되어 있었다는 결정적인 증거를 가지고 있었다.

Ⓒ 그가 남아메리카의 식물을 분류한 기준이 엄격했다.

Ⓓ 그는 지협이 유사한 식물들로 하여금 다른 지역으로 퍼질 수 있게 해주었다고 주장했다.

4.

3단락에 따르면, 쥐스가 가상의 초대륙을 곤드와나의 이름을 따서 명명한 이유는 무엇인가?

Ⓐ 곤드와나는 지구가 명백히 냉각되고 수축한 지역이었다.

Ⓑ 곤드와나가 중앙 인도의 전설적인 초대륙을 대표했다.

Ⓒ 그 지역이 초대륙의 중앙에 위치했다고 믿었다.

Ⓓ 곤드와나의 지질학적 특징과 화석들이 그에게 초대륙에 대한 실마리를 주었다.

5.

4단락에 따르면, 베게너의 이론이 다른 과학자들의 인정을 받지 못한 이유는 무엇인가?

Ⓐ 무엇이 대륙 이동을 야기했는지에 대한 확실한 설명을 제공하지 못했다.

Ⓑ 당시의 우세한 과학 패러다임에 맞서는 것이었다.

Ⓒ It was thought to be theoretically impossible despite all the evidence he had collected.

Ⓓ It was supported by pieces of evidence that were inconsistent with one another.

6. Vocabulary

The word "spreading" in paragraph 5 is closest in meaning to

Ⓐ **expansion**

Ⓑ circulation

Ⓒ separation

Ⓓ acceleration

7. Negative Fact

All of the following are mentioned in paragraph 5 EXCEPT

Ⓐ the way sonar helped the process of mapping.

Ⓑ the role of satellite mapping in researching the Earth's surface.

Ⓒ **the mineral composition of the crust.**

Ⓓ the mechanism behind plate tectonics.

8. Inference

Which of the following can be inferred from paragraph 5?

Ⓐ Only a few scientists in the past had the foresight to predict the future.

Ⓑ It sometimes requires time for an innovative idea to be widely accepted.

Ⓒ Some evidence has recently been discovered to refute the concept of tectonic plates.

Ⓓ **With advances in technology, it became possible to support the continental drift theory.**

9. Insertion

Look at the four squares [■] that indicate where the following sentence could be added to the passage.

This revealed that the Mid Atlantic Ridge was not simply a mountain range extending the length of the ocean.

Where would the sentence best fit? [■ B]

10. Summary

Directions: An introductory sentence for a brief summary of the passage is provided below. Complete the summary by selecting the THREE answer choices that express the most important ideas in the passage. Some sentences do not belong in the summary because they express ideas that are not presented in the passage or are minor ideas in the passage. *This question is worth 2 points.*

Ⓒ 그가 수집한 모든 증거들에도 불구하고 이론적으로 불가능한 것으로 여겨졌다.

Ⓓ 서로 불일치하는 증거들로 뒷받침되었다.

6.

5단락의 단어 "spreading(확장)"과 의미상 가장 가까운 것은?

Ⓐ 확장

Ⓑ 순환

Ⓒ 분리

Ⓓ 가속

7.

다음 중 5단락에서 언급되지 않은 것은?

Ⓐ 수중음파탐지기가 지도 제작 과정에 도움이 된 방법

Ⓑ 지구 표면의 연구에 있어 인공위성 지도 제작의 역할

Ⓒ 지각의 광물 조성

Ⓓ 판구조론의 메커니즘

8.

5단락에서 추론할 수 있는 것은 무엇인가?

Ⓐ 과거에 몇몇 과학자들만이 미래를 예측하는 선견지명을 가졌다.

Ⓑ 때때로 혁신적인 생각이 널리 받아들여지기까지는 시간이 걸린다.

Ⓒ 판구조론을 반박하는 증거들이 최근 발견되었다.

Ⓓ 기술의 발달로 인해 대륙이동설을 뒷받침하는 것이 가능해졌다.

9.

지문에 다음 문장이 들어갈 수 있는 위치를 나타내는 네 개의 사각형[■]을 확인하시오.

이것은 대서양 중앙산령이 그저 대양 길이만큼 뻗어 있는 산맥이 아님을 밝혀냈다.

이 문장이 들어가기에 가장 적합한 곳은? [■ B]

10.

지시문: 지문을 간략하게 요약한 글의 첫 문장이 아래 제시되어 있다. 지문의 가장 중요한 내용을 표현하는 세 개의 선택지를 골라 요약문을 완성하시오. 일부 문장들은 지문에 제시되지 않았거나 지문의 지엽적인 내용을 나타내기 때문에 요약문에 포함되지 않는다. *이 문제의 배점은 2점이다.*

Although it is widely accepted as fact today, the theory of continental drift faced strong opposition throughout its development.

B When the supercontinent hypothesis was first proposed, it was dismissed by most contemporary scientists due to lack of detailed evidence.

D The research and discoveries of Wegener and du Toit contributed to verifying the theory of continental drift.

E The development of science and technology helped reveal the mechanism behind continental drift.

A It was early European travelers who figured out the connection between the fossils they had found and the supercontinent Gondwana.

C Charles Darwin was one of the scientists who presumed that different continents had once formed one large landmass.

F Currents and winds dispersed the seeds and spores of plants, causing similar plant specimens to be found all over the world.

비록 오늘날에는 사실로서 널리 받아들여지고 있지만, 대륙이동설은 그 발달 과정 내내 강한 반대에 직면했다.

B 초대륙 가설이 처음 제시되었을 때, 대부분의 당대 과학자들은 자세한 증거 부족을 이유로 그것을 무시했다.

D 베게너와 두 토이의 연구와 발견은 대륙이동설을 입증하는 데 공헌했다.

E 과학과 기술의 발달은 대륙 이동의 메커니즘을 밝히는 데 도움이 되었다.

A 발견한 화석들과 초대륙 곤드와나의 연결성을 알아낸 것은 초기 유럽 탐험가들이었다.

C 찰스 다윈은 여러 다른 대륙들이 한때 하나의 큰 땅덩어리를 이루고 있었다는 것을 가정한 과학자 중 하나였다.

F 조류와 바람은 식물의 씨와 포자를 확산시켜 비슷한 식물 표본이 전 세계에 걸쳐 발견되도록 야기했다.

어휘

1 **exploit** ⓥ 활용[이용]하다, 개발하다 **| discovery** ⓝ 발견 **| cartographer** ⓝ 지도 제작자 **| document** ⓥ 기록하다 **| startling** 〔adj〕 깜짝 놀랄, 아주 놀라운 **| initially** 〔adv〕 처음에 **| intellectual** ⓝ 지식인 **| specimen** ⓝ 표본, 견본 **| diversity** ⓝ 다양성 **| landmass** ⓝ 땅덩어리, 대륙 **| observation** ⓝ 관찰 (결과) **| foundation** ⓝ 기반, 근거, 기초

2 **botanist** ⓝ 식물학자 **| extensively** 〔adv〕 널리, 광범위하게 **| hemisphere** ⓝ 반구 **| compile** ⓥ 엮다, 편집하다 **| classify** ⓥ 분류[구분]하다 **| surmise** ⓥ 추측[추정]하다 **| propose** ⓥ 제안[제의]하다 **| loosely** 〔adv〕 느슨하게, 헐겁게 **| geologic** 〔adj〕 지질학의, 지질의 **| force** ⓝ 힘, 물리력 **| climatic** 〔adj〕 기후의 **| discount** ⓥ 무시하다 **| dispersal** ⓝ 확산, 분산 **| migrate** ⓥ 이동하다

3 **solidify** ⓥ 굳히다, 굳어지다 **| geologist** ⓝ 지질학자 **| map** ⓥ (배치, 구조 등에 대한 정보를) 발견하다[보여주다] **| fragmented** 〔adj〕 조각난, 분열된, 조직이 파괴된 **| disappear** ⓥ 사라지다 **| formation** ⓝ 형성 (과정), 형성물 **| cool** ⓥ 식히다 **| contract** ⓥ 수축하다 **| disprove** ⓥ 틀렸음을 입증하다

4 **analyze** ⓥ 분석하다 **| detail** ⓥ 상세히 알리다[열거하다] **| observational** 〔adj〕 관측상의, 실측적인 **| ignore** ⓥ 무시하다 **| seafloor** ⓝ 해저 **| pursue** ⓥ 추구하다, 계속하다 **| bolster** ⓥ 북돋우다, 강화[개선]하다

5 **spreading** ⓝ 확장 **| reveal** ⓥ 드러내다, 밝히다 **| plunge** ⓥ 떨어지다, 돌진하다 **| confirm** ⓥ 사실임을 보여주다[확인해 주다] **| arrangement** ⓝ 배치, 배열 **| theorize** ⓥ 이론을 제시하다[세우다]

Altruism in Meerkats

1 ➡ Meerkats are small members of the mongoose family that live in the Kalahari and Namib Deserts of southern Africa. Scientists have studied them for centuries due to their complex societal structure and their altruism, which they practice to a level not often seen in nature. Meerkats breed cooperatively, which means that a group will consist of a dominant breeding pair and up to 40 male and female assistants who do not breed. These assistants spend most of their time taking care of the young by feeding them, training them, and protecting them from danger. As a social predator, it is not unusual that meerkats should do these things as a group, but the extent they carry this behavior to is remarkable.

2 ➡ Meerkats are primarily insectivores, but they will also eat small reptiles, mammals, fungi, and occasionally birds. The majority of the group will usually go out to gather food together, leaving a few to guard the young. Once the pack locates prey, it is difficult for that animal to escape as meerkats are extremely fast and excellent diggers. [■A] Surprisingly, one of their preferred prey animals is scorpions. [■B] While many members of the mongoose family are immune to various snake and insect venoms, it is unclear how much immunity meerkats possess, but this does not deter them. [■C] When a meerkat pounces on a scorpion, the arachnid often has no time to prepare a strike, and the meerkat circumvents any attack by swiftly biting off the scorpion's stinger. [■D] Then, it uses sand to wash away any venom that may remain on the scorpion's exoskeleton. The meerkat can then devour the disarmed creature at its leisure, or use it as a teaching tool for the young.

3 ➡ Young meerkats feed on milk like any other mammal as infants, but that milk is not always produced by their mother. If the mother is away hunting, other females will actually lactate to feed the infant young. Once they are weaned, however, they must be taught to forage with the adults. To teach them how to hunt dangerous prey like scorpions or centipedes, the adults will start with dead and disarmed prey. Once the young learn how to eat solid food, they will give them prey that has been disarmed

미어캣의 이타주의

1 ➡ 미어캣은 몽구스과에 속하는 작은 동물로, 아프리카 남부의 칼라하리 사막과 나미브 사막에 서식한다. 과학자들은 미어캣의 복잡한 사회 구조와 자연에서 흔히 볼 수 없는 수준의 이타주의 때문에 수 세기 동안 이들을 연구해왔다. 미어캣은 공동으로 새끼를 기르는데, 이는 한 무리가 번식하는 지배적인 한 쌍과 약 40마리의 번식하지 않는 수컷과 암컷 보조들로 이루어져 있다는 것이다. 이 보조들은 대부분의 시간을 새끼들을 먹이고 훈련시키고 위험으로부터 그들을 보호하며 지낸다. 사회적 포식자로서 미어캣이 이러한 것들을 집단적으로 하는 것은 그리 특이한 것이 아니지만, 그들이 이러한 행동을 행하는 범위는 놀랄 만하다.

2 ➡ 미어캣은 주로 곤충을 먹지만, 작은 파충류, 포유류, 버섯, 때로는 새도 먹는다. 무리의 대다수는 보통 함께 나가 먹이를 수집하고, 몇 마리가 남아 새끼를 보호한다. 일단 무리가 먹이를 발견하면 그 동물이 도망가는 것은 어려운데, 미어캣이 매우 빠르고 훌륭한 땅파기 기술자이기 때문이다. [■A] 놀랍게도 미어캣이 좋아하는 먹이 중 하나는 전갈이다. [■B] 몽구스과의 많은 동물들이 다양한 뱀과 곤충의 독에 대한 면역력이 있지만, 미어캣이 얼마만큼의 면역력을 가지고 있는지는 확실치 않다. 그러나 이것이 미어캣을 단념시키지는 않는다. [■C] 미어캣이 전갈을 덮치면 그 거미류 동물은 보통 공격을 준비할 시간이 없고, 미어캣은 전갈의 침을 빠르게 물어뜯어 공격을 피한다. [■D] 그리고 나서, 그것은 전갈의 외골격에 남아 있을지도 모르는 독을 씻어버리기 위해 모래를 이용한다. 그런 다음 미어캣은 그 무력해진 생물체를 느긋하게 집어삼키거나 새끼를 가르치기 위한 도구로 사용할 수 있다.

3 ➡ 어린 미어캣은 젖먹이일 때 다른 포유동물들처럼 젖을 먹지만, 그 젖이 항상 어미로부터 나오는 것은 아니다. 만약 어미가 사냥을 하러 나가면 다른 암컷이 젖먹이 새끼를 먹이기 위해 실제로 젖을 준비한다. 그러나 새끼들이 일단 젖을 떼면 그들은 다 자란 미어캣들과 함께 먹이를 찾는 법을 배워야 한다. 전갈이나 지네 같은 위험한 먹이를 사냥하는 법을 가르치기 위해 성체 미어캣은 죽거나 무력해진 먹이를 가지고 시작한다. 일단 새끼들이 딱딱한 먹이를 먹는 법을 배우게 되면 성체 미어캣은 새끼들에게 무력화되었지만 여전히 살아 있는 먹이를 준다. 새끼들이 자신의 먹

but remains very much alive. After they get used to killing their own food, the adults will then show them how to remove the stinger. At that point, it becomes the young animals' turn, and they either succeed or receive a painful and potentially fatal wound. Apart from this kind of training, the adults normally go to great lengths to protect all of the members of their clan.

4 ➡ While most of the clan goes foraging or tends to the young, a few animals will find a place to act as a sentry, either by standing on their hind legs on high ground or by climbing up into a nearby bush, but this also makes them visible to predators. If a sentry spots danger, it will bark, and the entire clan will flee to the nearest burrows. Some researchers have claimed that since the sentries often are the first animals to run, it shows that this behavior may not be entirely altruistic. However, the first animal to reemerge is usually the same sentry animal, and it will continue to give warning barks until it has confirmed that the surface is safe. This behavior is truly selfless, because the animal is not only exposing itself to potential danger, but also announcing its presence to any nearby predators with its barking.

5 ➡ When the clan is unable to avoid a threat in this way, they exhibit further altruistic behavior. If they are threatened in a group, the adults will bunch together and attack the creature en masse in an action called mobbing. This behavior is meant to scare away the predator by making the group appear to be a single larger animal. This is not always effective against snakes, and sometimes individuals get bitten. When there is danger, the babysitter will quickly usher the young underground, but this is not always possible. When there is no safe place to hide, she will gather the young into a group and then lie on top of them. Ideally, this will keep them from attracting attention, but it may result in the female sacrificing herself for the lives of the young.

이를 죽이는 데 익숙해지면, 성체 미어캣은 침을 제거하는 법을 알려준다. 그 시점에서 새끼의 차례가 되고, 새끼들은 성공하거나 아니면 고통스럽고 어쩌면 치명적일 수도 있는 상처를 입게 된다. 이러한 종류의 훈련 외에 성체 미어캣은 자기 무리의 모든 일원들을 보호하기 위해 많은 애를 쓴다.

4 ➡ 대부분의 무리가 먹이를 찾으러 가거나 새끼들을 돌보는 반면, 일부는 보초로 행동할 수 있는 장소를 찾아 높은 곳에 뒷다리로 서거나 가까운 덤불로 기어오르는데, 이는 또한 이들을 포식자들에게 보이게 한다. 만약 보초 미어캣이 위험을 알아차리면, 짖는 소리를 내고 모든 무리는 가까운 굴로 도망친다. 어떤 과학자들은 보초들이 대개 가장 먼저 도망치기 때문에 이 행동이 완전히 이타적이라고 볼 수 없다고 주장한다. 그러나 보통 가장 먼저 다시 나오는 것 역시 그 보초 미어캣이고, 밖이 안전하다는 것을 확인할 때까지 경고의 짖기를 계속한다. 보초가 잠재적인 위험에 자신을 노출할 뿐만 아니라 짖는 소리를 통해 가까이 있을지도 모르는 포식자에게 자신의 존재를 드러내기 때문에 이 행동은 진정으로 이타적이다.

5 ➡ 이러한 방법으로 무리가 위협을 피하지 못하면 그들은 더 이타적인 행동을 보인다. 만약 집단으로 위협을 받으면 성체 미어캣은 무리를 지어 모빙(mobbing)이라는 행동을 통해 단체로 상대를 공격한다. 이 행동은 무리를 하나의 더 큰 동물처럼 보이게 만들어 적을 쫓아내기 위한 것이다. 이는 뱀들에게 항상 효과적이지는 않고 때로 미어캣은 물리기도 한다. 위험이 있을 때 새끼를 돌보는 미어캣이 급히 새끼들을 땅속으로 인도하지만, 이것이 항상 가능한 것은 아니다. 숨을 만한 안전한 장소가 없을 때 새끼 돌보는 미어캣은 새끼들을 하나로 모아 그 위에 드러눕는다. 이상적으로 이것은 주의를 끄는 것을 막아주지만, 새끼들의 목숨을 위해 암컷이 자신을 희생하는 결과를 낳을 수도 있다.

1. **Fact**

According to paragraph 1, what sets apart the meerkats from other animals?

  (A) They are one of the few mammal species that breed cooperatively.

  (B) They are a popular subject of study for scientists.

1.

1단락에 따르면, 미어캣을 다른 동물들과 다르게 만드는 것은 무엇인가?

  (A) 공동으로 새끼를 기르는 얼마 안 되는 포유류 중 하나이다.

  (B) 과학자들에게 인기 있는 연구 대상이다.

ⓒ They are the smallest member of the mongoose family.
ⓓ **They are altruistic to an extent rarely observed.**

2. Sentence Simplification

Which of the sentences below best expresses the essential information in the highlighted sentence in the passage? *Incorrect* answer choices change the meaning in important ways or leave out essential information.

ⓐ Because many members of the mongoose family hold immunity to various venoms, meerkats do not fear venomous animals.

ⓑ **Unlike with other members of the mongoose family, we don't know how much immunity meerkats possess, but this isn't an obstacle for the meerkats.**

ⓒ Compared to many members of the mongoose family which have immunity to various venoms, meerkats are not aware if they possess immunity.

ⓓ While it is unclear how much immunity meerkats possess, other members of the mongoose family are weak against most venoms, and this discourages them.

3. Vocabulary

The word "**circumvents**" in paragraph 2 is closest in meaning to

ⓐ overcomes
ⓑ eradicates
ⓒ preserves
ⓓ **avoids**

4. Rhetorical Purpose

What is the purpose of paragraph 3 as it relates to paragraph 2?

ⓐ **To describe the training young meerkats go through to participate in hunting mentioned in paragraph 2**

ⓑ To provide an example of how young meerkats develop the immunity to venoms mentioned in paragraph 2

ⓒ To explain why meerkats prefer to hunt dangerous prey as mentioned in paragraph 2

ⓓ To differentiate the feeding practices of young meerkats from those of adults as discussed in paragraph 2

5. Fact

According to paragraph 4, what is the reasoning against regarding sentry behavior as altruistic?

ⓐ **Sentries are the first to enter their burrows.**

ⓑ Sentries do not participate in high-risk duties such as hunting dangerous prey.

ⓒ 몽구스과의 가장 작은 동물이다.
ⓓ 찾아보기 어려울 정도로 이타주의적이다.

2.

다음 중 지문의 음영 표시된 문장의 핵심 정보를 가장 잘 표현한 문장은 무엇인가? 오답은 의미를 크게 왜곡하거나 핵심 정보를 누락하고 있다.

ⓐ 몽구스과의 많은 동물들이 다양한 독에 대한 면역력을 가지고 있기 때문에 미어캣은 독이 있는 동물을 두려워하지 않는다.

ⓑ 몽구스과의 다른 동물들과 달리 우리는 미어캣이 얼마큼의 면역력을 가지고 있는지 모르지만 이것은 미어캣에게 장애가 되지 않는다.

ⓒ 다양한 독에 면역력을 가진 몽구스과의 다른 동물들과 비교하여, 미어캣은 그들이 면역력을 가지고 있는지 알지 못한다.

ⓓ 미어캣이 얼마큼의 면역력을 가지고 있는지 확실하지 않지만, 몽구스과의 다른 동물들은 대부분의 독에 취약하고, 이는 그들을 단념시킨다.

3.

2단락의 단어 "circumvents(피한다)"와 의미상 가장 가까운 것은?

ⓐ 극복한다
ⓑ 뿌리뽑는다
ⓒ 막는다
ⓓ 피한다

4.

2단락과의 관계에 비추어 3단락의 목적은 무엇인가?

ⓐ 새끼 미어캣이 2단락에서 묘사된 사냥에 참여하기 위해 통과하는 훈련을 서술하기 위해

ⓑ 2단락에서 언급된 독에 대한 면역력을 새끼 미어캣이 어떻게 키우는지에 대한 예시를 제공하기 위해

ⓒ 2단락에서 언급된 것처럼 왜 미어캣이 위험한 먹이 사냥을 선호하는지 설명하기 위해

ⓓ 2단락에서 거론된 것처럼 새끼 미어캣의 먹이를 먹는 행위와 성체 미어캣의 먹이를 먹는 행위를 구별하기 위해

5.

4단락에 따르면, 보초 행위를 이타적으로 보는 것에 반대하는 이유는 무엇인가?

ⓐ 보초들이 제일 먼저 굴에 들어간다.

ⓑ 보초들은 위험한 먹이를 사냥하는 것과 같은 위험 부담이 큰 직무에 참여하지 않는다.

© Sentries give false warnings to steal food.

D Sentries are safe from predator attacks.

6. Inference

Based on paragraph 4, what can be inferred about meerkats?

Ⓐ Meerkats are quite vulnerable to predator attacks.

Ⓑ Meerkats have poor vision.

Ⓒ Meerkats takes turns acting as sentries.

Ⓓ **Meerkats dig many burrows in their territory.**

7. Vocabulary

The word "usher" in paragraph 5 is closest in meaning to

Ⓐ move

Ⓑ **lead**

Ⓒ carry

Ⓓ push

8. Negative Fact

Which of the following is NOT mentioned in the passage about meerkats?

Ⓐ Defensive mechanisms

Ⓑ Foraging behavior

Ⓒ **Domestication by humans**

Ⓓ Breeding habits

9. Insertion

Look at the four squares [■] that indicate where the following sentence could be added to the passage.

Then, it uses sand to wash away any venom that may remain on the scorpion's exoskeleton.

Where would the sentence best fit? [■D]

10. Summary

Directions: An introductory sentence for a brief summary of the passage is provided below. Complete the summary by selecting the THREE answer choices that express the most important ideas in the passage. Some sentences do not belong in the summary because they express ideas that are not presented in the passage or are minor ideas in the passage. *This question is worth 2 points.*

Meerkats, one of the mostly widely studied mammals living in southern Africa, are well known for their exceptionally altruistic behavior.

© 보초들은 음식을 훔치기 위해 가짜 경고를 준다.

D 보초들은 포식자의 공격으로부터 안전하다.

6.

4단락에 근거하여 미어캣에 관해 추론할 수 있는 것은 무엇인가?

Ⓐ 미어캣은 포식자의 공격에 상당히 취약하다.

Ⓑ 미어캣은 시력이 좋지 않다.

Ⓒ 미어캣은 순번을 정해 보초 역할을 한다.

Ⓓ 미어캣은 자신들의 영역에 많은 굴을 판다.

7.

5단락의 단어 "usher(인도하다)"와 의미상 가장 가까운 것은?

Ⓐ 움직이다

Ⓑ 이끌다

Ⓒ 나르다

Ⓓ 밀다

8.

다음 중 지문에서 미어캣에 관해 언급되지 않은 것은 무엇인가?

Ⓐ 방어기제

Ⓑ 먹이를 찾는 행동

Ⓒ 인간에 의한 가축화

Ⓓ 번식 습성

9.

지문에 다음 문장이 들어갈 수 있는 위치를 나타내는 네 개의 사각형[■]을 확인하시오.

그리고 나서, 그것은 전갈의 외골격에 남아 있을지도 모르는 독을 씻어버리기 위해 모래를 이용한다.

이 문장이 들어가기에 가장 적합한 곳은? [■D]

10.

지시문: 지문을 간략하게 요약한 글의 첫 문장이 아래 제시되어 있다. 지문의 가장 중요한 내용을 표현하는 세 개의 선택지를 골라 요약문을 완성하시오. 일부 문장들은 지문에 제시되지 않았거나 지문의 지엽적인 내용을 나타내기 때문에 요약문에 포함되지 않는다. *이 문제의 배점은 2점이다.*

아프리카 남부에 서식하는 가장 널리 연구되는 포유류 중 하나인 미어캣은 그들의 유난히 이타적인 행동으로 잘 알려져 있다.

Ⓑ When sentries spot a predator, they issue a series of distinct barks until the danger has passed.

Ⓒ When meerkats are attacked by predators, they display altruistic behavior by mobbing the predator and placing the safety of their young first.

Ⓓ Every adult member of the group plays a role in feeding, training, and protecting the young, even though they are not their own offspring.

Ⓐ Male and female assistants in a group do not breed until the dominant pair permits them to.

Ⓔ The training for foraging and hunting for food is done in a multi-step process.

Ⓕ Meerkats bite off the scorpion's stinger first to ensure that the arachnid does not strike them with its venom.

Ⓑ 보초는 포식자를 발견하면 위험이 사라질 때까지 일련의 특징적인 짖는 소리를 낸다.

Ⓒ 미어캣은 포식자로부터 공격을 당할 때, 포식자를 모빙하고 새끼의 안전을 최우선으로 함으로써 이타적 행동을 보여준다.

Ⓓ 무리의 모든 성체 미어캣은 자신의 새끼가 아니더라도 새끼들을 먹이고, 훈련시키고, 보호하는 역할을 한다.

Ⓐ 무리의 수컷과 암컷 보조들은 지배적인 한 쌍이 허락할 때까지 새끼를 낳지 않는다.

Ⓔ 먹이 찾기와 먹이 사냥을 위한 훈련은 여러 단계의 과정으로 이루어진다.

Ⓕ 미어캣은 먼저 전갈의 침을 물어뜯는데 이는 그 거미류 동물이 독으로 자신들을 공격하지 못하도록 하기 위해서이다.

🔖 어휘

어휘

1 **societal** adj 사회의 I **altruism** n 이타주의 I **breed** v 새끼를 낳다, 기르다 I **cooperatively** adv 협력하여, 협조적으로 I **consist of** ~으로 이루어지다[구성되다] I **predator** n 포식자 I **extent** n 정도[규모] I **carry** v 갖다, (특징을) 지니다, 짊어지다 I **remarkable** adj 놀랄 만한, 놀라운

2 **primarily** adv 주로 I **immune** adj 면역성이 있는 I **deter** v 단념시키다 I **pounce** v 덮치다[덤비다] I **circumvent** v 피하다[면하다] I **venom** n 독 I **devour** v 집어삼키다 I **disarmed** adj 무장 해제된, 무력해진

3 **lactate** v 젖을 분비하다[젖이 나오다] I **wean** v 젖을 떼다 I **forage** v 먹이를 찾다 I **get used to** ~에 익숙해지다 I **potentially** adv 가능성 있게, 잠재적으로 I **fatal** adj 치명적인 I **wound** n 상처, 부상 I **clan** n 집단[무리]

4 **tend to** ~을 돌보다 I **hind** adj 뒤쪽의 I **spot** v 알아채다, 발견하다, 찾다 I **burrow** n 굴 I **claim** v 주장하다 I **reemerge** v 다시 나타나다 I **selfless** adj 이타적인 I **announce** v 알리다, 발표하다 I **presence** n 있음, 존재(함)

5 **exhibit** v 드러내다, 전시하다 I **threaten** v 협박[위협]하다 I **en masse** adv 집단으로[일제히] I **usher** v 안내하다, 인도하다 I **ideally** adv 이상적으로 I **sacrifice** v 희생하다

Actual Test 03

본서 | P. 98

Passage 1   Deep Sea Biology

1. Ⓐ	Vocabulary	6. Ⓑ	Rhetorical Purpose
2. Ⓒ	Sentence Simplification	7. Ⓐ	Negative Fact
3. Ⓒ	Inference	8. Ⓓ	Negative Fact
4. Ⓓ	Fact	9. Ⓒ	Insertion
5. Ⓐ	Fact	10. Ⓐ, Ⓓ, Ⓕ	Summary

Passage 2   Water in the Desert

1. Ⓓ	Sentence Simplification	6. Ⓑ	Rhetorical Purpose
2. Ⓐ	Inference	7. Ⓓ	Negative Fact
3. Ⓓ	Inference	8. Ⓓ	Fact
4. Ⓑ	Vocabulary	9. Ⓒ	Insertion
5. Ⓒ	Fact	10. Ⓑ, Ⓓ, Ⓔ	Summary

Passage 3   New York City Urban Planning

1. Ⓐ	Reference	6. Ⓓ	Fact
2. Ⓑ	Vocabulary	7. Ⓒ	Rhetorical Purpose
3. Ⓐ	Inference	8. Ⓓ	Negative Fact
4. Ⓐ	Fact	9. Ⓑ	Insertion
5. Ⓒ	Sentence Simplification	10. Ⓐ, Ⓑ, Ⓔ	Summary

● 내가 맞은 문제 유형의 개수를 적어 보고 어느 유형에 취약한지 확인해 봅시다.

문제 유형	맞은 개수
Sentence Simplification	3
Fact / Negative Fact	10
Vocabulary	3
Reference	1
Rhetorical Purpose	3
Inference	4
Insertion	3
Summary	3
Category Chart	0
Total	30

Deep Sea Biology

1 ➡ After centuries of exploration, scientists have revealed that life exists nearly everywhere on the surface of the Earth. This includes the deepest trenches in the ocean. However, proof of such life remained elusive for a long time because we lacked the technology to reach such depths. Therefore, many hypotheses that supposed that life could not survive there arose. These ideas were logical and convinced many experts that the reason that specimens could not be collected was because they did not exist. However, as evidence of organisms from the depths mounted, many of these ideas were proven wrong. One of the most famous mistaken theories about deep sea biology was created by Edward Forbes.

2 ➡ Edward Forbes was a naturalist and marine biologist from the Isle of Man who had a short but prolific career. He is best known for his time spent upon the HMS Beacon in the Aegean Sea on its survey voyage and the theory on oceanic life that he developed there. Using a dredging rig, he conducted a study of ocean life at varying depths, and came to the conclusion that life did not exist below 300 fathoms (1 fathom is about 2 meters). This belief became known as the azoic hypothesis and was widely accepted by the scientific community until it was disproven by later expeditions of discovery.

3 ➡ Forbes was invited to take part in the expedition by the commander of the ship, Captain Thomas Graves, in 1841. The majority of the trip was spent in the Greek Islands and Asia Minor, where Forbes devoted his time on land to botany. At sea, however, he was constantly dredging, completing at least 150 dredges at depths from 1 fathom to 130 fathoms. His goal was to catalogue how depth, pressure and the geology of the seafloor affected the sizes and types of organisms present. Unsurprisingly, his dredges proved that organisms became smaller and fewer in number the deeper he searched.

4 ➡ Based upon the specimens and data he recovered, Forbes divided the depths of the ocean into eight fairly distinct zones based upon the fauna present. However, due to the fact that he could only dredge up to a certain depth, he was forced

심해 생물학

1 ➡ 수 세기에 걸친 탐사 후에 과학자들은 지표면의 거의 모든 곳에 생명체가 존재한다는 사실을 밝혀냈다. 여기에는 바다의 가장 깊은 곳에 있는 해구도 포함된다. 그러나 그런 생명체가 존재한다는 증거는 오랫동안 불분명한 채 남아 있었는데, 그렇게 깊은 곳까지 도달할 수 있는 기술이 부족했기 때문이었다. 그래서 거기에서는 생명체가 생존할 수 없다고 가정하는 많은 가설들이 생겨났다. 이러한 생각들은 논리적이었고, 심해에서 생물 견본을 수집할 수 없었던 이유는 생물이 존재하지 않았기 때문이었다고 많은 전문가들을 설득시켰다. 그러나 해저 생물의 증거가 점점 발견되면서 이러한 많은 생각들이 잘못된 것으로 밝혀졌다. 심해 생물학에 대한 가장 잘 알려진 잘못된 이론은 에드워드 포브스에 의해 만들어졌다.

2 ➡ 에드워드 포브스는 맨 섬에서 온, 짧지만 다양한 경력을 소유한 동식물 연구가인 동시에 해양 생물학자였다. 그는 에게해에서 조사 항해를 한 HMS 비컨호에서 시간을 보낸 것과 그곳에서 그가 발전시킨 바다 생물에 관한 이론으로 가장 잘 알려져 있다. 준설 장비를 사용하여 다양한 깊이에서 해양 생물에 대한 연구를 했으며, 300패덤(fathom, 물의 깊이 측정 단위, 1패덤은 약 2미터) 아래로는 생명체가 존재하지 않는다는 결론을 내렸다. 이러한 믿음은 무생물 가설이라고 알려졌으며 이후의 탐사에 의해 사실이 아니라는 것이 증명되기 전까지 과학계에서 널리 받아들여졌다.

3 ➡ 포브스는 1841년에 토머스 그레이브스 선장에게서 그 탐험에 참여하도록 초대받았다. 그는 항해의 대부분을 그리스 섬들과 소아시아의 육지에서 식물학을 연구하는 데 보냈다. 그러나 바다에서는 계속해서 바다 채취 작업을 했는데, 1패덤에서 130패덤까지 적어도 150번의 바닥 채취 작업을 마쳤다. 그의 목표는 수심, 수압, 그리고 해저의 지질이 그곳에 존재하는 생명체의 크기와 종류에 어떤 영향을 미치는지 목록을 만드는 것이었다. 놀랄 것도 없이, 그의 바닥 채취 작업들은 수심이 더 깊어질수록 생명체가 더 작아지고 그 숫자가 줄어든다는 것을 증명했다.

4 ➡ 그가 얻은 생물 표본들과 자료를 바탕으로 포브스는 바다의 수심을 그곳에 존재하는 동물군에 기초하여 8개의 뚜렷한 구역으로 나누었다. 그러나 특정 깊이까지만 바다 채취를 할 수 있었던 탓에 그보다 더 깊은 곳의 조건이 어떠했는지는 추론할 수밖에 없었다. 이로 인해 그는 바다의

to extrapolate what conditions were like deeper down. This led him to believe that the deepest ocean abysses were utterly devoid of life. He could not conceive how organisms could withstand the brutal pressure, cold and absolute darkness that would be present, and his dredges seemed to support his logic. So, he called this the azoic zone, which literally means "without life." His hypothesis was greeted with general support, and became a dominant theory until it was proven utterly wrong many years later.

5 ➡ The reasons for his mistaken hypothesis come down to particular details of his investigation: the device he used to collect samples and the location. The dredge Forbes used was actually quite poorly designed for its intended use. The opening on the front of the dredge was actually fairly small, meaning that more animals were deflected by it than were captured. To make matters worse, the net on the back of it that was intended to hold the specimens until they were brought to the surface had holes that were large enough for many smaller organisms to freely pass through. In addition, the Aegean Sea had considerably lower levels of fauna than other seas of comparable size and depth. Combined, these factors actually limited the amount of data he could collect.

6 ➡ Another popular but erroneous hypothesis was created by the French naturalist François Peron. Prior to Forbes's survey of the Aegean, Peron explored the depths of the Baltic Sea, paying particular attention to the temperatures he recorded. He correctly noted that the temperature of the water falls as you descend. Pressure also increases with depth, so he believed that the water at the ocean floor was so cold and dense that there must be ice at the bottom of the ocean. These ideas led him to also conclude that the deep sea was lifeless. Like Forbes, Peron's theory also received wide support, even though it later turned out to be false.

7 ➡ As technology advanced, subsequent exploration of the ocean's depths revealed just how flawed these ideas were. [■A] Improved dredging equipment allowed much more effective collection of specimens, and organisms were found at depths well below 300 fathoms. [■B] Forbes's theory that life could not exist below that mark was shattered by Charles Wyville Thomson in 1868 when he collected specimens from over 2,400 fathoms (4,389 meters).

가장 깊은 심연에는 생명체가 아예 존재하지 않는다고 믿게 되었다. 그는 어떻게 생명체들이 혹독한 수압, 추위, 그리고 완전한 어둠을 견딜 수 있는지 이해할 수 없었으며, 그의 바닥 채취 작업은 그의 논리를 뒷받침하는 것처럼 보였다. 그래서 그는 이 구역을 무생물층이라고 불렀는데, 이는 말 그대로 '생명이 없는' 것을 의미한다. 그의 가설은 많은 지지를 받았으며 수 년 뒤 완전히 잘못된 것이라는 사실이 증명될 때까지 우세한 이론으로 자리잡았다.

5 ➡ 포브스의 가설이 잘못된 이유는 연구의 특정한 부분들, 즉 샘플을 수집하기 위해 그가 사용한 장비와 장소 때문이었다. 사실 포브스가 사용한 준설 장비는 원래 의도된 사용 목적에 전혀 맞지 않게 설계되었다. 장비 앞부분의 열리는 부분은 실제로 상당히 작은데, 그것은 장비에 잡히는 동물보다 장비에 부딪혀 방향을 바꾸는 동물들이 더 많았다는 것을 의미한다. 설상가상으로, 그 뒷부분에 있는 그물은 육지로 끌어올려질 때까지 생물들을 가둬 두도록 계획되었는데, 많은 작은 생명체들이 자유롭게 드나들 수 있을 정도로 크기가 큰 구멍이 있었다. 또한 에게해에는 비슷한 크기와 수심의 다른 바다들보다 상당히 낮은 수준의 동물군이 있었다. 이 요인들이 합쳐져서 포브스가 수집할 수 있었던 자료의 양을 사실상 제한시켰다.

6 ➡ 또 다른 유명하지만 잘못된 가설은 프랑스의 동식물 연구가인 프랑수아 페론에 의해 만들어졌다. 포브스의 에게해 조사가 있기 전에 페론은 발틱해의 수심을 탐험하며 자신이 기록한 바다의 온도에 특별한 관심을 가졌다. 그는 밑으로 내려갈수록 수온이 낮아진다는 사실을 정확하게 파악했다. 수심과 함께 수압 역시 증가하므로 그는 해저의 물이 너무나 차갑고 밀도가 높아서 바다 밑바닥에는 얼음이 있을 것이라고 믿었다. 이 생각은 그 역시 심해에는 생명체가 살고 있지 않을 것이라는 결론을 내리게 했다. 포브스와 마찬가지로 페론의 이론은 널리 지지를 받았지만 나중에 잘못된 것이라고 밝혀졌다.

7 ➡ 기술이 발전함에 따라 그 이후의 바다 수심 탐사는 이러한 생각이 얼마나 잘못된 것이었는지를 밝혀냈다. [■A] 향상된 준설 장비들은 생물 표본 수집을 훨씬 더 효율적으로 하게 했고, 생명체들은 300패덤 아래의 수심에서도 발견되었다. [■B] 그 깊이 이하에서는 생명체가 존재할 수 없다고 주장한 포브스의 이론은 1868년에 2,400패덤(4,389미터)에서 생물 표본을 수집한 찰스 위빌 톰슨에 의해 산산조각이 났다. [■C] 또한 과학자들은 바다가 자신들이 상상했던 것보다 훨씬 더 깊다는 것을 발견했다. 챌린저

[■C] Scientists also discovered that the oceans were far deeper than they had ever imagined. The Challenger expedition measured the Mariana Trench in 1875 and found that it was over 4,475 fathoms (8,184 meters) deep. [■D] Today, the trench is known to reach a maximum depth of 5,960 fathoms (10,900 meters), and life has been found even there.

호 탐사대는 1875년에 마리아나 해구를 측량했고 이 해구가 깊이 4,475패덤(8,184미터) 이상이라고 밝혔다. [■D] 오늘날 이 해구는 최대 5,960패덤(10,900미터)인 것으로 알려져 있으며 그곳에서도 생명체는 발견되고 있다.

---

1. Vocabulary

The word "elusive" in paragraph 1 is closest in meaning to

Ⓐ undefined
Ⓑ apparent
Ⓒ complicated
Ⓓ recognizable

2. Sentence Simplification

Which of the sentences below best expresses the essential information in the highlighted sentence in the passage? *Incorrect* answer choices change the meaning in important ways or leave out essential information.

Ⓐ After conducting expeditions of discovery, the scientific community was found to be wrong about the azoic hypothesis.
Ⓑ The discoveries and expeditions made by the scientific community helped to disprove the azoic hypothesis.
Ⓒ **The azoic hypothesis had been considered as true until it was proven to be erroneous by later discoveries.**
Ⓓ It was the scientific community that revealed the error of the azoic hypothesis, which had been widely accepted before.

3. Inference

According to paragraph 2, which of the following can be inferred about Edward Forbes?

Ⓐ As an experienced biologist, he took part in the survey voyage of the HMS Beacon.
Ⓑ During the survey in the Aegean Sea, he developed a theory about marine life.
Ⓒ **He became a well-respected member of the scientific community.**
Ⓓ He correctly concluded that there was no life in the deep sea.

1.

1단락의 단어 "elusive(불분명한)"와 의미상 가장 가까운 것은?

Ⓐ 확실하지 않은
Ⓑ 명백한
Ⓒ 복잡한
Ⓓ 알아볼 수 있는

2.

다음 중 지문의 음영 표시된 문장의 핵심 정보를 가장 잘 표현한 문장은 무엇인가? 오답은 의미를 크게 왜곡하거나 핵심 정보를 누락하고 있다.

Ⓐ 탐사 후에 과학계가 무생물 가설에 대해 틀렸다는 사실이 밝혀졌다.
Ⓑ 과학계의 발견과 탐험은 무생물 가설이 틀렸다고 증명하는 데 도움을 주었다.
Ⓒ 무생물 가설은 이후의 발견들에 의해 잘못된 것이라고 증명되기 전까지 사실인 것으로 여겨졌다.
Ⓓ 이전에 널리 인정받았던 무생물 가설의 잘못된 점을 밝혀낸 것은 과학계였다.

3.

2단락에 따르면, 다음 중 에드워드 포브스에 관해 추론할 수 있는 것은 무엇인가?

Ⓐ 경험이 풍부한 생물학자로서 HMS 비컨호의 조사 항해에 참여했다.
Ⓑ 에게해의 조사 중 해양 생물에 대한 이론을 발전시켰다.
Ⓒ 과학계에서 존중 받는 일원이 되었다.
Ⓓ 심해에는 생물체가 존재하지 않는다고 올바르게 결론을 내렸다.

4. Fact

According to paragraph 3, why did Forbes participate in the expedition?

Ⓐ To collect a variety of botanical samples in the Greek Islands and Asia Minor

Ⓑ To find evidence to support his hypothesis that organisms could not inhabit the deep sea

Ⓒ To develop an effective dredging device with which to study the seabed ecosystem

Ⓓ **To research the effects of depth, pressure and the geology under the sea on organisms**

5. Fact

According to paragraph 4, why did Forbes conclude that life did not exist in the deepest ocean?

Ⓐ **He thought the environment was too tough for organisms to survive.**

Ⓑ He was unable to discover anything when he reached a certain depth.

Ⓒ He faced unexpected obstacles while dredging.

Ⓓ He successfully classified the zones according to species diversity.

6. Rhetorical Purpose

Why does the author mention "the device he used to collect samples and the location" in paragraph 5?

Ⓐ To describe how poor the technology was in Forbes's time

Ⓑ **To point out what caused Forbes to draw an erroneous conclusion**

Ⓒ To explain how Forbes collected samples from the ocean

Ⓓ To emphasize the difficulty Forbes experienced during his exploration

7. Negative Fact

All of the following are mentioned in paragraph 5 as reasons for Forbes's mistaken hypothesis EXCEPT

Ⓐ **the dredge was originally designed for use on the surface of the sea rather than in the deep sea.**

Ⓑ the device Forbes used had a small hole which made it difficult to capture animals.

Ⓒ the net of the dredge did not function efficiently and failed to hold tiny organisms.

Ⓓ the Aegean Sea had lower levels of life compared to other seas.

4.

3단락에 따르면, 포브스가 탐사에 참여한 이유는 무엇인가?

Ⓐ 그리스 섬들과 소아시아에서 다양한 식물 견본을 수집하기 위해

Ⓑ 생명체가 심해에서 살 수 없다는 자신의 이론을 뒷받침할 증거를 찾기 위해

Ⓒ 해저 생태계를 연구하는 데 쓰일 효과적인 준설 장비를 개발하기 위해

Ⓓ 수심, 수압, 그리고 해저의 지질이 생명체에 주는 영향을 연구하기 위해

5.

4단락에 따르면, 포브스가 가장 깊은 심해에는 생명체가 존재하지 않는다는 결론을 내린 이유는 무엇인가?

Ⓐ 생명체가 살아남기에 환경이 너무 혹독하다고 생각했다.

Ⓑ 특정 수심에 도달했을 때 아무것도 발견할 수 없었다.

Ⓒ 바닥 채취 작업을 할 때 예상하지 못했던 장애물들에 부딪혔다.

Ⓓ 종의 다양성에 따라 구역을 성공적으로 분류했다.

6.

5단락에서 글쓴이가 "샘플을 수집하기 위해 그가 사용한 장비와 장소"를 언급한 이유는 무엇인가?

Ⓐ 포브스가 살았던 시대에 기술이 얼마나 부족했는지 묘사하기 위해

Ⓑ 포브스가 잘못된 결론을 내리도록 만든 것이 무엇인지 지적하기 위해

Ⓒ 포브스가 어떻게 바다에서 샘플을 수집했는지 설명하기 위해

Ⓓ 포브스가 탐사하는 동안 경험한 어려움을 강조하기 위해

7.

다음 중 5단락에서 포브스가 잘못된 가설을 세우게 된 이유로 언급되지 않은 것은?

Ⓐ 준설 장비는 원래 심해보다는 바다 표면에서 사용하도록 제작된 것이었다.

Ⓑ 포브스가 사용한 장비에는 작은 구멍이 있어 동물들을 포획하기 어려웠다.

Ⓒ 준설 장비의 그물이 제대로 작동하지 않았고 작은 생물들을 가두는 데 실패했다.

Ⓓ 에게해는 다른 바다에 비해 낮은 수준의 생물체를 가지고 있었다.

8. Negative Fact

According to paragraph 6, all of the following are true about Peron's hypothesis EXCEPT

(A) Peron's hypothesis was similar to that of Forbes in that it was lifeless in the deep sea.

(B) Peron found that the temperature becomes lower with depth by recording temperatures in the Baltic Sea.

(C) Peron thought ice was present at the bottom of the ocean due to the low seawater temperature.

(D) **Peron's hypothesis was correct in that the high pressure at the ocean floor makes it impossible for organisms to inhabit it.**

9. Insertion

Look at the four squares [■] that indicate where the following sentence could be added to the passage.

Scientists also discovered that the oceans were far deeper than they had ever imagined.

Where would the sentence best fit? [■ C]

10. Summary

Directions: An introductory sentence for a brief summary of the passage is provided below. Complete the summary by selecting the THREE answer choices that express the most important ideas in the passage. Some sentences do not belong in the summary because they express ideas that are not presented in the passage or are minor ideas in the passage. *This question is worth 2 points.*

Many hypotheses that have been presented to suggest that no life exists in the deepest ocean have since been disproven.

(A) Forbes divided the depths of the sea into eight regions based on the data he had collected and concluded it is lifeless in the abysmal depths of the ocean.

(D) The defective device Forbes used for his research and environmental conditions in the Aegean Sea led Forbes to the incorrect conclusion.

(F) Peron also developed a hypothesis that no living things existed in the depths of the ocean because of the low temperature and high pressure there.

8.

6단락에 따르면, 다음 중 페론의 가설에 대해 사실이 아닌 것은?

(A) 페론의 가설은 심해에 생명체가 살고 있지 않다는 점에서 포브스의 가설과 비슷했다.

(B) 발틱해의 수온을 기록함으로써 페론은 수심이 깊어질수록 온도가 더 낮아진다는 것을 발견했다.

(C) 바닷물의 낮은 수온 때문에 페론은 바다 밑바닥에는 얼음이 있을 것이라고 생각했다.

(D) 해저의 높은 수압이 해저에서 생명체가 사는 것을 불가능하게 만든다는 점에서 페론의 가설은 옳았다.

9.

지문에 다음 문장이 들어갈 수 있는 위치를 나타내는 네 개의 사각형[■]을 확인하시오.

또한 과학자들은 바다가 자신들이 상상했던 것보다 훨씬 더 깊다는 것을 발견했다.

이 문장이 들어가기에 가장 적합한 곳은? [■C]

10.

지시문: 지문을 간략하게 요약한 글의 첫 문장이 아래 제시되어 있다. 지문의 가장 중요한 내용을 표현하는 세 개의 선택지를 골라 요약문을 완성하시오. 일부 문장들은 지문에 제시되지 않았거나 지문의 지엽적인 내용을 나타내기 때문에 요약문에 포함되지 않는다. *이 문제의 배점은 2점이다.*

가장 깊은 심해에는 아무 생명체도 존재하지 않는다는 것을 뒷받침하기 위해 제기되었던 많은 가설들은 그 이후 사실이 아니라고 증명되었다.

(A) 포브스는 자신이 수집한 자료에 근거하여 바다의 수심을 8개의 구역으로 나누었고 바다의 가장 깊은 수심에서는 생명체가 살고 있지 않다는 결론을 내렸다.

(D) 포브스가 연구를 위해 사용한 결함이 있는 장비와 에게해의 환경적 조건이 포브스로 하여금 잘못된 결론을 내리게 했다.

(F) 페론 또한 낮은 수온과 높은 수압으로 인해 깊은 바다에는 생물이 존재하지 않는다는 가설을 발전시켰다.

Ⓑ Forbes found that the size and number of organisms decrease as you descend deeper into the sea.

Ⓒ Forbes's theory had been generally supported in the contemporary scientific field before it was revealed to be wrong.

Ⓔ Peron was the first to discover the link between the pressure and the temperature under the sea.

Ⓑ 포브스는 바다로 더 깊이 내려갈수록 생명체의 크기와 수가 줄어든다는 것을 발견했다.

Ⓒ 포브스의 이론은 잘못되었다는 것이 밝혀지기 전까지 당대 과학계로부터 일반적으로 지지를 받았다.

Ⓔ 페론은 바다 밑의 수압과 수온의 관계를 발견한 첫 번째 인물이었다.

📑 어휘

1 exploration ⋒ 탐험, 탐사 ┃ reveal ⓥ 밝히다, 드러내다 ┃ trench ⋒ 해구, 해자(垓子) ┃ roof ⋒ 지붕 ┃ elusive ⓐⓓⓙ 찾기 힘든 ┃ depth ⋒ 깊이 ┃ arise ⓥ 생기다, 발생하다 ┃ convince ⓥ 납득시키다, 확신시키다 ┃ specimen ⋒ 표본, 견본 ┃ evidence ⋒ 증거, 흔적 ┃ mount ⓥ 서서히 증가하다

2 prolific ⓐⓓⓙ 많은, 다작하는, 열매를 많이 맺는 ┃ dredging rig 준설 장비 ┃ varying ⓐⓓⓙ 바뀌는, 가지각색의 ┃ disprove ⓥ 틀렸음을 입증하다 ┃ expedition ⋒ 탐험, 원정

3 devote ⓥ 바치다, 쏟다, 기울이다

4 distinct ⓐⓓⓙ 뚜렷한, 분명한 ┃ extrapolate ⓥ 추론[추정]하다 ┃ abyss ⋒ 심연, 깊은 구렁 ┃ devoid of ~이 전혀 없는 ┃ conceive ⓥ 이해하다, 상상하다 ┃ withstand ⓥ 견뎌[이겨]내다 ┃ brutal ⓐⓓⓙ 혹독한, 잔혹한, 악랄한 ┃ absolute ⓐⓓⓙ 완전한, 완벽한 ┃ literally ⓐⓓⓥ 문자[말] 그대로 ┃ greet ⓥ 받아들이다, 맞다, 환영하다 ┃ utterly ⓐⓓⓥ 완전히, 순전히

5 intended ⓐⓓⓙ 의도된, 계획된 ┃ deflect ⓥ 방향을 바꾸다, 피하다[모면하다] ┃ considerably ⓐⓓⓥ 많이, 상당히 ┃ comparable ⓐⓓⓙ 비슷한, 비교할 만한

6 erroneous ⓐⓓⓙ 잘못된 ┃ descend ⓥ 내려오다, 하강하다 ┃ dense ⓐⓓⓙ 밀도가 높은, 빽빽한, 밀집한

7 flawed ⓐⓓⓙ 결함[결점/흠]이 있는 ┃ improved ⓐⓓⓙ 향상된, 개선된 ┃ collection ⋒ 수집(품), 소장품 ┃ shatter ⓥ 산산이 부수다

Passage 2

Water in the Desert

1 ➡ Despite their reputation as the most extreme environments on Earth, the world's great deserts have not always been so hostile. In fact, there is ample evidence suggesting that many of the driest places once flourished with life. The Sahara Desert, the Earth's largest desert, contains caves adorned with paintings of animals that only live in the grasslands of the savannah today. In addition, many species have specially adapted to the harsh conditions, and others like crocodiles linger on in the remnants of rivers and lakes that form oases. All of this evidence points to an environment that was very different from what prevails today, an environment that was blessed with far more water than what it currently possesses.

2 ➡ During a 1981 mission of the space shuttle Columbia, scientists used a radar array on board to scan the eastern Sahara, and they revealed a very different terrain beneath the dunes. They found that bedrock underlies the sand, and that ancient rivers had carved valleys through it. These features appear

사막의 물

1 ➡ 지구상 가장 극한 환경이라는 명성을 갖고 있지만 세상의 거대한 사막들이 항상 그렇게 적대적이지만은 않았다. 실제로, 가장 메마른 지역들도 과거에 생명체들이 번성했을 거라고 암시하는 충분한 증거가 있다. 지구상 가장 큰 사막인 사하라 사막에는 오늘날 사바나의 초원에서만 서식하는 동물들의 그림으로 장식된 동굴들이 있다. 그뿐만 아니라, 많은 종들은 혹독한 조건들에 특별히 적응했고, 악어와 같은 다른 동물들은 오아시스를 형성하는 강과 호수의 터에 머무른다. 이 모든 증거는 현재의 환경과는 매우 다른 환경, 즉 현재 보유하고 있는 것보다 훨씬 많은 양의 물을 가지고 있었던 축복 받은 환경을 가리킨다.

2 ➡ 1981년의 컬럼비아 우주왕복선 미션 중에 과학자들은 기내에 있는 배열 레이더를 사용하여 사하라 동쪽 지역을 스캔했고, 모래 언덕들 아래에 매우 다른 지형이 존재한다는 것을 밝혀냈다. 그들은 암반이 모래 아래에 있는 것을 발견했고, 고대 강물이 암반을 통과하여 계곡들을 만들었다는 것을 발견했다. 이 지형들은 대략 3,500만 년 전 제삼

---

to have been created during the Tertiary period around 35 million years ago. As they dried up about 2.5 million years ago, they began to fill with sand. Archaeological data shows that these sand sheets have advanced and retreated many times in a cycle that takes about 10,000 years, and that the region has had its current appearance for about 5,000 years. Further geological research was carried out by an Egyptian petroleum company using microwaves to penetrate the shifting sands in search of water. They subsequently drilled wells that revealed that freshwater aquifers are still present.

3 ➡ These massive climatic shifts are thought to be the result of plate tectonics. The surface of the planet is composed of plates of crust that move slowly but relentlessly, and over time they have moved entire continents great distances, resulting in massively different climates. In many cases, this movement has led to decreased precipitation, drying up rivers and lakes and transforming lush forests into barren wilderness. One extreme example of this is Antarctica, where dinosaurs once wandered through primeval forests but now ice sheets 2 kilometers thick dominate the landscape. Antarctica seems about as different from the Sahara as can be imagined, but it is also a desert as it only receives an average of 20 centimeters of precipitation per year. Both areas are subject to frequent wind storms, but Antarctica's polar location makes it extremely cold while the Sahara is in the tropics. Although water is scarcer in the Sahara, it is in a form more conducive to life.

4 ➡ Just as water manages to sustain life in the desert, it is also the major force behind continued changes there. In the rare event of actual rain, there is nothing to resist its power, and it rapidly carves new channels and forms great, shallow lakes. However, it usually affects the environment in a much more subtle way caused by the dramatic temperature changes between night and day. [■A] During the night and early morning, fog from the ocean and dew deposit their moisture on stones in the desert. [■B] This water is absorbed directly into the rocks, but the heat of day evaporates it once again. [■C] As this cycle repeats daily, the stones expand and contract, damaging them on a microscopic level. The results are not readily observable, but given enough time, it has a dramatic effect, causing the outer layers of the rocks to flake off. [■D] Sometimes, however, the process occurs more rapidly.

기에 형성된 것으로 보인다. 대략 250만 년 전에 말라버리면서 그것들은 모래로 채워지기 시작했다. 고고학 자료는 이러한 모래층들이 약 1만 년이 걸리는 주기 속에서 진전하고 후퇴하는 것을 많이 반복했으며, 이 지역이 약 5천 년 동안 현재의 모습을 유지해 왔다는 것을 보여준다. 이후 지질학적 연구가 한 이집트 석유 회사에 의해 행해졌는데 물을 찾기 위해 마이크로파를 사용해서 움직이는 모래를 투과하는 것이었다. 그 뒤에 그들은 우물을 파서 담수성 대수층이 여전히 존재한다는 것을 밝혀냈다.

3 ➡ 이러한 대대적인 기후 변화는 판구조론의 결과라고 생각된다. 지구의 표면은 느리지만 끊임없이 움직이는 지각판으로 구성되어 있으며, 시간이 지남에 따라 그것들은 대륙들을 멀리 이동시켰고, 이것은 엄청나게 다른 기후를 초래했다. 많은 경우 이러한 이동은 강수량 감소를 야기했으며, 강과 호수를 말라버리게 하며 우거진 숲을 척박한 황무지로 변화시켰다. 이것의 한 극단적인 예는 남극인데, 그곳은 공룡들이 한때 원시림을 거닐었지만 현재는 2킬로미터 두께의 빙상이 뒤덮고 있다. 남극은 상상할 수 있듯이 사하라 사막과는 전혀 다른 것 같지만, 연평균 강수량이 20센티미터이기 때문에 남극 또한 사막이다. 두 지역 모두 자주 폭풍에 시달리지만 남극은 극지방의 위치 때문에 매우 추운 반면 사하라 사막은 열대 지방에 있다. 물은 사하라 사막에서 더 부족하지만, 그것은 생명체에 좀 더 도움이 되는 형태로 존재한다.

4 ➡ 물은 사막에서 생명이 살아가게 하는 것만큼이나 그곳의 지속되는 변화를 야기하는 주요 요소이기도 하다. 실제로 비가 내리는 드문 경우에는 비의 위력에 저항할 수 있는 것이 없기에, 빗물은 재빠르게 새로운 수로를 만들어 내고 거대하고 얕은 호수들을 형성한다. 하지만 비는 밤과 낮 사이의 극적인 온도 차이로 야기되는 훨씬 더 미묘한 방법으로 환경에 영향을 미친다. [■A] 밤과 이른 아침 사이에, 바다에서 밀려오는 안개와 이슬은 사막의 바위에 수분을 스며들게 한다. [■B] 물은 바위로 곧장 흡수되지만, 낮의 열기는 그것을 다시금 증발시킨다. [■C] 이 순환이 매일 반복됨에 따라 바위들은 팽창하고 수축하면서 미세하게 손상을 입는다. 이것의 결과는 그 즉시 보여지지 않지만, 충분한 시간이 주어지면 바위의 바깥 층들이 떨어져 나가는 엄청난 영향을 미친다. [■D] 하지만 종종 이 과정은 더 빠르게 진행된다.

5 ➡ After a fierce downpour saturates stones already damaged by the daily water cycle, the rapid drying caused by the sun can sometimes shatter the stone. The energy released in such explosions can even split apart boulders. This explains how some rocks appear to move themselves without the help of wind or flowing water. Taken together, this evidence suggests that although deserts are defined by their lack of precipitation, water is the chief influence on their existence. It forms the terrain that underlies them, creates the oceans of sand that cover many, and continues to reshape them through both gradual and more rapid processes.

5 ➡ 세차게 내린 비가 매일 반복되는 물 순환으로 이미 손상된 바위를 가득 채운 후, 태양으로 인한 빠른 건조는 종종 바위를 산산조각 낼 수 있다. 이런 폭발에서 발산되는 에너지는 심지어 바위를 가를 수도 있다. 이 현상은 왜 몇몇 바위들이 바람이나 흐르는 물의 도움 없이 움직이는 것처럼 보이는지 설명한다. 종합적으로 봤을 때 이 증거가 시사하는 바는 비록 사막이 강수량의 부족에 의해 규정되지만 물은 사막의 존재에 주된 영향력을 끼친다는 것이다. 물은 사막 아래의 지형을 형성하고 그 지역을 뒤덮고 있는 무수히 많은 모래를 만들어 내며, 느리기도 하고 좀 더 빠르게도 진행되는 과정들을 통해 사막의 모양을 계속 바꿔나가고 있다.

---

1. Sentence Simplification

Which of the sentences below best expresses the essential information in the highlighted sentence in the passage? *Incorrect* answer choices change the meaning in important ways or leave out essential information.

- Ⓐ The environment, which was under water in the past, has gone through drastic changes.
- Ⓑ Various scientific findings show that unlike its current state, the environment used to be one of the driest places.
- Ⓒ Evidence shows that the environment will be blessed with far more water than what it currently contains and will become very different.
- Ⓓ **Evidence shows that the environment possessed more water in the past than it does today.**

2. Inference

What can be inferred about the Sahara Desert in paragraph 1?

- Ⓐ **It thrived with animal life in the past.**
- Ⓑ It has only recently become the Earth's largest desert.
- Ⓒ It was the home to many artists who drew cave paintings.
- Ⓓ It is home to many different species of crocodiles.

3. Inference

Based on paragraph 2, what can be inferred from the data collected on the Sahara Desert?

- Ⓐ It is one of the oldest deserts in the world.
- Ⓑ It was formed during the Tertiary period.
- Ⓒ It has bodies of seawater trapped in its bedrock.
- Ⓓ **It might have a different ecosystem 5,000 years from now.**

1.

다음 중 지문의 음영 표시된 문장의 핵심 정보를 가장 잘 표현한 문장은 무엇인가? 오답은 의미를 크게 왜곡하거나 핵심 정보를 누락하고 있다.

- Ⓐ 과거에 물 아래 잠겨 있던 그 지역 환경이 극적인 변화를 거쳤다.
- Ⓑ 다양한 과학적 연구 결과들은 그 지역 환경이 현재의 상태와는 다르게 가장 메마른 곳 중 하나였음을 보여준다.
- Ⓒ 증거는 그 지역 환경이 현재 보유하고 있는 것보다 훨씬 많은 양의 물을 보유하여 축복 받은 환경이 될 것이고, 매우 달라질 것임을 보여준다.
- Ⓓ 증거는 그 지역 환경이 현재 보유하고 있는 것보다 많은 양의 물을 과거에 보유하고 있었음을 보여준다.

2.

1단락에서 사하라 사막에 대해 추론할 수 있는 것은 무엇인가?

- Ⓐ 과거에 동물이 번성했다.
- Ⓑ 최근에서야 지구상 가장 큰 사막이 되었다.
- Ⓒ 동굴 벽화를 그리는 많은 화가들의 고향이었다.
- Ⓓ 많은 다양한 종류의 악어들의 서식지다.

3.

2단락에 근거하여 사하라 사막에 대해 수집된 데이터에서 추론할 수 있는 것은 무엇인가?

- Ⓐ 세계에서 가장 오래된 사막 중 하나다.
- Ⓑ 제삼기에 형성됐다.
- Ⓒ 암반에 바닷물이 갇혀 있다.
- Ⓓ 그곳의 생태계는 5,000년 후 다른 모습을 하고 있을 수 있다.

4. Vocabulary

The word "relentlessly" in paragraph 3 is closest in meaning to

- (A) conventionally
- **(B) interminably**
- (C) gradually
- (D) eventually

5. Fact

According to paragraph 3, what do Antarctica and the Sahara have in common?

- (A) Both were habitats for dinosaurs.
- (B) Both have shifted to different continents.
- **(C) Both have extreme climates.**
- (D) Both used to be deserts.

6. Rhetorical Purpose

What is the main purpose of paragraph 3?

- (A) To compare and contrast Antarctica and the Sahara
- **(B) To provide an explanation for the climate changes**
- (C) To suggest how dinosaurs became extinct
- (D) To introduce a new theory regarding plate tectonics

7. Negative Fact

All of the following are mentioned in paragraphs 4 and 5 as effects of water on the desert EXCEPT

- (A) shattering boulders
- (B) forming shallow lakes
- (C) creating sand
- **(D) forming aquifers**

8. Fact

According to paragraph 5, what is a key characteristic of a desert?

- (A) Stones damaged by the daily water cycle
- (B) Powerful solar energy
- (C) Oceans of sand
- **(D) Lack of precipitation**

9. Insertion

Look at the four squares [■] that indicate where the following sentence could be added to the passage.

As this cycle repeats daily, the stones expand and contract, damaging them on a microscopic level.

Where would the sentence best fit? [■C]

4.

3단락의 단어 "relentlessly(끊임없이)"와 의미상 가장 가까운 것은?

- (A) 관례적으로
- (B) 끝없이 계속
- (C) 서서히
- (D) 결국

5.

3단락에 따르면, 남극과 사하라 사막의 공통점은 무엇인가?

- (A) 둘 다 공룡의 서식지였다.
- (B) 둘 다 다른 대륙으로 이동했다.
- (C) 둘 다 극한 기후를 갖고 있다.
- (D) 둘 다 과거에 사막이었다.

6.

3단락의 주요 목적은 무엇인가?

- (A) 남극과 사하라 사막을 비교하고 대조하기 위해
- (B) 기후 변화에 대한 설명을 제공하기 위해
- (C) 공룡들이 어떻게 멸종했는지에 대해 암시하기 위해
- (D) 판구조론에 관한 새로운 이론을 소개하기 위해

7.

다음 중 4, 5단락에서 물이 사막에 미치는 영향으로 언급되지 않은 것은?

- (A) 바위를 산산조각 내는 것
- (B) 얕은 호수를 형성하는 것
- (C) 모래를 만드는 것
- (D) 대수층을 형성하는 것

8.

5단락에 따르면, 사막의 중요한 특징은 무엇인가?

- (A) 매일 일어나는 물의 순환으로 손상된 바위들
- (B) 강력한 태양 에너지
- (C) 무수히 많은 모래
- (D) 강수량 부족

9.

지문에 다음 문장이 들어갈 수 있는 위치를 나타내는 네 개의 사각형[■]을 확인하시오.

이 순환이 매일 반복됨에 따라 바위들은 팽창하고 수축하면서 미세하게 손상을 입는다.

이 문장이 들어가기에 가장 적합한 곳은? [■C]

10. Summary

Directions: An introductory sentence for a brief summary of the passage is provided below. Complete the summary by selecting the THREE answer choices that express the most important ideas in the passage. Some sentences do not belong in the summary because they express ideas that are not presented in the passage or are minor ideas in the passage. *This question is worth 2 points.*

Areas that are deserts today were once lush land inhabited by animals and even people.

Ⓑ **Over the years, advanced technology has allowed evidence of the ancient landscape beneath the desert dunes to be unearthed.**

Ⓓ **Changes in the Earth's plates have caused drastic climatic changes around the world, as is evident in Antarctica and the Sahara Desert.**

Ⓔ **Water, which is crucial for sustaining life in the desert, still plays a significant role in creating and reshaping the terrain there.**

Ⓐ An Egyptian petroleum company penetrated sand sheets to determine the presence of freshwater aquifers beneath the sand dunes.

Ⓒ Scientists have discovered that the region which is currently the Sahara Desert undergoes cyclic climatic changes every 10,000 years.

Ⓕ The phenomenon in which rocks in the desert appear to move on their own is explained by the shattering of boulders damaged by the daily water cycle.

10.

지시문: 지문을 간략하게 요약한 글의 첫 문장이 아래 제시되어 있다. 지문의 가장 중요한 내용을 표현하는 세 개의 선택지를 골라 요약문을 완성하시오. 일부 문장들은 지문에 제시되지 않았거나 지문의 지엽적인 내용을 나타내기 때문에 요약문에 포함되지 않는다. *이 문제의 배점은 2점이다.*

오늘날 사막인 지역들은 과거에 동물 및 심지어 인간도 거주하던 비옥한 땅이었다.

Ⓑ 시간이 지나면서 첨단 기술은 사막의 모래 언덕들 아래의 옛 지형들의 흔적을 찾아낼 수 있게 했다.

Ⓓ 지구의 판의 변화들은 남극과 사하라 사막에서 볼 수 있다시피 전 세계에 극적인 기후 변화를 가져왔다.

Ⓔ 사막에서 생명을 유지하는 데 결정적인 물은 그곳의 지형을 만들어 내고 새로운 모양으로 만드는 데 있어 여전히 중대한 역할을 하고 있다.

Ⓐ 이집트 석유 회사는 모래 언덕 아래에 담수성 대수층의 존재 여부를 밝히기 위해 모래층을 뚫었다.

Ⓒ 과학자들은 현재 사하라 사막이 위치한 지역이 1만 년마다 주기적으로 기후 변화를 겪는다는 것을 발견했다.

Ⓕ 사막에서 바위들이 자력으로 움직이는 것처럼 보이는 현상은 매일 일어나는 물의 순환 작용으로 인해 손상된 바위들이 산산조각 나는 것으로 설명된다.

📖 어휘

1 **reputation** ⓝ 평판, 명성 | **extreme** adj 극도의, 극심한 | **hostile** adj 적대적인 | **ample** adj 충분한 | **flourish** ⓥ 번창하다, 번성하다 | **adorn** ⓥ 꾸미다, 장식하다 | **grassland** ⓝ 풀밭, 초원 | **adapt** ⓥ 적응하다 | **harsh** adj 가혹한, 혹독한, 냉혹한 | **linger** ⓥ 남다[계속되다] | **remnant** ⓝ 남은 부분, 나머지 | **prevail** ⓥ 우세하다, 만연[팽배]하다 | **currently** adv 현재, 지금 | **possess** ⓥ 소유[소지/보유]하다

2 **terrain** ⓝ 지형, 지역 | **underlie** ⓥ ~의 아래에 있다, ~의 밑바닥에 잠재하다 | **carve** ⓥ 조각하다, 깎아서 만들다 | **advance** ⓥ 진전하다, 진격하다 | **retreat** ⓥ 후퇴[철수/퇴각]하다 | **penetrate** ⓥ 뚫고 들어가다, 관통하다, 투과하다 | **subsequently** adv 그 뒤에, 나중에

3 **massive** adj 거대한 | **relentlessly** adv 끈질기게, 가차없이 | **massively** adv 엄청나게 | **precipitation** ⓝ 강수(량) | **lush** adj 무성한, 우거진 | **wilderness** ⓝ 황야, 황무지 | **primeval** adj 태고의, 원시 시대부터 내려온 | **dominate** ⓥ 지배하다, 특징이 되다 | **landscape** ⓝ 풍경 | **polar** adj 북극[남극]의, 극지의 | **scarce** adj 부족한, 드문 | **conducive to** ~에 도움이 되는

4 **rare** adj 드문, 희귀한 | **resist** ⓥ 저항[반대]하다 | **subtle** adj 미묘한, 감지하기 힘든 | **change** ⓝ 변화 | **deposit** ⓥ 침전시키다 | **moisture** ⓝ 수분, 습기 | **evaporate** ⓥ 증발하다[시키다] | **readily** adv 손쉽게, 순조롭게 | **observable** adj 눈에 보이는, 식별[관찰]할 수 있는 | **flake off** 조각으로 떨어지다[벗겨지다]

5 **saturate** ⓥ 포화 상태를 만들다 | **boulder** ⓝ 바위 | **define** ⓥ 정의하다, 규정하다 | **gradual** adj 서서히 일어나는, 점진적인

New York City Urban Planning

1 ➡ Originally settled by the Dutch under the name of New Amsterdam, New York is one of the oldest planned cities in the United States. Like many early colonial cities, it began its existence as a fortification and was constructed along military guidelines. They eventually surrendered it to England, which in turn lost it when the United States achieved its independence. As the city expanded, a great deal of effort went into keeping the city organized. In fact, in 1811, the city council adopted a plan that divided up the mostly undeveloped northern portion of Manhattan Island and employed a strict grid pattern, regardless of terrain. However, due to the city's rampant growth, these measures often proved insufficient, and there were many serious problems involving health, sanitation and safety.

2 ➡ New York City has always been an important port city, but few anticipated the number of immigrants it would receive, and many buildings had to be rapidly constructed to accommodate the new arrivals. By 1800, the city's population had reached 30,000 people, most of whom lived in an area that only comprises a fraction of the modern city. Some historians estimate that New York's population increased at a rate of around 100 percent every ten years, which meant that even more people were forced to live in hastily constructed tenements. Such massive immigration and overcrowding inevitably created conditions that were perfect for infectious diseases to ravage the city. Epidemics of cholera, malaria, and typhoid swept through the population in the early 19th century, killing thousands in some of the worst outbreaks the country has ever seen. The demolition of many apartment buildings and the development of the northern part of the island served to alleviate the overcrowding, but these diseases would return again. One famous case was an outbreak of typhoid in the early 1900s. A woman whom the press labeled Typhoid Mary was a carrier of the disease who caused the deaths of over fifty people while working as a maid.

3 ➡ Along with overcrowding, New York also suffered from an inadequate sanitation system. All of the cabs and wagons that transported people

뉴욕 시의 도시 계획

1 ➡ 뉴암스테르담이란 이름으로 원래 네덜란드인들이 정착한 뉴욕은 미국에서 가장 오래된 계획 도시 중 하나이다. 초기의 많은 식민 도시들처럼 뉴욕도 요새로 존재했고 군사 가이드라인을 따라 건설되었다. 그들은 결국 영국에 뉴욕을 넘겼고, 영국은 다시 미국이 독립을 쟁취했을 때 그곳을 빼앗겼다. 도시가 확장함에 따라 도시를 정리하기 위한 많은 노력이 들어갔다. 사실 1811년에 시 의회는 거의 개발되지 않은 맨해튼섬의 북쪽 지역을 분리하고, 지형에 관계없이 엄격한 격자형을 이용하는 계획을 채택했다. 그러나 도시의 걷잡을 수 없는 발달로 이러한 조치들이 종종 불충분한 것으로 드러났고, 건강, 위생, 안전과 관련된 심각한 문제들이 있었다.

2 ➡ 뉴욕 시는 항상 중요한 항구 도시였지만 그것이 받아들이게 될 이민자의 수를 예측한 사람은 거의 없었고, 많은 건물들이 새로이 도착한 사람들을 수용하기 위해 빠르게 지어져야 했다. 1800년 즈음에 도시의 인구는 3만 명에 달했는데, 그들 대부분은 현재 도시의 일부에 해당하는 지역에 살았다. 일부 역사가들은 뉴욕의 인구가 10년마다 약 100퍼센트의 비율로 증가했다고 추산하는데, 이는 점점 더 많은 사람들이 급히 지어진 임대건물에 살아야만 했다는 것을 의미했다. 그러한 엄청난 이민과 과밀 거주는 전염병이 도시에 창궐하기에 완벽한 조건을 불가피하게 만들었다. 19세기 초에 콜레라, 말라리아와 장티푸스 같은 전염병이 사람들을 휩쓸었고, 일부 지역에서는 건국 이래 최악의 발생으로 수천 명이 사망했다. 많은 아파트 건물의 철거와 섬 북부의 개발이 과밀 거주를 완화하기 위해 이루어졌지만, 이런 전염병은 재발하곤 했다. 한 유명한 사례는 1900년대 초의 장티푸스 발생이었다. 언론이 장티푸스 메리라고 꼬리표를 붙인 어떤 여자가 병의 보균자였고, 가정부로 일하는 동안 50명이 넘는 사람들의 죽음을 야기했다.

3 ➡ 과밀 거주와 함께 뉴욕은 또한 부적절한 위생 체계로 고통을 받았다. 도시 거리를 가로질러 사람과 상품을 나르던 모든 택시와 수레들은 말이 끌었는데, 20세기 초까지

and goods through the city streets were pulled by horses, and an estimated 200,000 of them were living there by the beginning of the 20th century. By necessity, most of these animals lived on the island of Manhattan, often in residential areas. [■A] These animals generated large amounts of waste that piled up throughout the city due to a lack of infrastructure. [■B] Most often, waste was left in the middle of the street, as horse owners were far less likely to clean up after their horses if they were not on their own property. This waste made the streets reek in the summer, and it mixed with heavy snow in the winter, sometimes accumulating in frozen piles up to two meters high. [■C] Not only that, but the horses also were often overworked and otherwise mistreated to the extent that many of them died in the streets, where their bodies would remain since no one had the responsibility of cleaning them up. [■D] This situation was not remedied until 1909, when the Queensboro Bridge was opened to traffic. This allowed the waste to be transported over to rural Queens where it was used to fertilize farmland.

4 ➡ Waste from animals and humans led to an even more serious health problem: contaminated drinking water. Manhattan Island had never had a reliable water supply, with its brackish rivers forcing people to rely upon well water. Already insufficient, as the population grew, the aquifer those wells reached into became seriously polluted, which led to severe outbreaks of cholera. To cope with this problem, they had to look far outside of the city to find a viable source of water. The city undertook a large and complex project to bring fresh water from the Croton River to the island. Built between 1837 and 1842, the Old Croton Aqueduct brought water 66 kilometers to reservoirs in the city. Life in the city rapidly improved, but its growth did not slow down, and many additional aqueducts have been built since.

5 ➡ As serious as the health and sanitation issues were, a serious safety issue went largely ignored until disaster struck. After years of construction, the Erie Canal opened, successfully linking the Hudson River to the Great Lakes in 1825. This shipping lane dramatically increased trade in New York, and warehouses sprang up throughout the financial district to accommodate the merchants' goods. Unfortunately, like most of the city's other buildings, these warehouses were made of wood, and a

약 20만 마리의 말이 거기 살고 있던 것으로 추정된다. 필요에 의해 대부분의 말은 맨해튼섬에, 흔히 주거 지역에 살았다. [■A] 말은 기반 시설의 부족으로 도시 전체에 다량의 배설물을 배출했다. [■B] 대부분의 경우 배설물은 거리 중간에 방치되었는데, 말 주인들이 자신의 땅이 아니면 말의 배설물을 치우려고 하지 않았기 때문이었다. 이 배설물은 여름에는 거리에 냄새가 진동하게 했고, 겨울에는 많은 눈과 섞여 때로는 2미터 이상의 높이로 얼어 있었다. [■C] 그뿐만 아니라 말 역시 일을 과하게 하거나 혹사당하여 많은 말이 거리에서 죽었고, 누구도 그 사체를 치울 책임이 없었으므로 거리에 그냥 버려져 있곤 했다. [■D] 이러한 상황은 퀸즈버러 다리가 개통된 1909년까지 고쳐지지 않았다. 다리의 개통으로 배설물이 퀸즈의 시골 지역으로 옮겨져 농장을 비옥하게 하는 데 사용될 수 있었다.

4 ➡ 동물과 사람이 배출한 쓰레기는 더 심각한 건강 문제를 야기했는데, 그것은 오염된 식수였다. 맨해튼섬은 믿을 만한 식수 공급처를 가진 적이 없었는데, 염분이 섞인 강물은 사람들이 우물물에 의존하게 만들었다. 이미 불충분한 데다 인구가 늘어나자 그 우물들이 닿아 있는 대수층은 심각하게 오염되었고, 이는 심각한 콜레라 발생으로 이어졌다. 이 문제를 해결하기 위해 사람들은 이용 가능한 수자원을 찾기 위해 도시에서 멀리 떨어진 곳까지 찾아야 했다. 시는 담수를 크로턴강으로부터 맨해튼섬으로 끌어오는 복잡한 대형 프로젝트에 착수했다. 1837~1842년 사이에 건설된 올드 크로턴 송수관은 도시의 저수지로 물을 66킬로미터 끌어왔다. 도시의 삶은 급격히 개선되었지만 도시의 성장은 둔화되지 않았고, 추가로 많은 송수관들이 그 이후로 건설되었다.

5 ➡ 건강과 위생 문제가 심각했던 만큼 또 하나의 심각한 안전 문제가 큰 재난이 닥치기 전까지 대체로 무시되었다. 몇 년간의 공사 후, 1825년에 이리 운하가 개통되어 성공적으로 허드슨강과 5대호를 연결했다. 이 선박 항로는 뉴욕의 교역을 극적으로 증가시켰고, 상품을 수용하기 위해 금융가에 창고들이 속속 지어졌다. 불행히도 도시의 다른 대부분의 건물들처럼 이 창고들은 나무로 만들어졌고, 1835년 12월 16일 저녁, 매우 춥고 바람이 많이 불던 날 한 창고에서 재앙을 초래하는 화재가 발생했다. 불이 완전히 꺼지기까지 뉴욕 대화재는 맨해튼 남동부를 완전히 파괴하며,

calamitous fire started in a warehouse on the bitterly cold and windy evening of December 16, 1835. Before its flames were finally put out, the Great Fire of New York razed southeastern Manhattan, destroying most of the buildings in Wall Street and the New York Stock Exchange. The builders had ignored the dangers of constructing so many wooden buildings in such close proximity, and the fire took full advantage of their oversight. Following the conflagration, city planners regulated the minimum distance between buildings and created newer, stricter fire prevention policies.

월가의 대부분의 건물과 뉴욕 증권 거래소를 파괴했다. 건설자들은 그렇게 많은 목조 건물들을 아주 가깝게 건설하는 것의 위험성을 무시했으며, 화재는 그들의 간과를 충분히 이용했다. 대화재 이후 도시 기획자들은 건물 간의 최소 거리를 규제했고, 더 새롭고 더 엄격한 화재 예방 정책들을 세웠다.

---

1. Reference
The word "They" in paragraph 1 refers to
- Ⓐ the Dutch
- Ⓑ colonial cities
- Ⓒ guidelines
- Ⓓ the United States

2. Vocabulary
The word "inevitably" in paragraph 2 is closest in meaning to
- Ⓐ relentlessly
- Ⓑ unavoidably
- Ⓒ perversely
- Ⓓ allegedly

3. Inference
Based on paragraph 2, what can be inferred about epidemics in New York City in the early 19th century?
- Ⓐ They caused many people to resettle on the northern part of the island.
- Ⓑ Immigration declined due to the unsanitary conditions.
- Ⓒ The authorities were unable to locate the sources of outbreaks.
- Ⓓ Population growth slowed because of massive outbreaks of disease.

4. Fact
According to paragraph 3, what was the main role of horses in New York?
- Ⓐ Pulling cabs and wagons
- Ⓑ Disposing of waste in residential areas
- Ⓒ Fertilizing farmland
- Ⓓ Clearing snow in the winter

1.
1단락의 단어 "They(그들)"이 가리키는 것은?
- Ⓐ 네덜란드인들
- Ⓑ 식민 도시들
- Ⓒ 가이드라인
- Ⓓ 미국

2.
2단락의 단어 "inevitably(불가피하게)"와 의미상 가장 가까운 것은?
- Ⓐ 가차 없이
- Ⓑ 피할 수 없이
- Ⓒ 심술궂게
- Ⓓ 주장한 바에 의하면

3.
2단락에 근거하여 19세기 초반 뉴욕 시의 전염병에 대해 추론할 수 있는 것은 무엇인가?
- Ⓐ 많은 사람들이 섬의 북부에 다시 정착하게 만들었다.
- Ⓑ 비위생적인 환경 때문에 이민이 감소했다.
- Ⓒ 당국은 전염병 발생의 근원지를 밝혀낼 수 없었다.
- Ⓓ 대규모 전염병 발생 때문에 인구 증가가 둔화되었다.

4.
3단락에 따르면, 뉴욕에서 말의 주요 역할은 무엇이었는가?
- Ⓐ 택시와 수레 끌기
- Ⓑ 주거 지역의 배설물 처리
- Ⓒ 농장에 거름 주기
- Ⓓ 겨울에 눈 치우기

5. Sentence Simplification

Which of the sentences below best expresses the essential information in the highlighted sentence in the passage? *Incorrect* answer choices change the meaning in important ways or leave out essential information.

(A) The population was unable to filter the water from the polluted wells, leading to severe cholera outbreaks.

(B) The wells were used as sewers, polluting the aquifer and causing severe outbreaks of cholera amidst the growing population.

(C) **The aquifer which the wells reached into, already insufficient with population growth, became polluted and led to increased disease.**

(D) As the population grew, the wells could no longer reach the aquifer, which led to epidemics.

6. Fact

According to paragraph 4, what did the Old Croton Aqueduct achieve?

(A) It linked the Croton River to the Great Lakes.

(B) It provided an ample supply of clean water to the city.

(C) It paved the way for additional population growth.

(D) **It improved the quality of life in the city.**

7. Rhetorical Purpose

Why does the author mention "Great Fire of New York" in paragraph 5?

(A) To prove that fire has a more disastrous effect on society than poor sanitation

(B) To highlight the unexpected consequences of constructing the Erie Canal

(C) **To point out an aspect of urban planning the city planners neglected**

(D) To introduce the history of fire safety regulations in New York City

8. Negative Fact

Which of the following is NOT mentioned in the passage as a source of misfortune in New York City?

(A) Massive immigration

(B) Poor sanitation system

(C) Lack of drinking water

(D) **Wooden buildings**

5.

다음 중 지문의 음영 표시된 문장의 핵심 정보를 가장 잘 표현한 문장은 무엇인가? 오답은 의미를 크게 왜곡하거나 핵심 정보를 누락하고 있다.

(A) 사람들은 오염된 우물들의 물을 정수할 수 없었고, 이는 심각한 콜레라의 발생으로 이어졌다.

(B) 우물들은 하수도로 사용되어 대수층을 오염시키고 늘어나는 인구에 심각한 콜레라의 발생을 야기했다.

(C) 이미 인구 증가로 부족한 상태였던 우물들이 닿아 있던 대수층은 오염되었고 이는 질병 발생 증가로 이어졌다.

(D) 인구가 증가함에 따라 우물들은 더 이상 대수층에 도달할 수 없었고, 이는 전염병으로 이어졌다.

6.

4단락에 따르면, 올드 크로턴 송수관이 해낸 것은 무엇인가?

(A) 크로턴강과 5대호를 연결했다.

(B) 도시에 많은 양의 깨끗한 물을 공급했다.

(C) 추가적인 인구 증가를 위한 길을 닦았다.

(D) 도시의 삶의 질을 개선했다.

7.

5단락에서 글쓴이가 "뉴욕 대화재"를 언급하는 이유는 무엇인가?

(A) 화재가 열악한 위생 시설보다 사회에 더 파괴적인 영향을 미쳤다는 것을 증명하기 위해

(B) 이리 운하 건설에 따른 예상치 못한 결과를 강조하기 위해

(C) 도시 기획자들이 무시했던 도시 계획의 측면을 지적하기 위해

(D) 뉴욕 시 화재 안전 규정의 역사를 소개하기 위해

8.

다음 중 지문에서 뉴욕 시에 일어난 불운의 원인으로 언급되지 않은 것은 무엇인가?

(A) 대량 이민

(B) 열악한 위생 체계

(C) 식수 부족

(D) 목조 건물

9. Insertion

Look at the four squares [■] that indicate where the following sentence could be added to the passage.

Most often, waste was left in the middle of the street, as horse owners were far less likely to clean up after their horses if they were not on their own property.

Where would the sentence best fit? [■ B]

10. Summary

Directions: An introductory sentence for a brief summary of the passage is provided below. Complete the summary by selecting the THREE answer choices that express the most important ideas in the passage. Some sentences do not belong in the summary because they express ideas that are not presented in the passage or are minor ideas in the passage. ***This question is worth 2 points.***

New York, one of the oldest planned cities in the United States, underwent significant trial and error in tackling problems such as public health, sanitation, and fire safety during its development.

Ⓐ The huge number of immigrants settling down in New York rapidly increased the city's population, resulting in overcrowding and epidemic outbreaks.

Ⓑ The lack of a proper sanitation system or a reliable water supply resulted in outbreaks of cholera, prompting the city to transport clean water to the island.

Ⓔ After the fire in 1835, a greater awareness of fire safety led to stricter regulations about constructing buildings.

Ⓒ The horse owners did not clean up after their horses, and often left the remains of dead horses on the streets, providing a trigger for epidemic outbreaks.

Ⓓ Frequent outbreaks of infectious diseases led the city to demolish apartment buildings, and it was effective at curbing the death tolls.

Ⓕ The building of the Queensboro Bridge allowed the waste accumulated in Manhattan to be transported to Queens, where it was used as fertilizer.

9.

지문에 다음 문장이 들어갈 수 있는 위치를 나타내는 네 개의 사각형[■]을 확인하시오.

대부분의 경우 배설물은 거리 중간에 방치되었는데, 말 주인들이 자신의 땅이 아니면 말의 배설물을 치우려고 하지 않았기 때문이었다.

이 문장이 들어가기에 가장 적합한 곳은? [■ B]

10.

지시문: 지문을 간략하게 요약한 글의 첫 문장이 아래 제시되어 있다. 지문의 가장 중요한 내용을 표현하는 세 개의 선택지를 골라 요약문을 완성하시오. 일부 문장들은 지문에 제시되지 않았거나 지문의 지엽적인 내용을 나타내기 때문에 요약문에 포함되지 않는다. *이 문제의 배점은 2점이다.*

미국에서 가장 오래된 계획 도시 중 하나인 뉴욕은 발전 과정에서 공중 보건, 위생 시설, 화재 안전과 같은 문제들을 해결하는 데 상당한 시행 착오를 겪었다.

Ⓐ 뉴욕에 정착한 엄청난 수의 이민자들은 도시의 인구를 급증시켰으며, 이는 과밀 거주와 전염병 발생으로 이어졌다.

Ⓑ 적절한 위생 체계나 믿을 만한 물 공급의 부족은 콜레라의 발생으로 이어졌고 도시로 하여금 깨끗한 물을 맨해튼섬으로 끌어오게 했다.

Ⓔ 1835년의 대화재 이후, 화재 안전에 대한 더 큰 자각은 건물의 건설에 대한 더 엄격한 규정으로 이어졌다.

Ⓒ 말 주인들은 말의 배설물을 치우지 않았고, 종종 말의 사체를 거리에 그냥 내버려 두어 전염병 발생의 계기를 제공했다.

Ⓓ 빈번한 전염성 질병의 발생은 도시로 하여금 아파트 건물을 철거하게 했으며, 그것은 사망자 수를 억제하는 데 효과적이었다.

Ⓕ 퀸즈버러 다리의 건설은 맨해튼에 쌓인 쓰레기가 퀸즈로 옮겨져 그곳에서 비료로 사용될 수 있게 했다.

📘 어휘

1 **originally** adv 원래, 본래 | **settle** v 정착하다 | **construct** v 건설하다 | **surrender** v 항복하다, 포기하다, 넘겨주다 | **expand** v 확대[확장/팽창]되다 | **undeveloped** adj 미개발된 | **employ** v 고용하다, 이용하다 | **rampant** adj 걷잡을 수 없는, 만연[횡행]하는 | **insufficient** adj 불충분한 | **sanitation** n 위생 시설[관리], 공중 위생

2 **anticipate** v 예상하다, 예측하다 | **accommodate** v 수용하다 | **comprise** v ~으로 구성되다[이뤄지다] | **hastily** adv 급히, 서둘러서 | **inevitably** adv 필연적으로, 불가피하게 | **infectious** adj 전염되는 | **ravage** v 황폐[피폐]하게 만들다, 유린[파괴]하다 | **outbreak** n 발생[발발] | **demolition** n 파괴, 폭파, 철거 | **alleviate** v 완화하다 | **carrier** n 보균자, 나르는[운반하는] 사람[것]

3 **estimated** adj 추측의, 견적의 | **necessity** n 필요(성) | **generate** v 발생시키다, 만들어 내다 | **infrastructure** n 사회[공공] 기반 시설 | **accumulate** v 모으다, 축적하다 | **mistreat** v 학대[혹사]하다 | **fertilize** v 비옥하게 하다, 비료를 주다

4 **reliable** adj 믿을[신뢰할] 수 있는 | **pollute** v 오염시키다 | **cope** v 대처[대응]하다 | **viable** adj 실행 가능한, 성공할 수 있는 | **undertake** v 착수하다 | **reservoir** n 저수지

5 **largely** adv 크게, 대체로, 주로 | **ignore** v 무시하다 | **dramatically** adv 극적으로 | **spring up** 갑자기 생겨나다 | **financial** adj 금융[재정]의 | **calamitous** adj 재앙을 초래하는 | **bitterly** adv 몹시, 비통하게, 격렬히 | **raze** v 완전히 파괴하다 | **proximity** n 가까움[근접] | **take advantage** ~을 기회로 활용하다, ~을 이용하다 | **oversight** n 실수, 간과 | **conflagration** n 대화재 | **regulate** v 규제하다, 조절하다 | **fire prevention** 화재 예방 | **policy** n 정책

Actual Test 04

본서 | P. 111

Passage 1 Biodiversity in the Hawaiian Islands

1. Ⓓ	Fact	6. Ⓒ	Negative Fact
2. Ⓑ	Sentence Simplification	7. Ⓓ	Fact
3. Ⓒ	Negative Fact	8. Ⓓ	Inference
4. Ⓒ	Rhetorical Purpose	9. Ⓐ	Insertion
5. Ⓑ	Fact	10. Ⓐ, Ⓑ, Ⓔ	Summary

Passage 2 The Purpose of Extrafloral Nectar

1. Ⓓ	Fact	6. Ⓒ	Rhetorical Purpose
2. Ⓑ	Sentence Simplification	7. Ⓓ	Fact
3. Ⓑ	Inference	8. Ⓑ	Inference
4. Ⓓ	Negative Fact	9. Ⓓ	Insertion
5. Ⓐ	Vocabulary	10. Ⓒ, Ⓓ, Ⓕ	Summary

Passage 3 Population Distribution

1. Ⓑ	Fact	6. Ⓐ	Fact
2. Ⓑ	Rhetorical Purpose	7. Ⓒ	Sentence Simplification
3. Ⓑ	Inference	8. Ⓐ	Fact
4. Ⓐ, Ⓒ	Fact	9. Ⓐ	Insertion
5. Ⓓ	Vocabulary	10. Ⓐ, Ⓓ, Ⓖ / Ⓒ, Ⓔ	Category Chart

● 내가 맞은 문제 유형의 개수를 적어 보고 어느 유형에 취약한지 확인해 봅시다.

문제 유형	맞은 개수
Sentence Simplification	3
Fact / Negative Fact	12
Vocabulary	2
Reference	0
Rhetorical Purpose	3
Inference	4
Insertion	3
Summary	2
Category Chart	1
Total	30

Biodiversity in the Hawaiian Islands

1 ➡ The flora and fauna of the Hawaiian Islands display a level of biodiversity that is particularly remarkable due to their isolation. Located in the middle of the Pacific Ocean, the Hawaiian archipelago is about 4,000 kilometers from the nearest continent, and the islands were never attached to any large landmass. They are the tops of mountains created by a volcanic hot spot under the seafloor. None of the organisms found there could have taken an overland route from Asia, Australia, or the Americas, yet these areas share many of the same species. Some of the current species were introduced by humans, either when Polynesian people settled there around 500 CE or after Europeans reached the islands in the 1600s, but many of the organisms are different enough from other organisms that they must have arrived there much earlier and evolved in isolation. Therefore, the plants and animals that had lived there before humans arrived must have used other means of transportation to reach the islands.

2 ➡ The organisms that predate human colonization of Hawaii arrived by what are referred to as the "3 Ws." The first is "wind," which transported small, light seeds through the air. The second is "wings," which refers both to flying insects and birds and the seeds and other organisms that they carried with them. These animals did not deliberately transport seeds, but they did carry them lodged in their feathers and resting in their stomachs after eating fruit. After they reached the islands, the seeds were dislodged or released in their excrement. Many seeds actually require passing through an animal's digestive tract to germinate, so this method of transportation is widespread. The third "W" is "waves," which refers to all organisms that were brought over on ocean waves and currents. In some cases these were individual seeds like coconuts, but the category also includes rafts of tree branches and other drifting vegetation that carry their seeds and animal passengers. Such drifting rafts are how most land-based animals reach islands without human help.

3 ➡ The climate of Hawaii is typical for the tropics, but it varies with altitude and weather. The Hawaiian Islands sit atop volcanoes that range in age from

하와이 제도의 생물 다양성

1 ➡ 하와이 제도의 동식물상은 그곳의 지리적 고립 때문에 특별히 더 두드러지는 생물의 다양성을 보여준다. 태평양 중앙에 위치한 하와이 군도는 가장 가까운 대륙으로부터 약 4천 킬로미터 떨어져 있으며, 섬들은 그 어떤 큰 대륙과도 연결되었던 적이 없다. 그들은 해저의 화산의 핫 스폿에 의해 생성된 산의 꼭대기이다. 그곳에서 발견된 어느 생물도 아시아, 호주, 또는 미국 대륙으로부터 육로로 갔을 가능성은 없는데, 이 지역들은 동일한 종의 생물들을 많이 공유하고 있다. 현재 살고 있는 종들의 일부는 인간에 의해 유입되었는데, 그 시기는 폴리네시아 사람들이 서기 500년경에 거기 정착했을 때거나 또는 유럽인들이 1600년대에 그 섬에 도착한 후인데, 많은 생물체들이 다른 생물체들과 많이 다르므로 그들은 훨씬 더 일찍 거기에 도달해서 고립된 상태로 진화했음이 분명하다. 따라서 인간이 도착하기 전에 그곳에 살았던 동식물들은 섬에 도착하기 위해 다른 방법의 이동 수단을 사용했을 것이 틀림없다.

2 ➡ 인간보다 먼저 하와이를 점령한 생물체들은 소위 '3W'라고 불리는 것들에 의해 그곳에 도달했다. 첫 번째는 '바람'인데, 이는 작고 가벼운 씨앗들을 공기를 통해 이동시켰다. 두 번째는 '날개'인데, 날아다니는 곤충과 새, 그리고 그들이 함께 운반해 온 씨앗과 다른 생물체들을 모두 가리킨다. 이 동물들이 의도적으로 씨앗을 운반한 것은 아니고, 그들의 깃털에 붙어 있었거나 과일을 먹은 후에 위에 남아 있게 되었던 것들을 가져오게 된 것이다. 이러한 동물들이 섬에 도착한 후에, 씨앗은 떨어지거나 배설물과 함께 밖으로 나온다. 실제로 많은 씨앗들이 발아하기 위해 동물의 소화관을 통과해야만 하므로, 이러한 방식의 이동이 만연하다. 세 번째 W는 '파도'인데, 파랑과 해류에 밀려오는 모든 생물체를 가리킨다. 어떤 경우 이것들은 코코넛과 같은 개별적인 씨앗이었지만, 이 범주에는 이들의 씨앗과 동물 승객을 운반하는 나뭇가지 뗏목이나 다른 떠다니는 식물들 또한 포함된다. 이렇게 떠다니는 나뭇가지 뗏목은 대부분의 육지 동물들이 인간의 도움 없이 섬에 도달하는 방법이다.

3 ➡ 하와이의 기후는 열대 지방의 전형적인 기후이지만, 고도와 날씨에 따라 다양하다. 하와이 제도는 시간상으로 2천 8백만 년이 된 가장 북서쪽에 있는 쿠레 아톨에서부터

28 million years old for the northwestern-most Kure Atoll to a mere 400,000 years old for the main island. Despite the young geologic age of some, the islands have been heavily weathered, and they provide a wide variety of habitats. The smaller lower western islands are mostly rock with little protection from the wind. The larger eastern islands have peaks that reach up to 2.5 kilometers above sea level, which creates a variety of climatic zones. Since the islands are in the tropics, the temperature at sea level varies little throughout the year. At higher elevations, the climate becomes more temperate, and eventually transforms into alpine tundra at the summits of the tallest peaks. Some of the volcanoes are still active, which obviously puts pressure on any species that try to live in the immediate vicinity.

4 ➡ Being in the tropics also means that the islands are constantly buffeted by the trade winds that blow from the Eastern Pacific. Due to these winds, the eastern faces of the tall islands capture most of the rain that falls on the islands. This means that the windward side of an island supports much more plant life than the side that is out of the wind. Therefore, the windward sides are covered by lush rainforests filled with a myriad of species, while the leeward sides are open grassland with scattered shrubs. On the high mountain slopes, only hardy bushes and flowering plants can survive the colder weather that brings frequent frost and occasional snow.

5 ➡ The environmental extremes that characterize the Hawaiian Islands have forced any species that managed to survive there to adapt rapidly. [■A] About 90 percent of the organisms in Hawaii are native to the islands, and they exist nowhere else. The endemic species include a staggering array of plant, bird, and insect species, but there are no native reptiles or amphibians and only a few mammals. [■B] However, even among the categories with abundant species there is often a surprising lack of different types. [■C] For example, there are about 800 species of flies, but only about 15 percent of the world's insect families are represented, and termites, ants, and mosquitoes were wholly introduced by people. [■D] When new species successfully migrated to the islands, they adapted to fill many niches, which resulted in this kind of selective diversity. Since there are no large native predator species, most of the organisms also lack

생긴 지 40만 년 밖에 되지 않은 주요 섬에 걸친 화산 위에 앉아 있다. 지질학적으로 비교적 어린 나이에도 불구하고, 이 섬들은 심하게 풍화를 겪어 왔으며, 아주 다양한 서식지를 제공한다. 더 작고 낮은 서쪽 섬들은 대개 바람으로부터의 보호를 거의 받지 못하는 돌덩이다. 더 큰 동쪽 섬들은 그 봉우리가 해발 최대 2.5킬로미터까지 솟아 있는데, 그것은 다양한 기후대를 만들어 낸다. 이러한 섬들은 열대 지방에 위치해 있어서 해수면의 기온이 연중 거의 다르지 않다. 고도가 높은 곳에서는 기후가 온화해지다가, 결국 가장 높은 정상에서는 고산 툰드라로 바뀐다. 일부 화산들은 아직도 활동 중이며, 이는 분명 그 일대에 사는 생물들에게 압박을 가하고 있다.

4 ➡ 열대 지방에 있다는 것은 섬이 동태평양에서 불어오는 무역풍에 지속적으로 뒤흔들린다는 의미이다. 이 바람 때문에, 높은 섬들의 동쪽 면이 섬에 내리는 비의 대부분을 맞게 된다. 이는 섬에서 바람이 불어오는 쪽이 바람이 없는 쪽에 비해 식생이 훨씬 더 많다는 의미이다. 따라서 바람이 불어오는 쪽은 수많은 종들로 가득한 무성한 열대 우림으로 덮여 있는 반면, 바람이 가려지는 쪽은 드문드문 관목이 있는 열린 목초지이다. 높은 산의 경사면에는 오직 강인한 덤불과 꽃을 피우는 식물들만이 잦은 서리와 가끔 눈이 내리는 추운 날씨에서 살아남을 수 있다.

5 ➡ 하와이 제도의 특징인 극단적인 환경은 그곳에서 살아남은 생물체들이 빠르게 적응할 수밖에 없도록 만들었다. [■A] 하와이의 생물체의 약 90퍼센트가 섬의 토착 종들이며, 그 밖의 어떤 곳에서도 존재하지 않는다. 이러한 고유종에는 놀라울 정도로 다양한 식물, 새, 곤충 종들이 포함되어 있지만, 토착 파충류나 양서류는 없으며, 오직 소수의 포유동물들만이 있을 뿐이다. [■B] 하지만 심지어 풍부한 종을 보유하고 있는 범주 내에서도 다른 종들은 놀라울 정도로 결여되어 있는 경우가 종종 있다. [■C] 예를 들어, 파리는 약 800여 종이 있는 반면, 세계의 곤충 중 오직 약 15퍼센트만이 있을 뿐이며, 흰개미, 개미, 모기는 전적으로 사람에 의해 유입되었다. [■D] 새로운 종이 이 섬에 성공적으로 이주를 했고, 그들이 적응을 하여 많은 적소를 채우면서 이러한 일종의 선택적 다양성으로 이어졌다. 커다란 토종 포식자 종이 없기 때문에, 대부분의 생물체들은 그들의 먼 친척이 사용하는 위장술, 방호 기관, 그리고 독과 같은 방어 기제를 가지고 있지 않다. 그 결과 인간이 새로운 생물체들을 유입하기 시작하면서 많은 토종 동식물종들이 멸종했다.

the defensive mechanisms that their distant cousins use like camouflage, armor, and venom. As a result, many of the native flora and fauna species have gone extinct since humans began introducing new organisms.

1. Fact
Which of the following questions is answered by paragraph 1?

(A) Who named the islands?

(B) When were the Hawaiian Islands created?

(C) How many native species live in the Hawaiian Islands?

(D) **What caused the unique biodiversity of the Hawaiian Islands?**

2. Sentence Simplification
Which of the sentences below best expresses the essential information in the highlighted sentence in the passage? *Incorrect* answer choices change the meaning in important ways or leave out essential information.

(A) Both the Polynesians and European explorers introduced new species to the Hawaiian Islands.

(B) **Many of the species that live in Hawaii were introduced by people, but others are so unique that they must have evolved there on their own.**

(C) Most of the animals that live in Hawaii were brought there by people around 500 CE.

(D) Even though many species did not arrive there until the 1600s, they have rapidly adapted to their environment and become distinct from their original species.

3. Negative Fact
According to paragraph 2, which of the following is NOT a way seeds made their way to the Hawaiian archipelago?

(A) Transported through the air by wind

(B) Embedded in birds' feathers

(C) **Drifting with volcanic ash**

(D) Resting in animals' digestive organs

4. Rhetorical Purpose
What is the purpose of paragraph 3 as it relates to paragraph 2?

(A) To continue the explanation of the transportation of the organisms described in paragraph 2

(B) To suggest another way of transportation in addition to the ways mentioned in paragraph 2

1.
다음 중 1단락에서 답을 찾을 수 있는 질문은 무엇인가?

(A) 섬의 이름을 지은 사람은 누구인가?

(B) 하와이 제도는 언제 형성되었는가?

(C) 하와이 제도에는 얼마나 많은 토착종들이 살고 있는가?

(D) 하와이 제도 특유의 생물 다양성을 만들어낸 것은 무엇인가?

2.
다음 중 지문의 음영 표시된 문장의 핵심 정보를 가장 잘 표현한 문장은 무엇인가? 오답은 의미를 크게 왜곡하거나 핵심 정보를 누락하고 있다.

(A) 폴리네시아인들과 유럽 탐험가들 모두 하와이 제도로 새로운 종을 유입시켰다.

(B) 하와이에 서식하는 많은 종들이 인간에 의해 유입되었으나, 어떤 것들은 정말 독특해서 스스로 그곳에서 진화한 것임이 틀림없다.

(C) 하와이에 서식하는 대부분의 동물들은 서기 500년경에 인간에 의해 그곳으로 왔다.

(D) 많은 종들이 1600년대가 되어서야 비로소 거기에 도착했지만, 그들은 신속하게 환경에 적응하여 원래의 종들과 구별되었다.

3.
2단락에 따르면, 다음 중 식물의 씨앗이 하와이 군도로 오게 된 방법이 아닌 것은 무엇인가?

(A) 바람을 타고 공기 중으로 이동해서

(B) 새의 깃털에 박혀서

(C) 화산재와 함께 표류해서

(D) 동물의 소화 기관에 남아 있어서

4.
2단락과의 관계에 비추어 3단락의 목적은 무엇인가?

(A) 2단락에서 묘사된 생물체의 이동에 대한 설명을 계속하기 위해

(B) 2단락에서 언급된 방법들 외에 또 다른 이동 방법을 제안하기 위해

ants produced an average of 215 seeds, whereas the plants in the controlled environment produced a mere 45. The ants protected the flowers throughout their stages of development, thereby providing the plants with a better opportunity to reproduce.

7 ➡ As the research by Wheeler and Bentley shows, these organisms depend upon each other for their survival. The ants provide the plants with much needed protection, while the plants provide the ants with an easily digestible energy source and protection against their predators. Most insects have parasitic relationships with plants, wherein the plants suffer for the insect's benefit. However, the relationships between extrafloral nectarine plants and their protectors appear to be wholly beneficial to both species. This means that they have evolved to share a mutualistic form of symbiosis. When this occurred or how long it took to happen remains unclear, but their interaction is clearly observable.

겨우 45개만 생산했다. 개미들은 꽃의 발달 단계 내내 꽃들을 보호했고, 그로 인해 식물들에게 번식할 수 있는 더 좋은 기회를 제공했다.

7 ➡ 휠러와 벤틀리의 연구가 보여주는 것처럼 이런 생물들은 자신들의 생존을 위해 서로에게 의존한다. 개미들은 식물들이 절실히 필요로 하는 보호를 제공하는 한편, 식물들은 개미들에게 쉽게 소화되는 에너지원과 포식자로부터의 보호를 제공한다. 대다수의 곤충들은 식물들과 기생적 관계를 맺고 있는데, 거기서 식물들은 곤충의 이득을 위해 고통받는다. 하지만 꽃 밖 꿀샘 식물들과 보호자들 사이의 관계는 양쪽 종에게 온전히 유익한 것처럼 보인다. 이것은 그들이 상리 공생 형태의 공생을 함께하도록 진화했다는 의미이다. 이것이 언제 발생했는지 또는 발생하기까지 얼마나 오래 걸렸는지는 불확실하지만, 그들의 상호 작용은 명백하게 관찰된다.

---

1. **Fact**

According to paragraph 1, what is the primary function of extrafloral nectar?

Ⓐ It induces pollination.
Ⓑ It provides nutrients to insects.
Ⓒ It poisons organisms that feed on plants.
Ⓓ **It serves as a defense mechanism.**

2. **Sentence Simplification**

Which of the sentences below best expresses the essential information in the highlighted sentence in the passage? *Incorrect* answer choices change the meaning in important ways or leave out essential information.

Ⓐ Insects will move on to other tobacco plants after feeding on the nectar of one tobacco plant because it includes a certain amount of nicotine in its nectar.
Ⓑ **Because insects feeding on the nectar of tobacco plants find it bitter, they move on after only feeding once.**
Ⓒ Some insects are attracted to the nicotine present in tobacco plants because it is bitter and less aromatic, so they do not move on to other plants after feeding.
Ⓓ Because the nicotine in the nectar of tobacco plants is poisonous, insects will only feed eagerly on the nectar once before moving on.

1.

1단락에 따르면, 꽃 밖 꿀의 주요 기능은 무엇인가?

Ⓐ 수분을 유도한다.
Ⓑ 곤충들에게 영양분을 제공한다.
Ⓒ 식물들을 먹는 생물들을 독으로 죽인다.
Ⓓ 방어 기제로 사용된다.

2.

다음 중 지문의 음영 표시된 문장의 핵심 정보를 가장 잘 표현한 문장은 무엇인가? 오답은 의미를 크게 왜곡하거나 핵심 정보를 누락하고 있다.

Ⓐ 곤충들은 한 담배 식물의 꿀을 먹은 후 그것의 꿀에 특정 양의 니코틴이 함유되어 있기 때문에 다른 담배 식물로 옮겨간다.
Ⓑ 담배 식물들의 꿀을 먹는 곤충들은 그것이 쓰다는 것을 알게 되기 때문에, 한 번만 먹고 다른 곳으로 이동한다.
Ⓒ 어떤 곤충들은 담배 식물들에 있는 니코틴이 쓰고 덜 향기롭기 때문에 그것에 끌리고, 그 때문에 먹은 후 다른 식물들로 옮겨가지 않는다.
Ⓓ 담배 식물들의 꿀에 들어 있는 니코틴은 독성이 있기 때문에 곤충들은 그 꿀을 한 번만 열심히 먹은 후 이동한다.

3. Inference

Based on paragraph 2, it can be inferred that

(A) the chemical composition of nectar varies little from plant to plant.

(B) most plants do not want organisms to feed on their nectar indefinitely.

(C) nectars contain all the building blocks of proteins.

(D) flowers stop producing nectar after they have been fertilized.

4. Negative Fact

All of the following are mentioned in paragraph 3 EXCEPT

(A) ants can defend against animals much larger than them.

(B) aphids, which reproduce asexually, are a significant pest.

(C) the purpose of extrafloral nectaries is different from those in flowers.

(D) parasitic wasps provide protection against caterpillar eggs.

5. Vocabulary

The word "secrete" in paragraph 4 is closest in meaning to

(A) **emit**

(B) secure

(C) conclude

(D) absorb

6. Rhetorical Purpose

What is the function of paragraph 6 as it relates to paragraph 5?

(A) To show similarities between the work of Wheeler and Bentley

(B) To provide support for Delpino's work

(C) **To illustrate what Bentley's experiment was about**

(D) To cast doubt on the validity of Bentley's experiment

7. Fact

According to paragraph 6, Bentley conducted the experiment by

(A) introducing different types of insects to each environment.

(B) delaying the stages of development of plants in one environment.

(C) controlling the number of plants in each environment.

(D) **comparing plants in an ant-free environment to those in one with ants.**

3.

2단락에 근거하여 추론할 수 있는 것은?

(A) 꿀의 화학적 구성은 식물마다 별로 다르지 않다.

(B) 대부분의 식물은 생물이 자신의 꿀을 무한정 먹는 것을 원하지 않는다.

(C) 꿀은 단백질의 모든 구성 요소를 함유하고 있다.

(D) 꽃들은 수정된 뒤에 꿀 생산을 멈춘다.

4.

다음 중 3단락에서 언급되지 않은 것은?

(A) 개미들은 자신보다 훨씬 더 큰 동물들을 상대로 방어할 수 있다.

(B) 무성으로 번식하는 진딧물은 심각한 해충이다.

(C) 꽃 밖 꿀샘의 기능은 꽃 내부에 있는 꿀샘의 기능과 다르다.

(D) 기생 말벌은 애벌레 알로부터의 보호를 제공한다.

5.

4단락의 단어 "secrete(배출하다)"와 의미상 가장 가까운 것은?

(A) 내뿜다

(B) 확보하다

(C) 마치다

(D) 흡수하다

6.

5단락과의 관계에 비추어 6단락의 역할은 무엇인가?

(A) 휠러와 벤틀리의 연구의 유사성을 보여주기 위해

(B) 델피노의 연구에 대한 지지를 제공하기 위해

(C) 벤틀리의 실험이 무엇에 관한 것이었는지 묘사하기 위해

(D) 벤틀리의 실험의 타당성에 대해 의구심을 제기하기 위해

7.

6단락에 따르면, 벤틀리가 실험을 진행한 방법은?

(A) 각 환경에 다른 종류의 곤충을 도입함

(B) 한 환경에 있는 식물들의 발달 단계들을 지연시킴

(C) 각 환경에 있는 식물들의 수를 통제함

(D) 개미가 없는 환경의 식물들과 개미가 있는 환경의 식물들을 비교함

8. Inference

Based on paragraph 7, it can be inferred that

(A) extrafloral nectaries are a product of evolution.

(B) **a positive symbiotic relationship between insects and plants is rare.**

(C) over time, the ants developed enzymes that could easily digest the amino acids present in nectar.

(D) more careful observation is needed to fully understand the relationship between extrafloral nectarine plants and their predators.

9. Insertion

Look at the four squares [■] that indicate where the following sentence could be added to the passage.

Barbara Bentley conducted an experiment in 1977 that added further support to the theory.

Where would the sentence best fit? [■ D]

10. Summary

Directions: An introductory sentence for a brief summary of the passage is provided below. Complete the summary by selecting the THREE answer choices that express the most important ideas in the passage. Some sentences do not belong in the summary because they express ideas that are not presented in the passage or are minor ideas in the passage. *This question is worth 2 points.*

While nectar produced inside flowers attracts insects to help pollinate them, nectar produced on other parts of the plant attracts insects to protect the plant.

> (C) **While many scientists mistakenly assumed that extrafloral nectaries were excretory organs, Delpino was right in his argument that extrafloral nectar attracts insects to gain their protection.**
>
> (D) **Bentley's experiment, which showed that plants produced more seeds when ants were present, revealed the symbiotic relationship between insects and plants with extrafloral nectaries.**
>
> (F) **Insects such as parasitic wasps and ants feed on extrafloral nectar, consume pests which attack the plant, and deter larger herbivores from feeding on the plant.**

(A) Nectar, which is primarily composed of natural sugars, includes other chemical compounds that give off scents to attract insects.

8.

7단락에 근거하여 추론할 수 있는 것은?

(A) 꽃 밖 꿀샘들은 진화의 결과다.

(B) 곤충과 식물 간의 긍정적인 공생 관계는 드물다.

(C) 시간이 흐름에 따라 개미들은 꿀에 존재하는 아미노산들을 쉽게 소화시킬 수 있는 효소를 개발했다.

(D) 꽃 밖 꿀샘을 보유한 식물들과 그들의 포식자 간의 관계를 온전히 이해하기 위해서 더 세심한 관찰이 필요하다.

9.

지문에 다음 문장이 들어갈 수 있는 위치를 나타내는 네 개의 사각형[■]을 확인하시오.

바바라 벤틀리는 1977년에 이 이론에 추가로 힘을 실어주는 실험을 진행했다.

이 문장이 들어가기에 가장 적합한 곳은? [■ D]

10.

지시문: 지문을 간략하게 요약한 글의 첫 문장이 아래 제시되어 있다. 지문의 가장 중요한 내용을 표현하는 세 개의 선택지를 골라 요약문을 완성하시오. 일부 문장들은 지문에 제시되지 않았거나 지문의 지엽적인 내용을 나타내기 때문에 요약문에 포함되지 않는다. *이 문제의 배점은 2점이다.*

꽃 안에서 생산되는 꿀이 곤충을 끌어들여 수분되는 것을 돕게 한다면, 식물의 다른 부위에서 생산되는 꿀은 식물을 보호하기 위해 곤충을 끌어들인다.

> (C) 많은 과학자들이 꽃 밖 꿀샘들이 배설 기관이라고 잘못 생각할 때, 꽃 밖 꿀이 곤충의 보호를 받기 위해 곤충을 끌어들인다는 델피노의 주장은 옳았다.
>
> (D) 개미들이 있을 때 식물들이 더 많은 씨앗을 생산한다는 것을 보여준 벤틀리의 실험은 곤충과 꽃 밖 꿀샘을 보유한 식물들 간의 공생 관계를 드러냈다.
>
> (F) 기생 말벌과 개미와 같은 곤충들은 꽃 밖 꿀을 먹고, 그 식물을 공격하는 해충들을 잡아먹고, 크기가 더 큰 초식동물들이 그 식물을 먹으려고 하는 것을 막는다.

(A) 주로 천연당으로 구성된 꿀은 곤충들을 끌어들이기 위해 향기를 내뿜는 다른 화학 복합물들을 포함한다.

Ⓑ Both hydathodes and stomata are types of specialized plant tissues, but hydathodes secrete excess water while stomata regulate gas exchange.

Ⓔ In fact, plants exposed to ants produced an average of 215 seeds while those in an ant-free environment produced an average of 45 seeds.

Ⓑ 배수 조직과 기공은 둘 다 전문화된 식물 조직들이지만 배수 조직은 여분의 수분을 배출하는 반면 기공은 가스 교환을 조절한다.

Ⓔ 실제로 개미들에 노출된 식물들은 평균 215개의 씨앗을 생산한 반면에, 개미가 없는 환경에 있는 식물들은 평균 45개의 씨앗을 생산했다.

Passage 3

Population Distribution

1 ➡ All species of organisms that live on Earth inhabit an area that is referred to as that species' range. The boundaries of such an area are usually fluid as individuals may occasionally stray outside their normal range, and many species migrate seasonally. [■A] However, most organisms live within one or more fairly well-defined areas throughout their lifetimes. Within a species' range, the distribution of individuals usually takes on one of three forms of population distribution: clumped, regular, or random. [■B] These different types of distribution can greatly affect the population density of a species as they determine the number of animals that are going to be found in a given region within the species' range. [■C] The ways in which the population is distributed are determined by various factors that are categorized as abiotic or biotic. [■D]

2 ➡ Abiotic factors include any non-living physical or chemical factors in the environment. These factors

개체군 분포

1 ➡ 지구에 살고 있는 모든 생물체의 종들은 종의 영역이라고 불리는 구역에 서식한다. 이런 구역의 경계선은 개체들이 가끔 평소의 영역 밖으로 돌아다니기도 하고 많은 종이 계절에 따라 이동하기 때문에 보통 유동적이다. [■A] 하지만 대다수의 생물들은 비교적 구분이 뚜렷한 하나 혹은 그 이상의 구역 안에서 평생 생활한다. 종의 영역 내에서 개체의 분포는 흔히 세 가지의 개체군 분포 중 하나의 모습을 띠고 있다. 즉, 집괴 분포, 정규 분포, 그리고 마구잡이 분포 중 하나이다. [■B] 이러한 다른 종류의 분포는 한 종의 개체군 밀도에 큰 영향을 끼칠 수 있는데, 그것들이 그 종의 영역 내 특정 지역에서 볼 수 있는 동물들의 수를 결정하기 때문이다. [■C] 개체군이 분포하는 방법은 여러 가지의 요인들에 의해 결정되는데, 이는 비생물적 또는 생물적 요인으로 나뉜다. [■D]

2 ➡ 비생물적 요인들에는 환경 속에 있는 무생물의 물리적 또는 화학적 요인들이 모두 포함된다. 이러한 요인들은

are broken down into three subcategories: climatic factors, edaphic factors, and social factors. Climatic factors are those that determine the atmospheric environment, and they include the availability of sunlight, humidity, temperature, and salinity. Edaphic factors are those that determine the quality of the soil in a region, consisting of the local geology, the coarseness of the soil, acidity, and air penetration. Social factors that are categorized as abiotic include water availability and land use. Biotic factors are behaviors of organisms which directly or indirectly affect other organisms. These include competition for resources like mates, food, and water, predation, and disease. Taken together, these many factors determine which pattern of species distribution a population of a species will adopt.

3 ➡ The most common form of species distribution found in nature is clumped distribution, wherein space between individuals is minimized to form close groups that are separated from other groups of the same species. Clumped distribution is typically found in environments where resources are unevenly distributed. In very arid regions, where water is continuously in short supply, most species will clump together around permanent water sources called oases. In other areas where resource availability varies seasonally, animals will clump together around resources when they are scarce and disperse when they are plentiful. Clumped distribution is also useful in defending against predation or increasing the likelihood of capturing prey.

4 ➡ Prey animals often form into herds for protection through safety in numbers, and this can occur deliberately or accidentally. Many species of animals will organize into groups with the young in the center and large adults around the perimeter to deter predators. Others form what are called selfish herds, where safety is achieved by moving towards the middle of the group, increasing that organism's chances for survival with no thought for its fellow creatures. Predatory animals also form into groups such as wolf packs and prides of lions to maximize their hunting potential against prey herds. The greater the number of hunters working in coordination, the more likely they are to catch enough of their prey to survive.

5 ➡ Conversely, the availability of resources can also have an opposite effect, maximizing the distance

세 개의 세부 범주, 즉 기후 요인, 토양 요인, 그리고 사회적 요인으로 나뉜다. 기후 요인은 대기의 환경을 결정하는 것들이며, 여기에는 일조 가용성, 습도, 온도와 염도가 포함된다. 토양 요인은 어느 지역의 토양의 질을 결정하는 것들이며, 그 지역의 지질, 토양의 거칠기, 산도와 공기 침투를 포함한다. 비생물적인 것으로 분류된 사회적 요인에는 물의 가용성과 토지 활용이 포함된다. 생물적 요인들은 다른 생물들에 직접적으로 또는 간접적으로 영향을 미치는 생물의 행동들이다. 여기에는 짝, 먹이, 물과 같은 자원을 얻기 위한 경쟁, 포식과 질병이 포함된다. 종합적으로 이렇게 많은 요인들은 어느 종의 개체군이 어떤 개체군 분포를 취할지 결정한다.

3 ➡ 자연에서 발견되는 가장 흔한 형태의 개체군 분포는 집괴 분포인데, 거기에서는 개체 사이의 공간이 최소화되어 밀집된 집단을 형성하고 그 집단은 같은 종의 다른 집단과는 분리된다. 집괴 분포는 자원이 불균형적으로 분포된 환경에서 흔히 발견된다. 물 공급이 계속 부족한 매우 건조한 지역에서 대다수의 종은 오아시스라 불리는 영구적 수자원 주변에 모인다. 자원 가용성이 계절적으로 변하는 다른 지역에서는 동물들이 자원이 부족할 때 자원 주변으로 모이고, 자원이 풍부할 때는 흩어진다. 집괴 분포는 포식에 맞서 방어하거나 먹이를 포획할 가능성을 높이는 데 도움이 된다.

4 ➡ 사냥 당하는 동물들은 여럿이 함께 있어 안전하므로 방어하기 위해 무리를 형성하는데, 이것은 의도적으로 또는 우연하게 발생한다. 많은 동물 종들은 새끼를 무리의 중심에 두고 덩치가 큰 성체들이 포식자를 막기 위해 주위를 둘러싼다. 다른 동물들은 이기적 무리라고 불리는 것을 형성하는데, 무리의 중심으로 이동함으로써 안전을 얻고, 다른 동물들에 대한 배려는 전혀 없이 자신의 생존 가능성을 높인다. 사냥하는 동물들 또한 이리 떼 혹은 사자 무리처럼 무리를 형성하여 먹이 무리를 상대로 사냥의 가능성을 극대화한다. 함께 협력하는 사냥꾼의 숫자가 클수록, 그들이 생존할 만큼 충분한 양의 먹이를 사냥할 가능성이 높아진다.

5 ➡ 반대로, 자원의 가용성은 반대의 결과를 가져올 수도 있는데 개체군 내 개체 간의 사이를 극대화시켜서 정규

between individual members of a population, which results in regular or even distribution. Some species not only compete with their own population and others for resources, but they can effectively deny others from using their resources. This is particularly apparent in the trees which form the canopy of a forest. Their outstretched branches collect the maximum amount of sunlight possible, with only a small amount filtering through to the forest floor. This results in the widely spaced arrangement of trees that often appears to be deliberate or planned. In reality, it is the result of successful tree saplings utilizing resources more effectively than other members of their population, and discouraging the others from growing any further.

6 ➡ However, there are also species whose population distribution seems to have no inherent logic behind it. These organisms live in an environment where they have equal access to sufficient resources, so competition between members of the population is virtually nonexistent, and they are neither encouraged to group together nor to separate. Random distribution of a population is comparatively rare because abiotic and biotic factors typically cause populations to group together or to spread out. Therefore, this pattern of distribution is typically seen in organisms whose offspring disperse randomly throughout the environment. Plants whose seeds are carried on the wind often follow this pattern, as do animals with little social interaction apart from mating such as shellfish or arachnids.

혹은 균형 분포가 형성되는 결과를 초래한다. 몇몇 종은 자원을 놓고 자신이 속한 개체군과 다른 개체들과 경쟁할 뿐만 아니라, 다른 개체들이 그들의 자원을 쓰지 못하도록 효과적으로 막기도 한다. 이것은 특히 숲 지붕을 형성하는 나무들에게서 분명하다. 그들의 뻗어 있는 가지는 가능한 한 가장 많은 양의 햇살을 받으며 적은 양의 햇살만이 그 틈새로 숲 바닥을 비춘다. 이것은 나무가 널찍한 간격을 두고 자리잡게 만드는데, 때때로 이것은 마치 고의적 또는 계획적인 것처럼 보인다. 사실, 이것은 같은 개체군에 속한 다른 개체들보다 자원을 더 효과적으로 활용하고 다른 개체들이 더 자라는 것을 막는 성공적인 나무 묘목들의 결과다.

6 ➡ 하지만 내재된 논리가 없는 것처럼 보이는 개체군 분포를 갖고 있는 종들이 있다. 이 생물들은 충분한 자원에 동등하게 접근할 수 있는 환경에 살고 있기 때문에 그 개체군에 속한 개체들 사이의 경쟁은 거의 존재하지 않으며, 서로 무리를 짓거나 흩어지도록 유도되지도 않는다. 개체군의 마구잡이 분포는 상대적으로 드문데 왜냐하면 비생물적 요인들과 생물적 요인들이 흔히 개체군들이 무리를 짓거나 흩어지도록 만들기 때문이다. 그렇기 때문에 이런 패턴의 분포는 환경 전체에 걸쳐 자손이 무작위로 흩어지는 생물 사이에서 흔히 볼 수 있다. 바람에 씨앗이 운반되는 식물들이 흔히 이런 형태를 보이고, 교미 외에는 사회적 상호작용이 적은 갑각류와 거미류와 같은 동물들 또한 그렇다.

---

1. **Fact**
According to paragraph 1, the boundaries of some species' ranges are fluid due to
  Ⓐ population density
  Ⓑ **seasonal migration**
  Ⓒ average life span
  Ⓓ abiotic factors

2. **Rhetorical Purpose**
What is the function of paragraph 2 as it relates to paragraph 1?
  Ⓐ To outline the similarities and differences between biotic and abiotic factors

1.
1단락에 따르면, 몇몇 종의 영역이 유동적인 이유는?
  Ⓐ 개체군 밀도
  Ⓑ 계절에 따른 이동
  Ⓒ 평균 수명
  Ⓓ 비생물적 요인들

2.
1단락과의 관계에 비추어 2단락의 역할은 무엇인가?
  Ⓐ 생물적 요인들과 비생물적 요인들 간의 유사점과 차이점을 간략히 설명하기 위해

B To provide an explanation about factors influencing population distribution

C To give an example of how climatic factors affect the environment

D To suggest that abiotic factors are no different from biotic factors

3. Inference

What can be inferred about species distribution in paragraph 3?

A Animals form clumped groups with their kin.

B Animals in deserts typically display clumped distribution.

C Clumped distribution is found primarily amongst predators.

D Water is the main resource around which animals form clumps.

4. Fact

Which of the following tactics are mentioned in paragraph 4? Click on two answers.

A **Hunting in groups**

B Attacking a predator as a group

C **Forming selfish herds**

D Scattering when being hunted

5. Vocabulary

The word "apparent" in paragraph 5 is closest in meaning to

A peculiar

B obsolete

C pertinent

D **evident**

6. Fact

According to paragraph 5, what factor causes plants to grow in a uniform pattern?

A **Competition**

B Distribution of sunlight

C Size of roots

D Length of branches

7. Sentence Simplification

Which of the sentences below best expresses the essential information in the highlighted sentence in the passage? *Incorrect* answer choices change the meaning in important ways or leave out essential information.

B 개체군 분포에 영향을 미치는 요인들에 대한 설명을 제공하기 위해

C 기후 요인들이 환경에 어떻게 영향을 미치는지에 대한 예를 들기 위해

D 비생물적 요인들이 생물적 요인들과 전혀 차이가 없다는 것을 제안하기 위해

3.

3단락에서 종의 분포에 대해 추론할 수 있는 것은 무엇인가?

A 동물들은 그들의 친족들과 무리지어 지내는 집단을 형성한다.

B 사막의 동물들은 보통 집괴 분포를 선보인다.

C 집괴 분포는 대체적으로 포식자들 사이에서 발견된다.

D 물은 동물들이 무리를 형성하게 하는 주된 요인이다.

4.

다음 중 4단락에서 언급된 전략은 무엇인가? 보기 두 개를 고르시오.

A 무리를 지어 사냥하는 것

B 무리를 지어 포식자를 공격하는 것

C 이기적인 무리를 형성하는 것

D 사냥 당할 때 흩어지는 것

5.

5단락의 단어 "apparent(분명한)"와 의미상 가장 가까운 것은?

A 특이한

B 구식인

C 관련 있는

D 눈에 띄는

6.

5단락에 따르면, 식물들이 균일한 모습으로 성장하게 하는 요인은 무엇인가?

A 경쟁

B 햇빛의 분포

C 뿌리의 크기

D 가지의 길이

7.

다음 중 지문의 음영 표시된 문장의 핵심 정보를 가장 잘 표현한 문장은 무엇인가? 오답은 의미를 크게 왜곡하거나 핵심 정보를 누락하고 있다.

(A) When organisms live in an environment where competition between members of the population is virtually nonexistent, they are able to share access to resources.

(B) Living in an environment in which they have no access to resources, animals have no need to group together or disperse.

(C) **In an environment with access to sufficient resources, the pressure to gather together or disperse is absent because of the lack of competition.**

(D) When competition for resources between members of a population is nonexistent, there is no advantage for animals to either group together or separate.

(A) 개체군에 속한 개체들 간의 경쟁이 거의 존재하지 않는 환경에서 서식할 때, 생물들은 자원 접근을 공유할 수 있다.

(B) 자원에 접근할 수 없는 환경에 서식할 때, 동물들은 무리를 짓거나 흩어질 필요가 없다.

(C) 충분한 자원에 접근할 수 있는 환경에서는 경쟁이 없기 때문에 무리를 짓거나 흩어져야 하는 부담이 없다.

(D) 개체군에 속한 개체들 사이에서 자원을 향한 경쟁이 존재하지 않을 때, 동물들이 무리를 짓거나 흩어질 만한 이점이 없다.

8. Fact

According to paragraph 6, why is random distribution not common in nature?

(A) **In most environments, resources are unevenly distributed.**

(B) Not many organisms disperse their offspring randomly throughout the environment.

(C) Not all members of a population have equal access to resources.

(D) Animals like arachnids are not common in nature.

8.

6단락에 따르면, 마구잡이 분포가 자연에 흔치 않은 이유는 무엇인가?

(A) 대다수의 환경에서는 자원이 불균형하게 분포되어 있다.

(B) 환경 전체에 자손을 무작위로 퍼뜨리는 생물들이 많이 없다.

(C) 개체군의 모든 개체들이 자원에 동등한 접근을 갖고 있지 않다.

(D) 거미류와 같은 동물들은 자연에 흔하지 않다.

9. Insertion

Look at the four squares [■] that indicate where the following sentence could be added to the passage.

However, most organisms live within one or more fairly well-defined areas throughout their lifetimes.

Where would the sentence best fit? [■A]

9.

지문에 다음 문장이 들어갈 수 있는 위치를 나타내는 네 개의 사각형[■]을 확인하시오.

하지만 대다수의 생물들은 비교적 구분이 뚜렷한 하나 혹은 그 이상의 구역 안에서 평생 생활한다.

이 문장이 들어가기에 가장 적합한 곳은? [■A]

10. Category Chart

Directions: Complete the table by matching the sentences below. Select the appropriate phrases from the answer choices and match them to the category to which they relate. TWO of the answer choices will NOT be used. ***This question is worth 3 points.***

Climatic Factors
• (A) **availability of sunlight**
• (D) **temperature**
• (G) **salinity**
Edaphic Factors
• (C) **coarseness of the soil**
• (E) **local geology**

10.

지시문: 아래 문장들을 알맞게 넣어 표를 완성하시오. 선택지에서 적절한 구를 선택하여 관계 있는 범주에 연결하시오. 선택지 중 두 개는 정답이 될 수 없다. *이 문제의 배점은 3점이다.*

기후 요인
• (A) 일조 가용성
• (D) 온도
• (G) 염도
토양 요인
• (C) 토양의 거칠기
• (E) 지역의 지질

Ⓑ disease
Ⓕ average life span

Ⓑ 질병
Ⓕ 평균 수명

📋 어휘

1 **inhabit** ♥ (특정 지역에) 살다[거주/서식하다] Ⅰ **fluid** adj 유동[가변]적인 Ⅰ **stray** ♥ 제 위치[길]를 벗어나다 Ⅰ **migrate** ♥ 이주[이동]하다 Ⅰ **seasonally** adv 계절에 따라, 정기적으로 Ⅰ **well-defined** adj (정의가) 명확한, 윤곽이 분명한 Ⅰ **affect** ♥ 영향을 미치다 Ⅰ **determine** ♥ 결정하다, 알아내다

2 **atmospheric** adj 대기의 Ⅰ **coarseness** n 조악함, 거침 Ⅰ **penetration** n 침투, 관통 Ⅰ **predation** n 포식 Ⅰ **adopt** ♥ 채택하다, (특정한 방식이나 자세를) 쓰다[취하다]

3 **arid** adj 매우 건조한 Ⅰ **clump** ♥ 무리[떼]를 짓다, 함께 모이다[모으다] Ⅰ **permanent** adj 영구[영속]적인 Ⅰ **scarce** adj 부족한, 드문 Ⅰ **disperse** ♥ 흩어지다, 해산하다; 해산시키다 Ⅰ **defend** ♥ 방어[수비]하다 Ⅰ **prey** n 먹이[사냥감]

4 **herd** n 떼 Ⅰ **deliberately** adv 고의로, 의도[계획]적으로 Ⅰ **perimeter** n 주위, 주변 Ⅰ **selfish** adj 이기적인 Ⅰ **survival** n 생존 Ⅰ **potential** n 가능성, 잠재력

5 **conversely** adv 정반대로, 역으로 Ⅰ **deny** ♥ 부인[부정]하다, 거부하다[허락하지 않다] Ⅰ **apparent** adj 분명한, 누가 봐도 알 수 있는 Ⅰ **canopy** n 덮개, (숲의 나뭇가지들이) 지붕 모양으로 우거진 것 Ⅰ **outstretched** adj 펼친, 뻗친 Ⅰ **filter** ♥ 여과하다, 거르다 Ⅰ **sapling** n 묘목, 어린나무 Ⅰ **utilize** ♥ 활용[이용]하다

6 **inherent** adj 내재하는 Ⅰ **access** n 접근[입수] 방법, 이용[참가]할 권리 Ⅰ **virtually** adv 사실상, 거의 Ⅰ **nonexistent** adj 실재[존재]하지 않는 Ⅰ **comparatively** adv 비교적

Actual Test 05

본서 | P. 124

Passage 1　Fire Management

1. C	Rhetorical Purpose	6. A	Fact
2. C	Vocabulary	7. D	Negative Fact
3. B	Inference	8. A	Sentence Simplification
4. D	Fact	9. C	Insertion
5. B	Negative Fact	10. A, E, F	Summary

Passage 2　The Steam Engine in Britain

1. A	Negative Fact	6. B	Vocabulary
2. D	Rhetorical Purpose	7. A, D	Fact
3. A	Inference	8. C	Fact
4. D	Sentence Simplification	9. D	Insertion
5. C	Fact	10. B, D, E	Summary

Passage 3　Agricultural Pest Control

1. B	Negative Fact	6. D	Rhetorical Purpose
2. D	Sentence Simplification	7. B	Vocabulary
3. C	Negative Fact	8. A	Inference
4. B	Fact	9. C	Insertion
5. C	Fact	10. B, C, F	Summary

● 내가 맞은 문제 유형의 개수를 적어 보고 어느 유형에 취약한지 확인해 봅시다.

문제 유형	맞은 개수
Sentence Simplification	3
Fact / Negative Fact	12
Vocabulary	3
Reference	0
Rhetorical Purpose	3
Inference	3
Insertion	3
Summary	3
Category Chart	0
Total	30

Fire Management

1 ➡ Many people consider wildfires to be only a force of rampant destruction that devastates forests and consumes everything in its path. However, this is only partially true, as they actually play an important role in the life cycle of forests. Under normal circumstances, a wildfire will burn the dead plant matter that accumulates on the forest floor, and leave the adult trees largely intact. In doing so, they provide a readily available source of nutrients and space for new plants to grow. While it is true that many fires destroy large sections of forests as well as the homes of animals and humans alike, this is not part of the natural cycle. In fact, the severity of many wildfires and the massive destruction they cause is usually a direct result of human activity, much of which was undertaken with the goal of protecting the forests.

2 ➡ Without human intervention, wildfires play a vital role in the survival of forests. Although the damage they cause may seem severe, and it may take the forest an extended period to recover, they actually ensure the forest's survival. Over time, the trees in the forest drop branches, leaves and needles, which accumulate on the forest floor. This material takes about half a century to break down enough for other plants to utilize it, but if it burns it can be used much faster. This vegetable matter also piles up faster than it can decompose, often creating a thick layer that prevents new saplings from taking root in the soil and replacing the older trees. Not only that, but if periodic minor fires are prevented, this ever-thickening layer will only serve to intensify the magnitude of the inevitable blaze that will occur. A prime example of this situation is the fires that ravaged Yellowstone National Park in 1988.

3 ➡ Since its establishment as the first national park in 1872, efforts have been made to maintain the park and its many geological and natural wonders for future generations. Initially, this meant protecting its wildlife from poaching, the ground from miners, and its forests from logging. There was considerable opposition from nearby communities that wished to exploit the park's resources, but as its staff gradually increased, and its importance as a tourist attraction grew, this diminished. By 1940, the chief danger

화재 관리

1 ➡ 많은 사람들은 산불을 단지 산림을 파괴하고 지나가는 길목에 있는 모든 것을 전소시키는 걷잡을 수 없는 파괴적인 힘이라고 생각한다. 하지만 이것은 오직 부분적으로만 사실이다. 왜냐하면 산불은 실제로 산림의 생활 주기에 중요한 역할을 하기 때문이다. 보통의 환경에서 산불은 숲의 바닥에 쌓여 있는 죽은 식물 물질을 태우게 될 것이고, 다 큰 나무들은 거의 손상시키지 않는다. 그렇게 함으로써, 산불은 새로운 식물들이 자라는 데 쉽게 이용 가능한 영양 공급원과 공간을 제공한다. 많은 불들이 인간과 동물의 집뿐만 아니라 산림의 광범위한 지역을 파괴하는 것은 사실이지만, 이것은 자연적인 주기의 일부가 아니다. 사실 많은 산불의 가혹함과 그것들이 야기하는 대규모 파괴는 주로 인간 활동의 직접적인 결과이며, 그 활동 중 많은 부분이 산림을 보호한다는 목표를 가지고 행해졌다.

2 ➡ 인간의 개입이 없으면 산불은 산림의 생존에 필수적인 역할을 한다. 그들이 야기하는 피해가 심각하게 보이고, 숲이 회복되는 데 장기간에 걸친 기간이 걸릴지는 모르겠지만, 산불은 사실상 숲의 생존을 보장한다. 시간이 흐르면서 숲에 있는 나무들은 가지와 잎사귀, 솔잎을 떨어뜨리는데, 이것들은 숲의 바닥에 쌓이게 된다. 이 물질은 약 반세기에 걸쳐 다른 식물들이 이용할 수 있을 정도로 분해되지만, 만약에 탈 경우에는 훨씬 더 빠르게 사용될 수 있다. 또한 이러한 식물질은 분해되는 속도보다 쌓이는 속도가 더 빨라서 종종 두꺼운 층을 형성하여 새로운 묘목들이 토양에 뿌리를 내리고 늙은 나무들을 대체하는 것을 막는다. 그뿐만 아니라, 만약 정기적인 작은 불들이 예방된다면, 이렇게 계속 두꺼워지는 층은 후에 발생할 피할 수 없는 대형 화재의 강도를 심화하는 역할을 할 뿐이다. 이러한 상황의 아주 적절한 예는 1988년에 옐로스톤 국립공원을 파괴했던 화재이다.

3 ➡ 1872년에 최초의 국립공원으로 설립된 이후 미래 세대를 위해 이 공원과 그곳의 많은 지질학적, 자연적 경이로움을 유지하기 위한 노력들이 행해졌다. 처음에 이것은 야생 동물을 밀렵으로부터, 땅을 광부들로부터, 산림을 벌목으로부터 보호하는 것을 의미했다. 공원의 자원들을 이용하기 원하는 주변의 공동체들로부터 상당한 반대가 있었지만, 공원의 직원들이 점차 늘어나고 관광 명소로서의 중요성이 증가함에 따라 반대는 줄어들었다. 1940년까지 공원의 주된 위험 요소가 불이라고 여겨졌기에 화재 진압을 최우선 순위로 하는 법률이 통과되었다. 그리하여 국립공원

to the park was believed to be fire, so legislation was passed to make fire suppression a top priority. Therefore, the National Park Service extinguished any fires that started as quickly as possible. This policy allowed dead vegetation and thick undergrowth to accumulate for nearly 50 years, and set the stage for disaster.

4 ➡ In the summer of 1988, severe drought and strong, gusting winds made conditions in the park critical. Park officials admitted that they had knowledge of a number of small fires, but they had assumed that they would be put out naturally. As they looked on, those smaller fires merged into one of the largest conflagrations in the park's history. After raging for several months, the fire destroyed approximately 800,000 acres within the park boundaries, and more outside. Around 13,000 firefighters and military personnel were called upon to put out the blaze, and the effort cost the government 120 million dollars. Despite such efforts, they were unsuccessful, and the fire was ultimately defeated by precipitation that came in the fall and winter. This fire served as a wakeup call to fire control authorities, revealing how inadequate their current fire control policies were and how serious the need was for new techniques for protecting natural environments and managing forests.

5 ➡ Following the fires, a great deal of research was carried out to determine the exact role of fires in forest ecology and how they should be managed. Fires control growth in the understory of the forest, dispose of shed vegetation, and make way for new growth. In fact, some pinecones will not open to release their seeds unless exposed to fire. These conclusions led many people to provide more support for prescribed fire, which is also referred to as controlled burning. These fires are used in farming and grassland management to reduce the risk of wildfires. Some even condemned park officials for not having used controlled burns, saying that they could have prevented the firestorm in 1988. However, many scientists contend that in order for fires to be beneficial to forests, they would have to reach sizes that are uncontrollable.

6 ➡ [■A] The current policy is to let fires that begin naturally burn and monitor them closely. [■B] Fire management only intervenes when the parameters

관리청은 발생한 화재를 최대한 빨리 진압했다. 이 정책은 죽은 초목들과 두꺼운 덤불이 대략 50년 동안 축적되도록 만들었고, 재앙을 위한 무대를 마련한 셈이 되었다.

4 ➡ 1988년 여름에 극심한 가뭄과 거센 돌풍을 동반한 바람이 공원의 상태를 위태롭게 만들었다. 공원 관리자들은 자신들이 여러 작은 불들에 대해 알고 있었지만, 그 불들이 자연적으로 꺼질 것이라 생각했다는 것을 인정했다. 그들이 지켜보는 동안 그 작은 불들이 합쳐져 공원 역사상 가장 큰 규모의 대화재 중 하나가 되었다. 수개월에 걸쳐 맹렬히 계속된 후, 그 화재는 공원 경계 내의 약 80만 에이커에 해당하는 지역을 파괴했고, 경계 밖으로는 그 이상이었다. 약 1만 3천 명의 소방관과 군 인력이 대화재를 진압하기 위해 동원되었고, 이 복구 노력에 정부는 1억 2천만 달러를 썼다. 그러한 노력에도 불구하고 그들은 성공적이지 못했고, 화재는 결국 가을과 겨울에 내린 비에 의해 진압되었다. 이 화재는 화재 방재 당국에게 경고 신호의 역할을 했고, 당시 그들의 화재 방재 정책들이 얼마나 부적절했으며, 자연환경을 보호하고 산림을 관리하기 위한 새로운 기술에 대한 필요성이 얼마나 절박한지를 드러냈다.

5 ➡ 이 화재 사건 이후, 산림 생태계에서 불의 정확한 역할과 그것을 어떻게 관리해야 할지 알아내기 위해 수많은 연구가 행해졌다. 불은 숲의 하층 식생의 성장을 통제하고, 떨어진 초목을 없애며, 새로운 성장을 위한 길을 만든다. 사실 어떤 솔방울은 불에 노출되지 않으면 열리지 않아서 씨앗을 퍼뜨리지 못하기도 한다. 이러한 결론으로 많은 사람들은 통제 연소라고도 일컬어지는 사전 입화를 지지하게 되었다. 이러한 불은 농지와 초원을 관리하는 데 사용되어 들불의 위험을 줄였다. 심지어 어떤 사람들은 1988년의 대화재를 예방할 수도 있었다고 말하면서, 공원 관계자들이 통제 연소를 사용하지 않은 것을 비난했다. 하지만 많은 과학자들은 불이 산림에 혜택을 주기 위해서는 불이 통제 불가능한 규모에 도달해야 한다고 주장한다.

6 ➡ [■A] 최근의 정책은 자연적으로 발생한 불은 타도록 두고, 그것을 면밀하게 감시하는 것이다. [■B] 화재 관리는 날씨, 규모, 그리고 야생 동물과 주변 인간 공동체에 끼

of weather, size, and potential danger to wildlife and nearby human communities are exceeded. [■ C] Fires that are caused by humans are still quickly suppressed though. To protect park structures and nearby communities, underbrush and other fuel sources are manually removed within 400 feet of any structure. [■ D] They are also removed from risk areas as designated by the Hazard Fuels Reduction Plan. There have been around 300 natural fires since the late 1970s that officials have allowed to burn with little or no effort to control them, and the areas where they struck have since flourished.

치는 잠재적인 위험의 한도가 초과될 경우에만 개입한다. [■C] 인간에 의해 발생한 불은 여전히 서둘러 진압되기는 한다. 공원 시설물과 주변 공동체를 보호하기 위해, 덤불과 다른 연료 물질들은 모든 구조물의 400피트 이내에서 수동으로 제거된다. [■D] 그것들은 위험 연료원 감소 계획에 의해 지정된 위험 지역에서도 제거된다. 1970년대 후반 이후로 관계자들이 통제하려는 노력을 거의 안 하거나 혹은 아예 하지 않고 연소하도록 내버려 둔 자연적인 화재가 약 300여 건 있었고, 화재가 발생한 지역은 그 후에 나무들이 무성하게 자랐다.

---

1. **Rhetorical Purpose**

The author begins the passage by

(A) comparing two types of forest fires.
(B) giving an example of threatening wildfires.
(C) **refuting the common notion about wildfires.**
(D) emphasizing the importance of fire prevention.

2. **Vocabulary**

The word "extended" in paragraph 2 is closest in meaning to

(A) harsh
(B) uncertain
(C) **long**
(D) extreme

3. **Inference**

In paragraph 2, the author implies that

(A) wildfires hinder the decomposition process of dead leaves.
(B) **wildfires help forests by burning the layer of dead branches and leaves.**
(C) wildfires may develop into a conflagration unless preventative measures are taken.
(D) wildfires destroy old trees, allowing young ones to grow.

4. **Fact**

According to paragraphs 3 and 4, what is the underlying cause of the fire at Yellowstone National Park?

(A) The natural geological wonders of the park
(B) The opposition against wildlife protection
(C) The operation of the park as a tourist attraction
(D) **The fire suppression policy of the park**

1.
글쓴이가 지문을 시작하는 방법은?

(A) 두 가지 종류의 산불을 비교한다.
(B) 위협적인 산불의 예를 제시한다.
(C) 산불에 대한 통념을 반박한다.
(D) 화재 예방의 중요성을 강조한다.

2.
2단락의 단어 "extended(장기간에 걸친)"와 의미상 가장 가까운 것은?

(A) 거친
(B) 불확실한
(C) 오랜
(D) 극도의

3.
2단락에서 글쓴이가 암시하는 것은?

(A) 산불은 죽은 잎사귀의 분해 과정을 방해한다.
(B) 산불은 죽은 나뭇가지와 잎사귀 층을 태움으로써 산림을 돕는다.
(C) 산불은 예방 조치가 취해지지 않으면 대화재로 발전할 수 있다.
(D) 산불은 오래된 나무를 파괴하여 어린 나무들이 자라도록 돕는다.

4.
3, 4단락에 따르면, 옐로스톤 국립공원 화재의 근본 원인은 무엇인가?

(A) 공원의 자연 지질학적 경이로움
(B) 야생 동식물 보호에 대한 반대
(C) 관광 명소로서의 공원의 운영
(D) 공원의 화재 진압 정책

5. Negative Fact

According to paragraph 4, all of the following are true about the fire at Yellowstone National Park EXCEPT

(A) the weather conditions aggravated the situation.

(B) **the fire started from a small fire at one spot.**

(C) the efforts to extinguish the fire cost a great deal.

(D) natural phenomena helped to put out the fire.

6. Fact

According to paragraph 5, the purpose of using prescribed fire is

(A) **to lower levels of wildfire damage.**

(B) to learn how to control large-scale fires.

(C) to burn useless farms and grassland.

(D) to estimate the damage caused by wildfires more accurately.

7. Negative Fact

All of the following are mentioned in paragraph 5 EXCEPT

(A) the roles of fire in forest ecology.

(B) the changes in people's view of fire.

(C) the purpose of using controlled burning.

(D) **research conducted to find out the cause of wildfires.**

8. Sentence Simplification

Which of the sentences below best expresses the essential information in the highlighted sentence in the passage? *Incorrect* answer choices change the meaning in important ways or leave out essential information.

(A) **Since the late 1970s, officials have let around 300 natural fires burn out, which resulted in improvement in those areas.**

(B) Since the late 1970s, around 300 natural fires have struck flourishing areas, but officials could hardly control them.

(C) Since the late 1970s, officials have set around 300 fires in order to make the areas flourish.

(D) Since the late 1970s, around 300 natural fires which officials failed to control burned some thriving areas.

9. Insertion

Look at the four squares [■] that indicate where the following sentence could be added to the passage.

Fires that are caused by humans are still quickly suppressed though.

Where would the sentence best fit? [■C]

5.

4단락에 따르면, 다음 중 옐로스톤 국립공원 화재에 대해 사실이 아닌 것은?

(A) 기상 조건이 상황을 악화시켰다.

(B) 화재는 한 지점의 작은 화재로 시작되었다.

(C) 불을 끄려는 노력에 엄청난 비용이 들었다.

(D) 자연 현상이 불을 끄는 데 도움을 주었다.

6.

5단락에 따르면, 사전 입화를 이용하는 목적은?

(A) 산불로 인한 피해 정도를 낮추는 것이다.

(B) 대규모의 화재를 통제할 방법을 배우는 것이다.

(C) 쓸모 없는 농지와 초원을 태우는 것이다.

(D) 산불에 의해 야기된 피해를 더욱 정확하게 가늠하는 것이다.

7.

다음 중 5단락에서 언급되지 않은 것은?

(A) 산림 생태계에서의 불의 역할

(B) 불에 대한 사람들의 관점의 변화

(C) 통제 연소를 사용하는 목적

(D) 산불의 원인을 파악하기 위해 행해진 연구

8.

다음 중 지문에 음영 표시된 문장의 핵심 정보를 가장 잘 표현한 문장은 무엇인가? 오답은 의미를 크게 왜곡하거나 핵심 정보를 누락하고 있다.

(A) 1970년대 후반 이후로 관계자들은 약 300여 건의 자연적인 화재를 연소하도록 내버려 두었고, 그 결과 그 지역들이 개선되었다.

(B) 1970년대 후반 이후로 약 300여 건의 자연적인 화재가 나무들이 무성한 지역들을 강타했지만, 관계자들은 그것들을 거의 통제하지 못했다.

(C) 1970년대 후반 이후로 관계자들은 그 지역에 초목이 무성하게 자라도록 하기 위해 약 300여 차례 방화를 하였다.

(D) 1970년대 후반 이후로 관계자들이 통제하지 못한 약 300여 건의 자연적인 화재가 나무들이 무성한 지역들을 불타게 했다.

9.

지문에 다음 문장이 들어갈 수 있는 위치를 나타내는 네 개의 사각형[■]을 확인하시오.

인간에 의해 발생한 불은 여전히 서둘러 진압되기는 한다.

이 문장이 들어가기에 가장 적합한 곳은? [■C]

10. Summary

Directions: An introductory sentence for a brief summary of the passage is provided below. Complete the summary by selecting the THREE answer choices that express the most important ideas in the passage. Some sentences do not belong in the summary because they express ideas that are not presented in the passage or are minor ideas in the passage. *This question is worth 2 points.*

Wildfires can be beneficial to forests and the ecosystem when controlled properly.

Ⓐ **Occasional wildfires remove dead branches and leaves, thus stimulating the decay process and allowing new plants to flourish.**

Ⓔ **The conflagration in Yellowstone National Park provided an opportunity to change the pre-existing fire control policy.**

Ⓕ **The fire control policy of Yellowstone National Park provided an environment where a disastrous fire could break out.**

Ⓑ In order to prevent devastating fires, immediate and thorough fire suppression is required.

Ⓒ Through a number of research projects, misuse of prescribed fire was found to be the cause of the fire at Yellowstone National Park.

Ⓓ Causing extreme loss of life and property, the fire at Yellowstone National Park showed how important it was to prevent wildfires.

10.

지시문: 지문을 간략하게 요약한 글의 첫 문장이 아래 제시되어 있다. 지문의 가장 중요한 내용을 표현하는 세 개의 선택지를 골라 요약문을 완성하시오. 일부 문장들은 지문에 제시되지 않았거나 지문의 지엽적인 내용을 나타내기 때문에 요약문에 포함되지 않는다. *이 문제의 배점은 2점이다.*

산불은 적절히 통제되었을 때 산림과 생태계에 이로울 수 있다.

Ⓐ 이따금씩 발생하는 산불은 죽은 나뭇가지들과 잎사귀들을 제거하고 이렇게 하여 부패 과정을 활성화하고, 새로운 식물들이 무성하게 자라도록 해 준다.

Ⓔ 옐로스톤 국립공원에서의 대화재는 기존의 화재 방재 정책을 바꿀 계기를 제공했다.

Ⓕ 옐로스톤 국립공원의 화재 방재 정책은 재앙과 같은 화재가 발생할 수 있는 환경을 제공했다.

Ⓑ 파괴적인 화재를 예방하기 위해서는 즉각적이고 철저한 화재 진압이 필요하다.

Ⓒ 수많은 연구 프로젝트를 통해서 사전 입화의 오용이 옐로스톤 국립공원 화재의 원인이라는 것이 밝혀졌다.

Ⓓ 막대한 생명과 재산 손실을 야기한 옐로스톤 국립공원에서의 화재 사건은 산불을 예방하는 것이 얼마나 중요한지를 보여주었다.

📖 어휘

1 **rampant** adj 걷잡을 수 없는, 만연[횡행]하는 Ⅰ **destruction** n 파괴, 파멸, 말살 Ⅰ **devastate** v (한 장소나 지역을) 완전히 파괴하다 Ⅰ **consume** v (불이) 전소시키다, (특히 연료·에너지·시간을) 소모하다 Ⅰ **accumulate** v (서서히) 모으다, 축적하다 Ⅰ **intact** adj (하나도 손상되지 않고) 온전한, 전혀 다치지 않은 Ⅰ **severity** n 격렬, 혹독, 엄격 Ⅰ **undertake** v (책임을 맡아서) 착수하다[하다]

2 **intervention** n 개입, 개재, 조정, 중재 Ⅰ **severe** adj 극심한, 심각한 Ⅰ **ensure** v 반드시 ~하게[이게] 하다, 보장하다 Ⅰ **utilize** v 활용[이용]하다 Ⅰ **decompose** v 분해하다, 분해[부패]되다 Ⅰ **sapling** n 묘목, 어린나무 Ⅰ **periodic** adj 주기적인 Ⅰ **intensify** v 세게 하다, 강렬하게 만들다, 증대하다 Ⅰ **magnitude** n (엄청난) 규모[중요도] Ⅰ **inevitable** adj 불가피한, 필연적인 Ⅰ **ravage** v 황폐[피폐]하게 만들다, 유린[파괴]하다

3 **poaching** n 밀렵, (밀렵 따위를 하기 위해 남의 땅에 몰래 들어가는) 불법 침입 Ⅰ **logging** n 벌목 Ⅰ **exploit** v 활용[이용]하다 Ⅰ **diminish** v 줄어들다, 약해지다, 줄이다, 약화시키다 Ⅰ **legislation** n (의회에서 통과되는) 제정법, 법률 Ⅰ **suppression** n 진압, 억제 Ⅰ **priority** n 우선 사항

4 **critical** adj 위기의, 아슬아슬한; 결정적인, 중대한 Ⅰ **admit** v 인정[시인]하다 Ⅰ **assume** v 추정[상정]하다 Ⅰ **look on** (관여하지는 않고) 구경하다[지켜보다] Ⅰ **conflagration** n 대화재 Ⅰ **boundary** n 경계[한계](선), 분계선 Ⅰ **personnel** n (조직·군대의) 인원[직원들] Ⅰ **ultimately** adv 궁극적으로 Ⅰ **defeat** v 패배시키다[물리치다/이기다] Ⅰ **precipitation** n 강수 Ⅰ **inadequate** adj 부적절한, 불충분한

5 **ecology** n 생태계, 생태학 Ⅰ **dispose of** ~을 없애다, 정리하다, 처분(처리)하다 Ⅰ **expose** v 노출시키다, (보통 때는 가려져 있는 것을) 드러내다 Ⅰ **prescribed** adj 규정된, 미리 정해진 Ⅰ **condemn** v 비난하다, 힐난하다 Ⅰ **contend** v 주장하다

6 **monitor** v 추적 관찰하다, 감시하다 Ⅰ **parameter** n (일정하게 정한) 한도 Ⅰ **exceed** v 넘다[초과하다/초월하다] Ⅰ **manually** adv 손으로, 수동으로 Ⅰ **flourish** v (초목이) 무성하게 자라다, 번창하다

The Steam Engine in Britain

1 ➡ By the late 17th century, England was facing a crisis of a kind it had never faced before. Its rapidly growing population and expanding empire demanded huge amounts of timber to supply fuel to provide energy for homes and industry and wood for its mighty fleet of ships. Unfortunately, its own forests had already dwindled down far too low to meet the demand. [■A] To supplement their shipbuilding, timber was imported, but a new source of fuel had to be found. [■B] This need was met with coal, of which the British Isles had an ample supply. [■C] As the coal miners delved ever deeper, however, they encountered a new problem with water seeping into the shafts, making the work dangerous and often impossible. [■D] Initially, they used manually powered pumps driven by animals, but this soon proved insufficient. The creation of a viable steam engine ultimately not only resolved this dilemma, but also ushered in the modern industrial age.

2 ➡ The concept of a steam powered engine actually dates back to 1st century Roman Egypt. Writings describe a device called an aeolipile which created steam within a closed vessel and released it through opposite facing vents on a ball, making the ball rotate. While illustrating the principle of steam power, this primitive example served no real purpose. Over the intervening centuries, more sophisticated designs were developed, but few were ever built. In 1606, a Spanish engineer named Jeronimo de Ayanz y Beaumont made a steam operated pump that he used to drain flooded mines. Denis Papin later designed a piston that operated by boiling water and letting the steam condense, creating a vacuum. The action of this device was used to lift small weights, but his machine had to be completely reassembled for each use. He saw that the steam would need to be created in a separate boiler to create an automatic cycle of movement, but he took his research no further.

3 ➡ In 1698, Thomas Savery improved upon Beaumont's design, and came to the English miners' rescue. His machine consisted of a vessel where the water was boiled, and the steam was sent into a second chamber. When cold water was

---

영국의 증기 기관

1. ➡ 17세기 말에 영국은 지금까지 직면한 적이 없었던 위기에 직면하고 있었다. 영국의 급격하게 증가하는 인구와 확장되는 제국은 가정과 산업에 에너지를 제공하는 연료와 영국의 강력한 함대에 쓸 나무를 공급하기 위해 엄청난 양의 목재를 필요로 했다. 불행히도 영국의 숲은 이미 너무 줄어든 상태여서 그 수요를 충족시킬 수 없었다. [■A] 배를 만드는 작업에 보충하기 위해 목재가 수입되었지만 새로운 연료의 공급원을 찾아야만 했다. [■B] 이 필요는 영국 제도가 풍부하게 보유하고 있던 석탄을 통해 충족되었다. [■C] 하지만 광부들이 더 깊게 파고 들어갈수록, 그들은 물이 수갱에 스며드는 새로운 문제에 부딪혔고, 그것은 그 작업을 위험하고 종종 불가능하게 만들었다. [■D] 처음에 그들은 동물들에 의해 구동되는 수동 펌프를 사용했지만, 이것은 곧 충분하지 않은 것으로 드러났다. 실행 가능한 증기 기관의 발명은 이 딜레마를 궁극적으로 해결했을 뿐만 아니라 현대 산업 시대를 열었다.

2. ➡ 증기를 원동력 삼아 작동하는 기관의 개념은 사실 1세기 로마 통치 하의 이집트로 거슬러 올라간다. 기록들에는 기력계라고 불리는 장치가 묘사되어 있는데, 그것은 닫혀 있는 용기에서 증기를 만들어 반대측 통풍구로 배출해서 공이 회전하도록 만드는 것이다. 증기력의 원리를 묘사한 반면에, 이 원시적인 예는 아무 실질적인 용도가 없었다. 그 후 여러 세기에 걸쳐서 더 정교한 설계가 개발되었지만 실제로 만들어진 것은 거의 없었다. 1606년에 헤로니모 데 아얀스 이 보몽이라는 스페인 기술자가 증기로 작동하는 펌프를 만들어 침수된 탄광의 물을 빼내는 데 사용했다. 후에 드니 파팽은 물을 끓이고 그 증기가 응결되게 하여 진공을 만드는 피스톤을 설계했다. 이 장치의 움직임은 작고 무거운 것들을 들어올리는 데 사용됐지만, 그의 기계는 사용할 때마다 완전히 재조립되어야만 했다. 자동 이동 주기를 만들어 내려면 증기가 별도의 보일러에서 만들어져야만 된다는 것을 알았지만, 그는 더 이상 자신의 연구를 하지 않았다.

3 ➡ 1698년에 토머스 세이버리는 보몽의 설계를 개선해서 영국 광부들의 문제를 해결했다. 그의 기계는 물이 끓여지는 용기로 구성되어 있었고, 그 증기는 두 번째 챔버로 보내어졌다. 냉각수가 챔버 밖에 부어지면 증기가 급격하게 응결하면서 그로 인해 만들어진 진공이 밸브를 열어 그 챔

poured over the outside of the chamber, the steam rapidly condensed, creating a vacuum that opened the valve and sucked water up into the chamber. The valve only opened in this direction, so when it shut, it kept the water from falling back down the pipe. The water could then be drained off through a different valve. There were a few flaws with his design. Firstly, the vacuum could only pull water up from a short distance, so a series of pumps had to be used to draw water up to the surface. In addition, the condensing chambers had weak walls and sometimes exploded.

4 ➡ In 1712, Thomas Newcomen took Savery's design and incorporated Papin's piston. With his machine, the steam was driven into the piston chamber, and then a small injection of cold water condensed the steam creating a vacuum. However, instead of drawing up water into the chamber like in Savery's design, the vaccum pulled down the piston, which was attached to a chain. This chain was connected to a beam on an axle, and a chain at the other end of the beam operated the pump. When a new charge of steam filled the piston, it would rise and a weight on the pump end of the beam reset the system. Newcomen's steam engine could pull water up much farther, so it enjoyed great success, and over 100 had been installed by 1735.

5 ➡ Although Savery and Newcomen inarguably employed steam technology in their machines, the creation of the modern steam engine is usually attributed to one individual: James Watt. Watt was trained as an instrument maker in London and employed near Glasgow University. While there, he was asked to repair one of Newcomen's engines. As he worked, he realized why it was so inefficient: fuel, steam, and time were being wasted by having the steam condense inside of the piston. He remedied this by creating a separate condenser, and he partnered with Matthew Boulton.

6 ➡ They subsequently created two more improvements that not only further increased the engine's power output, but also allowed the engines to be used to power factories in addition to pumps. The first was a double-acting engine, which used steam to push the piston both up and down. This used steam that formerly was wasted and provided more power. The second was a spinning device

버 안으로 물을 빨아들였다. 그 밸브는 한 방향으로만 열렸기 때문에 그것이 닫히면 물이 다시 파이프를 따라 내려가는 것을 막았다. 챔버 안에 있는 물은 다른 밸브를 통해서 다시 빼내졌다. 그의 설계에는 몇 가지 약점이 있었다. 첫째, 진공은 물을 짧은 거리에서만 끌어올릴 수 있었기 때문에 물을 지면까지 끌어올리기 위해서는 일련의 펌프들이 사용되어야 했다. 그리고 냉각 챔버의 벽이 약했기 때문에 종종 폭발했다.

4 ➡ 1712년에 토머스 뉴커먼은 세이버리의 설계에 파팽의 피스톤을 접목시켰다. 그의 기계에서는 증기가 피스톤 챔버로 옮겨지고 작은 양의 냉각수의 투입이 증기를 응결시켜 진공을 만들었다. 하지만 세이버리의 설계에서처럼 물을 챔버로 끌어올리는 대신에, 그 진공은 체인에 달려 있는 피스톤을 끌어내렸다. 그 체인은 차축에 있는 기둥과 연결되어 있었고, 기둥의 반대쪽에 달려 있는 체인은 펌프를 작동시켰다. 증기가 새로 피스톤을 채우면, 그것은 뜨기 시작하면서 펌프와 연결된 기둥 쪽에 있는 추가 그 시스템을 초기화시켰다. 뉴커먼의 증기 기관은 물을 훨씬 더 높이 끌어올릴 수 있었기에 큰 성공을 누렸으며, 1735년까지 100대 이상 설치됐다.

5 ➡ 비록 세이버리와 뉴커먼이 논쟁의 여지 없이 증기 기술을 그들의 기계에 적용했지만, 현대 증기 기관 발명의 공은 보통 한 사람, 즉 제임스 와트에게 돌려진다. 와트는 런던에서 기구 제조자로 훈련을 받고 글래스고 대학교 근처에서 일하고 있었다. 거기에 있는 동안 그는 뉴커먼의 기계 중 하나를 수리해달라는 요청을 받았다. 그는 작업을 하면서 그 기계가 왜 그리 비효율적인지 깨닫게 됐다. 증기가 피스톤 안에서 응결하도록 함으로써 연료, 증기, 그리고 시간이 낭비되고 있었다. 그는 별도의 냉각기를 만들어서 이것을 개선했고, 매튜 볼튼과 협력했다.

6 ➡ 그들은 그 뒤에 추가로 개선된 것을 2개 더 만들었는데, 그것들은 기관의 동력 출력을 더 증가시켰을 뿐만 아니라 그 기관이 펌프와 함께 공장을 가동하는 데 사용될 수 있도록 해주었다. 첫 번째는 증기를 사용하여 피스톤을 위아래로 미는 복동 기관이었다. 이것은 기존에 낭비되던 증기를 사용하여 더 많은 동력을 제공했다. 두 번째는 원심조속기라고 불리는 회전하는 장치였다. 이 장치의 회전은 밸브를 자동으로 열고 닫는 데 사용됐으며, 기관의 앞뒤 움직

called a fly-ball governor. This device's rotation was used to open and close valves automatically, and it changed the engine's back-and-forth motion into a circular one. Before this invention, factories used water wheels to power their machines, but the rotating steam engine replaced them. This meant that factories could be built away from rivers, and Britain's manufacturing output skyrocketed. These innovations are why James Watt is typically given the most credit for modern steam engines.

임을 순환 움직임으로 변경했다. 이 발명 전에 공장들은 기계를 돌리는 데 물레바퀴를 사용했지만 회전하는 증기 기관이 그것들을 대체했다. 그것은 공장이 강에서 떨어진 곳에도 세워질 수 있다는 것을 의미했고, 영국의 제조업 생산량은 급등했다. 이러한 혁신은 흔히 현대 증기 기관 발명에 대해 제임스 와트가 가장 크게 인정받는 이유이다.

---

1. Negative Fact

According to paragraph 1, what is NOT one of the factors that led to the development of the steam engine in Britain?

Ⓐ **The dwindling supply of timber in Europe**

Ⓑ The growing population

Ⓒ The flooding in coal mines

Ⓓ The expanding British empire

1.

1단락에 따르면, 영국에서 증기 기관의 발전을 이끈 요인이 아닌 것은 무엇인가?

Ⓐ 유럽의 감소하는 목재 공급량

Ⓑ 증가하는 인구

Ⓒ 탄광의 침수

Ⓓ 확장되는 영국 제국

2. Rhetorical Purpose

Why does the author mention the "aeolipile" in paragraph 2?

Ⓐ To point out that the conceptual device served no real purpose

Ⓑ To explain Beaumont's source of inspiration for his steam operated pump

Ⓒ To prove that Roman Egypt was very advanced in science

Ⓓ **To illustrate how long the concept of steam power has existed**

2.

2단락에서 글쓴이가 기력계를 언급하는 이유는 무엇인가?

Ⓐ 그 개념적인 장치는 실질적인 용도가 없었다는 것을 지적하기 위해

Ⓑ 보몽으로 하여금 증기로 작동하는 펌프를 만들게 한 영감의 근원을 설명하기 위해

Ⓒ 로마 통치 하의 이집트가 과학이 매우 발달되어 있었다는 것을 증명하기 위해

Ⓓ 증기력의 개념이 얼마나 오랫동안 존재해 왔는지 묘사하기 위해

3. Inference

Based on paragraph 3, it can be inferred that

Ⓐ **Savery's machine did not achieve commercial success.**

Ⓑ Savery incorporated Papin's invention in his machine.

Ⓒ Savery eventually overcame the limitations of the chamber.

Ⓓ Savery's machine provided a final solution to the English miners.

3.

3단락에 근거하여 추론할 수 있는 것은?

Ⓐ 세이버리의 기계는 상업적인 성공을 거두지 못했다.

Ⓑ 세이버리는 파팽의 발명을 자신의 기계에 접목했다.

Ⓒ 세이버리는 결국 챔버의 한계를 극복했다.

Ⓓ 세이버리의 기계는 영국 광부들에게 최종 해결책을 제시했다.

4. Sentence Simplification

Which of the sentences below best expresses the essential information in the highlighted sentence in the passage? *Incorrect* answer choices change the meaning in important ways or leave out essential information.

4.

다음 중 지문의 음영 표시된 문장의 핵심 정보를 가장 잘 표현한 문장은 무엇인가? 오답은 의미를 크게 왜곡하거나 핵심 정보를 누락하고 있다.

(A) Condensation of steam inside the chamber caused water to be sucked up into the vacuum.

(B) When the cold water poured over the chamber rapidly condensed, the vacuum created by this opened the valve and sucked water up into the chamber.

(C) The vacuum created by the condensation of steam allowed cold water to be sucked up into the chamber through the valve.

(D) **When the cold water rapidly condensed the steam, the vacuum created inside the chamber caused water to be sucked up through the valve.**

5. Fact

According to paragraph 4, what was the main difference between Newcomen's and Savery's designs?

(A) Newcomen's engine relied on creating a vacuum in the chamber.

(B) Savery's engine could pull water up much farther than Newcomen's.

(C) **Savery's engine drew up water directly into the vacuum chamber.**

(D) Newcomen's engine was connected to a beam on an axle.

6. Vocabulary

The word "inarguably" in paragraph 5 is closest in meaning to

(A) incongruently

(B) **indisputably**

(C) irrevocably

(D) unlikely

7. Fact

According to paragraph 6, what effect did Watt's innovations have in Britain? Click on two answers.

(A) **They replaced water wheels in factories.**

(B) They automated the manufacturing process in British factories.

(C) They reduced Britain's dependency on timber.

(D) **They provided increased power output with the same amount of steam.**

8. Fact

According to the passage, why is the creation of the modern steam engine attributed to James Watt?

(A) He added a separate condenser to Newcomen's engines.

(B) He allowed factories to be built away from rivers.

(A) 챔버 내 증기의 응결은 물이 진공으로 빨려 올라가게 했다.

(B) 챔버 위에 부어진 냉각수가 급격하게 응결됐을 때, 이 것으로 인해 생긴 진공은 밸브를 열어 물을 챔버로 끌 어올렸다.

(C) 증기의 응결로 생긴 진공은 냉각수가 밸브를 통해 챔 버 안으로 빨려 들어가게 했다.

(D) 냉각수가 증기를 급격히 응결시켰을 때, 챔버 내에 생 긴 진공은 물이 밸브를 통해 빨려 올라가게 했다.

5.

4단락에 따르면, 뉴커먼의 설계와 세이버리의 설계의 주요 차이점은 무엇인가?

(A) 뉴커먼의 기관은 챔버 내에 진공을 만드는 것에 의존 했다.

(B) 세이버리의 기관은 뉴커먼의 기관보다 물을 훨씬 더 멀리 끌어올릴 수 있었다.

(C) 세이버리의 기관은 물을 곧장 진공 챔버로 끌어올렸 다.

(D) 뉴커먼의 기관은 차축에 있는 기둥과 연결되어 있었 다.

6.

5단락의 단어 "inarguably(논쟁의 여지 없이)"와 의미상 가장 가까운 것은?

(A) 일치하지 않게

(B) 반박의 여지 없게

(C) 변경할 수 없게

(D) 있음직하지 않은

7.

6단락에 따르면, 와트의 혁신은 영국에 어떠한 영향을 미 쳤는가? 보기 두 개를 고르시오.

(A) 공장의 물레바퀴를 대체했다.

(B) 영국 공장의 제조 과정을 자동화했다.

(C) 영국의 목재 의존성을 감소시켰다.

(D) 같은 양의 증기로 더 많은 동력 출력을 제공했다.

8.

지문에 따르면, 현대 증기 기관 발명의 공이 제임스 와트에 게 돌아가는 이유는 무엇인가?

(A) 그는 뉴커먼의 기관들에 별도의 냉각기를 추가했다.

(B) 그는 공장들이 강에서 떨어진 곳에 세워지는 것을 가 능하게 했다.

Ⓒ He made significant improvements to prior inefficient designs.

Ⓓ He trained as an instrument maker at Glasgow University.

9. Insertion

Look at the four squares [■] that indicate where the following sentence could be added to the passage.

Initially, they used manually powered pumps driven by animals, but this soon proved insufficient.

Where would the sentence best fit? [■ D]

10. Summary

Directions: An introductory sentence for a brief summary of the passage is provided below. Complete the summary by selecting the THREE answer choices that express the most important ideas in the passage. Some sentences do not belong in the summary because they express ideas that are not presented in the passage or are minor ideas in the passage. *This question is worth 2 points.*

Growing energy demands prompted England to turn from timber to coal and finally to the steam engine for a reliable source of energy, paving the way for the modern industrial age.

> Ⓑ Newcomen improved Savery's design by introducing pistons, and this modification increased the effectiveness of the steam engine.
> Ⓓ Utilizing steam power was a concept various engineers experimented with, but without significant application in real life.
> Ⓔ Watt's improvements to Newcomen's design transformed it into an efficient rotating steam engine, which contributed to the industrial age.

Ⓐ Because there was an abundant supply of coal in the British Isles, England was temporarily saved from a potentially disastrous energy crisis.

Ⓒ Together, the double-acting engine and the fly-ball governor changed the engine's motion into a circular pattern.

Ⓕ Because Watt made it possible for the steam engine to be applied in factories, he is called the creator of the steam.

Ⓒ 그는 기존의 비효율적인 설계에 상당한 개선을 이루어냈다.

Ⓓ 그는 글래스고 대학교에서 기구 제조자로 훈련을 받았다.

9.

지문에 다음 문장이 들어갈 수 있는 위치를 나타내는 네 개의 사각형[■]을 확인하시오.

처음에 그들은 동물들에 의해 구동되는 수동 펌프를 사용했지만, 이것은 곧 충분하지 않은 것으로 드러났다.

이 문장이 들어가기에 가장 적합한 곳은? [■ D]

10.

지시문: 지문을 간략하게 요약한 글의 첫 문장이 아래 제시되어 있다. 지문의 가장 중요한 내용을 표현하는 세 개의 선택지를 골라 요약문을 완성하시오. 일부 문장들은 지문에 제시되지 않았거나 지문의 지엽적인 내용을 나타내기 때문에 요약문에 포함되지 않는다. *이 문제의 배점은 2점이다.*

증가하는 에너지 수요는 영국으로 하여금 믿을 만한 에너지 지원을 찾아서 목재에서 석탄으로, 그리고 결국엔 증기 기관으로 돌아서게 했으며, 이것은 현대 산업 시대를 향한 길을 닦았다.

> Ⓑ 뉴커먼은 피스톤을 도입함으로써 세이버리의 설계를 개선했고, 이러한 변경은 증기 기관의 효율성을 높였다.
> Ⓓ 증기력의 활용은 여러 엔지니어들이 실험했던 개념인데, 실생활에서 중요한 적용은 없었다.
> Ⓔ 뉴커먼의 설계에 와트가 적용한 개선 사항들은 그것을 효율적인 회전 증기 기관으로 바꾸었고 그것은 산업 시대에 기여했다.

Ⓐ 영국 제도에 풍부한 양의 석탄이 있었기 때문에 영국은 잠재적으로 재앙에 가까운 에너지 위기에서 일시적으로 벗어나게 됐다.

Ⓒ 복동 기관과 원심조속기는 함께 기관의 움직임을 순환적 패턴으로 바꾸어놨다.

Ⓕ 증기 기관이 공장에 적용되는 것을 가능하게 했기 때문에, 와트는 증기 기관의 발명자라고 불린다.

어휘

1 **crisis** n 위기 | **expanding** adj 확장[팽창]하는 | **demand** v 요구하다, 필요로 하다 n 요구, 수요 | **dwindle** v (점점) 줄어들다 | **supplement** v 보충하다 | **delve** v 파다, 탐구하다, 깊이 파고들다 | **seep** v 스미다, 배다 | **initially** adv 처음에 | **insufficient** adj 불충분한 | **viable** adj 실행 가능한, 성공할 수 있는 | **ultimately** adv 궁극적으로 | **resolve** v (문제 등을) 해결하다 | **usher** v 안내하다, 인도하다, ~의 도래를 알리다 | **industrial** adj 산업[공업]의

2 **device** n 장치[기구] | **vessel** n 용기(容器), 그릇, (대형) 선박[배] | **facing** adj 마주 대하고 있는, 대면(對面)의 | **vent** n 통풍구, 환기구 | **rotate** v 회전하다[시키다] | **principle** n 원칙[원리] | **primitive** adj 원시 사회의, 원시적인 단계의 | **sophisticated** adj 세련된, 교양 있는 | **operate** v 작동[가동]되다 | **drain** v (물을) 빼내다, 따라 내다[흘러 나가다] | **mine** n 광산 | **condense** v 응결되다, 응결시키다 | **vacuum** n 진공 | **reassemble** v 재조립하다 | **separate** adj 분리된, 따로 떨어진, 독립된

3 **flaw** n 결함, 흠 | **chamber** n 방, (기계 속의) 실(室)

4 **incorporate** v 통합하다, 포함하다 | **attach** v 붙이다, 첨부하다 | **weight** n 추, 무게 | **reset** v (기기·조종 장치 등의) 시간·숫자 등을) 다시 맞추다

5 **inarguably** adv 논쟁의 여지 없이, 명백하게 | **employ** v 고용하다, 쓰다[이용하다] | **attribute** v 결과로[덕분으로] 보다 | **remedy** v 바로잡다, 개선[교정]하다

6 **subsequently** adv 그 뒤에, 나중에 | **formerly** adv 이전에, 예전에 | **circular** adj 원형의, 둥근 | **power** v 동력을 공급하다, 작동시키다 | **manufacturing** n 제조업 | **output** n 생산량, 산출량 | **skyrocket** v 급등하다 | **typically** adv 보통, 일반적으로 | **credit** n 명예, 공, 칭찬

Passage 3

Agricultural Pest Control

1 ➡ Without the adoption and subsequent development of agriculture, human society would never have been able to develop to the extent that it has, nor could our population have grown so rapidly. In order to farm, humans deliberately disrupt natural ecosystems to create the best possible conditions for the crops they wish to grow. [■A] They remove large numbers of the native species, alter the distribution of water, and enrich the soil with fertilizers. In addition, most farms practice monoculture to a certain extent, which means that one section to all of their land is used to grow the same plants. [■B] Such massive disruption of nature often leads to the explosion of species that consume those plants. [■C] These species that endanger crops are labeled as pests. In order to control pest organisms, farmers typically use chemical or biological controls; however, a more moderate approach appears to be the most effective in the long run. [■D]

2 ➡ Chemical controls are the most widely used method for limiting pest populations today, but they have a surprisingly long past. Around 2,500 BCE, ancient Sumerians used elemental sulfur powder to discourage pests, and a text called the Rig Veda, which dates back to around 4,000 years ago,

농업 병충해 방제

1 ➡ 농업의 채택과 계속되는 발전 없이 인간 사회는 결코 지금의 정도까지 발전하지 못했을 것이며, 인구도 이렇게 빨리 증가하지 못했을 것이다. 농사를 짓기 위해 인간은 재배하고자 하는 작물에 가능한 한 최상의 조건을 만들어주려고 자연 생태계를 의도적으로 교란한다. [■A] 그들은 다수의 토착종을 제거하고, 배수를 바꾸고, 비료로 토양을 비옥하게 한다. 게다가 대부분의 농장은 어느 정도의 단일재배를 실행하는데, 이것은 땅의 한 부분이 동일한 식물만을 재배하는 데 사용된다는 것을 의미한다. [■B] 그러한 자연의 엄청난 혼란은 종종 그러한 식물을 먹는 종의 폭발적인 증가로 이어진다. [■C] 농작물을 위태롭게 하는 이러한 종은 해충으로 분류된다. 해충을 방제하기 위해 농부들은 일반적으로 화학적 또는 생물학적 방제들을 사용한다. 그러나 장기적으로 봤을 때 더 온건한 접근이 가장 효과적인 것으로 보인다. [■D]

2 ➡ 화학적 방제는 오늘날 해충 개체수 제한을 위해 가장 널리 사용되는 방법이지만, 놀랍도록 오랜 역사를 가지고 있다. 기원전 2,500년경 고대 수메르인들은 해충을 억제하기 위해 원소 황 가루를 사용했고, 역사가 약 4,000년 전까지 거슬러 올라가는 리그 베다라고 불리는 서적은 비슷한 목적을 위해 독성이 있는 식물을 사용했다고 언급하고 있

mentions the use of poisonous plants for similar purposes. By the Renaissance, toxic chemicals like mercury, lead, and arsenic were being widely used to kill pests. Although these chemicals are toxic to humans as well, they were also used in makeup and medicines. At the time, people believed that small doses of poison were good for one's health, and no doubt thought that using them on crops would have little effect on them.

3 ➡ Beginning in the 17th century, people began extracting chemicals from plants to use as pesticides: nicotine sulfide from tobacco, pyrethrum from chrysanthemum flowers, and rotenone from the roots of tropical plants. All of these pesticides existed in nature, even the toxic elemental chemicals. However, in the early 20th century, synthesized chemicals became dominant. The first of these was DDT, which was initially used to control human parasites like mosquitoes and lice. Scientists soon learned to deliver DDT in any physical form, which led to its widespread use in agriculture. Since then, chemical pesticides have become the dominant control for agricultural pests, and their use has revealed many side effects of pest control.

4 ➡ Any attempt at controlling the population of a pest species entails the risk of affecting other species. Initially, this is caused by disrupting the predator-prey system. Even though local predators are unable to control the pest species, they may still depend upon them for food. However, chemical controls introduce additional problems. Firstly, the pesticides often kill organisms other than the intended pests, including their natural predators. Secondly, continuously exposing pests to chemicals will inevitably cause them to develop a resistance. Through natural immunity or repeated low level exposure, some will always survive to reproduce, and their population will rebound. Nearly every pesticide known to man has been used on mosquitoes, and they have always quickly adapted. Thirdly, pesticides spread into the surrounding environment, particularly through the water system. This can have far-reaching effects on organisms with no connection to the farms whatsoever, like birds that eat fish.

5 ➡ Thus, many farmers have decided to return to nature by introducing predatory species. Again, this is hardly a new idea as the Chinese are credited

다. 르네상스 시대까지 수은, 납, 비소와 같은 독성 화학물질들이 해충을 죽이기 위해 널리 사용되었다. 비록 이러한 화학물질들은 인간에게도 해롭지만 화장품과 약품에도 사용되었다. 당시 사람들은 소량의 독은 건강에 좋다고 믿었으며, 그것을 농작물에 사용하는 것 역시 영향이 거의 없을 거라고 생각했다.

3 ➡ 17세기 초부터 사람들은 살충제로 쓰기 위해 식물에서 화학물질을 추출하기 시작했다. 담배로부터는 니코틴 황화물을, 국화꽃에서는 제충국을, 열대식물의 뿌리에서는 로테논을 추출했다. 이러한 살충제들은, 심지어 독성 원소 화학물질들도, 자연에 존재했다. 그러나 20세기 초에 합성 화학물질들이 우세해지기 시작했다. 이 중에서 최초의 것은 DDT였는데, 이것은 원래 모기나 이 같은 인체 기생충을 억제하기 위해 사용되었다. 과학자들은 곧 DDT를 어떠한 물리적인 형태로든 만들어 내는 법을 알게 되었으며, 이는 농업에서의 광범위한 DDT 사용으로 이어졌다. 그 후로 화학 살충제는 농업 해충 방제에서 가장 우세하게 되었으며 사용은 해충 방제의 많은 부작용을 드러냈다.

4 ➡ 유해 동물종의 개체수를 억제하려는 어떤 노력도 다른 종에 영향을 미치는 위험을 수반한다. 처음에는 포식자와 피식자 시스템에 혼란을 일으킴으로써 야기된다. 비록 토착 포식동물이 유해 동물종을 억제할 수 없더라도, 그들은 여전히 먹이로서 그것들에 의존한다. 그러나 화학 방제는 부가적인 문제점들을 가져온다. 첫째로, 살충제는 종종 죽이려고 의도했던 해충 이외에 해충의 천적을 포함한 다른 종을 죽인다. 둘째, 지속적으로 해충을 화학물질에 노출시키는 것은 필연적으로 내성을 키우게 만들 것이다. 자연적인 면역이나 반복된 낮은 수치의 노출을 통해 언제나 일부는 번식할 정도로 살아남을 것이며, 개체수는 반등할 것이다. 인간에게 알려진 거의 모든 살충제가 모기에게 사용되었는데, 그들은 항상 빠르게 적응해 왔다. 셋째, 살충제는 이웃하는 환경으로 퍼지는데, 특히 하천의 수계를 통해 퍼진다. 이것은 농장과 아무런 관계도 없는 생물들, 예를 들어 물고기를 먹이로 하는 새들에게까지 널리 영향을 미칠 수 있다.

5 ➡ 따라서 많은 농부들은 천적을 도입함으로써 자연으로 돌아가기로 결정했다. 중국인들이 과수원에 개미집을 일부러 놓아두는 방법을 썼던 것으로 인정받기에 이는 전혀 새

with deliberately introducing ant hives to their fruit orchards. After noticing that a particular species of ants attacked insects on their citrus trees, they began collecting and transplanting the ants' nests into their trees. Today, many farmers introduce spiders, wasps and other predatory animals to their fields. However, they must take great care with the organisms which they select. The introduction of any non-indigenous species can have serious unforeseen side effects. These organisms often have no natural predators in their new environment, so their population can grow unchecked. In addition, there is no guarantee that they will eat the correct organisms, or even remain in the desired area. This has occurred widely with the cane toad, which often fled farmers' fields due to insufficient ground cover. Since the toads are poisonous, they have had a disastrous impact on local predatory animals with no immunity to their toxin.

6 ➡ In order to avoid such problems and still maintain maximum possible crop yield, many experts recommend an approach called Integrated Pest Management (IPM). IPM involves many tactics, but it begins with determining the threat level to the crops. Merely sighting a possible pest is not sufficient cause to begin using pesticides. The situation should be carefully monitored until an identified pest becomes an economic threat to the farm. At that point, preventative measures like removing the affected plants, rotating crops, or selecting more resistant varieties of a plant are recommended. If these are ineffective, then introducing reliable predator species may be an option, but spraying of broad-spectrum pesticides should only be used as a last resort.

로운 생각이 아니다. 특정 개미 종이 감귤류 나무의 벌레들을 공격하는 것을 알아차린 후, 중국인들은 개미 둥지를 모아서 나무에 옮기기 시작했다. 오늘날 많은 농부들이 거미, 말벌, 그리고 다른 포식동물들을 농장에 도입한다. 그러나 생물을 선택함에 있어 매우 조심해야 한다. 어떤 외래종의 도입이라도 예기치 못한 심각한 부작용을 불러일으킬 수 있다. 이러한 생물들은 새로운 환경에 천적이 없어서, 개체 수가 제재되지 않은 채 증가할 수 있다. 게다가 목적에 맞는 생물을 먹이로 하거나 심지어 원하는 지역에 남아 있으리라는 보장은 어디에도 없다. 이러한 경우가 수수두꺼비에게서 광범위하게 발생했는데, 그들은 부족한 지표식물로 인해 종종 농장에서 달아났다. 두꺼비는 독성이 있기 때문에 그들의 독에 면역이 없는 토착 포식동물들에게 처참한 영향을 주었다.

6 ➡ 그러한 문제점들을 피하면서도 최대 수확량을 유지하기 위해 많은 전문가들이 병충해 종합관리(IPM)라는 접근법을 추천하고 있다. IPM에는 많은 전략들이 포함되지만, 농작물에 대한 위협 수준을 결정하는 것으로부터 시작된다. 단순히 해충을 발견한 것은 살충제를 사용하기 시작하는 충분한 이유가 되지 못한다. 확인된 해충이 농장에 경제적인 위협이 될 때까지 상황이 유심히 관찰되어야 한다. 그 시점에 병충해를 입은 식물을 제거하거나, 농작물을 윤작하거나, 병충해에 더 강한 품종을 선택하는 것과 같은 예방 대책들이 추천된다. 만약 이러한 방법들이 효과가 없다면, 믿을 수 있는 포식종을 도입하는 것도 하나의 방법이 될 수 있지만, 광범위하게 살충제를 살포하는 것은 마지막 수단으로 사용되어야만 한다.

1. **Negative Fact**

All of the following are mentioned in paragraph 2 about past pest control EXCEPT

(A) Sumerians used powdered sulfur to deter pests.

(B) **farmers used toxins that made produce unsafe for consumption.**

(C) ancient farmers were aware of plants that are toxic to pests.

(D) texts on agriculture have been written for over 4,000 years.

1.

다음 중 2단락에서 과거의 해충 방제에 관해 언급되지 않은 것은?

(A) 수메르인들은 해충을 저지하기 위해 가루를 낸 황을 사용했다.

(B) 농부들은 농산물을 소비하기에 안전하지 않게 만드는 독성 물질을 사용했다.

(C) 고대 농부들은 해충에 독성을 가진 식물들을 알고 있었다.

(D) 농업에 관한 문헌은 4천 년이 넘는 동안 쓰여져 왔다.

2. Sentence Simplification

Which of the sentences below best expresses the essential information in the highlighted sentence in the passage? *Incorrect* answer choices change the meaning in important ways or leave out essential information.

Ⓐ At that time, people thought using a little poison on crops was helpful for their health.

Ⓑ At that time, people took small doses of poison for their health by using them on the crops that they grew.

Ⓒ At that time, the poisons which people used on their crops were not very dangerous, so they took them for their health.

Ⓓ **At that time, people thought that using poisons would not affect crops seriously since they were thought to be beneficial when used in small quantities.**

3. Negative Fact

According to paragraph 3, all of the following are true about DDT EXCEPT

Ⓐ DDT replaced natural chemicals from plants that had been used to kill pests.

Ⓑ DDT was the first synthetic pesticide, and it came to be used widely in the 20th century.

Ⓒ **DDT was originally synthesized to help agriculture by eliminating insects.**

Ⓓ DDT was adapted to be available in various physical forms.

4. Fact

According to paragraph 4, how does intentional control of pest populations affect the food chain?

Ⓐ Pesticides make it unnecessary for natural predators to depend upon pests for food.

Ⓑ **The use of pesticides may kill natural predators as well as pest species.**

Ⓒ Pesticides affect the whole ecosystem by causing mutations in natural predators.

Ⓓ Pesticides often weaken the immunity of predators, allowing pests to thrive.

5. Fact

According to paragraph 5, the Chinese introduced ant hives to their orchards to

Ⓐ identify the organisms affecting their trees.

Ⓑ remove undesired plants from the rows of trees.

Ⓒ **keep their citrus trees safe from fruit-damaging insects.**

2.

다음 중 지문의 음영 표시된 문장의 핵심 정보를 가장 잘 표현한 문장은 무엇인가? 오답은 의미를 크게 왜곡하거나 핵심 정보를 누락하고 있다.

Ⓐ 그 당시에 사람들은 농작물에 소량의 독을 사용하는 것이 건강에 이롭다고 생각했다.

Ⓑ 그 당시에 사람들은 재배하는 농작물에 독을 사용함으로써 건강을 위해 소량의 독을 섭취했다.

Ⓒ 그 당시에 사람들이 농작물에 사용한 독은 매우 위험하진 않았기 때문에 그들은 건강을 위해 독을 섭취했다.

Ⓓ 그 당시에 사람들은 독이 소량으로 사용되면 이롭다고 생각했기 때문에 독을 사용하는 것이 농작물에 심각하게 영향을 미치지 않을 거라고 생각했다.

3.

3단락에 따르면, 다음 중 DDT에 관해 사실이 아닌 것은?

Ⓐ DDT는 해충을 죽이는 데 사용되어 왔던 식물로부터 유래된 자연 화학물질을 대신했다.

Ⓑ DDT는 최초의 합성 살충제였고, 20세기에 널리 사용되었다.

Ⓒ DDT는 원래 곤충을 제거함으로써 농업을 돕기 위해 만들어졌다.

Ⓓ DDT는 다양한 형태로 이용 가능하게 응용되었다.

4.

4단락에 따르면, 의도적인 해충 개체수 억제는 어떻게 먹이 사슬에 영향을 주는가?

Ⓐ 살충제는 천적이 먹이로서 해충에 의존하는 것을 불필요하게 한다.

Ⓑ 살충제의 사용은 해충뿐만 아니라 천적도 죽일 수 있다.

Ⓒ 살충제는 천적에 돌연변이를 일으켜 전체 생태계에 영향을 미친다.

Ⓓ 살충제는 종종 포식자의 면역을 약화시켜 해충들이 번성하게 한다.

5.

5단락에 따르면, 중국인들이 자신들의 과수원에 개미집을 도입한 이유는?

Ⓐ 나무에 영향을 주는 생물을 알아내기 위해서

Ⓑ 줄지어 선 나무들에서 원하지 않는 식물을 제거하기 위해서

Ⓒ 감귤류 나무를 과실해충으로부터 안전하게 지키기 위해서

Ⓓ make their citrus trees more resistant to insects and disease.

Ⓓ 감귤류 나무를 해충과 병에 더 강하게 만들기 위해서

6. Rhetorical Purpose

Why does the author mention the "cane toad" in paragraph 5?

Ⓐ To give an example of a species with great adaptability

Ⓑ To explain how to domesticate introduced species effectively

Ⓒ To claim that any attempt to control a pest population is fruitless

Ⓓ **To show the danger of introducing foreign species indiscriminately**

6.

5단락에서 저자가 "수수두꺼비"를 언급하는 이유는 무엇인가?

Ⓐ 대단한 적응력을 가진 종의 예를 들기 위해

Ⓑ 도입된 종을 어떻게 효과적으로 길들이는지 설명하기 위해

Ⓒ 해충의 개체수를 억제하려는 어떤 시도도 효과가 없다는 것을 주장하기 위해

Ⓓ 외래종을 무차별적으로 도입하는 것의 위험성을 보여주기 위해

7. Vocabulary

The word "tactics" in paragraph 6 is closest in meaning to

Ⓐ alliances

Ⓑ **strategies**

Ⓒ standards

Ⓓ advantages

7.

6단락의 단어 "tactics(전략들)"와 의미상 가장 가까운 것은?

Ⓐ 동맹들

Ⓑ 전략들

Ⓒ 기준들

Ⓓ 장점들

8. Inference

What can be inferred about IPM from paragraph 6?

Ⓐ **It was designed to guarantee both ecological safety and productivity improvement.**

Ⓑ It aims to eradicate any kind of pest by introducing predator species.

Ⓒ It puts the highest priority on environmental value and the protection of species.

Ⓓ It was intended to expand agricultural fields and maximize crop yields.

8.

6단락에서 IPM에 대해 추론할 수 있는 것은 무엇인가?

Ⓐ 그것은 생태계의 안전과 생산성 향상 두 가지를 모두 보장하기 위해 고안되었다.

Ⓑ 그것은 포식종을 도입함으로써 모든 종류의 해충을 박멸하는 것을 목표로 한다.

Ⓒ 그것은 환경적 가치와 종의 보호를 최우선으로 한다.

Ⓓ 그것은 농경지를 확대하고 농작물 생산량을 극대화하기 위해 의도되었다.

9. Insertion

Look at the four squares [■] that indicate where the following sentence could be added to the passage.

These species that endanger crops are labeled as pests.

Where would the sentence best fit? [■C]

9.

지문에 다음 문장이 들어갈 수 있는 위치를 나타내는 네 개의 사각형[■]을 확인하시오.

농작물을 위태롭게 하는 이러한 종은 해충으로 분류된다.

이 문장이 들어가기에 가장 적합한 곳은? [■C]

10. Summary

Directions: An introductory sentence for a brief summary of the passage is provided below. Complete the summary by selecting the THREE answer choices that express the most important ideas in the passage. Some sentences do not belong in the summary because they express ideas that are not presented in the passage or are minor ideas in the passage. *This question is worth 2 points.*

10.

지시문: 지문을 간략하게 요약한 글의 첫 문장이 아래 제시되어 있다. 지문의 가장 중요한 내용을 표현하는 세 개의 선택지를 골라 요약문을 완성하시오. 일부 문장들은 지문에 제시되지 않았거나 지문의 지엽적인 내용을 나타내기 때문에 요약문에 포함되지 않는다. *이 문제의 배점은 2점이다.*

There have been various efforts to raise agricultural productivity by controlling pest organisms throughout human history.

Ⓑ In the past, a variety of chemicals from nature were generally used as pesticides.
Ⓒ To avoid the adverse effects of chemical pesticides on the ecosystem, some farmers began to make use of the predator-prey system.
Ⓕ IPM is an approach which requires care for the balance between economic values and the ecosystem.

Ⓐ Thanks to the development of agriculture, mankind could flourish and build civilizations.
Ⓓ Before the advent of DDT, people had mainly depended upon specific predator species to discourage pests.
Ⓔ These days, the introduction of non-indigenous species is recommended for pest eradication since it has few side effects.

인류 역사 내내 해충을 방제함으로써 농업 생산량을 늘리려는 다양한 노력들이 있었다.

Ⓑ 과거에 자연에서 얻은 다양한 화학물질들이 대개 살충제로 사용되었다.
Ⓒ 생태계에 미치는 화학 살충제의 부작용을 피하기 위해, 어떤 농부들은 포식자–피식자 시스템을 사용하기 시작했다.
Ⓕ IPM은 경제적 가치와 생태계의 균형을 위해 주의를 요하는 접근법이다.

Ⓐ 농업의 발달 덕분에 인류는 번창하고 문명을 건설할 수 있었다.
Ⓓ DDT의 등장 전에 사람들은 해충을 죽이기 위해 특정 포식종들에 주로 의존했다.
Ⓔ 오늘날 외래종의 도입은 부작용이 거의 없기 때문에 해충 박멸에 사용되도록 추천된다.

📘 어휘

1 **adoption** n (아이디어·계획 등의) 채택 ǀ **subsequent** adj 그[이] 다음의, 계속되는, 연속되는 ǀ **extent** n (크기·중요성·심각성 등의) 정도[규모] ǀ **native** adj 원산[토종/자생]의 ǀ **alter** v 바꾸다, 고치다, 변하다, 달라지다 ǀ **distribution** n 분배 (방식), 분포 ǀ **enrich** v (토지를) 비옥하게 하다, 풍요롭게 하다 ǀ **monoculture** n 단일재배 ǀ **consume** v 먹다, 마시다 ǀ **endanger** v 위험에 빠뜨리다, 위태롭게 만들다 ǀ **pest** n 해충, 유해 동물 ǀ **however** adv 하지만, 그러나 ǀ **moderate** adj 보통의, 중간의, 중도의[온건한] ǀ **long run** 장기간

2 **widely** adv 널리, 폭넓게 ǀ **dose** n (약의) 복용량[투여량]

3 **extract** v 뽑다[얻다], 추출하다 ǀ **pesticide** n 살충제 ǀ **elemental** adj 요소의, (물리, 화학) 원소의[같은] ǀ **synthesized** adj 합성화된 ǀ **dominant** adj 우세한, 지배적인 ǀ **parasite** n 기생충, 기생 동물[식물] ǀ **deliver** v 배달하다, 전하다, 넘겨 주다 ǀ **widespread** adj 광범위한, 널리 퍼진 ǀ **side effect** n 부작용

4 **entail** v 수반하다 ǀ **intended** adj 의도된, 계획된, 고의의 ǀ **continuously** adv 계속해서, 연속적으로, 끊임없이 ǀ **immunity** n 면역, 면역력 ǀ **exposure** n 노출 ǀ **survive** v 살아남다, 생존[존속]하다 ǀ **reproduce** v 번식하다 ǀ **rebound** v 반등하다, 되돌아오다 ǀ **far-reaching** adj (효과, 영향 등이) 멀리까지 미치는

5 **hardly** adv 거의 ~ 아니다[없다] ǀ **non-indigenous** adj (어떤 지역) 원산의[토착의] 것이 아닌 ǀ **unforeseen** adj 예측하지 못한, 뜻밖의 ǀ **unchecked** adj (유해한 것이 더 악화되지 않도록) 억제하지[손을 쓰지] 않고 놔 둔 ǀ **guarantee** n 보장 ǀ **desired** adj 바랐던, 희망했던, 훌륭한 ǀ **disastrous** adj 처참한, 형편없는 ǀ **immunity** n 면역력 ǀ **toxin** n 독소

6 **yield** n (농작물 등의) 산출[수확]량, 총수익 ǀ **recommend** v 추천[천거]하다 ǀ **threat** n 협박, 위협 ǀ **merely** adv 한낱, 그저, 단지 ǀ **identified** adj 확인된, 인정된, 식별된 ǀ **preventative** adj 예방[방지]을 위한 ǀ **measure** n 조치[정책] ǀ **resistant** adj 저항력 있는, ~에 잘 견디는[강한] ǀ **last resort** n 마지막 수단[방책, 수]

Actual Test 06

본서 | P. 137

Passage 1 The Development of Islamic Bookmaking

1. Ⓑ   Inference
2. Ⓐ   Rhetorical Purpose
3. Ⓓ   Fact
4. Ⓓ   Vocabulary
5. Ⓐ   Fact

6. Ⓐ   Vocabulary
7. Ⓒ   Sentence Simplification
8. Ⓑ   Inference
9. Ⓑ   Insertion
10. Ⓑ, Ⓒ, Ⓓ   Summary

Passage 2 The First Life on Earth

1. Ⓒ   Negative Fact
2. Ⓑ   Fact
3. Ⓓ   Fact
4. Ⓒ   Vocabulary
5. Ⓓ   Rhetorical Purpose

6. Ⓒ   Sentence Simplification
7. Ⓒ   Negative Fact
8. Ⓐ   Fact
9. Ⓒ   Insertion
10. Ⓑ, Ⓒ, Ⓕ   Summary

Passage 3 Soil Formation

1. Ⓐ   Reference
2. Ⓐ   Vocabulary
3. Ⓓ   Fact
4. Ⓐ   Sentence Simplification
5. Ⓓ   Inference

6. Ⓒ   Rhetorical Purpose
7. Ⓑ   Rhetorical Purpose
8. Ⓑ, Ⓓ   Fact
9. Ⓒ   Insertion
10. Ⓐ, Ⓒ, Ⓔ   Summary

● 내가 맞은 문제 유형의 개수를 적어 보고 어느 유형에 취약한지 확인해 봅시다.

문제 유형	맞은 개수
Sentence Simplification	3
Fact / Negative Fact	9
Vocabulary	4
Reference	1
Rhetorical Purpose	4
Inference	3
Insertion	3
Summary	3
Category Chart	0
Total	30

The Development of Islamic Bookmaking

1 ➡ Bookmaking flourished in the Middle East between the 9th and 15th centuries. Islamic books from this period were finely hand-crafted with luxurious materials and had detailed and artistically wrought covers and interior illustrations. This flowering of literary artistry was the result of two major events in the Muslim world. The first was the development of an official language with a codified alphabet and an accepted writing style. The second was the importation of paper-making technology, which allowed books to be produced on a vaster scale. These books were one of the main venues for artistic expression in the Arab world, and they employed not only calligraphers and painters, but also leather and paper makers and professional binders. This bookmaking industry was financially supported by princes and caliphs and lasted until printing presses were imported.

2 ➡ Islamic bookmaking extends back to the beginning of the religion it supports. According to the teachings of Islam, the Quran was imparted to the Prophet Muhammad by the archangel Gabriel between 610 and 632 CE, and he in turn translated the word of Allah into his own native Arabic. At first, his followers memorized his words and verbally relayed them to others, but this method of spreading the word was inconvenient, and worse yet, unreliable. In order to faithfully repeat his words, his assistants began writing down the Quran on any available material. These were eventually collected together, but a problem emerged: there was no unified Arabic alphabet. This was resolved during the rule of caliph Abd al-Malik, who made Arabic the official language of his empire and codified it into a single alphabet. This was eventually developed into calligraphy by Ibn Muqla in the 9th century, which was perfected by the 11th century calligrapher Ibn al-Bawwab.

3 ➡ [■A] What contributed most to the expansion of books throughout the Muslim world was an innovation from China that was introduced in the 9th century: paper. [■B] Paper was originally developed much earlier, but before this time the technology had not spread westward. Muslim forces that captured Chinese prisoners in Samarkand who knew how to make paper allowed this to happen. [■C] Their

이슬람교 서적 제조의 발달

1 ➡ 서적 제조는 9세기에서 15세기 사이에 중동에서 번창했다. 이 시기의 이슬람교 서적은 고급스러운 재료로 정교하게 수공예품으로 만들어졌으며 상세하고 예술적으로 만들어진 표지와 내부 삽화들을 갖추었다. 이러한 문학적 예술의 전성기는 이슬람 세계의 두 가지 중대 사건이 가져온 결과였다. 첫 번째는 성문화된 알파벳과 널리 받아들여진 문체를 가진 공용어의 발달이었다. 두 번째는 서적이 대규모로 생산되는 것을 가능하게 한 제지 기술의 도입이었다. 이런 서적은 아랍 세계에서 예술적 표현의 주된 통로 중 하나였으며, 서예가와 화가뿐만 아니라 가죽업자와 제지업자, 전문적인 제본 기술자도 고용했다. 이 서적 제조 산업은 왕자들과 칼리프들로부터 재정적인 후원을 받았으며 인쇄기가 수입될 때까지 지속됐다.

2 ➡ 이슬람교 서적 제조는 그것이 지원하는 종교의 시작으로 거슬러 올라간다. 이슬람교의 가르침에 의하면, 쿠란은 서기 610년과 632년 사이에 천사장 가브리엘을 통해 선지자 무함마드에게 전달됐고, 무함마드는 알라의 말씀을 자신의 모국어인 아랍어로 번역했다. 처음에 그의 제자들은 그의 말씀을 암기해 다른 사람들에게 구두로 전달했지만 이 방법으로 말씀을 전파하는 것은 불편했으며, 더 심각하게는 신뢰할 수 없었다. 그의 말씀을 온전히 반복하기 위해서 그의 조력자들은 구할 수 있는 모든 재료 위에 쿠란을 기록해 나가기 시작했다. 이것들은 시간이 흘러 취합됐지만 한 가지 문제가 생겨났다. 통일된 아랍어 알파벳이 없다는 것이었다. 이것은 압드 알 말리크 칼리프의 통치 기간 중에 해결되었는데, 그는 아랍어를 자신의 왕국의 공용어로 사용하고 하나의 알파벳으로 성문화했다. 이것은 결국 9세기에 이븐 무클라가 서예로 발달시켰으며, 11세기 서예가 이븐 알 바와브가 완벽하게 완성시켰다.

3 ➡ [■A] 이슬람 세계 전역에서 서적 확장에 가장 많이 기여한 것은 9세기에 소개된 중국의 혁신적인 제품, 즉 종이였다. [■B] 원래 종이는 훨씬 이전에 개발되었으나 이 시기 전에는 그 기술이 서방으로 퍼지지 않았다. 사마르칸드에서 종이를 만들 줄 아는 중국인 죄수들을 체포한 이슬람 세력들은 그 기술이 퍼질 수 있도록 했다. [■C] 그들의 종이 생산 방법에는 세 개의 주요 단계가 포함되었다. [■D] 첫째, 다양한 식물 종을 물에 끓여 펄프를 추출했다.

method of paper production involved three main steps. [■D] First, pulp was extracted from various plant types by boiling them down in water. Next, a fine mesh screen was used to catch these fibers and form a thin layer of pulp. Finally, these screens were carefully dried to make flexible sheets of paper. Despite the labor intensive process, this method actually produced writing material much more quickly and inexpensively than the prior method of curing goat hides. Qurans were soon being produced with pages made of this paper, and later other secular and scientific ideas were also spread through such books.

4 ➡ The first books produced in this way were religious texts, but later history, scientific treatises, poetry, and romantic literature were also written down and transformed into books. Many of these secular texts were just as richly decorated as the Quran, and many people were employed in their manufacture. They often featured leather covers that were embossed with gold in geometric and floral patterns. For the Qurans, this usually involved a fairly consistent pattern with a circle or oval at the center of the design that symbolized the sun. Of course, the degree of decoration varied, with books that were made for important patrons or public use being the richest, whereas those for personal use were often less ostentatious. These books became valuable trade goods, and often could be found far from where they were produced.

5 ➡ As paper spread through the Arab world, it revolutionized more than just bookmaking. Parchments were limited in size by the animals killed to make the original leather, but paper was limited only by the size of the screen it was dried upon. This meant that huge, incredibly detailed maps could be produced, and blueprints could be made large enough to clearly show building elements. In addition, the limitations of paper also made it popular for some purposes. Because the paper was so thin and absorbent, ink marks on it were nearly impossible to change, unlike parchment which allowed for corrections, or even worse, fraudulent alterations. For this reason, it quickly became the chief material used for official documents in Baghdad. Paper and its various uses rapidly spread throughout the Muslim world, stretching across northern Africa, and even into Spain, where it was first introduced to Europeans.

다음으로, 가는 철망 스크린을 사용하여 이 섬유를 받아서 얇은 펄프 막을 형성했다. 마지막으로, 이 스크린들을 조심스럽게 건조시켜서 유연한 종잇장들을 만들었다. 많은 노동력을 요하는 과정임에도 불구하고, 실제로 이 방법은 염소 가죽을 보존 처리하던 기존 방법보다 훨씬 더 빠르고 저렴하게 필기 재료를 생산해 냈다. 쿠란은 곧 이 종이로 만들어진 낱장들로 생산되기 시작했으며 나중에는 세속적이고 과학적인 아이디어 또한 이러한 책을 통해 확산되었다.

4 ➡ 이런 방법으로 제작된 첫 서적들은 종교 서적이었으나, 나중에는 역사 서적, 과학 논문, 시와 낭만주의 문학들 또한 글로 기록되어 책으로 탄생했다. 이런 세속적인 서적들 중 대다수는 쿠란만큼 화려하게 꾸며졌으며, 많은 사람들이 이 서적 제조에 고용되었다. 이 책들은 흔히 기하학적 무늬와 꽃무늬를 금으로 돋을새김한 가죽 표지를 선보였다. 쿠란의 경우엔 보통 태양을 상징하는 동그라미나 타원형을 디자인의 중앙에 둔 상당히 일관성 있는 패턴이 포함되었다. 물론 장식의 정도에 차이가 있었으며 중요한 고객을 위한 책이나 공용으로 사용되는 서적에는 장식이 더 화려했던 반면, 개인용으로 제작되는 책은 흔히 덜 호사스러웠다. 이런 책들은 귀중한 무역품이 되었고 제조된 곳에서 멀리 떨어진 장소에서 흔히 찾아볼 수 있었다.

5 ➡ 종이는 아랍 세계에 퍼지면서 서적 제조보다 더 많은 것들을 변화시켰다. 양피지는 원래 가죽을 만들기 위해 죽인 동물로 인해 크기가 제한되었지만, 종이는 종이를 건조시키는 스크린의 크기로만 제한되었다. 그것은 크고 엄청나게 상세한 지도들이 제작될 수 있고, 건축 재료들이 명확하게 보일 수 있을 정도로 큰 청사진이 만들어질 수 있다는 것을 뜻했다. 또한 종이가 지닌 한계로 인해 종이는 몇몇 용도 면에서 인기를 얻게 되었다. 종이는 매우 얇고 흡수력이 뛰어났기 때문에 종이 위의 잉크 자국은 수정하기가 거의 불가능했고, 수정이 가능하고 더 심하게는 사기성 변조가 가능했던 양피지와는 달랐다. 이러한 이유로 종이는 바그다드에서 공용 문서의 주된 재료로 빠르게 자리잡았다. 종이와 종이의 다양한 사용은 이슬람 세계 전역으로 빠르게 퍼졌고, 북아프리카와 심지어 스페인까지 퍼져서 거기서부터 유럽인들에게 종이가 처음 소개되었다.

1. **Inference**

Based on paragraph 1, it can be inferred that

(A) bookmaking flourished because of the varieties of writing styles.

(B) **printing presses were probably imported around the 15th century.**

(C) there were no other channels for artistic expression in the Arab world.

(D) the upper class did not support bookmaking.

2. **Rhetorical Purpose**

The author mentions "Ibn Muqla" in paragraph 2 to indicate who

(A) **developed the Arabic handwriting system**

(B) collected the Quran into a single volume

(C) made Arabic the official language of Islam

(D) codified the Arabic alphabet

3. **Fact**

According to paragraph 2, what was one problem of spreading the Quran?

(A) Verbally spreading the word was slow.

(B) Most of the recorded Quran were illegible.

(C) Calligraphy was not perfected until the 11th century.

(D) **There was no unified Arabic alphabet.**

4. **Vocabulary**

The word "extracted" in paragraph 3 is closest in meaning to

(A) converged

(B) purified

(C) accumulated

(D) **removed**

5. **Fact**

According to paragraph 4, what was the result of a flourishing bookmaking industry?

(A) **Books became trade goods in other parts of the world.**

(B) There was a growth in the number of literature writers.

(C) Secular texts became more popular than the Quran.

(D) Lower quality materials were used to keep up with demand.

6. **Vocabulary**

The word "ostentatious" in paragraph 4 is closest in meaning to

(A) **extravagant**

1.

1단락에 근거하여 추론할 수 있는 것은?

(A) 서적 제조는 다양한 문체로 인해 번성했다.

(B) 인쇄기는 아마도 15세기 즈음에 수입됐다.

(C) 아랍 세계에 다른 예술적 표현의 통로는 없었다.

(D) 상류층은 서적 제조를 지원하지 않았다.

2.

글쓴이가 2단락에서 언급하는 "이븐 무클라"는?

(A) 아랍어 필기 체계를 개발했다

(B) 쿠란을 한 권의 책으로 모았다

(C) 아랍어를 이슬람교의 공식 언어로 삼았다

(D) 아랍어 알파벳을 성문화했다

3.

2단락에 따르면, 쿠란을 전파하는 것의 한 가지 문제점은 무엇이었는가?

(A) 말씀을 구두로 퍼뜨리는 것은 느렸다.

(B) 기록된 쿠란의 대부분이 알아보기 힘들었다.

(C) 서예는 11세기까지 완성되지 않았다.

(D) 통일된 아랍어 알파벳이 없었다.

4.

3단락의 단어 "extracted(추출했다)"와 의미상 가장 가까운 것은?

(A) 모여들었다

(B) 정화했다

(C) 축적했다

(D) 꺼냈다

5.

4단락에 따르면, 번성하는 서적 제조 산업의 결과는 무엇이었는가?

(A) 서적은 세계의 다른 지역에서 무역품이 되었다.

(B) 문학가들의 수가 증가했다.

(C) 세속적인 서적이 쿠란보다 더 인기있었다.

(D) 수요를 따라잡기 위해 품질이 낮은 재료들이 사용되었다.

6.

4단락의 단어 "ostentatious(호사스러운)"와 의미상 가장 가까운 것은?

(A) 호화로운

B expensive
C decorated
D obnoxious

7. Sentence Simplification

Which of the sentences below best expresses the essential information in the highlighted sentence in the passage? *Incorrect* answer choices change the meaning in important ways or leave out essential information.

A While parchment allowed for the correction of ink marks, fraudulent alterations on paper were impossible to change because it was so thin and absorbent.

B Paper's resistance to ink allowed for criminal alterations, while corrections on parchment were nearly impossible.

C **While alterations could be made on parchment, the thin nature of paper made it impossible for corrections to be made.**

D Because it was thin and absorbent, parchment allowed for corrections, sometimes even fraudulent alterations.

8. Inference

Based on paragraph 5, what can be inferred about paper?

A Paper was introduced to Europe before the 9th century.

B **Using paper increased the sizes of books and documents.**

C The concept of drawing up blueprints was nonexistent until the widespread production of paper.

D The Chinese were unwilling to reveal the secrets of manufacturing paper to the Europeans.

9. Insertion

Look at the four squares [■] that indicate where the following sentence could be added to the passage.

Paper was originally developed much earlier, but before this time the technology had not spread westward.

Where would the sentence best fit? [■ B]

10. Summary

Directions: An introductory sentence for a brief summary of the passage is provided below. Complete the summary by selecting the THREE answer choices that express the most important ideas in the passage. Some sentences do not belong in the summary because they express ideas that are not presented in the passage or are minor ideas in the passage. *This question is worth 2 points.*

B 값비싼
C 장식된
D 불쾌한

7.

다음 중 지문에 음영 표시된 문장의 핵심 정보를 가장 잘 표현한 문장은 무엇인가? 오답은 의미를 크게 왜곡하거나 핵심 정보를 누락하고 있다.

A 양피지에는 잉크 자국의 수정이 가능했지만 종이는 매우 얇고 흡수력이 뛰어났기 때문에 종이 위의 사기성 변조는 수정하기 불가능했다.

B 잉크에 강한 종이는 범죄 관련 변조를 가능하게 한 반면, 양피지 위에 수정하는 것은 거의 불가능했다.

C 양피지 위에는 변조가 가능했던 반면, 얇은 특성으로 인해 종이는 수정이 불가능했다.

D 양피지는 얇고 흡수력이 뛰어났기 때문에 수정이 가능했고, 가끔은 심지어 사기성 변조도 가능하게 했다.

8.

5단락에 근거하여 종이에 대해 추론할 수 있는 것은 무엇인가?

A 종이는 9세기 전에 유럽에 소개됐다.

B 종이 사용은 서적과 서류의 크기를 늘렸다.

C 청사진을 그린다는 개념은 종이 생산이 널리 퍼지기 전까지는 존재하지 않았다.

D 중국인들은 종이 제조의 비밀을 유럽인들에게 밝히는 것을 원치 않았다.

9.

지문에 다음 문장이 들어갈 수 있는 위치를 나타내는 네 개의 사각형[■]을 확인하시오.

원래 종이는 훨씬 이전에 개발되었으나 이 시기 전에는 그 기술이 서방으로 퍼지지 않았다.

이 문장이 들어가기에 가장 적합한 곳은? [■B]

10.

지시문: 지문을 간략하게 요약한 글의 첫 문장이 아래 제시되어 있다. 지문의 가장 중요한 내용을 표현하는 세 개의 선택지를 골라 요약문을 완성하시오. 일부 문장들은 지문에 제시되지 않았거나 지문의 지엽적인 내용을 나타내기 때문에 요약문에 포함되지 않는다. *이 문제의 배점은 2점이다.*

Development of a unified alphabet and the introduction of paper-making technology allowed the bookmaking industry to flourish in the Middle East.

Ⓑ Widespread production of paper in the Middle East allowed non-religious literature to be made into books, and the use of paper quickly spread to other continents.

Ⓒ With a unified alphabet, the teachings of Muhammad could be written down, which was more convenient and reliable than the previous oral means.

Ⓓ Paper had many advantages over animal hides, and it quickly became the preferred writing material for books, blueprints, and official documents.

Ⓐ Arabic calligraphy wasn't perfected until the 11th century, crippling the caliph's effort at spreading the language.

Ⓔ The books were richly decorated with gold, with some books being more ostentatious than others.

Ⓕ While paper was invented much earlier, it wasn't until the 9th century that the technology spread westward.

통일된 알파벳의 개발과 종이 제작 기술의 도입은 서적 제조 산업이 중동에서 번성하게 만들었다.

Ⓑ 중동에서의 대대적인 종이 생산은 비종교적 문학이 책으로 만들어지는 것을 가능하게 했으며, 종이의 사용은 다른 대륙으로 빠르게 퍼져나갔다.

Ⓒ 통일된 알파벳으로 무함마드의 가르침은 기록될 수 있게 되었는데, 이는 기존의 구두로 전달하는 방식보다 더 편리하고 신뢰할 수 있는 방식이었다.

Ⓓ 종이는 동물 가죽보다 많은 장점을 갖고 있었으며, 빠르게 책, 청사진과 공문서에 선호되는 필기 재료가 되었다.

Ⓐ 아랍어 서예는 11세기가 되어서야 완성됐으며, 이것은 언어를 널리 알리고자 했던 칼리프의 노력을 좌절시켰다.

Ⓔ 책들은 금으로 화려하게 장식되었으며, 어떤 책들은 다른 것들보다 더 호사스러웠다.

Ⓕ 종이는 훨씬 일찍 발명되었지만 그 기술이 서방으로 퍼진 것은 9세기가 되어서였다.

어휘

1 **flourish** ⓥ 번창하다 | **finely** adv 섬세[정교]하게 | **hand-crafted** adj 수공예품인 | **luxurious** adj 아주 편안한; 호화로운, 사치스러운 | **artistically** adv 예술[미술]적으로 | **wrought** adj (철물 등이) 두들겨 만든, 단련한, 꾸민, 수놓은 | **interior** adj 내부의 | **illustration** ⓝ 삽화 | **flowering** ⓝ 전성기 | **literary** adj 문학의 | **artistry** ⓝ 예술가적 기교 | **codified** adj 성문화된 | **accepted** adj 일반적으로 인정된, 용인된 | **importation** ⓝ 수입 | **vast** adj (범위·크기·양 등이) 어마어마한[방대한/막대한] | **financially** adv 재정적으로 | **caliph** ⓝ 칼리프(과거 이슬람 국가의 통치자를 가리키던 칭호) | **last** ⓥ 계속되다

2 **extend** ⓥ (시간이) 계속되다, (~까지) 걸치다 | **impart** ⓥ (정보·지식 등을) 전하다 | **translate** ⓥ 번역[통역]하다, (다른 언어로) 옮기다 | **memorize** ⓥ 암기하다 | **verbally** adv 구두로 | **relay** ⓥ (정보 등을 받아서) 전달하다 | **inconvenient** adj 불편한[곤란한] | **unreliable** adj 믿을[신뢰할] 수 없는 | **faithfully** adv 충실히, 정확히 | **emerge** ⓥ 나오다, 드러나다 | **resolve** ⓥ 해결하다 | **perfect** ⓥ 완벽하게 하다

3 **innovation** ⓝ 혁신, 쇄신, 새로 도입한 것 | **capture** ⓥ 포로로 잡다 | **extract** ⓥ 뽑다[얻다], 추출하다 | **flexible** adj 신축성[융통성] 있는 | **intensive** adj 집중적인(짧은 시간에 많은 일·활동을 하는) | **inexpensively** adv 값싸게, 많은 비용을 들이지 않고 | **cure** ⓥ 보존 처리를 하다 | **secular** adj 세속적인

4 **treatise** ⓝ 논문 | **manufacture** ⓥ 제조[생산]하다 | **feature** ⓥ 특별히 포함하다, 특징으로 삼다 | **emboss** ⓥ 양각[돋을새김]하다 | **geometric** adj 기하학의; 기하학적인 | **consistent** adj 한결같은, 일관된 | **ostentatious** adj 대단히 비싼[호사스러운]

5 **revolutionize** ⓥ 대변혁[혁신]을 일으키다 | **limit** ⓥ 한정[제한]하다 | **incredibly** adv 믿을 수 없을 정도로, 엄청나게 | **detailed** adj 상세한 | **absorbent** adj 잘 빨아들이는, 흡수력 있는 | **fraudulent** adj 사기를 치는[치기 위한] | **alteration** ⓝ 변화, 개조 | **stretch** ⓥ 뻗어 있다[펼쳐지다/이어지다]

The First Life on Earth

1 ➡ Although there is still disagreement in scientific circles regarding what is the earliest evidence of life on Earth, the majority of experts agree that it could not have existed before the end of the Late Heavy Bombardment (LHB). The LHB was a period extending from approximately 4.1 to 3.8 billion years ago during which an unusually large number of asteroids collided with the inner planets of the solar system. Before this stellar assault, the inner planets had accreted most of their current mass and become fairly stable and solid. The severity of the LHB returned the Earth to a semi-molten state, and no evidence of life has been found that predates it. However, once the planet stabilized, life began gradually to take shape.

2 ➡ The popular theory of the origins of life held that it began in pools of water containing amino acids and other building blocks that were suddenly activated by an electric shock delivered by lightning. Indeed, subsequent laboratory experiments confirmed that such was possible. However, the planet's original atmosphere contained only trace amounts of oxygen, the element which so many organisms rely upon. Therefore, they concluded that these first life forms must have created the oxygen that permeates our atmosphere. They theorized that these organisms must have developed photosynthesis, the process by which plants use sunlight and carbon dioxide to sustain themselves and release oxygen as a byproduct.

3 ➡ However, there was a flaw in this theory. While the early atmosphere lacked oxygen, it was rich in water vapor, which readily reacts to ultraviolet radiation from the sun, splitting its molecules into hydrogen and oxygen. This means that the chemical soup from which life supposedly came would have been exposed to oxygen, which would have destroyed the amino acids. This means that the earliest life forms could not have formed in areas exposed to the atmosphere. So, life could only have started where the oxygenated atmosphere could not reach: deep in the ocean.

4 ➡ The cold, dark, high-pressure environment of the seafloor seems like the most inhospitable

지구 최초의 생명체

1 ➡ 지구상의 생명체에 대한 가장 초기의 증거가 무엇인지에 관해 과학계에서는 여전히 의견 충돌이 있지만, 대다수 전문가들은 그것이 후기 운석 대충돌기(LHB) 말 이전에 존재했을 리가 없다는 점에 동의한다. 후기 운석 대충돌기는 약 38억 년에서 41억 년 전에 걸친 기간으로, 이례적으로 많은 수의 소행성들이 태양계의 내행성들과 충돌했던 시기이다. 이러한 별들의 공격이 있기 전에, 내행성들은 오늘날 그들이 지닌 질량의 대부분을 부착시켜 커지게 하면서 꽤 안정적이고 단단해졌다. 후기 운석 대충돌기의 혹독함은 지구를 반고체 상태로 되돌려 놓았고, 그 시기를 앞선 그 어떤 생명체에 대한 증거도 발견되지 않았다. 하지만 일단 행성이 안정화되고 나자 생명체가 점차 형태를 갖추기 시작했다.

2 ➡ 생명의 기원에 대한 일반적인 이론은 번개에 의해 전달된 전기적 충격으로 갑작스럽게 활성화된 아미노산과 다른 구성요소들을 포함하고 있는 물 웅덩이에서 생명체가 시작되었다고 주장한다. 실제로 그 후의 실험실 실험들은 그러한 일이 가능하다는 것을 확인해 주었다. 그러나 행성의 원래 대기는 아주 많은 유기체들이 의존하는 원소인 산소를 극히 적은 양만 함유하고 있었다. 따라서 그들은 이러한 최초의 생명체들이 우리의 대기에 스며든 산소를 만들어냈음이 틀림없다고 결론지었다. 그들은 광합성, 즉 식물이 생존하기 위해 햇빛과 이산화탄소를 사용하고 그 부산물로 산소를 방출하는 과정을 이 유기체들이 발전시켰음이 틀림없다는 이론을 제시했다.

3 ➡ 하지만 이 이론에는 결점이 하나 있었다. 초기의 대기에는 산소가 없었지만 수증기가 풍부했는데, 수증기는 태양으로부터 방출된 자외선과 쉽게 반응하며, 그 결과 분자를 수소와 산소로 나눈다. 이것은 아마 생명체가 생겨난 화학물질이 산소에 노출되면서 아미노산을 파괴했을지도 모른다는 의미이다. 이것은 최초의 생명체가 대기에 노출된 지역에서는 형성될 수 없다는 뜻이다. 그래서 산소화된 대기가 도달할 수 없는 곳, 즉 바다 깊숙한 곳에서만 생명체가 시작됐을 것이다.

4 ➡ 춥고 어두운 고압의 해저 환경은 상상할 수 있는 가장 살기 힘든 공간으로 보이지만, 심지어 오늘날에도 그곳

environment imaginable, but even today life thrives there. The majority of the seabed is barren, but around volcanic vents, a whole ecosystem exists that depends upon them for warmth and the chemicals that pour out of them. Crustaceans feed upon worms, which in turn rely upon bacteria for their food. These bacteria are able to metabolize the chemicals that pour from crevices in the seabed, and they are very similar to their ancient cousins. Like their ancestors, they absorb the chemicals before they react to their new environment, and absorb the energy released when those inevitable reactions occur. The fossil record confirms that such bacteria existed up to 3.5 billion years ago, and they are called archaebacteria.

5 ➡ Despite their distant origins, archaebacteria still exist today, and they are typically found in harsh environments like the ocean floor, hot springs, and even highly acidic mine drainage. They share many similarities with bacteria and eukaryotes, the other two domains, but they are undeniably unique and have their own domain in the classification of organisms called prokaryotes, which is divided into four different phyla. They have no nucleus or any other form of organelles with membranes within their cells, but they do contain genes, which have allowed scientists to trace their lineage. Researchers have compared their genome to that of many extant bacteria, and the results have revealed that they share common ancestry.

6 ➡ [■A] Unfortunately, archaebacteria lack defined cell walls or shapes, so fossilized samples are impossible to find. [■B] Instead, scientists have found characteristic chemical fossils in the form of lipids that do not exist in other organisms. [■C] These samples vary in age from 2.7 to 3.8 billion years old, which makes them absolutely among the oldest organisms on the planet. Along with bacteria and other single-celled organisms, archaebacteria were the only life on Earth for around 2 billion years. [■D] Over time, these organisms evolved and became more complex, leading to the existence of all other life on the planet, including humans.

에서는 생명체가 번성한다. 해저의 대부분은 척박하지만, 화산 분화구 주변에는 그곳에서 쏟아져 나오는 온기와 화학물질에 의존하는 하나의 큰 생태계가 존재한다. 갑각류는 벌레들을 먹고 살며, 그 벌레들은 먹이로 박테리아에 의존한다. 이 박테리아들은 해저에 있는 틈들에서 뿜어져 나오는 화학물질을 대사할 수 있으며, 고대의 친척들과 매우 유사하다. 그들의 조상처럼 박테리아는 화학물질들이 새로운 환경에서 반응하기 전에 그것들을 흡수하고, 그러한 불가피한 반응이 일어날 때 방출되는 에너지를 흡수한다. 화석 기록은 이러한 박테리아들이 35억 년 전부터 존재했다는 것을 확인해 주었고 이들은 원시 박테리아라고 불린다.

5 ➡ 그들의 먼 기원에도 불구하고, 원시 박테리아는 오늘날까지도 여전히 존재하며 해저, 온천, 심지어는 산성도가 높은 광산 배수 시설과 같은 척박한 환경에서 주로 발견된다. 그들은 다른 두 역(域)인 박테리아 및 진핵생물과 많은 유사성을 공유하지만, 부인하기 어려울 정도로 고유하기도 하며, 원핵생물이라 불리는 그들만의 역(域)으로 분류되고, 이것은 네 가지 족(族)으로 나누어진다. 그것들은 세포 내에 핵이나 다른 종류의 막을 가진 세포기관을 가지고 있지 않지만, 유전자를 포함하고 있어서 그것을 통해 과학자들이 혈통을 추적해 낼 수 있었다. 연구자들은 그들의 게놈을 많은 현존하는 박테리아의 게놈과 비교한 결과, 그것들이 공통의 조상을 공유한다는 사실을 밝혀냈다.

6 ➡ [■A] 안타깝게도 원시 박테리아는 명확한 세포벽이나 형태가 없어서 화석화된 표본을 찾기가 불가능하다. [■B] 대신 과학자들은 다른 유기체에는 존재하지 않는 지방질 형태에서 특유의 화학 화석을 발견했다. [■C] 이 표본들은 27억 년에서 38억 년 정도로 나이가 다양하며, 이는 그들을 지구상 가장 오래된 생물 중 하나로 만들었다. 박테리아와 다른 단세포 생물들과 함께, 원시 박테리아는 약 20억 년 동안 지구상에 존재해 온 유일한 생명체였다. [■D] 시간이 흐름에 따라 이러한 유기체들이 진화하고 더욱 복잡해지면서 인간을 포함하여 이 지구상의 모든 다른 생명체들이 존재하게 만들었다.

1. Negative Fact

According to paragraph 1, all of the following are true about the LHB EXCEPT

(A) it lasted for about 300 million years.

(B) a great number of asteroid collisions occurred then.

(C) **it provided the appropriate environment for the birth of life on Earth.**

(D) life does not appear to have existed on Earth before it.

2. Fact

According to paragraphs 2 and 3, what did scientists incorrectly presume about the formation of life?

(A) They presumed that the first life forms did not need oxygen to metabolize.

(B) **They presumed that the first life forms created oxygen by photosynthesis.**

(C) They presumed that the early atmosphere contained little oxygen.

(D) They presumed that the early atmosphere was filled with water vapor.

3. Fact

According to paragraph 3, why did the earliest life forms start deep in the ocean?

(A) They needed oxygen to breathe and metabolize.

(B) The seawater contained abundant hydrogen and oxygen then.

(C) The ocean functioned as chemical soup which had the necessary materials.

(D) **The necessary chemicals for life were vulnerable to oxygen in the atmosphere.**

4. Vocabulary

The word "crevices" in paragraph 4 is closest in meaning to

(A) pebbles

(B) cliffs

(C) **gaps**

(D) flanks

5. Rhetorical Purpose

Why does the author mention "Crustaceans" in paragraph 4?

(A) To explain how life evolved around deep sea vents

(B) To indicate how organisms feed on volcanic chemicals

(C) To show the complexity of life in the deep ocean

(D) **To illustrate the food chain that exists near volcanic fissures**

1.

1단락에 따르면, 후기 운석 대충돌기(LHB)에 대해 사실이 아닌 것은?

(A) 약 3억 년 동안 지속됐다.

(B) 많은 소행성 충돌이 그 시기에 일어났다.

(C) 지구상의 생명체 탄생에 적당한 환경을 제공했다.

(D) 후기 운석 대충돌기 전에는 지구상에 생명체가 존재하지 않았던 것으로 보여진다.

2.

2, 3단락에 따르면, 과학자들이 생명체의 형성에 대해 잘못 추측한 것은 무엇인가?

(A) 그들은 최초의 생명체들이 신진대사를 하기 위해 산소를 필요로 하지 않았다고 추측했다.

(B) 그들은 최초의 생명체들이 광합성을 통해 산소를 만들어 냈다고 추측했다.

(C) 그들은 초기의 대기에는 산소가 거의 없었다고 추측했다.

(D) 그들은 초기의 대기가 수증기로 가득 차 있었다고 추측했다.

3.

3단락에 따르면, 최초의 생명체들이 바다 깊숙한 곳에서 시작된 이유는 무엇인가?

(A) 숨을 쉬고 신진대사를 하기 위해 산소를 필요로 했다.

(B) 그때 당시 바닷물에는 수소와 산소가 풍부했다.

(C) 바다가 필요한 물질들이 들어 있는 화학물질의 역할을 해주었다.

(D) 생명체에게 필요한 화학물질들이 대기 중의 산소에 취약했다.

4.

4단락의 단어 "crevices(틈들)"와 의미상 가장 가까운 것은?

(A) 조약돌들

(B) 절벽들

(C) 틈들

(D) 측면들

5.

4단락에서 글쓴이가 "갑각류 동물"을 언급하는 이유는 무엇인가?

(A) 심해 분화구 주변에서 생명체가 어떻게 진화했는지 설명하기 위해

(B) 생물이 어떻게 화산 화학물질을 먹고 사는지 알려주기 위해

(C) 심해에 사는 생명체의 복잡함을 보여주기 위해

(D) 화산 틈들 근처에 존재하는 먹이 사슬을 설명하기 위해

6. Sentence Simplification

Which of the sentences below best expresses the essential information in the highlighted sentence in the passage? *Incorrect* answer choices change the meaning in important ways or leave out essential information.

Ⓐ They share many similarities with bacteria and eukaryotes, which are definitely unique and classified as prokaryotes and further divided into four different phyla.

Ⓑ They are very similar to bacteria and eukaryotes, but these two domains are separately classified as prokaryotes, which are further divided into four different phyla.

Ⓒ **While they are similar to bacteria and eukaryotes in many ways, they are distinctly categorized as prokaryotes and further divided into four different phyla.**

Ⓓ They are very similar to bacteria and eukaryotes, which are the two domains with which they are classified as prokaryotes and further categorized into four different phyla.

7. Negative Fact

According to paragraph 5, all of the following are true about archaebacteria EXCEPT

Ⓐ they are similar to other bacteria and eukaryotes in many ways.

Ⓑ they are classified as prokaryotes and still exist today in severe environments.

Ⓒ **they are the oldest single-celled organisms to possess a nucleus.**

Ⓓ they have genes though they lack any organelles with membranes.

8. Fact

According to paragraph 6, why is it difficult to discover fossils of archaebacteria?

Ⓐ **They do not have cell walls, which makes it impossible to be fossilized.**

Ⓑ A long period of time has destroyed the remaining fossils.

Ⓒ They consist only of lipids which other organisms lack.

Ⓓ They are minuscule and invisible to the naked eye.

6.

다음 중 지문의 음영 표시된 문장의 핵심 정보를 가장 잘 표현한 문장은 무엇인가? 오답은 의미를 크게 왜곡하거나 핵심 정보를 누락하고 있다.

Ⓐ 그들은 박테리아 및 진핵생물과 많은 유사점을 공유하는데, 박테리아와 진핵생물은 명백하게 독특하고 원핵생물로 분류되며 거기서 더 나아가 네 가지 족(族)으로 나뉜다.

Ⓑ 그들은 박테리아 및 진핵생물과 매우 유사하지만, 이 두 개의 역(域)은 원핵생물로 따로 구별되어 분류되며, 거기서 네 가지 족(族)으로 더 나뉜다.

Ⓒ 많은 면에서 박테리아 및 진핵생물과 유사하지만, 그들은 원핵생물이라고 명백하게 분류되며, 거기서 네 가지 족(族)으로 더 나뉜다.

Ⓓ 그들은 박테리아 및 진핵생물과 매우 유사한데, 박테리아와 진핵생물은 원핵생물로 분류된 뒤 거기서 네 가지 족(族)으로 더 나뉘는 두 개의 역(域)이다.

7.

5단락에 따르면, 다음 중 원시박테리아에 대해 사실이 아닌 것은?

Ⓐ 그들은 많은 면에서 다른 박테리아 및 진핵생물과 비슷하다.

Ⓑ 그들은 원핵생물로 분류되고 오늘날에도 여전히 가혹한 환경에서도 존재하고 있다.

Ⓒ 그들은 핵을 가진 가장 오래된 단세포 유기체이다.

Ⓓ 그들은 막을 가진 세포기관이 없음에도 불구하고 유전자를 가지고 있다.

8.

6단락에 따르면, 원시박테리아의 화석을 발견하기 어려운 이유는 무엇인가?

Ⓐ 그들은 세포벽이 없어서 화석화되는 것이 불가능하다.

Ⓑ 긴 시간 동안 남아 있는 화석이 파괴되었다.

Ⓒ 그들은 다른 유기체에게 없는 지방질로만 구성되어 있다.

Ⓓ 그들은 매우 미세하고 육안으로는 보이지 않는다.

9. Insertion

Look at the four squares [■] that indicate where the following sentence could be added to the passage.

These samples vary in age from 2.7 to 3.8 billion years old, which makes them absolutely among the oldest organisms on the planet.

Where would the sentence best fit? [■ C]

10. Summary

Directions: An introductory sentence for a brief summary of the passage is provided below. Complete the summary by selecting the THREE answer choices that express the most important ideas in the passage. Some sentences do not belong in the summary because they express ideas that are not presented in the passage or are minor ideas in the passage. *This question is worth 2 points.*

The earliest life forms, which are called archaebacteria, arose in the deep sea.

B The first organisms are believed to have emerged in the deep sea since the early Earth's atmospheric conditions were improper for the birth of new life forms.
C The first life forms might have been able to feed from volcanic vents by absorbing the energy emitted in the process of chemical reactions.
F Archaebacteria are believed to be the first life forms on Earth because they share similarities with the genomes of extant bacteria.

A Scientists assumed that the first organisms came from small bodies of water that had materials necessary for starting life.
D Much about archaebacteria remains unknown since fossilized samples of them are unobtainable.
E The only way to trace the origin of archaebacteria is to compare their genetic information with that of other bacteria.

9.

지문에 다음 문장이 들어갈 수 있는 위치를 나타내는 네 개의 사각형[■]을 확인하시오.

이 표본들은 27억 년에서 38억 년 정도로 나이가 다양하며, 이는 그들을 지구상 가장 오래된 생물 중 하나로 만들었다.

이 문장이 들어가기에 가장 적합한 곳은? [■ C]

10.

지시문: 지문을 간략하게 요약한 글의 첫 문장이 아래 제시되어 있다. 지문의 가장 중요한 내용을 표현하는 세 개의 선택지를 골라 요약문을 완성하시오. 일부 문장들은 지문에 제시되지 않았거나 지문의 지엽적인 내용을 나타내기 때문에 요약문에 포함되지 않는다. *이 문제의 배점은 2점이다.*

원시 박테리아라고 불리는 최초의 생명체는 심해에서 발생했다.

B 최초의 유기체는 심해에서 생겨났을 것이라고 여겨지는데 초기의 지구 대기 상태가 새로운 생명체의 탄생에는 부적합했기 때문이었다.
C 최초의 생명체는 화학 반응의 과정에서 방출된 에너지를 흡수함으로써 화산 분화구에서 먹을 것을 제공받을 수 있었을지도 모른다.
F 원시 박테리아는 지구상 최초의 생명체라고 여겨지는데 그들이 현존하는 박테리아의 게놈과 유사성을 공유하기 때문이다.

A 과학자들은 최초의 유기체들이 생명이 시작되는 데 필요한 물질이 들어 있는 적은 양의 물에서 시작되었다고 가정했다.
D 화석화된 표본을 구할 수 없기 때문에 원시 박테리아에 대한 많은 것이 알려지지 않은 채로 남아 있다.
E 원시 박테리아의 기원을 추적할 수 있는 유일한 방법은 그들의 유전 정보를 다른 박테리아의 유전 정보와 비교하는 것이다.

📖 어휘

1 **asteroid** n 소행성 ǀ **collide** v 충돌하다, 부딪치다 ǀ **stellar** adj 별의 ǀ **assault** n 습격, 급습, 강습, 맹습 ǀ **accrete** v (부착시켜) 커지게 하다 ǀ **mass** n 질량 ǀ **severity** n 격렬, 혹독 ǀ **semi-molten** adj 반고체의 ǀ **predate** v ~보다 먼저[앞서] 오다 ǀ **stabilize** v 안정되다, 안정시키다 ǀ **shape** n 모양, 형태, 형(形)

2 **activate** v 작동하다, 활성화하다 ǀ **subsequent** adj 그[이] 다음의, 차후의 ǀ **trace** adj 극소량의 ǀ **permeate** v 스며들다, 침투하다 ǀ **theorize** v 이론을 제시하다[세우다] ǀ **sustain** v 살아가게[존재하게/지탱하게] 하다 ǀ **byproduct** n 부산물

3 **flaw** n 결함, 흠 ǀ **readily** adv 손쉽게, 순조롭게 ǀ **split** v 나뉘다[나누다] ǀ **molecule** n 분자 ǀ **supposedly** adv 추정상, 아마 ǀ **expose** v 노출시키다, 드러내다 ǀ **oxygenated** adj 산소화된

4 **inhospitable** adj 사람이 지내기[살기] 힘든 ㅣ **imaginable** adj 상상[생각]할 수 있는 ㅣ **thrive** v 번성하다; 잘 자라다 ㅣ **barren** adj 척박한, 황량한 ㅣ **vent** n 분출구, 배출구 ㅣ **metabolize** v 대사 작용을 하다 ㅣ **crevice** n 틈 ㅣ **inevitable** adj 불가피한, 필연적인
5 **distant** adj 먼, (멀리) 떨어져 있는 ㅣ **harsh** adj 가혹한, 냉혹한 ㅣ **acidic** adj 산성의 ㅣ **domain** n (지식·활동의) 영역[분야] ㅣ **undeniably** adv 명백하게, 틀림없이 ㅣ **classification** n 분류 ㅣ **nucleus** n (원자)핵 ㅣ **membrane** n (인체 피부·조직의) 막 ㅣ **trace** v 추적하다, (추적하여) 찾아내다, 밝혀내다 ㅣ **lineage** n 혈통 ㅣ **extant** adj 현존[잔존]하는 ㅣ **ancestry** n 가계, 혈통, 조상
6 **defined** adj 정의된, 명확한 ㅣ **fossilized** adj 화석화된 ㅣ **characteristic** adj 특유의, 특징적인, 독특한 ㅣ **evolve** v 진화하다[시키다] ㅣ **complex** adj 복잡한

Passage 3

Soil Formation

1 ➡ The definition of soil varies between different scientific disciplines, with the most basic being any loose material on the surface of the Earth. However, this ignores the complex nature of soil and the processes that are involved in its creation. Soil formation is determined by five main factors: the parent materials from which it forms, the weathering it is exposed to, the geography of the area, the flora and fauna that are present, and time. Changing the type or amount of any of these factors will dramatically affect the type and quality of soil that forms in a given region. However, the most significant factor as far as the soil's fertility is concerned is the life forms that are present.

2 ➡ The nature of soil depends first and foremost on the parent material from which it forms. All soils begin as bedrock, which is broken down into progressively smaller particles. The rocks that make up the Earth's crust are divided into three overall categories: igneous, sedimentary, and metamorphic. Igneous rocks like granite or basalt form directly from the cooling of magma, sedimentary rocks like sandstone and limestone aggregate from tiny particles of weathered material and minerals from organisms, and metamorphic rock is created by subjecting the other two kinds to extreme heat and pressure underground. Soils may be created on site from the weathering of parent material or from weathered rock that is transported from other areas.

3 ➡ Weathering of stone is caused by one of two processes: physical disintegration and chemical decomposition. In physical disintegration, the parent material is broken down without changing its molecular or crystalline structure; it simply becomes smaller pieces. This is caused by temperature

토양 생성

1 ➡ 토양의 정의는 다양한 과학 분야 사이에 차이가 있는데, 가장 기본적인 정의는 지표면의 단단하지 않은 물질이다. 그러나 이것은 토양의 복잡한 특성과 토양 생성에 관련된 과정들을 무시한 것이다. 토양 생성은 다섯 개의 주요 요인에 의해 결정된다. 토양이 생성되는 모재(parent material), 토양이 노출되는 풍화 작용, 그 지역의 지리, 존재하는 동물군과 식물군, 그리고 시간이다. 이 요인들 중 어떤 것에라도 종류나 양에 변화를 주면 그 지역에서 생성되는 토양의 종류와 질에 극적인 영향을 미칠 것이다. 그러나 토양의 비옥함과 관련하여 가장 중요한 요인은 그곳에 존재하는 생물체들이다.

2 ➡ 토양의 특성은 다른 무엇보다도 그것이 형성되는 모재에 달려 있다. 모든 토양은 기반암으로 시작하는데, 그것은 점점 더 작은 알갱이로 부서지게 된다. 지구의 지각을 형성하는 바위들은 일반적으로 화성암, 퇴적암, 그리고 변성암 등 3개의 범주로 분류된다. 화강암이나 현무암 같은 화성암은 마그마가 식으면서 직접적으로 형성되고, 사암과 석회암 같은 퇴적암은 풍화된 물질들의 미세한 입자들과 생물체의 미네랄이 모여 생기며, 변성암은 앞선 두 종류의 암석들을 지하에서 극한의 열과 압력에 놓이게 함으로써 형성된다. 토양은 모재의 풍화 작용으로 그 자리에 생성될 수도 있고, 다른 지역에서 운반된 풍화 작용을 받은 바위로 인해 생성되기도 한다.

3 ➡ 바위의 풍화 작용은 물리적 분해와 화학적 분해, 이 두 과정들 중 하나에 의해 발생한다. 물리적 분해에서 모재는 분자나 결정 구조의 변화 없이 부서져 그저 더 작은 조각이 된다. 이는 바위를 확장하고 수축하게 하는 온도 변화, 물이 바위에 스며든 뒤 증발하거나 얼고 녹는 순환 과정, 그리고 바람이나 물이 표면을 따라 운반하여 돌을 깎아

changes that make the rocks expand and contract, cycles where water permeates the rock then evaporates or freezes and thaws, and particles of rock that wind or water carry across the surface, abrading the stone. Chemical decomposition happens when reactions occur in the rock, breaking chemical bonds and causing the stone to fragment. Apart from wind weathering, these processes are directly dependent upon the amount of water an area has.

4 ➡ The amount of precipitation an area receives is important to soil composition, but the amount of water the soil can retain is even more important. This is determined by the geography of the region. Mountains and high plateaus do not tend to allow water to penetrate deeply, and their steepness means that it also will not collect on their surface. Instead it will pour down their sides, carrying away sediments and leaving little soil in place. This material collects further down slope, in valleys and plains where it forms layers of sediment that can make thick soil. However, while rich in minerals and nutrients released by chemical decomposition, soil at this point is still inorganic rock particles. In order to form fertile soil, organisms need to be present.

5 ➡ The first organisms that infiltrate soil are microscopic organisms, and there are usually millions of them living in just a cubic centimeter. These organisms include both flora and fauna, but the flora dominates. These organisms utilize the minerals and gases in the soil to create the nutrients that plants need in order to thrive. [■A] These include bacteria that fix nitrogen, combining it into compounds that the plants can use. [■B] They also help the soil particles to clump together, allowing more water and air to penetrate. [■C] Other bacteria are responsible for breaking down the dead material that plants shed, converting it into a rich mixture known as humus. These decomposers speed up a process that would otherwise take many years to accomplish, and they exist in huge numbers. [■D] In fact, 1 acre of soil, depending on depth, may contain 40 metric tons of bacteria.

6 ➡ While bacteria are of vital importance, other organisms also play important roles in fertile soil creation. The next most important organisms are earthworms, which tunnel through the soil by the

내는 바위 입자들로 인해 일어난다. 화학적 분해는 바위 내에서 화학 반응이 일어나 분자들 사이의 화학 결합을 깨뜨리고 바위를 부서지게 할 때 일어난다. 풍화 작용을 제외하고 이러한 과정들은 한 지역이 얼마만큼 물을 보유하고 있느냐에 직접적으로 달려 있다.

4 ➡ 한 지역의 강수량은 토양의 구성에 중요하지만, 그 토양이 보유할 수 있는 물의 양이 훨씬 더 중요하다. 이는 그 지역의 지리에 의해 결정된다. 산과 고원은 물이 깊이 침투하지 못하도록 하며 이들의 가파름은 표면에 물이 모이지 않는다는 것을 의미한다. 대신 물은 퇴적물과 함께 측면을 따라 흘러 토양을 거의 남기지 않는다. 이것은 경사지 더 아래로 내려가 골짜기와 평지에 쌓이고 거기에서 두꺼운 토양을 만들게 되는 퇴적물 층을 형성한다. 그러나 화학적 분해로 인해 방출되는 광물과 영양분이 풍부함에도 이때의 토양은 여전히 무기물의 바위 입자이다. 비옥한 토양이 되기 위해서는 생물이 있어야만 한다.

5 ➡ 토양에 침투하는 첫 번째 생물은 미생물이며, 한 입방 센티미터에 보통 수백만 개가 살고 있다. 이 미생물들에는 동물군과 식물군 둘 다 포함되지만 식물군이 우세하다. 미생물들은 토양 내의 광물과 가스를 이용하여 식물이 잘 자라나는 데 필요한 영양분을 만들어 낸다. [■A] 이것은 질소를 고정시키는 박테리아를 포함하는데, 이 박테리아는 식물들이 사용할 수 있도록 질소를 화합물로 결합시킨다. [■B] 이들은 또한 토양의 입자들이 서로 모이게 하여 더 많은 양의 물과 공기가 투입되도록 돕는다. [■C] 다른 박테리아는 식물들이 떨어뜨리는 죽은 물질을 분해하여 그것을 부엽토라고 알려진 풍부한 혼합물로 바꾸는 역할을 한다. 이 분해자들은 이들이 없었다면 수 년이 걸렸을 이 과정을 촉진하며, 어마어마한 수로 존재한다. [■D] 실제로 1에이커의 토양에는 깊이에 따라 40미터톤의 박테리아가 존재할 수 있다.

6 ➡ 박테리아는 대단히 중요하지만, 다른 생물들 역시 비옥한 토양을 만드는 데 중요한 역할을 한다. 다음으로 가장 중요한 생물은 지렁이들인데, 수천 마리가 토양에 구멍을 판다. 이들이 내는 구멍은 물과 공기가 토양을 통과하도록

thousands. Not only do their tunnels help water and air to spread through the soil, but they process the soil they move through their digestive tract. This chemically affects the soil, releasing even more nutrients, and the material they excrete as casts acts as natural fertilizer. Other burrowing animals like moles also mechanically mix the soil below the surface, while land mammals break down and mix the material above. Tree roots help water reach down into the soil, and shrubs and grasses hold the soil in place.

7 ➡ Of course, all of these factors require time to exert their influence on soil formation. In order to go from solid bedrock to fertile soil, many years must pass. The more time that the soil surface has seen exposure to precipitation and plant growth, the more developed the soil will be. Well-developed soil usually forms on stable, fairly flat areas and will often have distinct layers. Areas that are exposed to high levels of erosion usually form only thin soils, but the areas where those removed sediments are deposited may become very rich soil in the future.

도울 뿐만 아니라 그들은 소화관을 통해 이동하는 토양을 처리한다. 이것은 토양에 화학적으로 영향을 주며 더 많은 영양분을 발생시키고, 지렁이들이 허물로 벗어버리는 물질은 천연 비료의 역할을 한다. 두더지와 같은 땅을 파는 다른 동물들 또한 표면 아래에서 토양을 기계적으로 섞는 한편, 육지 포유동물들은 표면에서 물질을 분해하고 섞는다. 나무의 뿌리는 물이 내려가 토양까지 닿을 수 있도록 도우며, 관목과 풀들은 토양이 제자리에 고정되도록 도와준다.

7 ➡ 물론 이 모든 요인들이 토양 형성에 영향력을 행사하는 데에는 시간이 필요하다. 단단한 기반암에서 비옥한 토양이 되기 위해서는 오랜 시간이 흘러야만 한다. 토양 표면이 더 오래 강수와 식물 성장에 노출될수록 토양은 더욱 발달될 것이다. 잘 발달된 토양은 보통 안정적이며 상당히 평평한 지역에서 형성되며 종종 뚜렷한 층을 가진다. 침식에 많이 노출되는 지역은 보통 얇은 층의 토양만 형성되지만, 이렇게 제거된 퇴적물이 쌓이는 지역은 미래에 매우 비옥한 토양이 될 수도 있다.

---

1. Reference

The word "this" in paragraph 1 refers to

Ⓐ **definition**
Ⓑ material
Ⓒ surface
Ⓓ nature

1.

1단락의 단어 "이것"이 가리키는 것은?

Ⓐ 정의
Ⓑ 물질
Ⓒ 표면
Ⓓ 본성

2. Vocabulary

The word "subjecting" in paragraph 2 is closest in meaning to

Ⓐ **exposing**
Ⓑ absorbing
Ⓒ handling
Ⓓ subduing

2.

2단락의 단어 "subjecting(놓여지게 하는)"과 의미상 가장 가까운 것은?

Ⓐ 노출하는
Ⓑ 흡수하는
Ⓒ 다루는
Ⓓ 진압하는

3. Fact

In paragraph 2, what does the author indicate about the rocks that make up the Earth's crust?

Ⓐ Sedimentary rocks are the final phase of formation.
Ⓑ All of the rocks are formed inside of the Earth.
Ⓒ There are only two types of sedimentary rocks.
Ⓓ **Igneous rocks are formed directly from magma.**

3.

2단락에서 저자가 지구의 지각을 형성하는 바위들에 관해 언급하는 것은 무엇인가?

Ⓐ 퇴적암은 형성의 마지막 단계이다.
Ⓑ 모든 바위들은 지구 내부에서 형성된다.
Ⓒ 퇴적암에는 단지 두 종류만 있다.
Ⓓ 화성암은 마그마에서 직접적으로 형성된다.

4. **Sentence Simplification**

Which of the sentences below best expresses the essential information in the highlighted sentence in the passage? *Incorrect* answer choices change the meaning in important ways or leave out essential information.

Ⓐ **Temperature changes, water, and rock particles carried across the surface break down the stone.**

Ⓑ Expansion and contraction of rocks allows particles of rock to be carried across the rock surface.

Ⓒ The cycles of temperature change freezes the rock, making it stronger.

Ⓓ Temperature changes cause water that had permeated the rock to expand and contract.

5. **Inference**

Based on paragraph 4, what can be inferred about soil formation?

Ⓐ Sediments deposited in valleys and plains below mountains are composed of rich organic deposits.

Ⓑ The geography of a region does not play a minor role in determining where soil sediments are deposited.

Ⓒ Mountains are shaped by the amount of precipitation in that region.

Ⓓ **Sediments of rock particles on their own cannot be considered fertile soil.**

6. **Rhetorical Purpose**

What is the main purpose of paragraph 5?

Ⓐ To provide examples of how minerals and gases in soil are utilized by bacteria

Ⓑ To demonstrate the advantages of having decomposers speeding up the process of breaking down dead material into humus

Ⓒ **To explain how microscopic organisms help transform soil into an environment where plants can flourish**

Ⓓ To emphasize the sheer number of bacteria living in soil

7. **Rhetorical Purpose**

Why does the author mention "earthworms" in paragraph 6?

Ⓐ To prove that bacteria are not the most important organisms in soil development

Ⓑ **To provide an example of an organism that helps process soil**

Ⓒ To contrast earthworms with burrowing animals like moles

Ⓓ To discuss the various habitats of earthworms

4.

다음 중 지문의 음영 표시된 문장의 핵심 정보를 가장 잘 표현한 문장은 무엇인가? 오답은 의미를 크게 왜곡하거나 핵심 정보를 누락하고 있다.

Ⓐ 온도 변화, 물, 그리고 표면을 가로질러 운반된 바위 입자들이 바위를 부순다.

Ⓑ 바위의 확장과 수축은 바위 입자들이 바위 표면을 가로질러 운반되도록 한다.

Ⓒ 온도 변화의 주기가 바위를 얼려 더 단단하게 만든다.

Ⓓ 온도 변화가 바위를 침투한 물을 확장하고 수축하게 만든다.

5.

4단락에 근거하여 토양 형성에 대해 추론할 수 있는 것은 무엇인가?

Ⓐ 산 아래의 골짜기와 평원에 쌓인 퇴적물들은 풍부한 유기 퇴적물로 이루어져 있다.

Ⓑ 한 지역의 지리는 어디에 토양 퇴적물이 쌓이는지에 대해 작은 역할을 하지 않는다.

Ⓒ 산은 그 지역의 강수량에 따라 모양이 형성된다.

Ⓓ 바위 입자의 퇴적물들은 그 자체로는 비옥한 토양이라고 간주될 수 없다.

6.

5단락의 주요 목적은 무엇인가?

Ⓐ 토양 내의 광물과 가스가 박테리아에 의해 어떻게 이용되는지 예를 제공하기 위해

Ⓑ 분해자들이 죽은 물질을 부엽토로 분해하는 과정을 촉진하는 것의 이점을 보여주기 위해

Ⓒ 토양을 식물들이 잘 자랄 수 있는 환경으로 바꾸는 데 미생물들이 어떻게 도움이 되는지 설명하기 위해

Ⓓ 토양 내부에 사는 박테리아의 수를 강조하기 위해

7.

6단락에서 글쓴이가 "지렁이들"을 언급하는 이유는 무엇인가?

Ⓐ 토양 발달에 있어 박테리아가 가장 중요한 유기체가 아니라는 것을 증명하기 위해

Ⓑ 토양을 처리하는 데 도움을 주는 유기체의 예를 제시하기 위해

Ⓒ 두더지와 같은 땅을 파는 동물들과 지렁이들을 비교하기 위해

Ⓓ 지렁이들의 다양한 서식지를 논의하기 위해

8. Fact

In paragraph 7, what does the author mention about the development of fertile soil? Click on two answers.

Ⓐ Areas with high levels of erosion are not exposed to much precipitation.

Ⓑ **Well-developed fertile soil usually has distinct layers.**

Ⓒ Many years must pass for precipitation to create solid bedrock.

Ⓓ **Well-developed soil forms where sediments are deposited.**

9. Insertion

Look at the four squares [■] that indicate where the following sentence could be added to the passage.

Other bacteria are responsible for breaking down the dead material that plants shed, converting it into a rich mixture known as humus.

Where would the sentence best fit? [■C]

10. Summary

Directions: An introductory sentence for a brief summary of the passage is provided below. Complete the summary by selecting the THREE answer choices that express the most important ideas in the passage. Some sentences do not belong in the summary because they express ideas that are not presented in the passage or are minor ideas in the passage. *This question is worth 2 points.*

The development of soil unfolds over many years, with several key factors playing their roles in transforming solid bedrock into rich soil.

> Ⓐ **Wind and water abrade rocks into small particles, which are swept down by rainwater and deposited in plains.**
>
> Ⓒ **Microscopic organisms and other organisms work the inorganic sediment into an environment rich with nutrients that support a variety of plant life.**
>
> Ⓔ **The more time a given region is allowed for plant growth and development, the richer the soil will be.**

Ⓑ The amount of water retained in a region is fundamental in supporting the activity of microscopic organisms.

Ⓓ The material that earthworms excrete becomes natural fertilizer in important soil formation.

8.

7단락에서 저자가 비옥한 토양의 발전에 대해 언급한 것은 무엇인가? 보기 두 개를 고르시오.

Ⓐ 침식이 많이 일어나는 지역은 많은 강수량에 노출되지 않는다.

Ⓑ 잘 발달된 비옥한 토양은 보통 뚜렷한 층을 갖고 있다.

Ⓒ 강수가 단단한 기반암을 만들기 위해서는 오랜 시간이 지나야 한다.

Ⓓ 잘 발달된 토양은 퇴적물이 쌓여 있는 곳에 형성된다.

9.

지문에 다음 문장이 들어갈 수 있는 위치를 나타내는 네 개의 사각형[■]을 확인하시오.

다른 박테리아는 식물들이 떨어뜨리는 죽은 물질을 분해하여 그것을 부엽토라고 알려진 풍부한 혼합물로 바꾸는 역할을 한다.

이 문장이 들어가기에 가장 적합한 곳은? [■C]

10.

지시문: 지문을 간략하게 요약한 글의 첫 문장이 아래 제시되어 있다. 지문의 가장 중요한 내용을 표현하는 세 개의 선택지를 골라 요약문을 완성하시오. 일부 문장들은 지문에 제시되지 않았거나 지문의 지엽적인 내용을 나타내기 때문에 요약문에 포함되지 않는다. *이 문제의 배점은 2점이다.*

토양의 발달은 오랜 시간에 걸쳐 이루어지는데, 단단한 기반암을 비옥한 토양으로 변화시키는 데 몇 가지 중요한 요인들이 역할을 한다.

> Ⓐ 바람과 물이 바위를 작은 입자로 마모시키고, 이 입자들은 빗물에 의해 쓸려 내려가 평지에 퇴적된다.
>
> Ⓒ 미생물과 다른 유기체들은 무기 퇴적물을 다양한 식물들을 존재하게 하는 영양분이 풍부한 환경으로 만든다.
>
> Ⓔ 한 지역에 식물 성장과 발전을 위한 시간이 더 많이 주어질수록 토양은 더 비옥해질 것이다.

Ⓑ 한 지역에 보유된 물의 양은 미생물의 활동을 유지하게 하는 데 있어 핵심적이다.

Ⓓ 지렁이들이 분비하는 물질은 중요한 토양 형성에 천연 비료가 된다.

Ⓕ Harsh weather conditions have serious repercussions on the processes of soil formation.

Ⓕ 혹독한 기후 조건은 토양 형성 과정에 심각한 영향을 준다.

📖 어휘

1 **discipline** ⓝ 지식 분야, 학문 분야, 학과 | **loose** adj (흙 등이) 단단하지 않은 | **ignore** ⓥ 무시하다 | **weathering** ⓝ 풍화 (작용) | **fertility** ⓝ 비옥함; 생식력

2 **first and foremost** 다른 무엇보다도 | **progressively** adv (꾸준히) 계속해서 | **aggregate** ⓥ 모으다, 종합하다 | **subject** ⓥ 겪게 하다, 지배하에 두다 | **transport** ⓥ 수송하다, 옮기다

3 **disintegration** ⓝ 분해, 붕괴 | **decomposition** ⓝ 분해, 해체, 부패, 변질 | **structure** ⓝ 구조 | **expand** ⓥ 확대[확장/팽창]되다 | **contract** ⓥ 줄어들다, 수축하다 | **permeate** ⓥ 스며들다, 침투하다 | **evaporate** ⓥ 증발하다[시키다] | **thaw** ⓥ 녹다 | **abrade** ⓥ (암석 등을) 마멸시키다, 침식하다 | **fragment** ⓥ 산산이 부수다[부서지다] | **dependent** adj 의존하는

4 **composition** ⓝ 구성 | **retain** ⓥ (계속) 유지[보유]하다 | **plateau** ⓝ 고원 | **penetrate** ⓥ 뚫고 들어가다; 관통하다 | **steepness** ⓝ 가파름, 험준함 | **sediment** ⓝ 침전물, 앙금 | **slope** ⓝ 경사지, 비탈 | **inorganic** adj 무기물의

5 **infiltrate** ⓥ 잠입[침투]하다[시키다] | **microscopic** adj 미세한 | **dominate** ⓥ 우세하다, 지배하다 | **utilize** ⓥ 활용[이용]하다 | **thrive** ⓥ 번창하다; 잘 자라다 | **clump** ⓥ 무리[떼]를 짓다, 함께 모이다[모으다] | **break down** 허물어지다, 분해하다, 나누어지다 | **convert** ⓥ 변하게 하다, 전환하다 | **speed up** 속도를 더 내다[높이다] | **accomplish** ⓥ 완수하다, 성취하다, 해내다

6 **digestive** adj 소화의 | **excrete** ⓥ 배설[분비]하다, 방출하다 | **burrowing** adj 굴을 파는

7 **exert** ⓥ (권력·영향력을) 가하다[행사하다] | **precipitation** ⓝ 강수(량) | **deposit** ⓥ 침전시키다, 두다[놓다]

Actual Test 07

본서 I P. 150

Passage 1 Uneven Distribution of Gliding Animals

1. Ⓒ	Vocabulary		6. Ⓓ	Fact
2. Ⓑ	Fact		7. Ⓓ	Sentence Simplification
3. Ⓑ, Ⓓ	Fact		8. Ⓑ	Negative Fact
4. Ⓒ	Inference		9. Ⓑ	Insertion
5. Ⓒ	Fact		10. Ⓒ, Ⓔ, Ⓕ	Summary

Passage 2 Railroad Development in the United States

1. Ⓐ	Vocabulary		6. Ⓒ	Vocabulary
2. Ⓓ	Inference		7. Ⓓ	Fact
3. Ⓐ	Fact		8. Ⓒ	Sentence Simplification
4. Ⓒ	Rhetorical Purpose		9. Ⓒ	Insertion
5. Ⓓ	Inference		10. Ⓐ, Ⓒ, Ⓔ	Summary

Passage 3 Geographic Speciation

1. Ⓒ	Fact		6. Ⓐ	Rhetorical Purpose
2. Ⓓ	Vocabulary		7. Ⓓ	Negative Fact
3. Ⓓ	Sentence Simplification		8. Ⓒ	Negative Fact
4. Ⓑ	Negative Fact		9. Ⓒ	Insertion
5. Ⓒ	Reference		10. Ⓐ, Ⓔ, Ⓕ	Summary

● 내가 맞은 문제 유형의 개수를 적어 보고 어느 유형에 취약한지 확인해 봅시다.

문제 유형	맞은 개수
Sentence Simplification	3
Fact / Negative Fact	11
Vocabulary	4
Reference	1
Rhetorical Purpose	2
Inference	3
Insertion	3
Summary	3
Category Chart	0
Total	30

Uneven Distribution of Gliding Animals

1 ➡ Many species of animals around the world have developed gliding as a way to cover long distances, and this mode of transportation is typically used to avoid predation. It also provides a means to conserve the valuable energy that they would expend descending from one tree, crossing the forest floor, and climbing another when searching for scattered food sources. These organisms have provided intensely interesting subjects of study for scientists since gliding often requires extreme body modification. Biologists have also observed that the rainforests of Southeast Asia seem to have an unusually large concentration of such creatures in a surprising variety of animal classes. A number of theories have been suggested to explain why such proliferation exists in this particular region, and many of them focus on the particular flora of their environment.

2 ➡ The first theory focuses upon the extreme height of the dipterocarp trees and how this is conducive to gliding, so it is called the tall tree theory. [■A] As animals glide, they are engaged in a kind of controlled fall, so they lose altitude fairly rapidly as they move forward. [■B] Therefore, the taller the tree that they leap from, the longer the distance they could cover. However, observed animal behavior does not generally support this theory. [■C] Many gliders do not take off from the canopy of the trees they are in; rather, many initiate their trips from closer to the middle of the trunk. [■D] Not only that, but the gliders are not confined to these extremely tall forests and may be found in the relatively shorter canopy of the northern rainforests, on plantations, and even in urban areas. So, tall trees are not necessarily a requirement of gliding animals.

3 ➡ Another theory called the broken forest hypothesis speculates that Asian forests lack vegetation connecting them to one another because the dipterocarp trees are so much taller than the other trees in the canopy, which made gliding the most viable option. In the Central and South American rainforests, woody vines called lianas grow in profusion, creating a dense network of vines throughout the forest that animals exploit. However,

활공 동물들의 불규칙 분포

1 ➡ 전세계 많은 동물 종들은 장거리를 이동하기 위해 활공을 발달시켰고, 이런 형태의 이동 수단은 흔히 포식을 피하는 수단으로 사용된다. 이것은 또한 흩어져 있는 먹이를 구할 때 나무 아래로 내려와 숲 바닥을 가로질러 또 다른 나무를 오르면서 소모할 귀중한 에너지를 절약할 수 있는 방법을 제공한다. 이런 생물체들은 과학자들에게 매우 흥미로운 연구 대상을 제공하는데 이것은 활공이 흔히 극단적인 신체 변형을 필요로 하기 때문이다. 생물학자들은 동남아 우림에 이런 동물들이 유난히 많이 집중돼 있으며 그것도 놀랍게도 다양한 동물 종류들 사이에서 발견된다는 것을 관찰했다. 왜 이 특정 지역에서 그렇게 급증하는지 설명하는 여러 이론들이 있으며, 그 중 다수가 그 환경 고유의 식물군에 집중한다.

2 ➡ 첫 번째 이론은 용뇌향과 나무들의 매우 높은 키와 이것이 활공에 어떻게 도움이 되는지에 초점을 맞추므로 높은 나무 이론이라고 불린다. [■A] 동물들은 활공할 때 통제된 하강과 비슷하게 하기에 앞으로 이동하면서 꽤 빠르게 하강한다. [■B] 그렇기 때문에 그들이 뛰어내리는 나무가 더 높을수록 그들은 더 먼 거리를 이동할 수 있게 된다. 하지만 관찰된 동물 행동은 일반적으로 이 이론을 뒷받침하지 않는다. [■C] 많은 활공 동물들은 그들이 위치한 나무 꼭대기에서 활공을 시작하지 않으며, 오히려 나무 줄기 중간 부분에 가까운 곳에서 활공을 시작한다. [■D] 그뿐만 아니라, 활공 동물들은 매우 키가 큰 숲에 제한되지 않고, 비교적 높이가 더 낮은 숲 지붕을 갖고 있는 북쪽 우림, 농장, 심지어 도심에서도 발견된다. 그렇기 때문에 키가 큰 나무들이 반드시 활공 동물의 필수 조건인 것은 아니다.

3 ➡ 부서진 숲 가설이라고 불리는 또 다른 이론은 용뇌향과 나무들이 다른 나무들보다 훨씬 더 키가 크기 때문에 아시아 지역의 숲은 나무들 사이를 연결하는 식물들이 부족하다고 추측하며, 이것이 활공을 가장 가능성 있는 선택으로 만들었다고 한다. 중미와 남미의 우림에는 리아나(liana)라고 불리는 목본성 덩굴이 많이 자라며, 이것은 동물들이 활용하는 숲 전체에 고밀도 덩굴 네트워크를 형성한다. 하지만 세계의 다양한 지역에서 일하고 있는 식물학자들은 덩굴의 번성은 나무의 높이보다 기후, 토양, 고도,

botanists working in various parts of the world have concluded that vine proliferation is more dependent upon other conditions like climate, soil, elevation, and slope than the height of the trees. Indeed, many sections of Southeast Asian rainforests have dense liana growth, just as many parts of the Amazon possess very little. The many mammalian species that dwell in the canopy but do not glide or spend much time on the ground also detract from this theory.

4 ➡ A third explanation, called the food desert theory, purports that it is other aspects of dipterocarps that are providing such tremendous impetus for gliding adaptation. The majority of the gliding species are herbivores that subsist on leaves and fruit or carnivores that eat insects and some smaller vertebrates like frogs. Unfortunately for the mammals that prefer to feed upon leaves, the trees in the dipterocarp family often have poisonous leaves. In a habitat where 95 percent of the tall trees and over 50 percent of the total canopy foliage are dipterocarp trees, so much of their surroundings are inedible that they may as well be living in a desert. Gliding allows them to conserve energy while they seek out leaves that are palatable. There is a type of primate called the colugo that utilizes flaps of skin that extend from its front to rear paws to create a broad flat surface that includes its tail, granting it great control in the air. Unfortunately, this degree of control comes at a price as colugos are not very skilled climbers.

5 ➡ The herbivores that prefer to consume fruit encounter another problem entirely. The fruit that the trees produce contains much less toxin in comparison to the leaves, so it is actually edible. However, dipterocarps have very unusual reproductive cycles that recur every 2 to 7 years, and most of them bloom en masse. This makes fruit scarce most of the time, which also has a serious effect on the carnivorous gliders as these reptiles that eat insects and small vertebrates suffer since their prey feeds upon the fruit directly or indirectly as a vital part of their food chain. So, they must also travel extensively to locate their prey, and they are quite adept at gliding. Lizards in the genus Draco have greatly elongated ribs joined by skin which act as a very effective wing when extended. Some have even been observed to gain altitude while traveling from tree to tree.

경사와 같은 다른 조건들에 더 의존한다는 결론을 내렸다. 사실 동남아 우림의 많은 구역들에서는 리아나가 무성하게 자라는데 아마존의 많은 부분들에서는 매우 적다. 숲 지붕에 서식하지만 활공하거나 숲 바닥에서 많은 시간을 보내지 않는 많은 포유류 종들 또한 이 이론의 설득력을 떨어뜨린다.

4 ➡ 음식 사막 이론이라고 불리는 세 번째 설명은 용뇌향과 나무들의 다른 면들이 활공의 적응에 커다란 자극이 되었다고 주장한다. 활공 종의 대다수는 잎사귀와 과일을 먹는 초식동물이거나 곤충과 개구리 같은 작은 척추동물을 먹는 육식동물이다. 잎사귀 먹는 것을 선호하는 포유류에게는 불행하게도 용뇌향과 나무는 보통 독성이 있는 잎사귀를 갖고 있다. 키가 큰 나무의 95퍼센트와 전체 숲 지붕의 나뭇잎의 50퍼센트 이상이 용뇌향과 나무들인 서식지에서는 그들의 환경에 먹을 수 없는 것이 너무 많아서 이 동물들은 사막에 사는 것과 별반 차이가 없다. 활공은 맛있는 잎사귀를 구하러 나갈 때 에너지를 절약할 수 있게 해준다. 영장류 중 박쥐원숭이라고 불리는 동물은 앞발에서 뒷발까지 이어지는 피부막을 활용해서 꼬리를 포함한 넓고 평평한 표면을 만들어 공중에서 활동을 잘 제어할 수 있다. 안타깝게도 이런 수준의 제어에는 대가가 있어서 박쥐원숭이들은 기어오르는 것을 잘 하지 못한다.

5 ➡ 과일 먹는 것을 선호하는 초식동물은 완전히 다른 문제에 직면한다. 나무들이 생산하는 과일은 잎사귀에 비해 독성이 훨씬 없어서 사실은 먹을 수 있다. 하지만 용뇌향과 나무는 2~7년 주기로 반복되는 매우 특이한 생식 주기를 갖고 있으며, 대다수는 일제히 꽃을 피운다. 이것은 대부분의 경우에는 과일이 부족하게 만들며, 이는 육식 활공 동물들에게도 심각한 영향을 미친다. 곤충과 작은 척추동물을 먹는 파충류들은 그들의 먹이가 먹이 사슬의 필수적인 부분으로 과일을 직접적으로 혹은 간접적으로 섭취하기 때문에 피해를 입는다. 그래서 그들 또한 먹이의 위치를 찾기 위해 먼 거리를 이동해야 하며, 활공에 꽤 능숙하다. 드라코 속(屬)에 속한 도마뱀은 굉장히 긴 갈비뼈가 피부로 이어져 연결되어 있는데 그 피부는 펼쳐졌을 때 매우 효과적인 날개 역할을 한다. 심지어 몇몇은 나무에서 나무로 이동할 때 고도를 높이는 것으로 관찰됐다.

1. Vocabulary

The word "scattered" in paragraph 1 is closest in meaning to

(A) evenly distributed
(B) seasonally available
(C) **widely separated**
(D) hardly visible

2. Fact

According to paragraph 1, why have many species living in forests developed gliding?

(A) It is an energy-efficient way of climbing down the tree.
(B) **It makes them less vulnerable to predation.**
(C) It allows for extreme body modification.
(D) It means they can travel long distances that were not possible before.

3. Fact

According to paragraph 2, what evidence highlights the problems with the tall tree theory? Click on two answers.

(A) Gliding animals lose altitude swiftly as they descend.
(B) **Gliding animals begin their descent from the middle of the trunk.**
(C) More gliding species live in forests that have a relatively short canopy.
(D) **The gliding animals are found in other environments.**

4. Inference

Based on paragraph 3, what can be inferred about forests which have dense liana growth?

(A) Lack of sunlight on the forest floor limits the number of predators in the forest.
(B) The tree canopies of these forests are more uneven in height.
(C) **Animals utilize the vines to travel between trees.**
(D) Climatic conditions concentrate them in Central and South America.

5. Fact

According to paragraph 3, what is one problem with the broken forest hypothesis?

(A) The height difference between the tall dipterocarp trees and the other shorter trees makes gliding between trees more difficult, not easier.
(B) According to botanists, Southeast Asian rainforests have the most dense liana growth in the world.

1.

1단락의 단어 "scattered(흩어져 있는)"와 의미상 가장 가까운 것은?

(A) 균일하게 분포된
(B) 계절적으로 유용한
(C) 널리 떨어져 있는
(D) 거의 보이지 않는

2.

1단락에 따르면, 숲 속에 사는 많은 종들이 활공을 발달시킨 이유는 무엇인가?

(A) 나무를 내려오는 데 에너지 효율적인 방법이다.
(B) 동물들이 포식의 위험을 덜 받게 한다.
(C) 극단적인 신체 변형을 가능하게 한다.
(D) 과거엔 불가능했던 장거리 이동이 가능하다는 것을 뜻한다.

3.

2단락에 따르면, 높은 나무 이론의 문제점을 강조하는 증거는 무엇인가? 보기 두 개를 고르시오.

(A) 활공 동물은 내려오면서 빠르게 하강한다.
(B) 활공 동물은 나무 줄기 중간 부분에서 하강을 시작한다.
(C) 더 많은 활공 동물 종이 상대적으로 낮은 숲 지붕을 갖고 있는 숲에서 서식한다.
(D) 활공 동물은 다른 환경에서도 발견된다.

4.

3단락에 근거하여 덩굴이 무성하게 자라는 숲에 대해 추론할 수 있는 것은 무엇인가?

(A) 숲 바닥을 비추는 햇빛의 부족은 숲의 포식자의 숫자를 제한한다.
(B) 이런 숲의 숲 지붕 높이는 더 고르지 않다.
(C) 동물들은 덩굴을 활용하여 나무 사이를 이동한다.
(D) 기후 조건들이 그들을 중미와 남미에 집중 분포시킨다.

5.

3단락에 따르면, 부서진 숲 가설의 문제점 중 하나는 무엇인가?

(A) 높은 용뇌향과 나무와 더 낮은 다른 나무들 간의 높이 차이는 나무 사이의 활공을 더 쉽게 만드는 게 아니라 더 어렵게 만든다.
(B) 식물학자들에 따르면, 동남아 우림에서는 리아나가 세계에서 가장 무성하게 자란다.

Ⓒ There are other animal species in Southeast Asian rainforests that have not developed gliding abilities.

Ⓓ Contrary to popular belief, woody vines do not grow profusely in the Amazon rainforest.

6. Fact

Why is the theory explained in paragraph 4 called the food desert theory?

Ⓐ The majority of the gliding species living in Southeast Asian rainforests are also found living in deserts in other countries.

Ⓑ The poisonous dipterocarp leaves have caused other leaves in the forest to become inedible also.

Ⓒ Species like the colugo have adapted themselves to the dry, hot, desert-like surroundings.

Ⓓ **Herbivores are unable to eat the majority of the leaves in the region because they are poisonous.**

7. Sentence Simplification

Which of the sentences below best expresses the essential information in the highlighted sentence in the passage? *Incorrect* answer choices change the meaning in important ways or leave out essential information.

Ⓐ The lack of fruit means the reptiles that rely on them suffer, causing a serious effect on the carnivorous gliders.

Ⓑ Scarcity of fruit means that the insects and small vertebrates that feed upon them as a vital part of their diet suffer, causing a serious effect on the food chain.

Ⓒ The lack of fruit has a serious effect on the food chain because the carnivorous gliders compete with reptiles that eat insects and small vertebrates for food.

Ⓓ **When fruit is scarce, it affects the gliding carnivores which feed on herbivores that feed upon the fruit.**

8. Negative Fact

All of the following are mentioned in paragraphs 4 and 5 to be responsible for the lack of food in Southeast Asian forests EXCEPT

Ⓐ a forest comprised mainly of poisonous dipterocarp leaves.

Ⓑ **the relatively small number of carnivorous gliders.**

Ⓒ the unusual reproductive cycles of dipterocarp trees.

Ⓓ the extended periods when fruit is scarce.

Ⓒ 동남아 우림에는 활공 능력이 발달하지 않은 다른 동물 종들이 있다.

Ⓓ 일반적인 생각과는 다르게, 목본성 덩굴은 아마존 우림에서 많이 자라지 않는다.

6.

4단락에 설명되는 이론이 음식 사막 이론이라고 불리는 이유는 무엇인가?

Ⓐ 동남아 우림에 서식하는 활공 동물의 대다수는 다른 나라의 사막들에도 서식한다는 것이 발견됐다.

Ⓑ 독성이 있는 용뇌향과 나무 잎사귀는 숲의 다른 잎사귀들 또한 먹을 수 없는 것으로 만들었다.

Ⓒ 박쥐원숭이와 같은 종은 건조하고 덥고 사막과 같은 환경에 적응했다.

Ⓓ 초식동물은 그 지역 대다수의 잎사귀에 독성이 들어 있기 때문에 먹지 못한다.

7.

다음 중 지문의 음영 표시된 문장의 핵심 정보를 가장 잘 표현한 문장은 무엇인가? 오답은 의미를 크게 왜곡하거나 핵심 정보를 누락하고 있다.

Ⓐ 과일의 부족은 그것에 의존하는 파충류가 피해를 입고 육식 활공 동물에 심각한 영향을 미친다는 것을 뜻한다.

Ⓑ 과일의 부족은 과일을 필수 음식으로 먹는 곤충과 작은 척추동물이 피해를 입어 먹이 사슬에 심각한 영향을 미친다는 것을 뜻한다.

Ⓒ 과일의 부족은 먹이 사슬에 심각한 영향을 미치는데, 왜냐하면 육식 활공 동물이 곤충과 작은 척추동물을 먹는 파충류와 먹이를 놓고 경쟁하기 때문이다.

Ⓓ 과일이 부족하면, 그것은 그 과일을 먹는 초식동물을 먹는 육식 활공 동물에 영향을 미친다.

8.

다음 중 4, 5단락에서 동남아 우림의 식량 부족의 원인으로 언급되지 않은 것은?

Ⓐ 주로 독성이 있는 용뇌향과 나뭇잎으로 이루어진 숲

Ⓑ 상대적으로 적은 숫자의 육식 활공 동물

Ⓒ 용뇌향과 나무들의 특이한 생식 주기

Ⓓ 오랜 기간 동안의 과일 부족

9. Insertion

Look at the four squares [■] that indicate where the following sentence could be added to the passage.

Therefore, the taller the tree that they leap from, the longer the distance they could cover.

Where would the sentence best fit? [■ B]

10. Summary

Directions: An introductory sentence for a brief summary of the passage is provided below. Complete the summary by selecting the THREE answer choices that express the most important ideas in the passage. Some sentences do not belong in the summary because they express ideas that are not presented in the passage or are minor ideas in the passage. *This question is worth 2 points.*

Many theories have been put forth to explain why such proliferation of gliding animals exists in Southeast Asian rainforests.

- Ⓒ The extreme height of dipterocarp trees has led to the development of many gliding species.
- Ⓔ Dipterocarp trees create a desert-like environment that made it necessary for animals to develop gliding abilities to travel widely to find food.
- Ⓕ The canopy structure and the lack of woody vines in Southeast Asian forests are the main factors behind the concentration of gliding animals in the region.

Ⓐ Botanists have discovered that 95 percent of the tall trees in Southeast Asian forests have poisonous leaves.
Ⓑ Most gliding animals in the forest have gone through extreme body modifications, sometimes sacrificing the ability to climb.
Ⓓ The Amazon rainforest possesses very dense liana growth, and scientists say this explains the lack of gliding animals there.

9.

지문에 다음 문장이 들어갈 수 있는 위치를 나타내는 네 개의 사각형[■]을 확인하시오.

그렇기 때문에 그들이 뛰어내리는 나무가 더 높을수록 그들은 더 먼 거리를 이동할 수 있게 된다.

이 문장이 들어가기에 가장 적합한 곳은? [■ B]

10.

지시문: 지문을 간략하게 요약한 글의 첫 문장이 아래 제시되어 있다. 지문의 가장 중요한 내용을 표현하는 세 개의 선택지를 골라 요약문을 완성하시오. 일부 문장은 지문에 제시되지 않았거나 지문의 지엽적인 내용을 나타내기 때문에 요약문에 포함되지 않는다. *이 문제의 배점은 2점이다.*

동남아 우림에 왜 활공 동물들이 그렇게 급증하는지 설명하기 위해 많은 이론들이 제시되었다.

- Ⓒ 키가 매우 큰 용뇌향과 나무가 많은 활공 동물 종의 발달을 야기했다.
- Ⓔ 용뇌향과 나무는 사막과 같은 환경을 조성하여 동물들이 먹이를 찾으러 멀리 이동하기 위해 활공 능력을 발달시키는 것이 필요하도록 만들었다.
- Ⓕ 동남아 우림의 숲 지붕 구조와 목본성 덩굴 부족은 그 지역에 활공 동물들이 집중되어 있는 것의 주된 요인들이다.

Ⓐ 식물학자들은 동남아 우림의 키가 큰 나무의 95퍼센트 이상이 독성이 있는 잎사귀를 가지고 있다는 것을 밝혀냈다.
Ⓑ 숲의 활공 동물의 대다수는 극단적인 신체 변형을 겪었으며, 종종 기어오르는 능력을 희생했다.
Ⓓ 아마존 우림은 매우 무성하게 덩굴이 자라고 있는데, 과학자들은 이것이 그 지역의 활공 동물 부족을 설명한다고 말한다.

📑 어휘

1 **develop** Ⓥ 성장[발달]하다[시키다] ǀ **mode of transportation** 교통수단, 이동 수단 ǀ **predation** Ⓥ 포식 ǀ **conserve** Ⓥ 아끼다, 아껴 쓰다 ǀ **expend** Ⓥ 쏟다[들이다] ǀ **descend** Ⓥ 내려오다, 내려가다 ǀ **scattered** adj 뿔뿔이 흩어진, 산재해 있는, 드문드문 있는 ǀ **intensely** adv 몹시, 강렬하게, 격하게 ǀ **modification** Ⓝ 변형, 변경, 변용 ǀ **rainforest** Ⓝ (열대) 우림 ǀ **concentration** Ⓝ 집중, 농축 ǀ **proliferation** Ⓝ 급증, 확산, 증식

2 **conducive** adj ~에 좋은 ǀ **engaged** adj ~하고 있는, 바쁜 ǀ **controlled** adj 세심히 관리[통제/조정]된 ǀ **altitude** Ⓝ (해발) 고도 ǀ **rapidly** adv 빨리, 급속히 ǀ **observed** adj 관측된 ǀ **initiate** Ⓥ 시작하다, 착수하다 ǀ **trunk** Ⓝ 나무의 몸통 ǀ **confine** Ⓥ 국한시키다 ǀ **plantation** Ⓝ 농장 ǀ **not necessarily** 반드시[꼭] ~은 아닌

Passage 2

Railroad Development in the United States

1 ➡ The completion of the Transcontinental Railway in 1869 was a watershed event in United States history. Prior to the construction of railways, the primary means of transportation other than horses was by water. Boats traversed rivers and canals hauling both cargo and passengers. However, this meant that only cities that were on major waterways could benefit, and goods had to be transported by wagon to reach towns that were not. The earliest railways were short, dedicated routes that were used to connect things like quarries to rivers, and they were pulled by horses. When the steam engine was applied to railways in England, Americans were quick to follow suit. The first steam railways were built to connect cities in New England, but they soon spread both south and westward.

2 ➡ By 1850, approximately 14,400 kilometers of tracks had been laid down, but it was during the following decade that construction really began in earnest. By 1860, there was about 48,000 kilometers of railroad tracks, which meant that the United States had the most tracks in the world. The idea for a railroad that would connect the Atlantic and Pacific coasts dates back to 1832, but it did not receive government approval until 1862. The railway was built in three sections: from Oakland, California to Sacramento, California, from Sacramento to Promontory Summit, Utah, and from Omaha, Nebraska to Promontory Summit. When the two lines met at Promontory Summit, Utah, they were connected with a ceremonial golden spike on May 10, 1869.

미국 철도의 발달

1 ➡ 1869년 대륙횡단 철도 완공은 미국 역사에서 분수령 이 되는 사건이었다. 철도 부설 이전에는 말 이외의 주요 운송 수단은 배였다. 배는 화물과 승객을 싣고 강과 운하 를 가로질렀다. 그러나 이것은 주요 수로상에 있는 도시들 만 혜택을 받았고, 그렇지 않은 마을에 상품이 도달하려면 마차로 운반되어야 했음을 의미했다. 가장 초기 철도들은 채석장 같은 것들을 강까지 연결하는 데 사용되는 짧은 전 용 노선들이었으며 말이 끌었다. 증기 기관이 영국에서 철 도에 적용되었을 때, 미국인들은 재빨리 이를 따라했다. 첫 번째 증기 철도는 뉴잉글랜드의 도시들을 연결하기 위해 부설되었으나, 곧 남쪽과 서쪽으로 확장되었다.

2 ➡ 1850년까지 약 14,400킬로미터의 철로가 놓였지만 부설이 본격적으로 시작된 것은 그 다음 10년 간이었다. 1860년이 되자 약 48,000킬로미터 가량의 철로가 놓였고, 이는 전 세계에서 미국에 가장 많은 철로가 놓여 있었음을 의미했다. 대서양과 태평양 해안을 연결하는 철도에 대한 발상은 1832년으로 거슬러 올라가지만, 이는 1862년까지 는 정부의 승인을 받지 못했다. 철도는 세 구역에 부설되었 는데, 캘리포니아주 오클랜드에서 캘리포니아주 새크라멘 토까지, 새크라멘토에서 유타주 프로몬터리 서밋까지, 그 리고 네브라스카주 오마하에서 프로몬터리 서밋까지였다. 1869년 5월 10일 유타주 프로몬터리 서밋에서 두 노선이 만났을 때 그것들은 기념식을 위한 금으로 된 못으로 연결 되었다.

3 ➡ The benefits of railway construction were many, but the most significant was their effect on the economy. [■A] They allowed the rapid transportation of food and other products to areas that previously had little to no access to such items. [■B] Previously, dairy products had to be produced and consumed locally, but now they could be transported long distances, allowing people to also increase production. [■C] Seafood could also be transported further inland than ever before. Most of the farmers in the western territories had practiced subsistence agriculture before, selling what little surplus they produced to local markets or using it for barter with neighbors. [■D] The railways allowed them to plant cash crops that they could send all over the country. Along with improvements in plow and harvester technology, this allowed the farms in the Midwest to expand rapidly, transforming the prairie into oceans of wheat and corn.

4 ➡ The railroads also facilitated settlement of the vast reaches of the West. Prior to the completion of the Transcontinental Railway, the only way to reach the West Coast was by wagon trail or by sailing around South America, both of which took many months. By rail, it could be achieved in a matter of days. The railroads also helped these people keep in touch with their families back east as mail came to be transported by train. Settlers flooded into the West, displacing Native Americans as they rapidly established cities and towns. Towns that already existed along the route also grew in response as they became important layovers where trains were supplied with fuel and water. As populations swelled, more states were admitted to the Union, and maps had to be redrawn to reflect the new boundaries.

5 ➡ The extensive rail system also proved to have significant military value. During the American Civil War, both sides transported troops to the front by train whenever possible, and many battles were fought in order to secure vital railway hubs. The North's ability to exploit its more extensive railway network was an important factor in its ultimate victory in 1865. Their importance is further clarified by General Sherman's infamous March to the Sea, wherein his troops specifically targeted railroad tracks for destruction to economically weaken the Confederacy. Later, they helped transport mounted

3 ➡ 철도 부설의 이점은 많았으나, 가장 중대한 것은 철도가 경제에 미친 영향이었다. [■A] 그것들은 이전에는 식량과 다른 상품에 접근성이 없었던 지역에 이것들을 빠르게 운반하도록 해주었다. [■B] 전에는 유제품이 지역적으로 생산되고 소비되어야 했으나, 이제 장거리로 운반할 수 있게 됐으며 이는 사람들이 생산량을 늘릴 수 있게 해 주었다. [■C] 해산물 또한 그 어느 때보다도 내륙 지역 깊숙이 운반되었다. 서부 지역의 농부들 대부분은 이전에는 자급 농업을 실시했으며, 그들이 생산한 것 중 얼마 안 되는 여분의 농산물을 지역 시장에 내다 팔거나 이웃과 물물교환을 하는 데 이용했다. [■D] 철도 덕분에 그들은 국가 전역으로 보낼 수 있는 환금성 작물을 심을 수 있었다. 경작과 수확 기술의 향상에 따라, 이는 미국 중서부의 농장이 빠르게 확장하도록 했으며, 대초원을 밀과 옥수수의 바다로 바꾸어 놓았다.

4 ➡ 철도는 또한 서부 광활한 지역의 정착을 용이하게 했다. 대륙횡단 철도 완공 이전에는 서부 해안으로 가는 유일한 길은 마차 길이나 남미를 돌아 항해하는 것뿐이었으며, 두 방법 모두 몇 달이 소요되었다. 기차로는 며칠 만에 도달할 수 있었다. 우편물이 기차로 오가게 되면서 철도는 사람들이 동부의 가족들과 연락을 취하는 데도 도움을 주었다. 정착민들은 서부로 몰려 들었고 도시와 마을을 급속도로 건설하면서 북미 원주민들을 몰아냈다. 노선을 따라 이미 존재하던 마을들은 기차가 연료와 물을 공급받는 중요한 기착지가 되었으므로 이에 대응하여 성장했다. 인구가 늘어남에 따라 더 많은 주들이 미국으로 편입되었고, 새로운 경계선을 반영하기 위해 지도들이 다시 그려져야 했다.

5 ➡ 광범위한 철도 시스템은 또한 중대한 군사적 가치를 지닌 것으로 증명되었다. 남북전쟁 시기에 양측은 가능할 때면 언제나 병력을 기차로 전선까지 실어 날랐고, 중요한 철도 중심지를 확보하기 위해 많은 전투가 치러졌다. 좀 더 광범위한 철도 네트워크를 활용하는 북부의 능력은 1865년 궁극적 승리의 중요 요인이었다. 철도의 중요성은 셔먼 장군의 악명 높은 대행진(March to the Sea)에 의해서도 명확해지는데, 여기서 그의 병력은 남부 연합군을 경제적으로 약화시키기 위해 특별히 철로의 파괴를 목적으로 삼았다. 이후 인디언 전쟁의 여러 전투에서 그것들은 서부 전역의 기병 수송에 도움을 주었다.

cavalry throughout the West during the many conflicts of the Indian Wars.

6 ➡ By 1880, there were 17,800 locomotives transporting freight and 22,200 of them transporting passengers all over the country. The industrialists who owned these railways became incredibly wealthy as some of the larger companies spanned across many states. However, the federal government viewed such complete control as monopolistic, and it disapproved of some of the owners' excesses, particularly when they were lax about regulations. Congress responded to the situation by establishing the Interstate Commerce Commission, which controlled their business activities through heavy regulation. This was effective for a while, but then disaster struck.

7 ➡ In 1893, railroad overbuilding and unstable railroad financing resulted in the largest economic crisis ever at that time. By the middle of 1894, one quarter of the railroad companies had failed, and as they collapsed, they took a series of banks with them. This led to a distrust of the railroad companies that only intensified when the remaining owners joined forces to gain control of the railroad tracks left without management. Eventually, the invention of the automobile created competition that the railroads couldn't cope with, and passenger trains dwindled. In the United States today, most of the trains carry only freight.

6 ➡ 1880년에는 전국에 화물을 운송하는 기관차 17,800대와 승객을 실어 나르는 기관차 22,200대가 있었다. 큰 회사들 중 일부가 여러 주를 가로지르게 되면서 이러한 철도를 소유한 기업가들은 엄청나게 부유해졌다. 그러나 연방 정부는 그런 완전한 지배권을 독점으로 간주했고, 일부 소유주들의 월권행위, 특히 그들이 규제에 대해 해이하게 구는 것을 못마땅해 했다. 의회는 주간 통상위원회를 설립함으로써 이러한 상황에 대처했는데, 이것은 엄중한 규제를 통해 그들의 사업 활동을 통제했다. 이것은 한동안은 효과가 있었으나 그 후 재앙이 닥쳤다.

7 ➡ 1893년에 철도의 과잉 부설과 불안정한 철도 재정이 그 당시 어느 때보다도 가장 큰 경제 위기를 가져왔다. 1894년 중반에 철도 회사들의 1/4이 도산했고, 그것들이 붕괴되면서 일련의 은행들 또한 그렇게 되었다. 이는 철도 회사에 대한 불신으로 이어졌고 이것은 남은 소유주들이 관리 없이 방치된 철로들을 장악하려고 힘을 합쳤을 때 더욱 강화되었다. 결국 자동차의 발명은 철도로서는 대응할 수 없었던 경쟁을 낳았고 여객 열차는 줄어들었다. 오늘날 미국에서 대부분의 열차는 화물만을 실어 나른다.

---

1. **Vocabulary**

The word "dedicated" in paragraph 1 is closest in meaning to

(A) reserved

(B) staunch

(C) resolute

(D) purposeful

2. **Inference**

Based on paragraph 2, it can be inferred that

(A) the construction of the Transcontinental Railway lasted for more than 10 years.

(B) England had the most tracks in the world before the development of the Transcontinental Railway.

(C) the government dictated the route of the railroad that would connect the Atlantic and Pacific coasts.

1.

1단락의 단어 "dedicated(전용의)"와 의미상 가장 가까운 것은?

(A) 지정된

(B) 견고한

(C) 단호한

(D) 결의에 찬

2.

2단락에 근거하여 추론할 수 있는 것은?

(A) 대륙횡단 철도의 부설은 10년 이상 동안 계속되었다.

(B) 대륙횡단 철도 개발 이전에는 영국이 세계에서 가장 많은 철로를 갖고 있었다.

(C) 정부가 대서양과 태평양 해안을 연결하는 철도 노선을 지시했다.

Ⓓ the construction of the Transcontinental Railway began from both California and Nebraska simultaneously.

3. Fact
According to paragraph 4, what effect did railroad construction have on the West?

Ⓐ **Existing towns along the railroad became important hubs.**
Ⓑ Displaced Native Americans established new cities and towns.
Ⓒ It forced mail to be transported along wagon trails during the period of railroad construction.
Ⓓ Maps had to be redrawn to include locations where trains stopped to replenish their supplies.

4. Rhetorical Purpose
Why does the author mention "Indian Wars" in paragraph 5?

Ⓐ To discuss the negative effects of targeting railroad tracks for destruction
Ⓑ To explain the role General Sherman played in the military after the American Civil War
Ⓒ **To provide further support for the argument that the railroads had significant military value**
Ⓓ To provide an earlier example of how railroads played a strategic role in warfare

5. Inference
Based on paragraph 5, it can be inferred that

Ⓐ the South's railway network was more extensive than the North's.
Ⓑ General Sherman fought in the South's army.
Ⓒ the March to the Sea was a failed military operation.
Ⓓ **the South's lack of infrastructure contributed to its defeat.**

6. Vocabulary
The word "freight" in paragraph 6 is closest in meaning to

Ⓐ weapons
Ⓑ vehicles
Ⓒ **cargo**
Ⓓ mail

7. Fact
According to paragraph 7, what is true about the railroad companies?

Ⓐ The railroad companies were owned by the same group of people that owned the banks.

Ⓓ 대륙횡단 철도의 부설은 캘리포니아주와 네브라스카주에서 동시에 시작했다.

3.
4단락에 따르면, 철도 부설은 서부에 어떤 영향을 미쳤는가?

Ⓐ 철도를 따라 자리잡고 있는 기존의 마을들이 중요한 거점이 되었다.
Ⓑ 쫓겨난 북미 원주민들이 새로운 도시와 마을을 건설했다.
Ⓒ 철도가 부설되는 기간 동안 마차 길을 따라서 우편물이 운송되도록 했다.
Ⓓ 열차가 물자를 보충하기 위해 멈추었던 위치를 포함시키기 위해 지도가 다시 그려져야 했다.

4.
글쓴이가 5단락에서 "인디언 전쟁"을 언급하는 이유는 무엇인가?

Ⓐ 철도 파괴를 목적으로 삼는 것의 부작용을 논하기 위해
Ⓑ 남북전쟁 후 군대에서의 셔먼 장군의 역할을 설명하기 위해
Ⓒ 철도가 중대한 군사적 가치를 지녔다는 주장에 대한 근거를 더 제시하기 위해
Ⓓ 철도가 전쟁에서 어떻게 전략적 역할을 했는지에 관한 이전의 예를 제시하기 위해

5.
5단락에 근거하여 추론할 수 있는 것은?

Ⓐ 남부의 철도 네트워크는 북부의 것보다 더 광범위했다.
Ⓑ 셔먼 장군은 남부 군대에서 싸웠다.
Ⓒ 대행진은 실패한 군사 작전이었다.
Ⓓ 남부의 사회 기반시설 부족이 패배의 원인이 되었다.

6.
6단락의 단어 "freight(화물)"와 의미상 가장 가까운 것은?

Ⓐ 무기
Ⓑ 탈것
Ⓒ 화물
Ⓓ 우편물

7.
7단락에 따르면, 다음 중 철도 회사에 대해 사실인 것은 무엇인가?

Ⓐ 철도 회사들은 은행을 소유했던 사람들과 똑같은 집단에 의해 소유되었다.

(B) The Interstate Commerce Commission was successful in regulating the railroad companies.

(C) The federal government bought railroad tracks that were left without management.

(D) **Railroad companies eventually allocated more locomotives to transporting freight than passengers.**

8. Sentence Simplification

Which of the sentences below best expresses the essential information in the highlighted sentence in the passage? *Incorrect* answer choices change the meaning in important ways or leave out essential information.

(A) Distrust led owners of remaining railroad companies to gain control of tracks left without management.

(B) Distrust of railroad companies arose when railroad company owners sold tracks that were left without management.

(C) **This resulted in distrust of railroad companies which grew stronger after other company owners teamed up to buy the abandoned tracks.**

(D) Distrust grew as other railroad company owners fought to gain control over railroad tracks that were left without management.

9. Insertion

Look at the four squares [■] that indicate where the following sentence could be added to the passage.

Seafood could also be transported further inland than ever before.

Where would the sentence best fit? **[■ C]**

10. Summary

Directions: An introductory sentence for a brief summary of the passage is provided below. Complete the summary by selecting the THREE answer choices that express the most important ideas in the passage. Some sentences do not belong in the summary because they express ideas that are not presented in the passage or are minor ideas in the passage. *This question is worth 2 points.*

The Transcontinental Railway, which was completed in 1869, greatly impacted the United States, which already had the most tracks in the world by the mid-19th century.

(B) 주간 통상위원회는 철도 회사들을 규제하는 데 성공했다.

(C) 연방 정부가 관리 없이 방치된 철로들을 사들였다.

(D) 철도 회사들은 결국 여객들보다는 화물을 운송하는 데 더 많은 기관차를 할당했다.

8.

다음 중 지문의 음영 표시된 문장의 핵심 정보를 가장 잘 표현한 문장은 무엇인가? 오답은 의미를 크게 왜곡하거나 핵심 정보를 누락하고 있다.

(A) 불신은 남아 있던 철도 회사의 소유주들로 하여금 관리 없이 방치된 철로들을 장악하게 했다.

(B) 철도 회사 소유주들이 관리 없이 방치된 철로들을 팔았을 때 철도 회사에 대한 불신이 일었다.

(C) 이것은 철도 회사에 대한 불신을 초래했고 이는 다른 회사의 소유주들이 버려진 철로를 사들이기 위해 협력한 이후 더 강해졌다.

(D) 관리 없이 방치된 철로를 장악하기 위해 다른 철도 회사 소유주들이 경쟁했을 때 불신이 커졌다.

9.

지문에 다음 문장이 들어갈 수 있는 위치를 나타내는 네 개의 사각형[■]을 확인하시오.

해산물 또한 그 어느 때보다도 내륙 지역 깊숙이 운반되었다.

이 문장이 들어가기에 가장 적합한 곳은? [■C]

10.

지시문: 지문을 간략하게 요약한 글의 첫 문장이 아래 제시되어 있다. 지문의 가장 중요한 내용을 표현하는 세 개의 선택지를 골라 요약문을 완성하시오. 일부 문장들은 지문에 제시되지 않았거나 지문의 지엽적인 내용을 나타내기 때문에 요약문에 포함되지 않는다. *이 문제의 배점은 2점이다.*

1869년도에 완성된 대륙횡단 철도는 미국에 큰 영향을 주었는데, 미국은 19세기 중반에 이미 세계에서 가장 많은 철로를 보유하고 있었다.

Ⓐ Despite the government's efforts to regulate the monopoly, railroad company owners retained their dominance until it was broken by the automobile.

Ⓒ Not only did increased accessibility encourage settlers to rush into the West, but the railway system also proved to be of strategic military value.

Ⓔ The railway system allowed farmers to increase crop production as products could be transported to other areas rapidly.

Ⓐ 독점을 규제하려는 정부의 노력에도 불구하고 철도 회사 소유주들은 자동차로 무너질 때까지 우세를 점했다.

Ⓒ 개선된 접근 용이성이 정착민들로 하여금 서부로 몰려들게 했을 뿐만 아니라, 철도 시스템은 또한 전략상 중요한 군사적 가치도 지닌 것으로 증명되었다.

Ⓔ 철도 시스템은 상품이 다른 지역으로 신속히 운송될 수 있게 되면서 농부들이 작물 생산량을 늘릴 수 있게 해 주었다.

Ⓑ Prior to railway construction, farmers could not attempt mass production because produce had to be consumed locally, with any surplus being sold to neighbors.

Ⓓ The construction of the railway began in 1862, and it eventually spanned across the continent, connecting the cities in New England to Promontory Summit.

Ⓕ During the American Civil War, General Sherman focused on destroying railway tracks to prevent troops from being transported to the frontlines.

Ⓑ 철도 부설 이전에는 농작물이 지역적으로 소비되고, 여분의 농산물은 이웃에게 판매되어야만 했기 때문에 농부들은 대량 생산을 시도할 수 없었다.

Ⓓ 철도 부설은 1862년에 시작되었고, 마침내는 대륙 전역에 걸쳐 이어졌고 뉴잉글랜드의 도시들과 프로몬터리 서밋을 연결시켰다.

Ⓕ 남북전쟁 시기에 셔먼 장군은 군대가 전선으로 수송되는 것을 막기 위해 철로를 파괴하는 데 중점을 두었다.

📋 어휘

1 **completion** n 완성, 완료 | **transcontinental** adj 대륙횡단의 | **watershed** adj 분수계[분기점]를 이루는, 획기적인 n 분수령 | **primary** adj 주된 | **transportation** n 운송, 수송 | **traverse** v 가로지르다 | **haul** v 운반하다, 끌다 | **cargo** n 화물 | **benefit** v 혜택[이익]을 얻다 | **dedicated** adj 특정 작업용으로 만들어진, 전용의 | **quarry** n 채석장 | **follow suit** 전례를 따르다

2 **in earnest** 본격적으로 | **ceremonial** adj 의식용의

3 **previously** adv 이전에 | **consume** v 소비하다 | **inland** adv 내륙으로 | **territory** n 지역, 구역, 영역 | **subsistence agriculture** 자급 농업 | **surplus** n 잉여 농산물, 잉여, 과잉 | **barter** v 물물교환하다 | **cash crop** 환금성 작물 | **plow** n 경작 | **rapidly** adv 신속히 | **transform** v 변형시키다, 완전히 바꿔놓다[탈바꿈시키다]

4 **facilitate** v 용이하게 하다 | **displace** v 쫓아내다 | **in response (to)** ~에 대응하여 | **layover** n 기착지, 도중하차 | **swell** v 늘다, 팽창하다 | **boundary** n 경계선

5 **value** n 가치 | **troop** n 부대, 병력 | **front** n 전선 | **secure** v 확보하다 | **hub** n 중심지 | **exploit** v 활용하다 | **extensive** adj 광범위한 | **clarify** v 명확히 하다 | **ultimate** adj 궁극적인 | **infamous** adj 악명 높은 | **target** v 목표로 삼다, 겨냥하다 | **weaken** v 약화시키다 | **mounted** adj 말에 탄, 기동의 | **cavalry** n 기사 | **conflict** n 충돌, 갈등, 전투

Passage 3

Geographic Speciation

1 ➡ The evolutionary paths of all species are influenced by three factors: mutation, natural selection, and genetic drift. A mutation occurs when there is a random, sudden change in an individual's genetic code, making it distinct from other members of its species. This may occur at any time, but if it does not give the organism any advantage over other

지리적 종분화

1 ➡ 모든 종들의 진화적 경로는 세 가지 요소에 영향을 받는다. 돌연변이, 자연 선택, 그리고 유전적 부동이다. 돌연변이는 한 개체의 유전자 코드에 무작위적이고 갑작스러운 변화가 있을 때 발생하며, 그 개체가 그 종의 다른 구성원들과 구별되도록 만든다. 이것은 어느 때나 발생할 수 있지만, 만약 그것이 그 생물에게 그 종의 다른 구성원보다 나은 이익을 주지 못할 때에는, 그 변화가 여러 세대에

Actual Test 07

Actual Test 07 **115**

members of the species, the change is unlikely to be passed down for many generations. Genetic drift also involves chance, but it is a much more gradual process. Genes govern particular traits of an organism, but they can yield different results each time the organisms reproduce. These possible results are called alleles, but as a species evolves, the number of possible alleles becomes smaller, gradually homogenizing the species. Natural selection, often referred to as survival of the fittest, occurs when environmental factors force organisms to adapt in order to survive and reproduce, which inevitably changes the species as a whole. These factors often act in combination, and the end result of the changes they cause are new species. Therefore, this evolutionary process is called speciation.

2 ➡ Each species is the result of its own genetic history and how it was influenced by unpredictable interactions. Every genetic history is unique, but they can be grouped according to some recurring patterns. The origin of any new species can usually be traced back to a physical separation of the original population, which is called allopatric speciation. The separation is usually caused by an impassable physical object like a river, canyon, mountain range, or ocean. Once the population is divided into two or more groups, they begin to take separate evolutionary paths from each other as different traits become dominant, gradually altering them into populations that can no longer successfully mate when reintroduced, thereby creating new species.

3 ➡ The likelihood of a physical barrier dividing a species is completely dependent upon that organism's regular means of travel. For example, small rivers in the Amazon have proven sufficient to create new species of leaf-cutter ants, but much larger barriers are usually required. This means that speciation due to geographic isolation is usually a very slow process. The Grand Canyon took millions of years to form, but it eventually divided a rodent population, resulting in different species living to the north and south of it. A similarly slow geological process occurred in Central America. Originally, North and South America were not connected, and a species of shrimp lived in the ocean between them. However, a chain of volcanoes grew, creating what is now the Isthmus of Panama, separating the population into two groups which evolved differently.

걸쳐 전해질 가능성은 낮다. 유전적 부동 역시 가능성을 포함하고 있지만, 그것은 훨씬 더 점진적인 과정이다. 유전자는 한 생물의 특정한 특성을 지배하지만, 생물이 번식할 때마다 다른 결과를 낼 수 있다. 이러한 가능한 결과들을 대립 유전자라고 부르는데, 종이 진화함에 따라 가능한 대립 유전자의 수가 줄어들고, 점차적으로 그 종을 균일화한다. 종종 적자생존으로도 일컬어지는 자연 선택은 환경적인 요소가 생물이 생존하고 번식하기 위해 적응을 하도록 강요할 때 일어나는데, 그로 인해 불가피하게 종 전체가 변화하게 된다. 이러한 요소들은 결합하여 작용하는 경우가 많으며, 그것이 일으키는 변화의 최종 결과는 새로운 종들이다. 따라서 이러한 진화의 과정은 종분화라고 불린다.

2 ➡ 각각의 종은 자신들의 유전적 역사와 그것이 예측할 수 없는 상호작용에 어떻게 영향을 받았는지에 대한 결과이다. 모든 유전적 역사는 고유하지만, 몇 가지 반복되어 발생하는 패턴에 따라 분류될 수 있다. 새로운 종의 기원은 보통 기존 개체들의 물리적인 분리로 거슬러 올라갈 수 있는데, 그것을 이소적 종분화라고 부른다. 이 종분화는 주로 강, 협곡, 산맥, 또는 대양과 같은 지나갈 수 없는 물리적인 사물에 의해 생겨난다. 일단 그 개체군이 둘 이상의 집단으로 분리되면, 다른 특성들이 우세하게 되면서 그 집단들은 서로 다른 진화적 경로를 밟기 시작하고, 이는 그들을 점차적으로 바꾸어 그들이 과거 지역으로 다시 전해질 때 더 이상 성공적으로 짝짓기를 할 수 없는 개체군으로 만들고, 결과적으로 새로운 종을 탄생시키게 된다.

3 ➡ 물리적인 장벽이 종을 나눌 가능성은 전적으로 그 생물의 규칙적인 이동 수단에 의존한다. 예를 들어, 아마존의 작은 강들은 절엽 개미의 새로운 종을 만들어 내기에 충분한 것으로 증명이 되었지만, 보통 훨씬 더 큰 장벽들이 필요하다. 이것은 지리적인 고립에 의한 종분화가 보통 매우 느린 과정이라는 의미이다. 그랜드 캐니언은 만들어지는 데 수백만 년이 걸렸지만, 결과적으로 설치류 개체들을 나누었으며, 그 결과 그것의 북부와 남부에 사는 서로 다른 종을 만들어 냈다. 이와 유사하게 느린 지질학적 과정이 중미에서 발생했다. 원래 북미와 남미는 연결되어 있지 않았고, 어떤 종의 새우가 그것들 사이에 있는 대양에서 살았다. 하지만 연속된 화산이 생성되어 현재의 파나마 지협을 만들었고, 그 개체군을 서로 다르게 진화한 두 집단으로 분리했다.

4 ➡ Within this larger concept there are two subgroups. In the first, one of the populations is much smaller than the other, which causes it to change much more rapidly. A smaller population equals a smaller gene pool, meaning that certain traits can become dominant much faster. As a result, the larger parent population remains largely unchanged, while the isolated smaller group may be radically different. This form of speciation is called peripatric. In the other, the population is not divided or isolated by a physical barrier, but by distance. The parent population is spread out over a vast area, and while they are capable of mating with members of any other group, members of a particular group only mate with each other. These small groups often exist in different environments than the rest of the population, causing them to express different genetic traits. This form of speciation is called parapatric.

5 ➡ One of the best areas to observe these forms of speciation is within archipelagos like the Galapagos Islands or the Hawaiian Islands. These island chains are located neither too far from the continents around the Pacific Ocean nor too close to them. So, when animals do survive the journey to them, they usually remain. If they manage to reproduce, then they have the potential to become firmly established on the islands. [■A] This is because they left their natural predators behind on the mainland, and their population is often only limited by the available food supply. [■B] One example of this is the Galapagos finches, which contributed greatly to Darwin's theories regarding evolution. [■C] These birds came to the islands from South America, effectively isolating themselves from their parent population. As they settled in their new home, they began to change physically to exploit the local food supply (allopatric speciation). [■D] Individual islands could not support a large population, so the necessary traits to eat the food available on each quickly became dominant. Large, blunt beaks developed to eat seeds and nuts, long, thin ones to feed on nectar, and medium ones to eat insects (peripatric speciation). And, although the finches were perfectly capable of traveling to other islands, the majority of them did not, which resulted in the 15 species that eventually developed (parapatric speciation).

4 ➡ 이 큰 개념 내에 두 가지 하위 집단이 있다. 첫 번째 하위 집단에서는 개체군들 중 하나가 다른 개체군보다 훨씬 더 작기 때문에 훨씬 더 급속하게 변화한다. 더 작은 개체군은 더 작은 유전자 풀과 같으며, 이는 특정 특성들이 훨씬 더 빨리 우세하게 될 수 있다는 것을 의미한다. 결과적으로 더 큰 모집단은 주로 변화하지 않은 채로 남아 있는 반면, 고립된 더 작은 집단은 급진적으로 달라질 수 있다. 이러한 형태의 종분화를 근소적 종분화라고 부른다. 두 번째 하위 집단에서는 개체군이 물리적인 장벽에 의해서가 아니라 거리에 의해서 분화되거나 격리된다. 모집단은 거대한 지역에 퍼지고, 다른 집단의 개체들과 짝짓기를 할 수 있지만, 특정 집단의 개체들은 오직 자기들끼리만 짝짓기를 한다. 이러한 작은 집단들은 종종 다른 개체군의 나머지와는 다른 환경에서 존재하며, 그것들이 다른 유전적 특성을 나타내도록 만든다. 이러한 형태의 종분화를 근지역 종분화라고 부른다.

5 ➡ 이러한 형태들의 종분화를 관찰할 수 있는 가장 좋은 지역 중 하나가 갈라파고스 제도나 하와이 제도와 같은 제도 내이다. 이러한 열도들은 태평양 주변의 대륙으로부터 너무 멀리 떨어져 있지도 않고, 또 너무 가깝지도 않은 곳에 위치해 있다. 그래서 동물들은 그곳으로 이동하는 여정에서 살아남으면, 보통 떠나지 않고 남아 있다. 만약 그들이 번식에 성공한다면, 그 군도에 확고하게 자리를 잡을 잠재력을 갖게 된다. [■A] 이것은 그들이 본토에 자신의 천적들을 남겨두고 왔고, 그들의 개체군은 보통 이용 가능한 식량 공급에 의해서만 제한되기 때문이다. [■B] 이것의 한 가지 예가 갈라파고스의 핀치인데, 이것은 진화와 관련된 다윈의 이론에 크게 기여했다. [■C] 이 새들은 남미에서 그 군도로 왔으며, 스스로를 모집단으로부터 효과적으로 격리시켰다. 새로운 서식지에 정착했을 때, 그들은 그 지역의 먹이 공급을 이용하기 위해 물리적으로 변화하기 시작했다(이소적 종분화). [■D] 각각의 군도는 큰 개체군을 부양할 수 없어서 해당 군도에서 입수 가능한 음식을 먹기 위해 필요한 특성들이 재빨리 우세하게 되었다. 크고 뭉툭한 부리가 씨앗과 견과류를 먹기 위해 발달했고, 길고 얇은 부리는 꽃의 꿀을 먹기 위해, 중간 부리는 곤충을 먹기 위해 발달되었다(근소적 종분화). 그리고 핀치는 충분히 다른 군도로 이동할 수 있었지만, 대다수가 이동하지 않았으며, 그 결과 15개의 종들이 생겨났다(근지역 종분화).

1. Fact

According to paragraph 1, what is the difference between mutation and natural selection?

Ⓐ Natural selection is a much quicker process than mutation.

Ⓑ Mutation is a result of an organism's attempt to accommodate itself to sudden changes.

Ⓒ **Natural selection is a result of environmental changes while mutation is one of genetic changes.**

Ⓓ Natural selection occurs randomly, whereas mutation occurs only when there is a great change in the genes of organisms.

2. Vocabulary

The word "recurring" in paragraph 2 is closest in meaning to

Ⓐ developing

Ⓑ limiting

Ⓒ laboring

Ⓓ **reappearing**

3. Sentence Simplification

Which of the sentences below best expresses the essential information in the highlighted sentence in the passage? *Incorrect* answer choices change the meaning in important ways or leave out essential information.

Ⓐ After the population divides into different groups, this prevents them from successfully mating with each other, and as a result, different traits become dominant.

Ⓑ As the population divides into several groups, this results in the creation of new species that take separate evolutionary paths by successfully mating with each other to become populations with different dominant traits.

Ⓒ Once the population is reunited, each group exhibits different traits that have become dominant that make the species stronger after they mate successfully.

Ⓓ **The division of a population into different groups essentially creates new species that display different dominant traits and are unable to successfully mate with each other.**

4. Negative Fact

According to paragraph 2, all of the following are true about allopatric speciation EXCEPT

Ⓐ it occurs due to a physical separation.

Ⓑ **it refers to changes caused by encounters between two different species.**

1.

1단락에 따르면, 돌연변이와 자연 선택의 차이점은 무엇인가?

Ⓐ 자연 선택은 돌연변이보다 훨씬 더 빠른 과정이다.

Ⓑ 돌연변이는 한 유기체가 갑작스러운 변화에 적응하고자 하는 시도의 결과이다.

Ⓒ 자연 선택은 환경 변화의 결과인 반면, 돌연변이는 유전적인 변화의 하나이다.

Ⓓ 자연 선택은 무작위적으로 일어나는 반면, 돌연변이는 유기체의 유전자에 큰 변화가 있을 때에만 일어난다.

2.

2단락의 단어 "recurring(반복되어 발생하는)"과 의미상 가장 가까운 것은?

Ⓐ 발달하는

Ⓑ 제한하는

Ⓒ 힘든

Ⓓ 다시 나타나는

3.

다음 중 지문의 음영 표시된 문장의 핵심 정보를 가장 잘 표현한 문장은 무엇인가? 오답은 의미를 크게 왜곡하거나 핵심 정보를 누락하고 있다.

Ⓐ 그 개체군이 여러 집단으로 분리된 후, 이것은 그들이 서로 성공적으로 짝짓기를 할 수 없게 하고, 그 결과 다른 특성들이 우세하게 된다.

Ⓑ 그 개체군이 여러 집단으로 분리되면서, 서로와 성공적으로 짝짓기를 하여 다른 우세한 특성들을 지닌 개체군들이 됨으로써 서로 다른 진화적 경로를 밟는 새로운 종을 탄생시키게 된다.

Ⓒ 일단 그 개체군이 다시 만나면, 각 집단은 서로와 성공적으로 짝짓기를 한 후 그 종을 더 강하게 만드는 각각 다른 우세해진 특성들을 나타낸다.

Ⓓ 개체군이 여러 집단으로의 분리되면, 근본적으로 새로운 종들을 탄생시키는데, 그 종들은 다른 우세한 특성들을 나타내며 서로 성공적으로 짝짓기를 할 수 없다.

4.

2단락에 따르면, 다음 중 이소성 종분화에 대해 사실이 아닌 것은?

Ⓐ 물리적인 분리로 생겨난다.

Ⓑ 두 가지 다른 종의 만남에 의해 야기되는 변화를 일컫는다.

Ⓒ each group steadily develops traits which are different from the other.

Ⓓ geographic factors such as rivers, mountain ranges, and oceans contribute to it.

5. Reference

The word "it" in paragraph 3 refers to

Ⓐ speciation

Ⓑ process

Ⓒ **Grand Canyon**

Ⓓ population

6. Rhetorical Purpose

Why does the author mention "Isthmus of Panama" in paragraph 3?

Ⓐ **To give an example of geographic isolation that caused the speciation of an organism**

Ⓑ To show what affects the speciation of marine species as opposed to terrestrial species

Ⓒ To demonstrate the consequences of long-term geological changes on rodent populations

Ⓓ To point out how important volcanic eruptions are in the evolution of species

7. Negative Fact

According to paragraph 4, all of the following are true EXCEPT

Ⓐ both peripatric and parapatric speciation occur in small groups which are separated from the rest of the parent population.

Ⓑ a group with a smaller population is likely to develop specific traits faster due to its smaller gene pool.

Ⓒ parapatric speciation occurs when members of a small group that lives away from the rest mate only with each other.

Ⓓ **parapatric speciation involves a physical barrier which divides the larger population of organisms into smaller groups.**

8. Negative Fact

According to paragraph 5, all of the following are true EXCEPT

Ⓐ Darwin's theory of evolution is based upon the finches in the Galapagos Islands.

Ⓑ some archipelagos in the Pacific Ocean are ideal places to observe the evolution of species.

Ⓒ **the Galapagos Islands were a proper place to observe speciation because of their climate.**

Ⓒ 각 집단은 서로 다른 특성들을 꾸준히 발전시킨다.

Ⓓ 강, 산맥, 대양과 같은 지리적인 요소들이 그것의 원인이 된다.

5.

3단락의 단어 "그것"이 가리키는 것은?

Ⓐ 종분화

Ⓑ 과정

Ⓒ 그랜드 캐년

Ⓓ 개체군

6.

3단락에서 글쓴이가 "파나마 지협"을 언급하는 이유는 무엇인가?

Ⓐ 한 유기체의 종분화를 일으킨 지리적인 격리의 예를 들기 위해

Ⓑ 육생 생물과 반대로 해양 생물의 종분화에 영향을 주는 것이 무엇인지 보여주기 위해

Ⓒ 장기적인 지질학적 변화가 설치류 개체에 끼친 결과를 보여주기 위해

Ⓓ 화산 분출이 종의 진화에 얼마나 중요한지를 지적하기 위해

7.

4단락에 따르면, 다음 중 사실이 아닌 것은?

Ⓐ 근소적 종분화와 근지역 종분화 모두 모집단의 나머지와 분리된 작은 집단에서 발생한다.

Ⓑ 더 작은 개체군을 가진 집단은 그것의 작은 유전자 풀 때문에 특정한 특성을 더 빠르게 발전시키기 쉽다.

Ⓒ 근지역 종분화는 다른 것들과 떨어진 곳에 사는 작은 집단이 오직 구성원끼리만 짝짓기할 때 일어난다.

Ⓓ 근지역 종분화는 유기체의 더 큰 개체군을 더 작은 집단으로 나누는 물리적인 장벽을 포함한다.

8.

5단락에 따르면, 다음 중 사실이 아닌 것은?

Ⓐ 다윈의 진화론은 갈라파고스 제도의 핀치를 기반으로 한다.

Ⓑ 태평양의 몇몇 군도들은 종의 진화를 관찰하기에 이상적인 장소이다.

Ⓒ 갈라파고스 제도는 기후 때문에 종분화를 관찰하기에 적합한 장소이다.

Ⓓ the physical traits of the finches changed in response to the environment of the islands.

9. Insertion

Look at the four squares [■] that indicate where the following sentence could be added to the passage.

These birds came to the islands from South America, effectively isolating themselves from their parent population.

Where would the sentence best fit? [■ C]

10. Summary

Directions: An introductory sentence for a brief summary of the passage is provided below. Complete the summary by selecting the THREE answer choices that express the most important ideas in the passage. Some sentences do not belong in the summary because they express ideas that are not presented in the passage or are minor ideas in the passage. *This question is worth 2 points.*

Speciation is the evolutionary process that occurs when a group of organisms is geographically isolated from the original population.

Ⓐ **Mutation, genetic drift, and natural selection take place in combination, thus causing species to evolve.**
Ⓔ **Physical barriers separate a species into two or more groups, and speciation gradually progresses afterward.**
Ⓕ **The Galapagos finches, which were provided with an ideal environment for evolution, are a great example of speciation.**

Ⓑ The advent of new species is the result not of genetic alteration, but of a physical separation.
Ⓒ The definition of a species includes organisms which can mate and produce viable offspring.
Ⓓ It is not easy to observe how a new species emerges since there are various forms of speciation.

Ⓓ 핀치의 신체적 특징은 섬의 환경에 대한 반응으로 변화했다.

9.

지문에 다음 문장이 들어갈 수 있는 위치를 나타내는 네 개의 사각형[■]을 확인하시오.

이 새들은 남미에서 그 군도로 왔으며, 스스로를 모집단으로부터 효과적으로 격리시켰다.

이 문장이 들어가기에 가장 적합한 곳은? [■ C]

10.

지시문: 지문을 간략하게 요약한 글의 첫 문장이 아래 제시되어 있다. 지문의 가장 중요한 내용을 표현하는 세 개의 선택지를 골라 요약문을 완성하시오. 일부 문장들은 지문에 제시되지 않았거나 지문의 지엽적인 내용을 나타내기 때문에 요약문에 포함되지 않는다. *이 문제의 배점은 2점이다.*

종분화는 한 집단의 생물들이 원래의 개체군에서 지리적으로 격리되었을 때 일어나는 진화 과정이다.

Ⓐ 돌연변이, 유전적 부동, 자연 선택은 결합하여 일어나며, 따라서 종의 진화를 야기한다.
Ⓔ 물리적인 장벽이 한 종을 두 가지 이상의 집단으로 나누고, 종분화는 그 이후 점차적으로 진행된다.
Ⓕ 진화를 위한 이상적인 환경을 제공받은 갈라파고스의 핀치는 종분화의 훌륭한 예이다.

Ⓑ 새로운 종의 출현은 유전적 변화의 결과가 아니라 물리적인 분리의 결과이다.
Ⓒ 종의 정의에는 짝짓기를 할 수 있고 독자 생존 가능한 자손을 생산할 수 있는 유기체가 포함된다.
Ⓓ 다양한 형태의 종분화가 있기 때문에 새로운 종이 어떻게 생겨나는지 관찰하기는 쉽지 않다.

어휘

1 **evolutionary** adj 진화의; 점진적인 I **mutation** n 돌연변이 (과정) I **genetic** adj 유전의, 유전적인 I **distinct** adj 뚜렷이 다른[구별되는], 별개의 I **advantage** n 유리한 점, 이점, 장점 I **pass down** 물려주다[전해주다] I **chance** n 가능성, 우연 I **trait** n 특성 I **yield** v 내다[산출하다], (결과를) 가져오다 I **allele** n 대립 형질[유전자] I **homogenize** v 균질[동질]이 되게 하다, 균질화하다 I **refer to** ~을 나타내다 I **survival of the fittest** 적자 생존 I **inevitably** adv 불가피하게, 필연적으로 I **end result** 최종 결과

2 **unpredictable** adj 예측할 수 없는, 예측이 불가능한 I **interaction** n 상호작용 I **recurring** adj 되풀이하여 발생하는 I **trace back** ~의 기원이 ~까지 거슬러 올라가다 I **physical** adj 물질의, 물질[물리]적인 I **separation** n 분리, 구분 I **impassable** adj 통행할 수 없는, 폐쇄된 I **gradually** adv 서서히 I **alter** v 변하다, 달라지다, 바꾸다, 고치다 I **successfully** adv 성공적으로 I **mate** v 짝짓기를 하다

3 **likelihood** n 공산[가능성] I **barrier** n 장벽, 장애물 I **means of travel** 이동 수단 I **sufficient** adj 충분한 I **geological** adj 지질학의 I **occur** v 일어나다, 발생하다 I **evolve** v 진화하다, 발달[진전]하다

4 **concept** n 개념 I **isolated** adj 고립된, 외떨어진, 외딴 I **radically** adv 급진적으로 I **vast** adj 거대한, 어마어마한, 방대한 I **capable** adj ~할 수 있는

5 **archipelago** n 군도 I **continent** n 대륙 I **survive** v 살아남다, 생존[존속]하다 I **mainland** n 본토 I **limit** v 제한[한정]하다 I **contribute** v 기여하다 I **isolate** v 격리하다, 고립시키다 I **exploit** v 활용[이용]하다 I **blunt** adj 무딘, 뭉툭한 I **eventually** adv 결국, 마침내

PAGODA TOEFL 90+

READING

Actual Test

PAGODA TOEFL 90+

READING

Actual Test

PAGODA TOEFL 90+

READING

Actual Test

PAGODA
TOEFL
90+ Reading
Actual Test